Better Homes and Gardens®

the *ultimate* cookie book

Meredith® Books

Des Moines, Iowa

Better Homes and Gardens® The Ultimate Cookie Book
Editor: Lois White
Contributing Project Editor: Annie Krumhardt-Peterson
Contributing Graphic Designer: Jill Budden
Copy Chief: Terri Fredrickson
Copy Editor: Kevin Cox
Publishing Operations Manager: Karen Schirm
Senior Editor, Asset & Information Management: Phillip Morgan
Edit and Design Production Coordinator: Mary Lee Gavin
Editorial Assistant: Cheryl Eckert
Book Production Managers: Pam Kvitne, Marjorie J. Schenkelberg,
  Rick von Holdt, Mark Weaver
Imaging Center Operator: Ryan Alexander
Contributing Copy Editor: Michelle Bolton King
Contributing Proofreaders: Pegi Bevins, Sarah Enticknap,
  Gretchen Kauffman, Donna Segal
Contributing Indexer: Elizabeth T. Parson
Test Kitchen Director: Lynn Blanchard
Test Kitchen Home Economists: Elizabeth Burt, R.D., L.D.; Juliana
  Hale; Laura Harms, R.D.; Maryellyn Krantz; Greg Luna; Jill Moberly;
  Dianna Nolin; Colleen Weeden; Lori Wilson

Meredith® Books
Executive Director, Editorial: Gregory H. Kayko
Executive Director, Design: Matt Strelecki
Managing Editor: Amy Tincher-Durik
Executive Editor: Jennifer Darling
Senior Editor/Group Manager: Jan Miller
Senior Associate Design Director: Mick Schnepf
Marketing Product Manager: Toye Guinn Cody

Publisher and Editor in Chief: James D. Blume
Editorial Director: Linda Raglan Cunningham
Executive Director, Marketing: Kevin Kacere
Executive Director, New Business Development: Todd M. Davis
Executive Director, Sales: Ken Zagor
Director, Operations: George A. Susral
Director, Production: Douglas M. Johnston
Director, Marketing & Publicity: Amy Nichols
Business Director: Jim Leonard

Vice President and General Manager: Douglas J. Guendel

Better Homes and Gardens® Magazine
Editor in Chief: Gayle Goodson Butler
Deputy Editor, Food and Entertaining: Nancy Hopkins

Meredith Publishing Group
President: Jack Griffin
Senior Vice President: Karla Jeffries

Meredith Corporation
Chairman of the Board: William T. Kerr
President and Chief Executive Officer: Stephen M. Lacy
In Memoriam: E. T. Meredith III (1933–2003)

All of us at Meredith® Books are dedicated to providing you with the information and ideas you need to create delicious foods. We welcome your comments and suggestions. Write to us at: Meredith Books, Cookbook Editorial Department, 1716 Locust St., Des Moines, IA 50309–3023.

Our seal assures you that every recipe in *The Ultimate Cookie Book* has been tested in the Better Homes and Gardens® Test Kitchen. This means that each recipe is practical and reliable, and meets our high standards of taste appeal. We guarantee your satisfaction with this book for as long as you own it.

Better Homes and Gardens®

Test Kitchen

Cover photography: Blaine Moats
Food Stylist: Tami Leonard
Prop Stylist: Sue Mitchell
Pictured (top row, from left): Chocolate Chip Cookie, page 39, Sugar Cookie Star Cutout, page 129, Chocolate Almond-Apricot Cookie, page 141; (middle row, from left): Coconut-Raspberry Delight, page 64, Pumpkin-Pecan Cookie, page 28, Chocolate-Mint Snow-Top Cookie, page 193; (bottom row, from left): Chocolate-Cherry Pocket, page 100, Lemon-Ginger Meringue, page 256, Ultimate Chocolate-Dipped Cookie, page 43.

Pictured above and on page 5: Chocolate Chip Cookies, page 39

table of
contents

One good bite leads to another.

Loved for their buttery-rich flavor and tender bite, cookies are one of those tempting treats people just can't resist. If you're a cookie baking enthusiast, you will value this book as a collection of extraordinarily good recipes and baking wisdom. It covers everything! In the first chapter, you'll discover the hows and whys of successful cookie baking from the expert bakers in the Better Homes and Gardens® Test Kitchen. The knowledge you gain as you read about ingredients, equipment, and techniques will help transform you into a top-notch baker. Never again will you have cookies that spread too much, have burned bottoms, or taste tough or hard. What's equally valuable are the chapters full of the very best cookie creations—everything from tried-and-true classics to new flavor twists and ingredient combinations. And because every recipe has been thoroughly tested, you can trust that your cookies will turn out scrumptiously delicious every time.

Enjoy this unique collection of recipes. May you have many happy memories of baking cookies in your kitchen.

cookie

bas

This pictorial guide is dedicated to every
cookie baker who's ever had questions about
ingredients, equipment, and techniques.
Use these helpful pointers to ensure success
in all of your cookie baking ventures.

ics

cookie dough tips

*super slicing When making cookies that are formed into a log, chilled, and sliced, form the log into an evenly round roll. Then place the log into a drinking glass or baguette pan to help keep its shape. If the dough is still too soft to slice after chilling, quick-chill it in the freezer for 20 minutes. Use a sharp, thin-bladed knife to slice the dough. Rotate the roll between cuts to prevent one side from flattening.

*divine drops Minimize spreading of drop cookies by greasing the cookie sheets with shortening only if the recipe directs. Also be sure to cool the cookie sheets completely between each batch. To make your drops evenly sized, use a small ice cream scoop instead of a spoon to scoop the dough.

*righteous rolling When making cutout cookies, work with only half of the dough at a time; chill the rest to keep it from getting too soft. Dip cookie cutters into flour between cuts to avoid sticking. Make cutouts close together so fewer rerolls will be needed; chill scraps before rerolling. Use a plastic spatula to transfer cutouts to a baking sheet. Bake similar-size cutouts together so they will all be done at once.

In the Better Homes and Gardens® Test Kitchen, all the cookie recipes are tested with large eggs. If you wish, you can use refrigerated egg substitute instead of whole eggs. Just follow the directions on the package.

eggs-actly

batch **baking**: Bake cookies on a large cookie sheet one batch at a time on the center rack or on two small cookie sheets set on two oven racks and baked at the same time. If using two cookie sheets, switch them halfway through the baking time for even baking.

the **oven temperature** test: To check your oven temperature for accuracy using a freestanding oven thermometer, set the oven at 350°F and let it heat up for at least 10 minutes. Place the thermometer inside the oven. Close the door and heat the thermometer for at least five minutes. If the thermometer reads higher than 350°F, then reduce the oven setting by the number of degrees' difference each time you bake. If the thermometer reads lower than 350°F, then increase the oven setting by the number of degrees' difference. If your oven is more than 50 degrees off, it's a good idea to have a service technician adjust the thermostat.

great **greasing**: When a recipe calls for greased cookie sheets, dip a ball of waxed paper in shortening and wipe the sheets with a light coating. Or use a light coating of nonstick cooking spray. You may also use parchment paper or a silicone mat in place of greasing the cookie sheet.

Treat your family to the very best cookies you can bake.

spaced out: Be sure to leave enough space between cutout cookies and dough balls so the cookies do not bake into one another. Follow guidelines in recipes.

master **mixing**: All of the recipes in this book can be made using either a portable hand mixer or a stand mixer. If you use a hand mixer, when you add the flour beat in as much as you can. Stir in the remaining flour using a wooden spoon.

ready or not? Check cookies for doneness after the minimum baking time called for in your recipe. If they appear done, use a thin plastic spatula to transfer cookies to a cooling rack. (A metal spatula may scratch cookie sheets.) Some cookies need to set for one or two minutes before moving them.

Correctly measuring ingredients is one of the simplest secrets to successful cookie baking. To get the best results from your baking projects, follow these measuring cues.

measuring up

Sugar: Granulated sugar should be spooned into a dry measuring cup or spoon and then leveled off with the straight edge of a knife or spatula. Powdered sugar is measured the same way but should be sifted beforehand. Brown sugar should be pressed into a dry measuring cup until it holds the shape of the cup or spoon when it is inverted.

Shortening: Measure solid shortening by pressing it into a dry measuring cup or measuring spoon with a rubber scraper. Level off the excess with the straight edge of a knife. Shortening is also sold in sticks with markings on the wrapper that indicate tablespoon and cup measures.

Flour: To measure flour, stir it in the bag or canister to fluff it up. (Sifting is not necessary, except with cake flour.) Gently spoon the flour into a dry measuring cup or spoon, filling it to overflowing. Level off the top with the straight edge of a knife or spatula. Avoid packing the flour into the cup or tapping the cup to level it.

Liquids: Pour liquid in a glass or clear plastic liquid measuring cup placed on a level surface. Read the markings on the cup by bending down so you see them at eye level.

sheet smarts

If the cookie sheets in your cupboard are lightweight, warped, or dark with baked-on grease, then it's time for some new ones. Here are some tips to help you choose cookie sheets.

✳ Look for shiny, heavy pans that have very low or no sides.

✳ Avoid dark-color cookie sheets, which can easily cause cookies to overbrown.

✳ Use jelly-roll pans (four-sided, 15×10×1-inch baking pans) for bar cookies only. Other types of cookies will not brown evenly in these pans.

✳ Be sure to choose a cookie sheet that fits comfortably in your oven. There should be at least one to two inches of space all around the pan. You want a cookie sheet that handles easily, so pay close attention to its size and weight.

✳ Insulated cookie sheets tend to yield pale, too-soft cookies, so steer clear of this type of sheet for cookie baking purposes.

✳ Perforated cookie sheets and accompanying silicone mats are not all they're cracked up to be. They do not help cookies bake any more evenly than on a standard cookie sheet, and cleanup is difficult due to crumbs becoming lodged in the perforated mat.

✳ Cookie baking stones are not necessary to bake cookies. Testing shows that cookies baked on stones take longer to bake and don't brown enough on the bottom. The weight of baking stones, as well as the fact that they are very breakable, makes them less convenient to handle than metal pans.

Heavyweight cookie sheets can stand up to high temperatures—they won't warp or bend in the oven's heat.

Parchment Paper: *Use this moistureproof paper to line baking pans and cookie sheets to make cookies easier to remove. In addition parchment paper makes cleanup a breeze. After use just toss it in the garbage.*

sticking solutions

Aluminum Foil: *Lining baking pans with foil makes removing the bars from the pan easier. Foil also helps keep pans from being damaged from knife cuts and makes cleanup much easier. Just shape the foil over the outside of the pan, extending it over the edges about one inch, then place the shaped foil inside the pan. If your recipe calls for a greased pan, grease the foil inside the pan (or choose no-stick foil). Bake and cool the bars as usual, then grasp the extra foil at the edges to pull the uncut bars out of the pan.*

high-altitude cookie baking: *Cookies need less adjustment for high altitude than other baked goods. Start by increasing the oven temperature by 25°F and decreasing the baking time by a minute or two. If further adjustment is necessary, reduce the sugar by a couple of tablespoons. If a recipe calls for baking powder or baking soda, you may need to reduce the amount by ⅛ teaspoon. Make just one recipe change at a time.*

Less Fat, More Applesauce! If you experiment with applesauce or fruit puree as a substitute for fat in drop or bar cookie recipes, replace no more than half the butter or shortening with the fruit product. The cookies will be moist and cakelike because the fruit holds moisture. Applesauce or fruit puree does not work in cutout or slice-and-bake cookies because it makes dough too soft to hold its shape.

finds

cookie **basics**

Candied citrus peel and crystallized ginger are sold in packages in the spice aisle, baking aisle, or the produce section.

Chocolate-hazelnut spread, such as Nutella brand, can be found in the grocery store near the peanut butter.

Edible glitter and luster dust are sold at crafts stores in the cake decorating section and through mail order catalogs.

Lemon, lime, and orange curd are found next to the jams, preserves, and jellies in larger supermarkets.

Mini phyllo cups are sold in the bakery department of larger supermarkets or with specialty items.

Meringue powder is sold at crafts stores in the cake decorating section and in mail order catalogs.

Phyllo sheets are in your grocer's freezer case near frozen desserts.

Pine nuts and pistachio nuts can be found in the produce section or in the snack aisle of your grocery store.

fun dried fruit: *Don't stop with raisins (dried grapes). You can purchase apples, apricots, bananas, carambolas (star fruit), cherries, cranberries, currants, dates, figs, mangoes, papayas, peaches, pears, persimmons, pineapples, and plums in dried form. They're all intensely sweet, chewy, and great for cookie baking. Once you've opened a package, wrap the remaining dried fruit airtight and store it in the freezer for up to 6 months.*
✱ *Either a sharp knife or kitchen shears make quick work of cutting large pieces of dried fruits into bite-size pieces. Dip the knife or shears into hot water or lightly spray with nonstick cooking spray to keep the fruit from sticking.*

Peanut Butter Facts

By law peanut butter must be 90 percent peanuts; no artificial flavor, colors, and preservatives are allowed. Peanut butter usually contains stabilizers to keep the oil from separating. Natural peanut butter, made only with peanuts and oil, must be stored in the refrigerator and stirred before use. Either type makes delicious cookies.

what's the
difference?

Butter versus margarine: Butter is the first choice for cookies because it contributes a rich flavor and consistent results. Stick margarine will work if it contains at least 80 percent fat. Avoid low-fat, liquid, and soft spreads.

Pure vanilla extract versus imitation vanilla: Vanilla extract comes from long, slender seedpods called vanilla beans. Circulating diluted alcohol through finely chopped vanilla beans makes pure vanilla extract. Imitation vanilla is an artificial flavoring made of synthetic flavors and coloring and is an inexpensive substitute for extract. For most uses measure the same amount of imitation vanilla as you would pure vanilla extract.

Dark molasses versus light molasses: Thick, dark, syrupy molasses is a byproduct of refining cane or beet sugar. When describing molasses, light refers only to flavor, not color or calorie or sugar content. Light molasses, also called mild-flavor molasses, comes from the first boiling of the refining process and is sweet in flavor. Dark molasses, from the second boiling, is not as sweet as light molasses but has a distinctive, robust flavor. Light and dark molasses can be used interchangeably in recipes.

Evaporated milk versus sweetened condensed milk: Evaporated milk is made by removing the water from whole milk. Sweetened condensed milk is milk that has had the water removed and then sugar added. They are not to be used interchangeably in recipes.

Baking soda versus baking powder: Baking soda is an alkaline leavening agent that is used in conjunction with acidic ingredients, such as buttermilk or brown sugar, to form bubbles of air that make cookies rise. Baking powder is not used in conjunction with an acidic ingredient in recipes because it already contains the acidifying agent (cream of tartar). Do not use these products interchangeably for baking.

Liquid food coloring versus food coloring paste: Liquid food coloring, usually available in just four colors—red, green, yellow, and blue—has a relatively low concentration of dye. Paste food coloring is highly concentrated and available in a wide variety of colors. Use less paste coloring than you would liquid.

Savvy Storage Make sure the cookies have cooled completely on a wire rack before storing. If they are still warm, they are likely to stick together. Use storage containers with tight-fitting lids. Never store crisp cookies and soft cookies in the same container; crisp cookies will soften and soft cookies will harden. To store most cookies, bars, and candy, layer them between waxed paper in an airtight container. Unless a recipe directs otherwise, store cookies and candy at room temperature for up to three days (up to two days for meringue-base cookies) or freeze (unfrosted, unfilled, and/or undrizzled) for up to three months. Store bars at room temperature for up to three days or in the refrigerator as specified in recipe. You can freeze bars (unfrosted or undrizzled) for up to three months. Be sure to store cookies or bars topped with creamy frostings or delicate toppings in a single layer.

Freeze with Ease Use these tips to freeze your cookies.
✳ Cookie Containers: Use sturdy containers with tight-fitting lids. Keep a variety of shapes and sizes on hand for different types and amounts of cookies—any extra air in the container makes the cookies prone to freezer burn.
✳ Store Smart: Separate layers of cooled cookies with pieces of waxed paper. The paper protects from crumbing and provides insulation against freezer burn. Label each container, listing the name of the cookies and the date they were made. If the cookies need to be filled or frosted before serving, add a note with clear instructions.
✳ Proper Thawing: Thaw cookies in the refrigerator or on the countertop. Leave the cookies in their storage container to avoid damage due to condensation. Frost them, fill them, and/or serve them after they have completely thawed.

what is freezer burn? *Freezer burn occurs when food dries out in the freezer, which affects the food's flavor and texture. To minimize these effects, store cookies in airtight containers designed for the freezer. However, anything stored too long will suffer from freezer burn. Store cookies no longer than three months for best quality.*

store ingredients wisely

Here are storage guidelines for various baking ingredients.

baking powder and baking soda: Store at room temperature; check expiration dates on packages.

brown sugar: Store in a sturdy container with a tightly fitting lid at room temperature for up to six months.

butter: Refrigerate in original packaging for up to one month. To freeze, thoroughly wrap the package with plastic wrap and freeze for up to six months.

chocolate: Store baking chocolate wrapped in plastic wrap and foil in a cool, dark place. Store chocolate pieces in a resealable bag or storage container. Store milk chocolate and dark chocolate for up to a year and white chocolate for up to eight months.

coconut: After opening, tightly close package or put in a resealable bag and store in the refrigerator for up to two months.

eggs: Store whole eggs in the carton in the coldest part of the refrigerator for up to five weeks after the packing date.

flour: Store all-purpose flour in an airtight container in a cool, dry place for 10 to 15 months. Store whole grain flours for up to five months. For longer storage, refrigerate or freeze flour in a moistureproof container.

granulated and powdered sugars: Store these types of sugar indefinitely in airtight containers in a cool, dry place.

spices: Store in airtight containers in a dry place away from sunlight and heat. Most whole spices keep for one to two years; ground spices keep up to a year.

Cookie Packaging

Sending cookies to loved ones is a great way to show you care. Use these tips to ensure your treats arrive unharmed.

* Choose crisp or firm cookies, such as sliced, drop, or bar cookies. Avoid moist, frosted, or filled ones.

* Wrap cookies in plastic wrap individually, in back-to-back pairs, or in stacks.

* Line a sturdy cardboard box with plastic bubble wrap and pack cookies in layers of packing peanuts or tissue paper. Fill the box completely so the cookies do not shift. Seal the box with packing tape and mark it "perishable."

ahh, nuts!

Many people like the flavor and texture nuts give to cookies. But if your kitchen is a nut-free zone, for most recipes you can simply leave them out. There are exceptions, however. If a recipe calls for ground nuts, they take the place of some flour and fat, so they are essential to the structure of the cookies. If nuts are the primary ingredient, omitting them leaves a bland, unappealing cookie. Here are some cookie-friendly nuts.

Almonds
These nuts have pale, smooth meat and a delicate flavor. Almonds come whole, sliced, slivered, or chopped. Toasting them helps retain their crunch.

Pecans Sweet, buttery pecans have the highest fat content of any nut. Use them interchangeably with walnuts.

Peanuts Not technically nuts, peanuts are legumes that grow beneath the ground. In cookies use unsalted, roasted peanuts unless otherwise specified.

Walnuts Mild-flavor English walnuts are the best nut for all kinds of baking. Black walnuts have a distinctive and intense flavor and can be slightly bitter.

Cashews Buy these rich, buttery nuts raw or roasted, salted or plain. For baking, use unsalted roasted cashews unless otherwise specified.

Macadamia Nuts Native to Australia but grown primarily in Hawaii, macadamia nuts taste rich, sweet, and buttery. Use them whenever you would use cashews.

Pistachios Their mild and sweet flavor is similar to almonds, which make a suitable substitute. The shells may be tan or colored red with vegetable dye. The nut meat is green.

Toasting heightens the flavor of nuts, seeds, and coconut. To toast, spread the nuts, seeds, or coconut in a single layer in a shallow baking pan. Bake in a 350°F oven for 5 to 10 minutes or until light golden brown and fragrant; watch carefully and stir once or twice.

Hazelnuts Also called filberts, hazelnuts have a mild, sweet flavor. Remove the bitter skins by rubbing the nuts between your hands before baking.

chocolate
and more
chocolate

Smooth, rich chocolate comes in many forms.
Here's a rundown on some basic varieties.

Unsweetened chocolate
Sometimes called baking or bitter chocolate, this product is pure chocolate with no added sugar.

Semisweet chocolate Pure chocolate with added cocoa butter and sugar, this versatile product is available in bars, blocks, and pieces.

Bittersweet chocolate There are no legal guidelines for this term, but the product is usually darker and less sweet than semisweet chocolate.

Milk chocolate This product consists of pure chocolate with added cocoa butter, sugar, and milk solids.

Sweet baking chocolate Made of pure chocolate with added cocoa butter and sugar, this chocolate is sweeter than bittersweet chocolate but less sweet than semisweet chocolate.

Unsweetened cocoa powder This product is pure chocolate with most of the cocoa butter removed. Cocoas labeled "Dutch-process" or "European-style" have been treated to neutralize the natural acids, giving them a mellow flavor and a reddish color.

what exactly is white chocolate?

All the white baking products you can find at the supermarket (such as baking squares, baking pieces, baking chunks, and white candy or confectioners' coating) are not created equal. Some contain cocoa butter, while others do not. The only products that are true white chocolate contain cocoa butter. Read your recipe before heading to the store. When a recipe specifies white chocolate baking squares with cocoa butter, be sure to check the product for the words "cocoa butter."

chips to try

You'll be in for a yummy change of pace when you try new flavors of chips in your cookie recipes.

 cinnamon: These are slightly smaller than the standard chip and deliver an intense sweet-spicy flavor.

 semisweet: These classic chips were introduced by Nestlé Co. in 1939. You'll also find milder, sweeter milk chocolate morsels and darker, richer bittersweet chips. All are interchangeable in recipes.

 white chocolate: These aren't true chocolate— they contain no chocolate liquor, a paste from which all versions of the real thing are made. They have a mild, sweet vanilla flavor and a creamy texture.

 cappuccino: These chips take on the flavor and color of sweetened coffee and cream. Coffee lovers are in for a treat.

 mint: You're probably familiar with the chocolate-mint-flavor chip. These pastel green chips have a more delicate mint flavor.

 raspberry-chocolate: These semisweet morsels are laced with a luscious and tangy berry flavor that adds a touch of sophistication to cookies.

 cherry: Any size—regular or miniature—bursts with fruity flavor and festive red color.

 butterscotch: These blond bits contribute a buttery brown sugar flavor to cookies and bars.

---

tips on storing chips
* Store chips in a cool, dry place for up to three months.
* After opening the package, transfer remaining chips to an airtight container.
* The morsels keep best in constant temperatures. When exposed to temperature changes, the surface of the chips can develop a film called "bloom." It's actually just fine traces of melted cocoa butter that has rehardened, and it won't affect the flavor or performance of the chip.

decorating guide

A punchy color palette, swirls and pipes of frosting, and sprinkles of sparkly sugars and candies work hand in hand to create exquisite cookies that look almost too beautiful to eat.

decorating tools

Tweezers This versatile tool comes in handy for adding decorative embellishments such as dragées or candies to your cookies.

Fluted pastry wheel Create decorative scalloped edges with a pastry wheel, which also works nicely to cut geometric shapes out of cookie dough.

Decorator bags For ease and convenience, use plastic disposable decorator bags to pipe frosting. When you are finished decorating your cookies, simply discard the bag.

Decorating tips Tips for decorating bags come in several shapes and sizes, but you actually need only three—a round tip, a star, and a leaf—to decorate cookies. Choose tips with small or medium holes to pipe frosting.

Brushes The quickest way to glaze or ice cookies is with a brush. Use a large pastry brush to apply an egg wash on unbaked cookies; once baked, the glazed cookies have a nice sheen. Use small paintbrushes for detail work, such as applying thin strokes of frosting or luster dust to cookies.

cookie **basics**

How to work with Buttercream Frosting (recipe on page 96):

To pipe Buttercream Frosting, fill a decorator bag about two-thirds full of frosting. Fold the corners over and roll the bag down to the frosting. With one hand grip the bag near the roll above the frosting. Apply pressure with the palm of your hand, forcing frosting toward the tip. Use your other hand to guide the tip of the bag.

Star Tip: Besides stars, a star tip creates shells, zigzags, and decorative borders.

Leaf Tip: To form leaves, hold the bag at a 45-degree angle, keeping the top opening parallel to the surface. Squeeze out some frosting to make the base of a leaf. Continue squeezing but ease up on the pressure as you pull toward the leaf tip. Stop the pressure, then pull away.

Round Tip: The round tip is ideal for writing and creating dots, lines, stems, and vines.

How to work with Royal Icing (recipe on page 128):

1 Use a small round tip to pipe an icing outline around the cookie. The piped edge creates a border to hold the icing inside.

2 Using a large paintbrush, spread the icing to reach the piped outline icing. This is your base coat.

3 To create the wet-on-wet effect, pipe squiggles of a second color on still-wet icing. The decorative pipes sink into the base coat, creating a smooth top. To create a marbled effect, use a toothpick to pull swirls of the piped icing through the base coat. Decorate one cookie at a time to ensure the icings dry evenly.

4 To create a multidimensional effect on cookies, ice the cookies and let dry. Then pipe additional icing on top and add dragées or sprinkles to the pipes.

assorted toppers

Sugars Several types of sugars add sparkle and color to cookies. Fine sanding sugar gives the cookies a highly dramatic sparkle. Decorating or coarse sugar contains granules that are about four times larger than regular granulated sugar. Raw sugar, or Demerara sugar, contributes a delicate molasses flavor to cookies along with its brownish color and texture. Top iced cookies with sugars when they are slightly dry but still tacky.

Luster dust This shimmering powder comes in gold, silver, and pearl tones as well as many colors. Add luster dust to icing for a metallic sheen. You may also brush it onto dried icing for a shimmery finish by mixing ½ teaspoon luster dust with 2 teaspoons vodka. The alcohol in the vodka evaporates, leaving a paintable mixture ready to apply to dried icing with a small paintbrush.

Edible glitter Much flakier than sugar, edible glitter makes cookies glisten when sprinkled onto icing that is still wet.

Candies, nonpareils, and dragées Tiny candies and other small embellishments provide fun decorating effects on cookies. Nonpareils are tiny opaque balls that give texture to cookies. They come in a wide range of colors.

edible glitter

jimmies

gel paste food coloring

coarse sugar

luster dust

nonpareils

raw sugar

fine sanding sugar

metallic dragées

egg painting: *Use egg paint to apply color to cookies only before baking. In a small bowl stir together 1 egg yolk and a few drops of water. Divide the mixture among several bowls. Mix a little paste food coloring into each. Use a small, clean brush to paint various colors onto unbaked cutouts. If the egg paint thickens while you're working with it, stir in water, one drop at a time.*

delicious

dro

2

Time-pressed cooks have long appreciated the ease of the drop cookie, not to mention the smiles the cookies bring. Fill your jar to brimming with cookies from this collection, which offers both familiar and fun new flavors.

drops

If you like pumpkin pie, you'll love these cookies. Toasted pecans accentuate the spiced flavors wonderfully.

pumpkin-pecan cookies

prep: 30 min. **bake:** 10 min. per batch **oven:** 375°F **makes:** about 40 cookies

2 cups all-purpose flour
1½ teaspoons baking powder
1 teaspoon ground cinnamon
¼ teaspoon baking soda
¼ teaspoon ground allspice
1 cup butter, softened
1 cup sugar
1 egg
1 cup canned pumpkin
1 cup chopped toasted pecans (see tip, page 19)
1 recipe Brown Sugar-Butter Frosting
Toasted coconut (see tip, page 19) (optional)

1 Preheat oven to 375°F. In a medium bowl stir together flour, baking powder, cinnamon, baking soda, and allspice. Set aside.

2 In a large mixing bowl beat the butter with an electric mixer on medium to high speed for 30 seconds. Add sugar. Beat until combined, scraping sides of bowl occasionally. Beat in egg until combined. Stir in pumpkin and the flour mixture. Stir in pecans.

3 Drop dough by rounded teaspoons 2 inches apart onto an ungreased cookie sheet. Bake for 10 to 12 minutes or until bottoms are light brown. Transfer to a wire rack and let cool. Frost cooled cookies with Brown Sugar-Butter Frosting. If desired, sprinkle toasted coconut onto each frosted cookie.

brown sugar-butter frosting: *In a medium saucepan heat 6 tablespoons butter and ⅓ cup packed brown sugar over medium heat until butter is melted. Remove from heat. Stir in 2 cups powdered sugar and 1 teaspoon vanilla. Stir in enough hot water (2 to 3 teaspoons) to make a smooth, spreadable frosting. Frost cookies immediately after preparing frosting. If frosting becomes grainy, add a few more drops of hot water and stir frosting until it is smooth.*

From top to bottom:
Peanut Butter-Oatmeal Rounds (recipe, page 30),
Fudge Ecstasies, and
Pumpkin-Pecan Cookies

These rich and fudgy cookies, featuring two kinds of chocolate, are sure to become a family favorite.

fudge ecstasies

prep: 20 min. **bake:** 8 min. per batch **oven:** 350°F **makes:** about 36 cookies

1	12-ounce package semisweet chocolate pieces (2 cups)
2	ounces unsweetened chocolate, chopped
2	tablespoons butter
2	eggs
⅔	cup sugar
¼	cup all-purpose flour
1	teaspoon vanilla
¼	teaspoon baking powder
1	cup chopped nuts

1 Preheat oven to 350°F. Lightly grease a cookie sheet; set aside.

2 In a medium heavy saucepan heat and stir 1 cup of the chocolate pieces, the unsweetened chocolate, and butter over low heat until smooth. Remove from heat. Add eggs, sugar, flour, vanilla, and baking powder. Beat until combined, scraping sides of pan occasionally. Stir in remaining 1 cup chocolate pieces and the nuts.

3 Drop dough by rounded teaspoons 2 inches apart onto the prepared cookie sheet. Bake for 8 to 10 minutes or until edges are firm and surfaces are dull and crackled. Transfer to a wire rack and let cool.

If you're a fan of sweet-salty flavor combinations, opt for the cocktail peanuts option, rather than chocolate chips, in this recipe.

peanut butter-oatmeal rounds

prep: 30 min. bake: 10 min. per batch oven: 375°F makes: about 48 cookies

¾ cup butter, softened
½ cup peanut butter
1 cup granulated sugar
½ cup packed brown sugar
1 teaspoon baking powder
½ teaspoon baking soda
2 eggs
1 teaspoon vanilla
1¼ cups all-purpose flour
2 cups rolled oats
1 cup chopped cocktail peanuts or semisweet chocolate pieces

1 Preheat oven to 375°F. In a large mixing bowl beat butter and peanut butter with an electric mixer on medium to high speed for 30 seconds. Add granulated sugar, brown sugar, baking powder, and baking soda. Beat until combined, scraping sides of bowl occasionally. Beat in eggs and vanilla until combined. Beat in as much of the flour as you can with the mixer. Stir in any remaining flour. Stir in oats and peanuts.

2 Drop dough by rounded teaspoons 2 inches apart onto an ungreased cookie sheet. Bake about 10 minutes or until edges are light brown. Transfer cookies to a wire rack and let cool.

chocolate-peanut butter-oatmeal rounds: *Prepare as above, except melt and cool 3 ounces unsweetened chocolate. After beating in the eggs and vanilla, stir in chocolate.*

Brandy, a liquor distilled from wine, adds an elegant touch to the icing on these sweet yet tangy cranberry-studded drops.

brandied **cranberry** drops

prep: 25 min. **bake:** 8 min. per batch **stand:** 1 min. per batch **oven:** 375°F
makes: about 30 cookies

½	cup dried cranberries
1	tablespoon brandy or orange juice
½	cup butter, softened
½	cup shortening
1	cup sugar
1	teaspoon baking powder
¼	teaspoon salt
1	egg
1	teaspoon vanilla
2¼	cups all-purpose flour
2	tablespoons finely chopped candied ginger
1	recipe Brandy Icing

1 Preheat oven to 375°F. In a small bowl combine cranberries and brandy; let stand while preparing dough.

2 In a large mixing bowl beat butter and shortening with an electric mixer on medium to high speed for 30 seconds. Add sugar, baking powder, and salt. Beat until combined, scraping sides of bowl occasionally. Beat in egg and vanilla until combined. Beat in as much of the flour as you can with the mixer. Stir in any remaining flour. Stir in cranberry mixture and the ginger.

3 Drop dough by rounded teaspoons 2 inches apart onto an ungreased cookie sheet. Bake for 8 to 10 minutes or until light brown. Let stand for 1 minute on cookie sheet. Transfer to a wire rack and let cool. Drizzle cooled cookies with Brandy Icing.

brandy icing: *In a bowl stir together 1½ cups powdered sugar, 2 tablespoons brandy or milk, and ¼ teaspoon vanilla. Stir in additional brandy or milk, 1 teaspoon at a time, until icing is of drizzling consistency.*

Serve a batch of these dreamy white-chocolate-studded treats at your next party and watch them disappear.

dream cookies

prep: 30 min. **bake:** 12 min. per batch **stand:** 1 min. per batch **oven:** 350°F
makes: about 24 cookies

½	cup shortening
½	cup butter, softened
¾	cup granulated sugar
¾	cup packed brown sugar
½	teaspoon baking powder
¼	teaspoon baking soda
¼	teaspoon salt
2	eggs
1	teaspoon vanilla
1⅓	cups all-purpose flour
⅓	cup unsweetened cocoa powder
2½	cups rolled oats
1	cup semisweet chocolate pieces
1	cup white baking pieces or peanut butter-flavor pieces
1	cup chopped macadamia nuts or pecans

1 Preheat oven to 350°F. Lightly grease a cookie sheet; set aside.

2 In a large mixing bowl beat shortening and butter with an electric mixer on medium to high speed for 30 seconds. Add granulated sugar, brown sugar, baking powder, baking soda, and salt. Beat until combined, scraping sides of bowl occasionally. Beat in eggs and vanilla until combined. Beat in flour and cocoa powder. Stir in oats, chocolate pieces, white baking pieces, and nuts.

3 Drop dough by a ¼-cup measure (or 2-ounce ice cream scoop portions) 3 inches apart onto the prepared cookie sheet. Flatten dough mounds into 3-inch circles. Bake for 12 to 14 minutes or until just set. Let stand for 1 minute on cookie sheet. Transfer to a wire rack and let cool.

Kitchen shears are great for snipping the dried apricots. To keep the fruit from sticking, spray the shears with nonstick cooking spray.

apricot-raisin drops

prep: 40 min. **bake:** 10 min. per batch **oven:** 350°F **makes:** 48 to 60 cookies

⅔ cup snipped dried
  apricots
⅔ cup golden raisins
½ cup apricot nectar
½ cup butter, softened
1 cup granulated sugar
1 teaspoon baking
  powder
½ teaspoon salt
¼ teaspoon ground
  ginger
1 egg
1 teaspoon vanilla
2¼ cups all-purpose flour
1¼ cups chopped
  walnuts
  Powdered sugar
  (optional)

1 In a small bowl stir together apricots, raisins, and nectar. Let stand for 15 minutes to soften fruit. Preheat oven to 350°F. Lightly grease a cookie sheet; set aside.

2 In a large mixing bowl beat butter with an electric mixer on medium to high speed for 30 seconds. Add granulated sugar, baking powder, salt, and ginger. Beat until combined, scraping sides of bowl occasionally. Beat in egg and vanilla until combined. Beat in as much of the flour as you can with the mixer. Stir in fruit mixture. Stir in any remaining flour and the walnuts.

3 Drop dough by rounded teaspoons 2 inches apart onto the prepared cookie sheet. Bake for 10 to 12 minutes or until edges are light brown. Transfer to a wire rack and let cool. If desired, sift powdered sugar over tops of cooled cookies.

Apricot nectar gives these cookies their deliciously fruity flavor.

Pudgy cocoa cookies topped with roly-poly marshmallows, crisp pecans, and a drizzle of caramel form an intriguingly ingenious treat.

marshmallow snappers

prep: 1 hr. **bake:** 10 min. per batch **stand:** 2 min. per batch **oven:** 350°F
makes: 48 cookies

1   12-ounce package
    semisweet or
    bittersweet
    chocolate pieces
¾   cup butter, softened
1½ cups all-purpose flour
½   cup unsweetened
    cocoa powder
1   teaspoon baking
    powder
1   teaspoon salt
1½ cups packed brown
    sugar
3   eggs
1   teaspoon vanilla
2   cups pecan halves,
    toasted (see tip,
    page 19)
24 large marshmallows,
    halved*
    Caramel ice cream
    topping (optional)

1 In a medium saucepan combine the chocolate pieces and 2 tablespoons of the butter. Heat and stir over low heat until smooth. Let stand at room temperature for 20 to 30 minutes or until cooled. Preheat oven to 350°F. Meanwhile, in a medium bowl stir together flour, cocoa powder, baking powder, and salt; set aside.

2 In a large mixing bowl beat the remaining butter with an electric mixer on medium to high speed for 30 seconds. Beat in brown sugar. Add eggs, one at a time, beating and scraping bowl after each addition. Beat in the melted chocolate mixture and the vanilla. Add the flour mixture, beating on low speed until mixture is combined.

3 Drop dough by heaping teaspoons 2 inches apart onto an ungreased cookie sheet. Bake for 8 minutes. Remove from oven. Lightly press three or four pecan halves onto each cookie, arranging pecans evenly apart and with ends pointing toward center of the cookie. Place a marshmallow half, cut side down, in the center of each cookie, with pecan ends under marshmallow.

4 Return cookies to oven for 2 minutes. Remove from oven. Lightly press a pecan half on top of each marshmallow. Let stand 2 minutes on cookie sheet. Transfer to a wire rack; cool. If desired, drizzle cookies with caramel ice cream topping just before serving.

*Use kitchen shears lightly coated with nonstick cooking spray to halve the marshmallows.

note: *Store undrizzled cookies as directed on page 16. Drizzle cookies with caramel ice cream topping just before serving.*

Purchase unsalted, roasted cashews for this recipe. Their buttery, sweet flavor is delicious with the creamy yet crisp meringue.

cashew meringues

prep: 15 min. **bake:** 15 min. per batch **oven:** 325°F **makes:** 60 cookies

4   egg whites
1   teaspoon vanilla
¼   teaspoon cream of
     tartar
4   cups powdered sugar
2   cups chopped
     cashews or mixed
     nuts

1 Place egg whites in a large mixing bowl; let stand at room temperature for 30 minutes. Preheat oven to 325°F. Lightly grease a cookie sheet; set aside.

2 Add vanilla and cream of tartar to egg whites. Beat with an electric mixer on medium speed until soft peaks form (tips curl). Add powdered sugar, ¼ cup at a time, beating on medium speed just until combined. Beat for 1 or 2 minutes more or until soft peaks form. (Do not continue beating until stiff peaks form [tips stand straight].) Using a spoon, gently fold in the nuts.

3 Drop egg white mixture by rounded teaspoons 2 inches apart onto the prepared cookie sheet. Bake about 15 minutes or until edges are light brown. Transfer to a wire rack and let cool.

note: *Store as directed on page 16. Store at room temperature for up to 2 days.*

These crisp and airy meringue cookies are sure to please the nut lovers in your family.

Toasted hazelnut flour, in combination with the Browned Butter Frosting, gives these cookies a distinctly nutty flavor.

browned butter hazelnut drops

prep: 25 min. **bake:** 10 min. per batch **stand:** 1 min. per batch **oven:** 350°F
makes: 30 cookies

½	cup butter
⅔	cup packed brown sugar
¼	cup milk
1½	cups all-purpose flour
1	cup toasted hazelnut flour*
1	recipe Browned Butter Frosting

1 Preheat oven to 350°F. In a medium saucepan heat butter over medium heat until butter turns the color of light brown sugar, stirring frequently. Remove from heat. Stir in brown sugar and milk. Stir in all-purpose flour and hazelnut flour until combined.

2 Drop dough by rounded teaspoons 2 inches apart onto an ungreased cookie sheet. Flatten slightly with back of spoon. Bake for 10 to 12 minutes or until edges just begin to brown. Let stand for 1 minute on cookie sheet. Transfer to a wire rack and let cool. Frost cooled cookies with Browned Butter Frosting.

✱ Look for toasted hazelnut flour at specialty food stores and through mail order catalogs.

browned butter frosting: *In a small saucepan heat and stir 3 tablespoons butter over medium-low heat until butter turns golden brown. (Do not scorch.) Remove from heat. Whisk in 2 cups powdered sugar, 1 teaspoon vanilla, and enough milk (2 to 3 tablespoons) to make a frosting of spreading consistency.*

Plain or chocolate cookies studded with white baking chips and semisweet chocolate chunks are a special treat.

chocolate chunk cookies

prep: 20 min. **bake:** 8 min. per batch **oven:** 375°F **makes:** 48 cookies

1	cup butter, softened
¾	cup granulated sugar
¾	cup packed brown sugar
1	teaspoon baking soda
1	egg
1	teaspoon vanilla
2½	cups all-purpose flour
11	to 12 ounces white baking chips and/or semisweet chocolate, coarsely chopped

1 Preheat oven to 375°F. In a large mixing bowl beat butter with an electric mixer on medium to high speed for 30 seconds. Add granulated sugar, brown sugar, and baking soda. Beat until combined, scraping sides of bowl occasionally. Beat in egg and vanilla until combined. Gradually beat in flour. Stir in white baking chips and/or chopped chocolate.

2 Drop dough by rounded teaspoons 2 inches apart onto an ungreased cookie sheet. Bake for 8 to 10 minutes or until edges are light brown. Transfer to a wire rack; cool.

note: *Store cookies as directed on page 16. Refrigerate up to 3 days. Do not freeze.*

double-chocolate chunk cookies: *Prepare as above, except use 2 eggs. Add 2 ounces unsweetened chocolate, melted and cooled, to the egg mixture. Substitute ½ cup unsweetened cocoa powder for ½ cup of the flour.*

Grated semisweet chocolate, chopped pecans, and ground cinnamon enhance the flavor of these chewy cookies.

cinnamon-chocolate
macaroons

prep: 1 hr. **bake:** 20 min. **stand:** 1 min. **oven:** 325°F **makes:** 26 cookies

2	egg whites
½	teaspoon vanilla
⅔	cup sugar
1	teaspoon ground cinnamon
1	cup flaked or shredded coconut
½	cup chopped pecans
½	ounce semisweet chocolate, grated

1 Place egg whites in a medium mixing bowl; let stand at room temperature for 30 minutes. Preheat oven to 325°F. Lightly grease 2 large cookie sheets or line them with parchment paper; set aside.

2 Add vanilla to egg whites. Beat with an electric mixer on high speed until soft peaks form (tips curl). In a small bowl combine sugar and cinnamon. Add the sugar mixture to the egg whites, 1 tablespoon at a time, beating until stiff peaks form (tips stand straight). Gently fold in coconut, pecans, and grated chocolate.

3 Drop egg white mixture by rounded teaspoons 2 inches apart onto the prepared cookie sheets. Bake both sheets on separate racks about 20 minutes or until set and dry. Let stand for 1 minute on cookie sheets. Transfer to a wire rack and let cool.

note: *Store cookies as directed on page 16. Store at room temperature for up to 1 day or freeze up to 1 month.*

With morsels of semisweet chocolate nestled in rich butter cookie dough, these cookies are a longtime favorite.

chocolate chip cookies

prep: 40 min. **bake:** 8 min. per batch **oven:** 375°F **makes:** about 60 cookies

¾ cup butter, softened
¼ cup shortening
1 cup packed brown sugar
½ cup granulated sugar
¾ teaspoon baking soda
½ teaspoon salt
2 eggs
1 teaspoon vanilla
2½ cups all-purpose flour
1 12-ounce package (2 cups) semisweet chocolate pieces or miniature candy-coated semiswect chocolate pieces
1½ cups chopped walnuts or pecans (optional)

1 Preheat oven to 375°F. In a large mixing bowl beat butter and shortening with an electric mixer on medium to high speed for 30 seconds. Add the brown sugar, granulated sugar, baking soda, and salt. Beat until combined, scraping sides of bowl occasionally. Beat in eggs and vanilla until combined. Beat in as much of the flour as you can with the mixer. Stir in any remaining flour. Stir in chocolate pieces and, if desired, nuts.

2 Drop dough by rounded teaspoons 2 inches apart onto an ungreased cookie sheet. Bake for 8 to 9 minutes or until edges are light brown. Transfer to a wire rack; cool.

chocolate chip cookie bars: *Prepare as above, except press dough into an ungreased 15×10×1-inch baking pan. Bake in a 375°F oven for 15 to 20 minutes or until golden. Cool on a wire rack. Cut into bars. Makes 48 bars.*

big chocolate chip cookies: *Prepare as above, except place ¼-cup mounds (or 2-ounce ice cream scoop portions) of dough about 4 inches apart on ungreased cookie sheet. If desired, flatten dough mounds to circles about ¾ inch thick. Bake in a 375°F oven for 10 to 12 minutes or until edges are light brown. Let cool on cookie sheets for 1 minute. Transfer to a wire rack and let cool. Makes about 18 cookies.*

When shredding the lemon peel, be sure to remove only the yellow part of the peel; the white pith tends to be bitter.

lemon drops

prep: 25 min. **bake:** 8 min. per batch **oven:** 375°F **makes:** 36 cookies

½ cup butter, softened
¾ cup granulated sugar
4 teaspoons finely shredded lemon peel
½ teaspoon baking powder
½ teaspoon baking soda
⅛ teaspoon salt
1 egg
½ cup dairy sour cream
⅓ cup lemon juice
2 cups all-purpose flour
1 recipe Lemon Glaze
   Yellow gumdrops, chopped (optional)
   Coarse sugar (optional)

1 Preheat oven to 375°F. In a large mixing bowl beat butter with an electric mixer on medium to high speed for 30 seconds. Add the ¾ cup sugar, the lemon peel, baking powder, baking soda, and salt. Beat until combined, scraping sides of bowl occasionally. Beat in egg, sour cream, and lemon juice until combined. Beat in as much of the flour as you can with the mixer. Stir in any remaining flour.

2 Drop dough by slightly rounded tablespoons 3 inches apart onto an ungreased cookie sheet. Bake about 8 minutes or until tops are firm. Transfer to a wire rack. Brush the tops of warm cookies with Lemon Glaze. If desired, sprinkle tops of cookies with chopped gumdrops and coarse sugar. Let cookies cool.

lemon glaze: *In a small bowl stir together ¼ cup granulated sugar and 2 tablespoons lemon juice.*

All the rage in Paris a hundred years ago, these chewy coconut bites are still a popular treat to savor.

chewy COCONUT macaroons

prep: 15 min. **bake:** 20 min. per batch **oven:** 325°F **makes:** 30 cookies

2	3.5-ounce cans (2⅔ cups total) flaked coconut
⅔	cup sugar
⅓	cup all-purpose flour
¼	teaspoon salt
4	egg whites
½	teaspoon almond extract
2	ounces semisweet chocolate (optional)
½	teaspoon shortening (optional)

1 Preheat oven to 325°F. Lightly grease and flour a large cookie sheet; set aside.

2 In a medium bowl stir together coconut, sugar, flour, and salt. Stir in egg whites and almond extract.

3 Drop egg white mixture by rounded teaspoons 2 inches apart onto the prepared cookie sheet. Bake for 20 to 25 minutes or until edges are golden brown. Transfer to a wire rack and let cool. If desired, in a small heavy saucepan heat and stir chocolate and shortening over low heat until smooth. Drizzle melted chocolate over the cooled cookies.

Wheat flakes cereal, though unexpected, adds a pleasant texture and toasty flavor to these cherry-crowned cookies.

cherry winks

prep: 30 min. **bake:** 7 min. per batch **oven:** 400°F **makes:** 36 cookies

½ cup sugar
⅓ cup shortening
½ teaspoon baking powder
¼ teaspoon salt
1 egg
1 tablespoon milk
1 teaspoon vanilla
1 cup all-purpose flour
½ cup chopped raisins
½ cup chopped walnuts
1 teaspoon finely shredded lemon peel
2 cups wheat flake cereal, crushed
18 candied cherries, halved

1 Preheat oven to 400°F. In a large mixing bowl beat sugar, shortening, baking powder, and salt with an electric mixer on medium to high speed for 30 seconds. Beat in egg, milk, and vanilla until combined. Beat in as much of the flour as you can with the mixer. Stir in any remaining flour. Stir in raisins, walnuts, and lemon peel.

2 Place crushed cereal in a shallow dish. Drop a rounded teaspoon of dough into cereal; toss lightly to coat dough with flakes. Place dough drops 2 inches apart onto an ungreased cookie sheet. Press a candied cherry half into each dough drop. Bake for 7 to 8 minutes or until bottoms are light brown. Transfer to a wire rack and let cool.

With a crunchy cereal coating and a sweet cherry center, these treats have been around for years for a good reason. They're truly delicious.

These cookies are made with melted chocolate and whole chips, then dipped in a velvety ganache for complete chocolate decadence.

ultimate chocolate-dipped cookies

prep: 40 min. bake: 8 min. per batch oven: 350°F makes: about 72 cookies

1½	cups all-purpose flour
½	cup unsweetened cocoa powder
1	teaspoon baking powder
1	teaspoon salt
1	12-ounce package (2 cups) semisweet or bittersweet chocolate pieces
¾	cup butter, softened
1½	cups packed brown sugar
3	eggs
1	teaspoon vanilla
1	cup semisweet chocolate pieces or white baking pieces
1	recipe Chocolate Ganache

1 Preheat oven to 350°F. In a medium bowl stir together flour, cocoa, baking powder, and salt. Set aside.

2 In a medium heavy saucepan combine the 2 cups chocolate pieces and 2 tablespoons of the butter. Heat and stir over low heat until smooth. Set aside to cool slightly.

3 In a large mixing bowl beat remaining butter for 30 seconds. Add brown sugar. Beat until combined; scrape sides of bowl. Beat in eggs, one at a time, scraping sides of bowl after each addition. Beat in melted chocolate mixture and the vanilla until combined. Add the flour mixture and beat on low speed until well combined. Stir in the 1 cup chocolate pieces.

4 Drop dough by rounded teaspoons 2 inches apart onto an ungreased cookie sheet. Bake for 8 to 10 minutes or until edges are firm and surface is slightly cracked. Transfer to a wire rack; cool. Dip each cooled cookie one-third to halfway into Chocolate Ganache. Place on wire rack until ganache is set.

chocolate ganache: *In a saucepan combine ½ cup whipping cream, 1 tablespoon butter, and 1 tablespoon granulated sugar. Bring just to boiling, stirring to dissolve sugar. Remove from heat. Place 1 cup semisweet chocolate pieces in a bowl. Pour hot cream mixture over chocolate; let stand 5 minutes. Stir until smooth. Let cool before using.*

*These cookies burst
with flavor—three
kinds of chocolate
make them exciting
and indulgent.*

chock-full of chips

prep: 40 min. **bake:** 10 min. per batch **stand:** 1 min. per batch **oven:** 350°F
makes: about 48 cookies

2½ cups all-purpose flour
1 cup quick-cooking
   rolled oats
1 cup wheat flake
   cereal
1 teaspoon baking
   powder
1 teaspoon baking soda
¼ teaspoon salt
1 cup butter, softened
1 cup granulated sugar
1 cup packed brown
   sugar
2 eggs
1½ teaspoons vanilla
1 cup semisweet
   chocolate pieces
½ cup miniature
   candy-coated milk
   chocolate pieces
½ cup white baking
   pieces

1 Preheat oven to 350°F. In a medium bowl
stir together flour, oats, cereal, baking
powder, baking soda, and salt; set aside. In a
very large mixing bowl beat butter with an
electric mixer on medium to high speed for
30 seconds. Add granulated sugar and brown
sugar. Beat until combined, scraping sides of
bowl occasionally. Beat in eggs and vanilla
until combined. Beat in as much of the flour
mixture as you can with the mixer. Stir in any
remaining flour mixture. Stir in the semisweet
chocolate pieces, candy-coated chocolate
pieces, and white baking pieces.

2 Drop dough by rounded teaspoons
2 inches apart onto an ungreased cookie
sheet. Bake for 10 to 12 minutes or until
golden brown. Let stand for 1 minute on
cookie sheet. Transfer to a wire rack; cool.

Want a new spin on old-fashioned chocolate chip cookies? Stir in some honey-roasted peanuts and chocolate-covered peanut butter cups.

chocolate-peanut blowouts

prep: 30 min. bake: 10 min. per batch oven: 350°F makes: about 30 cookies

½	cup butter, softened
½	cup peanut butter
½	cup packed brown sugar
¼	cup granulated sugar
1	teaspoon baking soda
¼	teaspoon salt
1	egg
¼	cup milk
1	teaspoon vanilla
2	cups all-purpose flour
¾	cup semisweet chocolate pieces
¾	cup honey-roasted peanuts
¾	cup coarsely chopped bite-size chocolate-covered peanut butter cups (about 15)*

1 Preheat oven to 350°F. In a large mixing bowl beat butter and peanut butter with an electric mixer on medium to high speed for 30 seconds. Add brown sugar, granulated sugar, baking soda, and salt. Beat until combined, scraping sides of bowl occasionally. Beat in egg, milk, and vanilla until combined. Beat in as much of the flour as you can with the mixer. Stir in any remaining flour. Stir in the chocolate pieces, peanuts, and chopped peanut butter cups.

2 Drop dough by generously rounded teaspoons 2 inches apart onto an ungreased cookie sheet. Bake about 10 minutes or until light brown. Transfer to a wire rack and let cool.

*For easier chopping, freeze miniature chocolate-covered peanut butter cups in their wrappers for 1 hour. Remove wrappers before chopping the candies.

jumbo cookies: *Place ¼-cup mounds (or 2-ounce ice cream scoop portions) of dough about 4 inches apart on an ungreased cookie sheet. Bake for 12 to 15 minutes or until golden brown. Let stand for 2 minutes on cookie sheet. Transfer to a wire rack and let cool. Makes about 20 cookies.*

These melt-in-your-mouth drop cookies are super-rich with bittersweet chocolate and macadamia nuts.

chocolate dreams

prep: 45 min. **bake:** 8 min. **oven:** 350°F **makes:** about 40 cookies

8 ounces bittersweet chocolate, chopped
2 tablespoons butter
3 tablespoons all-purpose flour
¼ teaspoon baking powder
2 eggs
⅔ cup sugar
1 teaspoon vanilla
2 cups chopped macadamia nuts
1½ cups semisweet chocolate pieces

1 In a medium saucepan cook and stir bittersweet chocolate and butter over low heat until melted and smooth. Remove from heat and cool mixture about 20 minutes. Meanwhile, preheat oven to 350°F. Line two large cookie sheets with foil or parchment paper; set aside.

2 In a small bowl stir together flour and baking powder; set aside. In a large mixing bowl beat eggs, sugar, and vanilla with an electric mixer on medium speed about 5 minutes or until thickened and pale yellow. Gently stir in flour mixture and cooled melted chocolate. Stir in nuts and chocolate pieces.

3 Immediately, using a small cookie scoop (1½ inches in diameter), drop dough in mounds 1 inch apart onto prepared cookie sheets. (Dough will thicken as it stands.) Bake both sheets of cookies at the same time on separate racks for 8 to 9 minutes or until edges are set but centers are soft, switching sheets to the opposite racks halfway through baking. Cool cookies completely on cookie sheets set on wire racks. Peel cooled cookies off the foil or parchment paper.

Make this recipe when you want to send someone cookies via mail. This sturdy favorite holds up to anything that shipping can dish out.

peanut butter oatmeal drops

prep: 30 min. bake: 10 min. per batch stand: 1 min. per batch oven: 350°F
makes: about 48 cookies

1 cup butter, softened
1 cup creamy or chunky peanut butter
2 cups packed brown sugar
1 teaspoon baking soda
1 teaspoon baking powder
½ teaspoon salt
2 eggs
2 teaspoons vanilla
2¼ cups all-purpose flour
2 cups rolled oats
1 cup milk chocolate pieces (optional)

1 Preheat oven to 350°F. In a large mixing bowl beat butter and peanut butter with an electric mixer on medium to high speed for 30 seconds. Add brown sugar, baking soda, baking powder, and salt. Beat until combined, scraping sides of bowl occasionally. Beat in eggs and vanilla until combined. Beat in the flour. Stir in the oats and, if desired, the milk chocolate pieces.

2 Drop dough by rounded teaspoons 2 inches apart onto ungreased cookie sheet. Bake for 10 to 12 minutes or until golden brown. Let stand for 1 minute on cookie sheet. Transfer to a wire rack; cool.

Make someone's day special by giving a friend a batch of these irresistible cookies.

Greet out-of-town guests with these spiced pecan and raisin-filled cookies, which are a traditional Southern favorite.

hermits

prep: 25 min. **bake:** 8 min. per batch **oven:** 375°F **makes:** about 48 cookies

¾   cup butter
¾   cup packed brown
      sugar
1   teaspoon ground
      cinnamon
½   teaspoon baking soda
¼   teaspoon ground
      cloves
¼   teaspoon ground
      nutmeg
1   egg
¼   cup strong brewed
      coffee, cooled
1½ cups all-purpose flour
2   cups raisins
1   cup chopped pecans

1 Preheat oven to 375°F. In a large mixing bowl beat butter with an electric mixer on medium to high speed for 30 seconds. Add brown sugar, cinnamon, baking soda, cloves, and nutmeg. Beat until combined, scraping sides of bowl occasionally. Beat in egg and coffee until combined. Beat in as much of the flour a you can with the mixer. Stir in any remaining flour. Stir in raisins and pecans.

2 Drop dough by rounded tablespoons 2 inches apart onto an ungreased cookie sheet. Bake for 8 to 10 minutes or until edges are light brown. Transfer to a wire rack; cool.

These delicate golden meringues melt away in your mouth to reveal a surprise hidden inside. Kids and grown-ups alike will love them.

orange surprise meringues

prep: 1 hr. **bake:** 15 min. **stand:** 30 min. **oven:** 325°F
makes: about 30 cookies

2   egg whites
½   teaspoon vanilla
⅛   teaspoon cream of
    tartar
½   cup granulated sugar
8   orange slice-shape
    jelly candies, each
    cut into 4 pieces
    Orange colored sugar

1 Place egg whites in a medium bowl; let stand at room temperature for 30 minutes. Preheat oven to 325°F. Line two large cookie sheets with parchment paper; set aside.

2 Add vanilla and cream of tartar to egg whites. Beat until soft peaks form (tips curl). Add granulated sugar 1 tablespoon at a time, beating on high speed until stiff peaks form (tips stand straight).

3 Drop egg white mixture by rounded teaspoons 1½ inches apart onto prepared cookie sheets. Press one candy piece into each mound. With a knife, swirl meringue over candy to cover. Sprinkle with orange sugar.

4 Bake sheets on separate racks 15 minutes. Turn oven off and let cookies dry in closed oven for 30 minutes. Transfer to wire rack; cool.

note: *Store cookies as directed on page 16. Store at room temperature for up to 2 days.*

chocolate chip meringues

prep: 50 min. **bake:** 20 min. per batch **oven:** 300°F **makes:** 36 cookies

2   egg whites
½   teaspoon vanilla
⅛   teaspoon cream of
    tartar
⅔   cup sugar
⅔   cup miniature
    semisweet
    chocolate pieces

1 Place egg whites in a medium mixing bowl; let stand at room temperature for 30 minutes. Preheat oven to 300°F. Lightly grease a cookie sheet; set aside.

2 Add vanilla and cream of tartar to egg whites. Beat until soft peaks form (tips curl). Add sugar, 1 tablespoon at a time, beating until stiff peaks form (tips stand straight). Fold in the chocolate pieces.

3 Drop by rounded teaspoons 2 inches apart onto prepared cookie sheet. Bake 20 minutes or until firm and bottoms are light brown. Transfer to a wire rack; cool.

note: *Store cookies as directed on page 16. Store at room temperature for up to 2 days.*

Orange Surprise Meringues

*Malted milk balls and malted milk powder give these cookies
old-time flavor, sure to bring back favorite childhood memories.*

malted milk cookies

prep: 30 min. **bake:** 10 min. per batch **stand:** 1 min. per batch **oven:** 375°F
makes: about 36 cookies

1	cup butter, softened
¾	cup granulated sugar
¾	cup packed brown sugar
1	teaspoon baking soda
2	eggs
1	teaspoon vanilla
2	ounces unsweetened chocolate, melted and cooled
2¼	cups all-purpose flour
½	cup instant malted milk powder
1	cup chopped malted milk balls

1 Preheat oven to 375°F. In a large mixing bowl beat butter with an electric mixer on medium to high speed for 30 seconds. Add granulated sugar, brown sugar, and baking soda. Beat until combined, scraping sides of bowl occasionally. Beat in eggs, vanilla, and melted chocolate until combined. Beat in as much of the flour as you can with the mixer. Stir in any remaining flour and the malted milk powder. Stir in chopped malted milk balls.

2 Drop dough from rounded teaspoons 2½ inches apart onto an ungreased cookie sheet. Bake about 10 minutes or until edges are firm. Let stand for 1 minute on cookie sheet. Transfer to a wire rack and let cool.

Counterclockwise from top:
**Peanut Brittle Cookies,
Malted Milk Cookies**

If you don't share your grandmother's knack for candy making,
simply purchase the peanut brittle at a candy shop.

peanut brittle cookies

prep: 25 min. **bake:** 12 min. per batch **stand:** 2 min. per batch **oven:** 350°F
makes: about 24 cookies

½ cup butter, softened
¼ cup shortening
1 cup packed dark
   brown sugar
½ teaspoon baking
   powder
¼ teaspoon baking soda
1 egg
1 teaspoon vanilla
1¼ cups all-purpose flour
1¼ cups quick-cooking
   rolled oats
4 ounces bittersweet
   or semisweet
   chocolate, chopped
1 cup crushed peanut
   brittle

1 Preheat oven to 350°F. Line two cookie sheets with foil; grease the foil. Set aside.

2 In a large mixing bowl beat butter and shortening with an electric mixer on medium to high speed for 30 seconds. Add brown sugar, baking powder, and baking soda. Beat until combined, scraping sides of bowl occasionally. Beat in egg and vanilla until combined. Beat in as much of the flour as you can with the mixer. Stir in any remaining flour. Stir in oats, chopped chocolate, and ½ cup of the peanut brittle.

3 Drop dough by rounded teaspoons 2 inches apart onto the prepared cookie sheets. Flatten each mound slightly. Bake one sheet at a time for 8 minutes. Remove from oven. Sprinkle cookies with the remaining ½ cup crushed peanut brittle, carefully pressing in slightly. Bake for 4 to 5 minutes more or until edges are light brown. Let stand for 2 minutes on cookie sheet. Transfer to a wire rack and let cool.

Imagine the buttery flavor and
delightful crunch of peanut brittle encased in a soft,
chewy (and easy-to-make) oatmeal cookie.

These chocolate drop cookies get a fun flavor twist with the help of instant coffee crystals and slivered almonds.

chocolate-coffee-almond cookies

prep: 45 min. **bake:** 8 min. per batch **stand:** 1 min. per batch **oven:** 350°F
makes: about 40 cookies

½	cup instant coffee crystals
2	tablespoons hot water
1	cup butter, softened
1¼	cups sugar
¾	teaspoon baking soda
½	teaspoon salt
2	eggs
1	teaspoon vanilla
2⅔	cups all-purpose flour
2	cups semisweet chocolate pieces
¾	cup slivered almonds, toasted (see tip, page 19)

1 Preheat oven to 350°F. Lightly grease a cookie sheet; set aside. In a small bowl dissolve coffee crystals in the hot water; set aside. In a large mixing bowl beat butter, sugar, baking soda, and salt with an electric mixer on medium speed until well combined, scraping sides of bowl occasionally. Beat in coffee mixture, eggs, and vanilla until combined. Beat in as much of the flour as you can with the mixer. Stir in any remaining flour. Stir in chocolate pieces and almonds.

2 Drop dough by heaping teaspoons 2 inches apart onto a greased cookie sheet. Bake for 8 to 10 minutes or until edges are firm and light brown. Let stand for 1 minute on cookie sheet. Transfer to a wire rack and let cool.

Frozen orange juice concentrate imparts the sunshine-fresh flavor to these cookies. Use one can for both the dough and the frosting.

orange snowdrops

prep: 25 min. bake: 8 min. per batch stand: 1 min. per batch oven: 375°F
makes: about 36 cookies

½ cup butter
½ cup shortening
1 cup powdered sugar
½ teaspoon baking soda
1 egg
½ of a 6-ounce can
   (⅓ cup) frozen
   orange juice
   concentrate,
   thawed
1 teaspoon vanilla
2 cups all-purpose flour
1 recipe Orange
   Frosting
   Finely shredded
   orange peel
   (optional)

1 Preheat oven to 375°F. In a large mixing bowl beat butter and shortening with an electric mixer on medium to high speed for 30 seconds. Add powdered sugar and baking soda. Beat until combined, scraping sides of bowl occasionally. Beat in egg, orange juice concentrate, and vanilla until combined. Beat in as much of the flour as you can with the mixer. Stir in any remaining flour.

2 Drop dough by rounded teaspoons 2 inches apart onto an ungreased cookie sheet. Bake about 8 minutes or until edges are light brown. Let stand for 1 minute on cookie sheet. Transfer to a wire rack and let cool. Frost cooled cookies with Orange Frosting. If desired, sprinkle with orange peel.

orange frosting: *In a small bowl stir together ½ of a 6-ounce can (⅓ cup) frozen orange juice concentrate, thawed; ½ teaspoon finely shredded orange peel; and 3 cups powdered sugar until mixture is smooth.*

This cookie dazzles with its irresistible Browned Butter Frosting. If you haven't tried this kind of frosting, now is the time to discover a classic.

frosted **butterscotch** cookies

prep: 35 min. **bake:** 10 min. per batch **oven:** 375°F **makes:** about 60 cookies

2½ cups all-purpose flour
1 teaspoon baking soda
½ teaspoon baking powder
½ teaspoon salt
1½ cups packed brown sugar
½ cup shortening
2 eggs
1 teaspoon vanilla
1 8-ounce carton dairy sour cream
⅔ cup chopped walnuts
1 recipe Browned Butter Frosting
 Walnut halves or chopped walnuts (optional)

1 Preheat oven to 375°F. Lightly grease a cookie sheet; set aside.

2 In a medium bowl stir together flour, baking soda, baking powder, and salt; set aside. In a large mixing bowl beat the brown sugar and shortening with an electric mixer on medium speed until combined. Beat in eggs and vanilla until combined. Alternately add flour mixture and sour cream, beating in after each addition. Stir in the ⅔ cup chopped nuts.

3 Drop dough by rounded teaspoons 2 inches apart onto the prepared cookie sheet. Bake for 10 to 12 minutes or until edges are light brown. Transfer to a wire rack and let cool. Frost cooled cookies with Browned Butter Frosting. If desired, top with walnut halves or chopped walnuts.

browned butter frosting: *In a medium saucepan heat and stir ½ cup butter over medium-low heat until butter turns golden brown. (Do not scorch.) Remove from heat. Whisk in 3½ cups powdered sugar, 5 teaspoons boiling water, and 1½ teaspoons vanilla. Beat until frosting is easy to spread. Immediately spread on cookies. If frosting begins to get stiff, stir in a small amount of boiling water.*

When chocolate-loving friends come to visit, delight them with a batch of these deep chocolate cookies.

frosted sour cream
and chocolate drops

prep: 35 min. bake: 8 min. per batch oven: 350°F makes: about 42 cookies

½ cup butter, softened
1 cup packed brown
    sugar
½ teaspoon baking soda
¼ teaspoon salt
1 egg
1 teaspoon vanilla
2 ounces unsweetened
    chocolate, melted
    and cooled
1 8-ounce carton dairy
    sour cream
2 cups all-purpose flour
1 recipe Chocolate
    Butter Frosting

1 Preheat oven to 350°F. In a large mixing bowl beat butter with an electric mixer on medium to high speed for 30 seconds. Add brown sugar, baking soda, and salt. Beat until combined, scraping sides of bowl occasionally. Beat in egg and vanilla until combined. Add melted chocolate; beat until combined. Beat in sour cream. Beat in as much of the flour as you can with the mixer. Stir in any remaining flour.

2 Drop dough by slightly rounded teaspoons about 2 inches apart onto an ungreased cookie sheet. Bake cookies for 8 to 10 minutes or until edges are firm. Transfer to a wire rack and let cool. Frost cooled cookies with Chocolate Butter Frosting.

chocolate butter frosting: *In a medium mixing bowl beat ¼ cup butter with an electric mixer on medium to high speed until fluffy. Gradually beat in ⅓ cup unsweetened cocoa powder and 1 cup powdered sugar. Slowly beat in 3 tablespoons milk and 1 teaspoon vanilla. Slowly beat in an additional 1½ cups powdered sugar. If necessary, beat in additional milk to make a frosting of spreading consistency.*

Counter clockwise from top:
**Frosted Sour Cream
and Chocolate Drops,
Stuffed Date Drops**

*A brown sugar-sour cream
dough encapsulates a
pecan-stuffed date in each
of these chewy cookies.*

stuffed date drops

prep: 35 min. bake: 8 min. per batch oven: 375°F makes: 60 cookies

1	pound pitted dates
60	to 70 pecan halves
¼	cup butter, softened
¾	cup packed brown sugar
½	teaspoon baking powder
½	teaspoon baking soda
¼	teaspoon salt
1	egg
1¼	cups all-purpose flour
½	cup dairy sour cream
1	recipe Browned Butter Icing

1 Preheat oven to 375°F. Stuff each date with a pecan half; set aside. In a large mixing bowl beat butter with an electric mixer on medium to high speed for 30 seconds. Add brown sugar, baking powder, baking soda, and salt. Beat until combined, scraping sides of bowl occasionally. Beat in egg until combined. Alternately add flour and sour cream, beating in after each addition. Stir in stuffed dates.

2 Drop dough by teaspoons 2 inches apart onto an ungreased cookie sheet, allowing one date per cookie. Bake for 8 to 10 minutes or until golden brown. Transfer to a wire rack and let cool. Drizzle cooled cookies with Browned Butter Icing.

browned butter icing: *In a saucepan heat and stir ½ cup butter over medium heat until golden brown. (Do not scorch.) Remove from heat. Whisk in 3 cups powdered sugar and 1 teaspoon vanilla. Add enough water (2 to 3 tablespoons) to make an icing of drizzling consistency.*

Chocolate-covered raisins are the secret ingredient in these tasty oatmeal cookie concoctions.

favorite oatmeal cookies

prep: 25 min. **bake:** 8 min. per batch **oven:** 350°F **makes:** 36 cookies

2 cups rolled oats
⅓ cup butter
⅓ cup shortening
¾ cup granulated sugar
¾ cup packed brown sugar
1 teaspoon baking soda
2 eggs
1 teaspoon vanilla
1 cup all-purpose flour
1 cup coarsely chopped walnuts
1 cup chocolate-covered raisins

1 Preheat oven to 350°F. For oat flour, place ½ cup of the oats in a blender or 1 cup in a food processor. Cover and blend or process until oats turn into a powder. Transfer powder to a small bowl. If using a blender, repeat with ½ cup more oats. Set aside.

2 In a large mixing bowl beat butter and shortening with an electric mixer on medium to high speed for 30 seconds. Add granulated sugar, brown sugar, and baking soda. Beat until combined, scraping sides of bowl occasionally. Beat in eggs and vanilla until combined. Beat in oat flour and all-purpose flour. Stir in remaining 1 cup rolled oats, the walnuts, and raisins.

3 Drop dough by heaping teaspoons 2 inches apart onto an ungreased cookie sheet. Bake for 8 to 10 minutes or until edges are light brown. Transfer to a wire rack; cool.

Whether you choose to use hickory nuts, black walnuts, or toasted pecans, the powder-white meringue creates the perfect base.

hickory nut macaroons

prep: 25 min. bake: 15 min. per batch oven: 325°F makes: about 36 cookies

4   egg whites
4   cups sifted powdered
     sugar
2   cups chopped
     hickory nuts,* black
     walnuts, or toasted
     pecans (see tip,
     page 19)

1 Preheat oven to 325°F. Lightly grease a cookie sheet; set aside. In a large mixing bowl beat egg whites with an electric mixer on high speed until soft peaks form (tips curl). Gradually add powdered sugar, about ¼ cup at a time, beating at medium speed just until well combined. Beat on high speed about 2 minutes more or until stiff peaks form (tips stand straight). Gently stir in the nuts.

2 Drop egg white mixture by rounded teaspoons 2 inches apart onto the prepared cookie sheet. Bake about 15 minutes or until very light brown (cookies will puff and sides will split during baking). Transfer to a wire rack and let cool.

✳ Look for hickory nuts at your local farmer's market or at specialty food stores.

note: *Store cookies as directed on page 16. Store at room temperature for up to 2 days.*

These melt-in-your-mouth cookies are ever so easy to make and packed with protein-rich nuts.

Crispy yet chewy, these cranberry cookies are extra special with chopped almonds, shredded orange peel, and white chocolate.

crisp **cranberry** rounds

prep: 20 min. **bake:** 8 min. per batch **stand:** 2 min. per batch **oven:** 350°F
makes: about 30 cookies

⅓   cup butter, cut up
⅓   cup milk
¼   cup sugar
¾   cup finely chopped
     almonds, toasted
     (see tip, page 19)
⅔   cup dried cranberries,
     finely snipped
¼   cup all-purpose flour
1   teaspoon finely
     shredded orange
     peel
½   of a 6-ounce package
     white chocolate
     baking squares or
     white baking bars
2   teaspoons shortening

1 Preheat oven to 350°F. Grease and flour two cookie sheets; set aside.

2 In a medium heavy saucepan combine butter, milk, and sugar. Bring to boiling over medium-high heat, stirring occasionally. Remove from heat. Stir in almonds, cranberries, flour, and orange peel.

3 Drop cranberry mixture by slightly rounded teaspoons about 3 inches apart onto the prepared cookie sheets. Using the back of a spoon, spread each mound into a 2½-inch round.

4 Bake for 8 to 10 minutes or until edges are deep golden brown. (Do not underbake, or the cooled cookies may be limp rather than crisp.) Let stand for 2 minutes on cookie sheets. Carefully loosen edges and transfer to waxed paper to cool.

5 In a small heavy saucepan heat and stir the white baking squares and shortening over low heat until melted and smooth. Drizzle over the cooled cookies.

Granola and dried fruit bits lend distinctive flavor and crunch to this chip-based cookie.

fruit and chip cookies

prep: 25 min. **bake:** 10 min. per batch **stand:** 1 min. per batch **oven:** 350°F
makes: about 60 cookies

1	cup butter, softened
¾	cup packed brown sugar
½	cup granulated sugar
1	teaspoon baking soda
2	eggs
1	teaspoon vanilla
2	cups all-purpose flour
2	cups granola cereal
1	6-ounce package mixed dried fruit bits (1½ cups)
1	cup chopped hazelnuts (filberts) or walnuts
1	cup white baking pieces

1 Preheat the oven to 350°F. In a medium mixing bowl beat butter with an electric mixer on medium to high speed for 30 seconds. Add brown sugar, granulated sugar, and baking soda. Beat until combined, scraping sides of bowl occasionally. Beat in eggs and vanilla until combined. Beat in as much of the flour as you can with the mixer. Stir in any remaining flour and the granola. Stir in dried fruit bits, nuts, and baking pieces.

2 Drop dough by rounded teaspoons 2 inches apart onto an ungreased cookie sheet; flatten slightly. Bake about 10 minutes or until edges are golden. Let stand for 1 minute on cookie sheet. Transfer to a wire rack and let cool.

The indulgent flavors of chocolate, toasted coconut, and tangy raspberries mesh beautifully in these cookies.

coconut-raspberry delights

prep: 45 min. **bake:** 20 min. per batch **stand:** 30 min. **oven:** 325°F
makes: about 40 cookies

1   7-ounce package
    flaked coconut
    (2⅔ cups)
⅔   cup sugar
⅓   cup all-purpose flour
¼   teaspoon salt
3   egg whites, lightly
    beaten
½   teaspoon almond
    extract
4   ounces chocolate-
    flavor candy
    coating, chopped
¼   cup seedless
    raspberry jam or
    preserves

1 Preheat oven to 325°F. Line a cookie sheet with parchment paper; set aside. In a medium bowl stir together coconut, sugar, flour, and salt. Stir in the egg whites and almond extract.

2 Drop coconut mixture by rounded teaspoons 1 inch apart onto the prepared cookie sheet, making ¾- to 1-inch mounds. Lightly flour your thumb and press it into the center of each mound to make an indentation.

3 Bake about 20 minutes or until edges are golden. If necessary, use the rounded side of a teaspoon to press indentations again. Cool cookies completely on cookie sheet on a wire rack. Carefully remove cooled cookies from the cookie sheets.

4 In a small heavy saucepan heat and stir candy coating over low heat until melted. Carefully dip the bottom of each cooled cookie into the melted candy coating, letting excess drip off. Place cookies, candy coating sides up, on parchment paper or waxed paper; let stand about 30 minutes or until candy coating sets.

5 To fill cookies, just before serving spoon about ¼ teaspoon of the preserves into the indentation in each cookie.

note: *Store unfilled cookies as directed on page 16. Refrigerate for up to 1 week. Fill with jam before serving.*

It is hard to believe that just five ingredients add up to such a moist, delicious cookie, full of intense flavors.

cherry-coconut drops

prep: 20 min. **bake:** 12 min. per batch **stand:** 1 min. per batch **oven:** 325°F
makes: about 24 cookies

1 7-ounce package (2⅔ cups) flaked coconut

2 tablespoons cornstarch

½ cup sweetened condensed milk

1 teaspoon vanilla

½ cup chopped candied cherries

1 Preheat oven to 325°F. Grease and flour a cookie sheet; set aside.

2 In a medium bowl stir together coconut and cornstarch. Stir in sweetened condensed milk and the vanilla until combined. Stir in candied cherries.

3 Drop dough by slightly rounded teaspoons about 1 inch apart onto the prepared cookie sheet. Bake for 12 to 15 minutes or until light brown on bottoms. Let stand for 1 minute on cookie sheet. Transfer to a wire rack and let cool.

This luscious cookie works with any flavor of honey. Or substitute maple or dark corn syrup, if you prefer.

honeydoodles

prep: 30 min. **bake:** 8 min. per batch **oven:** 375°F **makes:** about 30 cookies

⅓ cup butter, softened

⅔ cup honey

¾ teaspoon baking soda

½ teaspoon cream of tartar

¼ teaspoon salt

1 egg

1½ cups all-purpose flour

1 tablespoon granulated sugar (optional)

½ teaspoon ground cinnamon (optional)

1 Preheat oven to 375°F. Lightly grease a cookie sheet; set aside. In a large mixing bowl beat butter with an electric mixer on medium to high speed for 30 seconds. Add honey, baking soda, cream of tartar, and salt. Beat until combined, scraping sides of bowl occasionally. Beat in egg until combined. Beat in as much of the flour as you can with the mixer. Stir in any remaining flour.

2 If desired, in a small bowl stir together sugar and cinnamon. Drop dough by rounded teaspoons 2 inches apart onto the prepared cookie sheet. If desired, sprinkle tops of dough mounds with sugar-cinnamon mixture. Bake for 8 to 10 minutes or until edges are just firm. Immediately transfer to a wire rack and let cool.

The spiced pumpkin dough beautifully showcases the dried currants in these iced cookies.

spiced and iced pumpkin cookies

prep: 25 min. **bake:** 8 min. per batch **oven:** 375°F **makes:** 42 cookies

1	cup shortening
½	cup granulated sugar
½	cup packed brown sugar
1½	teaspoons pumpkin pie spice
½	teaspoon baking powder
¼	teaspoon baking soda
1	egg
1	cup canned pumpkin
2	cups all-purpose flour
½	cup dried currants
1	recipe Brown Sugar Icing

1 Preheat oven to 375°F. In a large mixing bowl beat shortening with an electric mixer on medium to high speed for 30 seconds. Add granulated sugar, brown sugar, pumpkin pie spice, baking powder, and baking soda. Beat until combined, scraping sides of bowl occasionally. Beat in egg and pumpkin until combined. Beat in as much of the flour as you can with the mixer. Stir in any remaining flour and the currants.

2 Drop dough by rounded teaspoons 2 inches apart onto an ungreased cookie sheet. Bake for 8 to 10 minutes or until tops are firm. Transfer to a wire rack and let cool. Frost cooled cookies with Brown Sugar Icing.

brown sugar icing: *In a small saucepan combine ½ cup packed brown sugar, 3 tablespoons butter, and 1 tablespoon milk. Heat and stir until butter melts. Remove from heat. Stir in 1 cup powdered sugar and 1 teaspoon vanilla. Frost cookies immediately after preparing frosting. If frosting begins to set, stir in a few drops of hot water.*

Coffee-flavor dough flecked with chocolate and chocolate dough flecked with chopped nuts bake side by side, giving the cookies a yin-yang effect.

coffee-and-cream drops

prep: 30 min. **bake:** 8 min. per batch **stand:** 1 min. per batch **oven:** 375°F
makes: about 48 cookies

2	tablespoons instant coffee crystals
3	tablespoons light cream or half-and-half
1	cup butter, softened
⅔	cup granulated sugar
⅔	cup packed brown sugar
1	teaspoon baking soda
¼	teaspoon salt
1	egg
1	teaspoon vanilla
2¼	cups all-purpose flour
¼	cup unsweetened cocoa powder
½	cup chopped nuts
½	cup miniature semisweet chocolate pieces

1 Preheat oven to 375°F. In a small bowl dissolve coffee crystals in 1 tablespoon of the light cream; set aside.

2 In a large mixing bowl beat butter with an electric mixer on medium to high speed for 30 seconds. Add granulated sugar, brown sugar, baking soda, and salt. Beat until combined, scraping sides of bowl occasionally. Beat in the coffee mixture, egg, and vanilla until combined. Beat in as much of the flour as you can with the mixer. Using a wooden spoon, stir in any remaining flour.

3 Divide the dough in half. Set one portion aside. Stir the remaining 2 tablespoons light cream and the cocoa powder into the remaining portion. Stir nuts into chocolate dough. Stir chocolate pieces into plain dough.

4 Drop scant teaspoons of each dough side by side onto an ungreased cookie sheet. Press dough pairs together. Bake for 8 to 9 minutes or until just set. Let stand for 1 minute on cookie sheet. Transfer to a wire rack and let cool.

This variation of basic brown sugar cookie dough shines with dried cranberries, almonds, and a zesty orange drizzle.

cranberry jumbles

prep: 25 min. **bake:** 12 min. per batch **oven:** 350°F **makes:** 32 cookies

1 cup all-purpose flour
⅓ cup whole wheat flour
¾ cup packed brown sugar
¾ teaspoon baking powder
⅛ teaspoon baking soda
½ teaspoon ground cinnamon
½ cup shortening
1 egg, lightly beaten
2 tablespoons cranberry juice or orange juice
1 cup dried cranberries
½ cup slivered almonds
1 recipe Orange Icing

1 Preheat oven to 350°F. In a large mixing bowl stir together the all-purpose flour, whole wheat flour, brown sugar, baking powder, baking soda, and cinnamon. Cut in shortening until mixture resembles fine crumbs. Stir in egg and juice until combined. Stir in cranberries and almonds.

2 Drop dough by rounded teaspoons 2 inches apart onto an ungreased cookie sheet. Bake for 12 to 14 minutes or until bottoms are light brown. Transfer to a wire rack and let cool. Drizzle cooled cookies with Orange Icing.

orange icing: *In a small bowl stir together 1 cup sifted powdered sugar, ½ teaspoon finely shredded orange peel, and enough orange juice (1 to 2 tablespoons) to make an icing of drizzling consistency.*

With fudgy centers, chocolate pieces, nuts, and a drizzle of chocolate, it is plain to see how these cookies came by their name.

ultimate chocolate cookies

prep: 25 min. **bake:** 8 min. per batch **stand:** 1 min. per batch **oven:** 350°F
makes: 36 cookies

¼ cup all-purpose flour
¼ teaspoon baking
   powder
   Dash salt
1 12-ounce package
   (2 cups) semisweet
   chocolate pieces
2 ounces unsweetened
   chocolate
2 tablespoons butter
2 eggs
⅔ cup granulated sugar
1 teaspoon vanilla
1 cup chopped nuts
4 ounces semisweet
   chocolate, melted

1 Preheat oven to 350°F. Lightly grease a cookie sheet; set aside. In a small bowl stir together flour, baking powder, and salt. Set aside.

2 In a heavy saucepan heat and stir 1 cup of the chocolate pieces, the unsweetened chocolate, and butter until smooth. Transfer to a large mixing bowl; cool slightly. Beat in eggs, sugar, and vanilla until combined. Beat in flour mixture. Stir in remaining 1 cup chocolate pieces and the nuts.

3 Drop dough by heaping teaspoons onto the prepared cookie sheet. Bake for 8 to 10 minutes or until edges are firm and surface is dull and cracked. Let stand for 1 minute on cookie sheet. Transfer to a wire rack; cool. Drizzle melted chocolate over cooled cookies.

Delight chocolate-loving friends with a batch of these decadent cookies.

The magical melding of white chocolate and raspberries adds magic to these cookies.

white chocolate and
raspberry cookies

prep: 35 min. **bake:** 7 min. per batch **stand:** 1 min. per batch **oven:** 375°F
makes: about 48 cookies

11	ounces white baking bar
½	cup butter, softened
1	cup sugar
1	teaspoon baking soda
¼	teaspoon salt
2	eggs
2¾	cups all-purpose flour
½	cup seedless raspberry jam
½	teaspoon shortening

1 Preheat oven to 375°F. Lightly grease a cookie sheet; set aside. Chop 4 ounces of the white baking bar; set aside. In a small heavy saucepan heat and stir 4 ounces of the remaining white baking bar over low heat until smooth; cool.

2 In a large mixing bowl beat butter with an electric mixer on medium to high speed for 30 seconds. Add sugar, baking soda, and salt. Beat until combined, scraping sides of bowl occasionally. Beat in eggs and melted white baking bar until combined. Beat in as much of the flour as you can with the mixer. Stir in any remaining flour. Stir in the 4 ounces chopped white baking bar.

3 Drop dough by rounded teaspoons 2 inches apart onto the prepared cookie sheet. Bake for 7 to 9 minutes or until cookies are light brown around edges. Let stand for 1 minute on cookie sheet. Transfer to a wire rack and let cool.

4 Just before serving, melt the raspberry jam in a small saucepan over low heat. Spoon about ½ teaspoon of jam on top of each cookie. In a small heavy saucepan heat and stir the remaining 3 ounces white baking bar and the shortening until smooth; drizzle over cookies. If necessary, refrigerate cookies about 15 minutes or until drizzle is firm.

note: *Store cookies as directed on page 16. Refrigerate for up to 3 days.*

Flaked coconut gives these peanutty oatmeal cookies substantial flavor and texture that your family is sure to love.

vanilla salted peanut cookies

prep: 30 min. **bake:** 7 min. per batch **stand:** 2 min. per batch **oven:** 375°F
makes: about 60 cookies

¾	cup shortening
2	cups packed brown sugar
½	teaspoon baking soda
¼	teaspoon salt
2	eggs
1	tablespoon vanilla
1½	cups all-purpose flour
2	cups rolled oats
1	cup dry-roasted peanuts
½	cup raisins
½	cup flaked coconut

1 Preheat oven to 375°F. In a large mixing bowl beat shortening with an electric mixer on medium to high speed for 30 seconds. Add brown sugar, baking soda, and salt. Beat until combined, scraping sides of bowl occasionally. Beat in eggs and vanilla until combined. Beat in flour. Stir in oats. Stir in peanuts, raisins, and coconut.

2 Drop dough by rounded teaspoons 2 inches apart onto an ungreased cookie sheet. Bake for 7 to 9 minutes or until edges are light brown. Let stand for 2 minutes on cookie sheet. Transfer to a wire rack; cool.

delicious **drops**

Bits of dried fruit, nuts, and coconut give these simple drop cookies pleasing flavor and chewy texture.

tropical snowdrops

prep: 40 min. **bake:** 9 min. per batch **oven:** 375°F **makes:** about 60 cookies

½ cup butter, softened
½ cup shortening
1 cup sugar
½ teaspoon baking soda
¼ teaspoon salt
2 eggs
½ teaspoon vanilla
¼ teaspoon rum extract
2½ cups all-purpose flour
1 cup tropical-blend mixed dried fruit bits
1 cup flaked coconut
½ cup chopped macadamia nuts or pecans
   Coconut, whole macadamia nuts, or pecan halves (optional)

1 Preheat oven to 375°F. In a large mixing bowl beat butter and shortening with an electric mixer on medium to high speed for 30 seconds. Add sugar, baking soda, and salt. Beat until combined, scraping sides of bowl occasionally. Beat in eggs, vanilla, and rum extract until combined. Beat in as much of the flour as you can with the mixer. Stir in any remaining flour, the fruit bits, the 1 cup coconut, and the ½ cup nuts.

2 Drop dough by teaspoons 2 inches apart onto an ungreased cookie sheet. If desired, lightly press additional coconut onto tops of cookies or top each with a macadamia nut or pecan half. Bake for 9 to 11 minutes or until edges are light brown. Transfer to a wire rack and let cool.

note: *Store cookies as directed on page 16. Store at room temperature for up to 2 days.*

These oversize, oat-filled treats are sure to satisfy even the hungriest cookie munchers.

oatmeal jumbos

prep: 35 min. **bake:** 15 min. per batch **stand:** 1 min. per batch **oven:** 350°F
makes: 26 cookies

1 cup peanut butter
½ cup butter, softened
1½ cups packed brown
   sugar
½ cup granulated sugar
1½ teaspoons baking
   powder
½ teaspoon baking soda
3 eggs
2 teaspoons vanilla
4 cups quick-cooking
   rolled oats
¾ cup chopped peanuts,
   walnuts, or pecans
1½ cups candy-coated
   milk chocolate
   pieces

1 Preheat oven to 350°F. In a large mixing bowl beat the peanut butter and butter with an electric mixer on medium to high speed for 30 seconds. Add the brown sugar, granulated sugar, baking powder, and baking soda. Beat until combined, scraping sides of bowl occasionally. Beat in the eggs and vanilla until combined. Stir in the oats, nuts, and candy-coated milk chocolate pieces.

2 Place ¼-cup mounds (or 2-ounce ice cream scoop portions) of dough 4 inches apart on an ungreased cookie sheet. Bake about 15 minutes or until edges are light brown. Let stand for 1 minute on cookie sheet. Transfer to a wire rack and let cool.

small cookies: *Prepare as above, except drop dough by heaping teaspoons 2 inches apart onto an ungreased cookie sheet. Bake about 10 minutes or until edges are light brown. Let stand for 1 minute on cookie sheet. Transfer to a wire rack and let cool. Makes about 60 cookies.*

If your family members are fans of all kinds of dried fruits, make these cookies extra special by using a mixture of dried fruit bits.

ranger cookies

prep: 25 min. bake: 8 min. per batch stand: 1 min. per batch oven: 375°F
makes: about 48 cookies

½	cup butter, softened
½	cup granulated sugar
½	cup packed brown sugar
½	teaspoon baking powder
¼	teaspoon baking soda
1	egg
1	teaspoon vanilla
1¼	cups all-purpose flour
1	cup quick-cooking rolled oats
1	cup flaked coconut
1	cup raisins, dried cherries, dried cranberries, or mixed dried fruit bits

1 Preheat oven to 375°F. In a large mixing bowl beat butter with electric mixer on medium to high speed for 30 seconds. Add granulated sugar, brown sugar, baking powder, and baking soda. Beat until combined, scraping sides of bowl occasionally. Beat in egg and vanilla until combined. Beat in as much of the flour as you can with the mixer. Stir in any remaining flour. Stir in oats, coconut, and raisins.

2 Drop dough by rounded teaspoons 2 inches apart onto an ungreased cookie sheet. Bake for 8 to 10 minutes or until edges are golden and centers are set. Let stand for 1 minute on cookie sheet. Transfer to a wire rack and let cool.

big ranger cookies: *Place ⅓-cup mounds of dough 2 inches apart on an ungreased cookie sheet. Press into 3-inch circles. Bake for 10 to 12 minutes or until edges are golden and centers are set. Let stand for 1 minute on cookie sheet. Transfer to a wire rack and let cool. Makes about 10 cookies.*

Instead of placing a pecan half on each cookie, you can stir ⅔ cup chopped pecans into the dough along with the chocolate pieces.

chocolate-oatmeal cookies

prep: 25 min. **bake:** 8 min. per batch **oven:** 375°F **makes:** about 48 cookies

1	cup butter, softened
1½	cups sugar
1	teaspoon baking powder
½	teaspoon baking soda
3	ounces unsweetened chocolate, melted and cooled
1	egg
1	teaspoon vanilla
1¼	cups all-purpose flour
1½	cups quick-cooking rolled oats
1	6-ounce package semisweet chocolate pieces (1 cup)
	Pecan halves

1 Preheat the oven to 375°F. In a large mixing bowl beat butter with an electric mixer on medium to high speed for 30 seconds. Add the sugar, baking powder, and baking soda. Beat until combined, scraping sides of bowl occasionally. Beat in melted chocolate, egg, and vanilla until combined. Beat in as much of the flour as you can with the mixer. Stir in any remaining flour, the oats, and chocolate pieces.

2 Drop dough by slightly rounded teaspoons about 3 inches apart onto an ungreased cookie sheet. Top each dough mound with a pecan half. Bake for 8 to 10 minutes or until edges are firm. Transfer to a wire rack; cool.

These double-chocolate goodies are so good, your friends will be asking for the recipe. Any doubts? Bake a batch to share and see for yourself.

Be sure to purchase pure maple syrup for these confections—imitation just won't do.

maple-oatmeal drops

prep: 25 min. **bake:** 13 min. per batch **stand:** 1 min. per batch **oven:** 350°F
makes: about 40 cookies

½ cup shortening
1½ cups all-purpose flour
1 cup pure maple syrup
1 egg
¼ cup milk
2 teaspoons baking powder
¼ teaspoon salt
1½ cups rolled oats
½ cup raisins
½ cup chopped walnuts or pecans

1 Preheat the oven to 350°F. Lightly grease a cookie sheet; set aside. In a large mixing bowl beat shortening with an electric mixer on medium to high speed for 30 seconds. Beat in half of the flour. Add maple syrup, egg, milk, baking powder, and salt. Beat until combined, scraping sides of bowl occasionally. Stir in remaining flour and the oats. Stir in raisins and nuts (dough will be soft).

2 Drop dough by heaping teaspoons 2 inches apart onto the prepared cookie sheet. Bake about 13 minutes or until edges are light brown. Let stand for 1 minute on cookie sheet. Transfer to a wire rack; cool.

top: **Maple-Oatmeal Drops**
bottom: **Chocolate-Oatmeal Cookies**

The flavors of peanut butter and caramel stand out in these irresistible goodies.

peanut butter and
caramel chip cookies

prep: 35 min. **bake:** 8 min. per batch **stand:** 1 min. per batch **oven:** 375°F
makes: about 30 cookies

⅔ cup crunchy peanut
butter
½ cup butter, softened
½ cup granulated sugar
½ cup packed brown
sugar
1 egg
2 cups packaged
biscuit mix
1 10-ounce package
milk-chocolate-and-
caramel-swirled
pieces, or 1½
cups semisweet
chocolate pieces
or milk-chocolate-
and-peanut-butter
pieces
1 teaspoon shortening

1 Preheat oven to 375°F. In a large mixing bowl combine peanut butter, butter, granulated sugar, and brown sugar. Beat on medium speed with an electric mixer until creamy. Beat in egg until combined. Beat in biscuit mix on low speed just until combined. Stir in 1 cup of the chocolate pieces.

2 Drop dough by rounded teaspoons 2 inches apart onto an ungreased cookie sheet. Bake for 8 to 10 minutes or until bottoms begin to brown. Let stand for 1 minute on cookie sheet. Transfer to a wire rack and let cool.

3 In a small heavy saucepan heat and stir the remaining chocolate pieces and the shortening over low heat until smooth. Cool slightly. Drizzle melted chocolate over the cooled cookies.

note: *Store cookies as directed on page 16. Refrigerate up to 3 days. Do not freeze.*

These treats double your cooking-eating enjoyment by packing both chocolate and butterscotch chips into an oatmeal dough.

double-whammy
oatmeal chews

prep: 40 min. **bake:** 8 min. per batch **stand:** 1 min. per batch **oven:** 375°F
makes: about 50 cookies

1	cup butter, softened
1	cup granulated sugar
1	cup packed brown sugar
1	teaspoon baking soda
½	teaspoon salt
2	eggs
1	teaspoon vanilla
1¾	cups all-purpose flour
3	cups rolled oats
1	cup semisweet chocolate pieces
1	cup butterscotch-flavored pieces

1 Preheat oven to 375°F. In a very large mixing bowl beat butter with an electric mixer on medium to high speed for 30 seconds. Add granulated sugar, brown sugar, baking soda, and salt. Beat until combined, scraping sides of bowl occasionally. Beat in eggs and vanilla until combined. Beat in flour. Stir in oats. Stir in chocolate and butterscotch pieces.

2 Drop dough by rounded teaspoons 2 inches apart onto an ungreased cookie sheet. Bake for 8 to 10 minutes or until golden. Let stand for 1 minute on cookie sheet. Transfer to a wire rack and let cool.

These surprising cookies smell and taste just like the traditional pie.
Toast the nuts to enhance the aroma and flavor even more.

pumpkin pie drops

prep: 30 min. **bake:** 10 min. per batch **oven:** 375°F **makes:** about 48 cookies

1 cup butter, softened
½ cup granulated sugar
½ cup packed brown
   sugar
2 teaspoons pumpkin
   pie spice
1 teaspoon baking
   powder
½ teaspoon baking soda
¼ teaspoon salt
1 egg
1 cup canned pumpkin
2 tablespoons
   finely chopped
   crystallized ginger
2 cups all-purpose flour
½ cup chopped
   almonds, toasted
   (see tip, page 19)
   (optional)
1 recipe Browned
   Butter Drizzle
   Chopped almonds,
   toasted (optional)
   Finely chopped
   crystallized ginger
   (optional)

1 Preheat oven to 375°F. In a large mixing bowl beat butter with an electric mixer on medium to high speed for 30 seconds. Add granulated sugar, brown sugar, pumpkin pie spice, baking powder, baking soda, and salt. Beat until combined, scraping sides of bowl occasionally. Beat in egg, pumpkin, and the 2 tablespoons crystallized ginger. Gradually add flour, beating until combined. If desired, stir in ½ cup almonds.

2 Drop dough by rounded teaspoons 2 inches apart onto ungreased cookie sheet. Bake for 10 to 12 minutes or until bottoms are light brown. Transfer to a wire rack and let cool.

3 Place Browned Butter Drizzle in a heavy resealable plastic bag. Seal bag and snip a small hole in one corner. Drizzle icing over cooled cookies. If desired, sprinkle cookies with additional chopped almonds and crystallized ginger, pressing additions lightly into icing. Let cookies stand until drizzle sets.

browned butter drizzle: *In a medium saucepan heat and stir ⅓ cup butter over medium-low heat until butter turns golden brown. (Do not scorch.) Remove from heat. Whisk in 2½ cups powdered sugar, 1 teaspoon vanilla, and enough milk (2 to 3 tablespoons) to make an icing of drizzling consistency.*

Rolled oats in a sweetly spiced dough make this cookie wholesome but indulgent. No wonder it's an all-time pleaser.

classic oatmeal cookies

prep: 25 min. **bake:** 8 min. per batch **stand:** 1 min. per batch **oven:** 375°F
makes: about 48 cookies

¾ cup butter, softened
1 cup packed brown sugar
½ cup granulated sugar
1 teaspoon baking powder
¼ teaspoon baking soda
¼ teaspoon salt
½ teaspoon ground cinnamon (optional)
¼ teaspoon ground cloves (optional)
2 eggs
1 teaspoon vanilla
1½ cups all-purpose flour
2 cups rolled oats

1 Preheat oven to 375°F. In a large mixing bowl beat butter with an electric mixer on medium to high speed for 30 seconds. Add brown sugar, granulated sugar, baking powder, baking soda, salt, and, if desired, cinnamon and cloves. Beat until combined, scraping sides of bowl occasionally. Beat in eggs and vanilla until combined. Beat in as much of the flour as you can with the mixer. Stir in any remaining flour. Stir in oats.

2 Drop dough by rounded teaspoons 2 inches apart onto an ungreased cookie sheet. Bake for 8 to 10 minutes or until edges are lightly browned. Let stand for 1 minute on cookie sheet. Transfer to a wire rack; cool.

oatmeal raisin cookies: *Prepare as above, except after stirring in oats, stir in 1 cup raisins or snipped dried tart cherries. Makes about 54 cookies.*

Cocoa drop cookies become the ultimate treat with white chocolate, dried cherries, and chopped pecans stirred into the dough.

white chocolate chunk
and cherry cookies

prep: 40 min. **bake:** 7 min. per batch **oven:** 350°F **makes:** about 60 cookies

2   cups all-purpose flour
½   cup unsweetened
    cocoa powder
2   teaspoons baking
    powder
½   teaspoon salt
1   cup butter, softened
1½ cups sugar
2   eggs
1   teaspoon vanilla
6   ounces white
    chocolate baking
    squares, coarsely
    chopped or 1 cup
    white baking pieces
1   cup chopped pecans,
    toasted if desired
    (see tip, page 19)
½   cup dried cherries

1 Preheat oven to 350°F. Lightly grease a cookie sheet; set aside. In a medium bowl stir together flour, cocoa powder, baking powder, and salt. Set aside.

2 In a large mixing bowl beat butter with an electric mixer on medium to high speed for 30 seconds. Add sugar. Beat until combined, scraping sides of bowl occasionally. Beat in eggs and vanilla until combined. Beat in as much of the flour mixture as you can with the mixer. Stir in any remaining flour mixture, the white chocolate pieces, chopped pecans, and dried cherries.

3 Drop dough by rounded teaspoons 2 inches apart onto the prepared cookie sheet. Bake for 7 to 9 minutes or until edges are just firm (do not overbake). Transfer cookies to a wire rack and let cool.

Enhanced with cinnamon and candy-coated milk chocolate pieces, these whoppers are every bit as big in flavor as they are in size.

giant multigrain cookies

prep: 30 min. **bake:** 12 min. per batch **stand:** 2 min. per batch **oven:** 350°F
makes: 24 cookies

⅔	cup butter, softened
¾	cup granulated sugar
½	cup packed brown sugar
½	teaspoon baking soda
½	teaspoon ground cinnamon
1	egg
⅓	cup cooking oil
¼	cup honey
1	teaspoon vanilla
1¼	cups all-purpose flour
½	cup toasted wheat germ
2½	cups rolled oats
2	cups candy-coated milk chocolate pieces

1 Preheat the oven to 350°F. In a large mixing bowl beat butter with an electric mixer on medium to high speed for 30 seconds. Add granulated sugar, brown sugar, baking soda, and cinnamon. Beat until combined, scraping sides of bowl occasionally. Beat in egg, oil, honey, and vanilla until combined. Beat in flour and wheat germ. Stir in oats and candies.

2 Drop dough by a ¼-cup measure (or 2-ounce ice cream scoop portions) 4 inches apart onto an ungreased cookie sheet; flatten slightly. Bake about 12 minutes or until golden brown. Let stand for 2 minutes on cookie sheet. Transfer to a wire rack; cool.

delicious **drops**

Calling for two kinds of coconut and a bit of honey, this macaroon recipe will please everyone in your household.

golden macaroons

prep: 20 min. **chill:** 30 min. **bake:** 17 min. per batch **oven:** 300°F
makes: about 40 cookies

2½ cups flaked
    sweetened coconut
    (about 7 ounces)
2   cups unsweetened
    finely shredded
    coconut*
1   cup sugar
3   tablespoons all-
    purpose flour
¼   teaspoon salt
4   egg whites
1   tablespoon honey
1   teaspoon vanilla

1 In a bowl combine flaked and shredded coconut until evenly mixed. (Flaked coconut should be broken into separate flakes with only a few very small clumps.)

2 In a bowl combine sugar, flour, and salt. Add egg whites, honey, and vanilla. Whisk until smooth. Pour sugar mixture over coconut mixture. Stir with a wooden spoon, then use your hands to blend until evenly mixed. Cover with plastic wrap; chill 30 minutes.

3 Preheat oven to 300°F. Line a large cookie sheet with parchment paper. Drop batter by rounded tablespoons 2 inches apart onto the prepared cookie sheet. Gently pinch mounds into shaggy pyramid shapes. Bake for 17 to 19 minutes or until golden brown. Immediately transfer to a wire rack; cool.

*Look for unsweetened finely shredded coconut in natural-foods stores or in the bulk-food section of your supermarket.

note: *Store cookies as directed on page 16. Store at room temperature for up to 2 days or freeze up to 1 month.*

Simple as ever and utterly delicious, these smooth, chocolate-studded peanut butter cookies are an all-time kid favorite.

super peanut butter drops

prep: 25 min. **bake:** 10 min. per batch **stand:** 5 min. per batch **oven:** 325°F
makes: 24 cookies

1   cup peanut butter
½   cup granulated sugar
½   cup packed brown
    sugar
1   teaspoon baking soda
2   eggs
½   cup all-purpose flour
1   cup semisweet
    chocolate pieces

1 Preheat oven to 325°F. In a medium mixing bowl beat peanut butter, granulated sugar, brown sugar, and baking soda with an electric mixer on medium speed until combined. Beat in eggs until combined. Stir in flour. Stir in chocolate pieces.

2 Shape dough into 1¼-inch balls. Place balls 2 inches apart on an ungreased cookie sheet. (Do not use an insulated cookie sheet.) Flatten balls slightly with fingers.

3 Bake about 10 minutes or until cookies are slightly puffed and light brown around edges (centers will be soft). Let stand for 5 minutes on cookie sheet. Transfer to a wire rack and let cool.

chocolate-hazelnut macaroons

prep: 25 min. **bake:** 20 min. per batch **oven:** 325°F **makes:** 30 cookies

2⅔ cups flaked coconut
    (7 ounces)
¾   cup sugar
⅓   cup chopped toasted
    hazelnuts* (filberts)
    (see tip, page 19)
⅓   cup dried cranberries
¼   cup all-purpose flour
3   tablespoons
    unsweetened cocoa
    powder
¼   teaspoon salt
4   egg whites, lightly
    beaten
1   teaspoon vanilla

1 Preheat oven to 325°F. Line two large cookie sheets with parchment paper; set aside. In a medium bowl stir together coconut, sugar, hazelnuts, cranberries, flour, cocoa powder, and salt. Stir in egg whites and vanilla until combined.

2 Drop coconut mixture by rounded teaspoons 2 inches apart onto the prepared cookie sheets. Bake for 20 to 25 minutes or until set. Transfer to a wire rack and let cool.

✱ After toasting hazelnuts, place the warm nuts in a clean kitchen towel. Rub nuts with the towel to remove loose skins.

creative

3

cuto

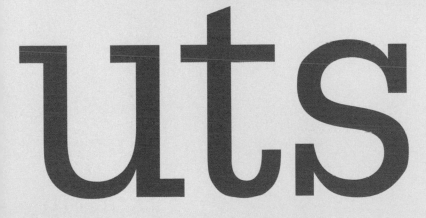

Shapely cookies are as much fun to prepare as they are to eat—especially when you enlist junior chefs' help. From rolling and cutting the dough to frosting and embellishing, these works of art yield a deliciously good time.

uts

Roll and fold the rich, buttery dough to make flaky layers that puff slightly during baking.

jam diamonds

prep: 30 min. chill: 20 min. bake: 10 min. per batch oven: 400°F
makes: 28 cookies

2	cups all-purpose flour
¼	cup sugar
1	cup butter, cut into ½-inch-thick slices
1	cup small-curd cottage cheese
¼	cup strawberry or cherry jam
	Strawberry or cherry jam (optional)
1	recipe Powdered Sugar Icing

1 In a large mixing bowl stir together flour and sugar. Using a pastry blender, cut in butter and cottage cheese just until mixture clings together (butter should remain in large pieces). Form dough into a ball. Place dough on a floured pastry cloth. With floured hands, gently knead dough for eight strokes. Using a well-floured rolling pin, roll dough into a 12×10-inch rectangle. Fold dough crosswise into thirds to form a 4×10-inch rectangle. Give the dough a quarter turn and roll into a 12×10-inch rectangle. Fold, roll, and fold one more time as before. Wrap dough in plastic wrap. Chill in the freezer for 20 to 30 minutes or until firm but not stiff.

2 Preheat oven to 400°F. Lightly grease a cookie sheet; set aside. On the floured pastry cloth, roll dough into a 15×11-inch rectangle. Using a pastry wheel or sharp knife, cut lengthwise into 1½-inch strips. Cut diagonally into about 1½-inch strips, forming diamonds. Place diamonds on the prepared cookie sheet. Press an indentation in center of each diamond. Spoon about ¼ teaspoon jam into each indentation.

3 Bake about 10 minutes or until edges are golden. Transfer to a wire rack and let cool. If desired, spoon a little additional jam onto cookies. Drizzle cooled cookies with Powdered Sugar Icing.

powdered sugar icing: *In a small bowl stir together 1 cup powdered sugar and enough milk (1 to 2 tablespoons) to make an icing of drizzling consistency.*

A creamy dough made with cashews and brown sugar turns ordinary sugar cookie cutouts into ultrabuttery, golden treats.

cashew-butter leaves

prep: 1 hr. chill: 3 hr. bake: 6 min. per batch oven: 375°F makes: 60 cookies

⅔ cup lightly salted cashews

⅓ cup butter-flavor shortening or shortening

⅓ cup butter, softened

¾ cup granulated sugar

½ cup packed brown sugar

1 teaspoon baking powder

½ teaspoon baking soda

2 eggs

1 teaspoon vanilla

2⅔ cups all-purpose flour

8 ounces white chocolate baking squares or white baking bars, chopped

4 teaspoons butter-flavor shortening or shortening

¾ cup very finely chopped lightly salted cashews

1 Place the ⅔ cup cashews in a food processor. Cover and process for 2 to 3 minutes or until a smooth butter forms, scraping down sides of bowl occasionally. Transfer cashew butter to a large mixing bowl. Add the ⅓ cup shortening and the butter. Beat with an electric mixer on medium to high speed for 30 seconds. Add granulated sugar, brown sugar, baking powder, and baking soda. Beat until combined, scraping sides of bowl occasionally. Beat in eggs and vanilla until combined. Beat in as much of the flour as you can with the mixer. Stir in any remaining flour. Divide dough in half. Cover and chill dough about 3 hours or until easy to handle.

2 Preheat oven to 375°F. On a lightly floured surface, roll half of the dough at a time until ¼ inch thick. Using a 2½-inch leaf-shape cutter, cut out dough; place 2 inches apart on an ungreased cookie sheet. Bake for 6 to 8 minutes or until edges are firm and bottoms are light brown. Transfer to a wire rack; cool.

3 In a small heavy saucepan heat and stir white chocolate and the 4 teaspoons shortening over low heat until smooth. Spread or pipe white chocolate mixture onto cooled cookies. Immediately sprinkle with the chopped cashews. Let stand until set.

This new rendition of classic s'mores is sure to bring out everyone's inner camper. Be sure to toast the marshmallows just before serving.

chocolate s'mores

prep: 1 hr. chill: 1 hr. bake: 8 min. per batch stand: 1 min. per batch
oven: 375°F makes: 25 s'mores

1 cup butter, softened
1¼ cups granulated sugar
½ teaspoon baking powder
¼ teaspoon salt
2 ounces bittersweet chocolate, melted and cooled
2 eggs
1 tablespoon milk
1½ teaspoons vanilla
¼ cup unsweetened cocoa powder
3 cups all-purpose flour
1 egg white, lightly beaten
2 tablespoons water
Coarse sugar or granulated sugar
12½ 1.55-ounce milk chocolate bars
25 large marshmallows, toasted (toast as for nuts; see tip, page 19)

1 In a large bowl beat butter for 30 seconds. Add the 1¼ cups granulated sugar, the baking powder, and salt. Beat until combined; scrape sides of bowl. Beat in melted chocolate. Beat in eggs, milk, and vanilla until combined. Beat in cocoa powder and as much of the flour as you can with the mixer. Stir in any remaining flour. Divide dough in half. Cover and chill dough 1 hour or until easy to handle.

2 Preheat oven to 375°F. On a lightly floured surface, roll half of the dough at a time into a 13-inch square. Using a fluted pastry wheel, cut dough square into twenty-five 2½- to 3-inch squares. Using a 1½-inch desired-shape cutter, make a cutout in the center of half of the squares.* Place squares on an ungreased cookie sheet.

3 Whisk together egg white and the water; brush tops of squares lightly with egg white mixture and sprinkle with coarse sugar. Bake for 8 to 10 minutes or just until tops are firm. Let stand for 1 minute on cookie sheet. Transfer to a wire rack; cool.

4 To assemble s'mores, break each chocolate bar in half crosswise; place one half on top of each solid cookie. Top each with a toasted marshmallow (still warm). Top each marshmallow with a cutout cookie; press down gently and serve immediately.

＊Bake small dough cutouts on an ungreased cookie sheet in the 375°F oven for 3 to 5 minutes or just until tops are firm. Transfer to a wire rack and let cool.

note: *If not serving immediately, prepare cookies through Step 3. Store as directed on page 16. Thaw (if frozen) and assemble as directed in Step 4.*

Using rum extract is a great way to add the distinct essence of rum to cookies without the alcohol.

butter-rum cutouts

prep: 35 min. bake: 8 min. per batch oven: 350°F makes: 50 to 60 cookies

1 cup butter, softened
⅔ cup packed brown
   sugar
1 teaspoon baking
   powder
1 teaspoon ground
   nutmeg
¼ teaspoon salt
1 egg
1 teaspoon rum extract
   or vanilla
2⅔ cups all-purpose flour
1 recipe Royal Icing
   (page 128)

1 In a large mixing bowl beat butter with an electric mixer on medium to high speed for 30 seconds. Add brown sugar, baking powder, nutmeg, and salt. Beat until combined, scraping sides of bowl occasionally. Beat in egg and rum extract until combined. Beat in as much of the flour as you can with the mixer. Stir in any remaining flour. Divide dough in half. If necessary, cover and chill dough about 1 hour or until easy to handle.

2 Preheat oven to 350°F. On a lightly floured surface, roll half of the dough at a time until ⅛ inch thick. Using cookie cutters, cut dough into desired shapes. Place cutouts 1 inch apart on an ungreased cookie sheet. Bake for 8 to 10 minutes or until edges are light brown. Transfer to a wire rack and let cool. Decorate cookies with Royal Icing. Let stand until dry.

One sweet whiff from the oven will tell you that these are no ordinary cookies.

You'll love the delicious flavor the apple butter filling gives to these cookies—it's similar to that of homebaked apple pie.

apple butter crescents

prep: 35 min. chill: 3 hr. bake: 8 min. per batch oven: 375°F
makes: 32 cookies

⅔ cup butter, softened
1 cup sugar
1 teaspoon baking powder
¼ teaspoon salt
2 eggs
1 teaspoon vanilla
3 cups all-purpose flour
⅔ cup apple butter or seedless raspberry jam
2 tablespoons sugar
½ teaspoon ground cinnamon

1 In a large mixing bowl beat butter with an electric mixer on medium to high speed for 30 seconds. Add the 1 cup sugar, the baking powder, and salt. Beat until combined, scraping sides of bowl occasionally. Beat in eggs and vanilla until combined. Beat in as much of the flour as you can with the mixer. Stir in any remaining flour. Divide dough in half. Cover and chill dough about 3 hours or until easy to handle.

2 Preheat oven to 375°F. Line a cookie sheet with foil or parchment paper; set aside. On a lightly floured surface, roll half of the dough at a time into a 12-inch square. Cut dough into sixteen 3-inch squares.

3 Spread about 1 teaspoon apple butter down the middle of each square. Fold one edge of the dough over the filling. Fold over the other edge. Place on prepared cookie sheet. Make three cuts halfway through dough on each cookie. Curve cookies slightly to separate cuts.

4 In a small bowl stir together the 2 tablespoons sugar and the cinnamon. Brush cookies lightly with a little water. Sprinkle cinnamon-sugar mixture over cookies. Bake for 8 to 10 minutes or until golden brown. Transfer to a wire rack and let cool.

A few splashes of coffee liqueur give these gingerbread cutouts a touch of sophistication, making them perfect for a special occasion.

festive gingerbread cookies

prep: 30 min. chill: 3 hr. bake: 6 min. per batch stand: 1 min. per batch
oven: 375°F makes: about 36 cookies

⅓ cup butter, softened
⅓ cup shortening
1 cup granulated sugar
½ cup packed light brown sugar
1 teaspoon baking soda
1 teaspoon ground ginger
½ teaspoon ground cinnamon
½ teaspoon ground nutmeg
1 egg
¼ cup light-color molasses
2 tablespoons coffee liqueur, strong coffee, or milk
2¼ cups all-purpose flour
1 recipe Lemon Meringue Icing
Colored sugar or edible glitter (optional)

1 In a large mixing bowl beat butter and shortening with an electric mixer on medium to high speed for 30 seconds. Add granulated sugar, brown sugar, baking soda, ginger, cinnamon, and nutmeg. Beat until combined, scraping sides of bowl occasionally. Beat in egg, molasses, and coffee liqueur until combined. Beat in as much of the flour as you can with the mixer. Stir in any remaining flour. Divide dough in half. Cover and chill dough about 3 hours or until easy to handle.

2 Preheat oven to 375°F. Lightly grease a cookie sheet; set aside. On a lightly floured surface, roll half of the dough at a time until ¼ inch thick. Using desired cookie cutters, cut out dough. Place cutouts 1 inch apart on the prepared cookie sheet. Bake for 6 to 8 minutes or until edges are light brown. Let stand for 1 minute on cookie sheet. Transfer to a wire rack and let cool.

3 Decorate cooled cookies with Lemon Meringue Icing. Pipe icing onto cookies or use a clean, fine-tip brush to paint icing onto cookies. If desired, sprinkle with colored sugar or edible glitter. Let stand until icing sets.

lemon meringue icing: *In a medium mixing bowl combine ⅓ cup warm water, 2 tablespoons meringue powder, and 1 tablespoon lemon juice. Beat lightly with a fork until blended. Add 3 to 3¼ cups powdered sugar, beating with an electric mixer on high speed until the icing is the consistency of soft whipped cream. Divide icing, if desired, and color each portion with a different food coloring. Store, tightly covered, in the refrigerator.*

*Creamy and bursting with vanilla flavor, these cookies are delicious
on their own but even better paired with a Buttercream Frosting.*

vanilla rounds

prep: 30 min. chill: 2 hr. bake: 6 min. per batch oven: 375°F
makes: about 30 sandwich cookies

½ cup butter, softened
1 3-ounce package
   cream cheese,
   softened
1 cup sugar
½ teaspoon baking soda
¼ teaspoon salt
2 eggs
1½ teaspoons vanilla
2¾ cups all-purpose flour
   Sugar (optional)
1 recipe desired flavor
   of Buttercream
   Frosting
   (pages 96–97)

1 In a large mixing bowl beat butter and cream cheese with an electric mixer on medium speed for 30 seconds. Add the 1 cup sugar, the baking soda, and salt. Beat until combined, scraping sides of bowl occasionally. Beat in eggs and vanilla until combined. Beat in as much of the flour as you can with the mixer. Stir in any remaining flour. Divide dough in half. Cover and chill dough about 2 hours or until easy to handle.

2 Preheat oven to 375°F. On a lightly floured surface, roll half of the dough at a time until ⅛ inch thick. Using a 1½-inch round cookie cutter, cut out dough. Place cutouts 1 inch apart on an ungreased cookie sheet. If desired, sprinkle cutouts lightly with additional sugar. Bake for 6 to 7 minutes or until bottoms are light brown. Transfer to a wire rack; cool.

3 Spread desired flavor of Buttercream Frosting onto the bottoms of half of the cooled cookies. Top with the remaining cookies, bottom sides down.

What's more indulgent than rich, creamy
frosting sandwiched between two
soft, chewy cookies?

The vibrant combination of cream cheese and chocolate makes these classic rounds taste delightfully rich and a little tangy.

chocolate rounds

prep: 30 min. chill: 2 hr. bake: 6 min. per batch oven: 375°F
makes: about 30 sandwich cookies

2½ cups all-purpose flour
¼   cup unsweetened
      cocoa powder
½   teaspoon baking soda
¼   teaspoon salt
½   cup butter, softened
1   3-ounce package
      cream cheese,
      softened
1   cup sugar
2   eggs
1½ teaspoons vanilla
1   recipe desired flavor
      of Buttercream
      Frosting
      (pages 96–97)

1 In a medium bowl stir together flour, cocoa powder, baking soda, and salt. Set aside. In a large mixing bowl beat butter and cream cheese with an electric mixer on medium speed for 30 seconds. Add sugar. Beat until combined, scraping sides of bowl occasionally. Beat in eggs and vanilla until combined. Beat in as much of the flour mixture as you can with the mixer. Stir in any remaining flour mixture. Divide dough in half. Cover and chill dough about 2 hours or until easy to handle.

2 Preheat oven to 375°F. On a lightly floured surface, roll half of the dough until ⅛ inch thick. Using a 1½-inch round cookie cutter, cut out dough. Place cutouts 1 inch apart on an ungreased cookie sheet. Bake for 6 to 7 minutes or until edges are firm. Transfer to a wire rack and let cool.

3 Spread Buttercream Frosting on bottoms of half of the cookies. Top with remaining cookies, bottom sides down. If desired, roll edges in additional embellishments (see pages 96–97).

Pair your favorite buttercream with the ginger rounds below or the vanilla or chocolate rounds on pages 94 and 95. Dip the edges into chopped nuts, crushed hard candies, or jimmies as shown on page 97.

spicy ginger rounds

prep: 30 min. chill: 4 hr. bake: 8 min. per batch stand: 1 min. per batch
oven: 350°F makes: about 32 sandwich cookies

½ cup butter, softened
¼ cup shortening
¾ cup packed brown
   sugar
2 tablespoons grated
   fresh ginger
1 teaspoon ground
   cinnamon
½ teaspoon salt
¼ teaspoon baking soda
¼ teaspoon ground
   nutmeg
1 egg
⅓ cup molasses
3 cups all-purpose flour
1 egg white, beaten
1 tablespoon water
1 recipe desired flavor
   of Buttercream
   Frosting (see below
   and page 97)

1 In a large bowl beat butter and shortening on medium speed for 30 seconds. Add brown sugar, ginger, cinnamon, salt, baking soda, and nutmeg. Beat until combined. Beat in whole egg and molasses. Beat in as much of the flour as you can. Stir in any remaining flour. Divide dough in half. Cover and chill for 4 to 24 hours or until dough is easy to handle.

2 Preheat oven to 350°F. Lightly grease cookie sheets or line cookie sheets with parchment paper; set aside.

3 On a lightly floured surface, roll half the dough at a time to ¼-inch thickness. Using a 1½-inch round cutter, cut out dough. Place cutouts 1 inch apart on prepared cookie sheets. Combine egg white and water. Lightly brush top of each dough shape with mixture.

4 Bake about 8 minutes or until edges are firm and bottoms just begin to brown. Let stand on cookie sheet for 1 minute. Transfer cookies to a wire rack and let cool.

5 Spread desired Buttercream Frosting onto the bottoms of half of the cookies. Top with the remaining cookies, bottom sides down.

buttercream frosting

start to finish: 10 min. makes: about 1¼ cups

½ cup butter, softened
1 teaspoon vanilla
2½ cups powdered sugar
1 to 2 tablespoons milk

1 In a bowl beat butter with an electric mixer on medium speed until fluffy. Add vanilla. Beat in half of the powdered sugar. Beat in 1 tablespoon of the milk. Beat in the remaining powdered sugar until smooth. Beat in enough of the remaining milk to make a frosting of spreading consistency.

frosting variations

citrus buttercream:
Prepare Buttercream Frosting, substituting finely shredded lemon, orange, or lime peel for the vanilla, and lemon, orange, or lime juice for the milk.

chocolate buttercream:
Prepare Buttercream Frosting, substituting ¼ cup cocoa powder for ¼ cup of the powdered sugar.

coffee buttercream:
Prepare Buttercream Frosting, omitting vanilla and substituting 2 tablespoons coffee liqueur or strong-brewed coffee for the milk. Stir in additional powdered sugar as needed to make a frosting of spreading consistency.

peppermint buttercream:
Prepare Buttercream Frosting, substituting ½ teaspoon peppermint extract for the vanilla. If desired, stir in 2 tablespoons crushed peppermint candies.

almond buttercream:
Prepare Buttercream Frosting, substituting ¼ teaspoon almond extract for the vanilla.

When shredding lime peel, be sure to remove only the green part of the rind. The white pith gives the cookies an undesirable bitter flavor.

lime-basil cookies

prep: 30 min. chill: 1 hr. bake: 7 min. per batch oven: 375°F
makes: 32 cookies

⅔	cup butter, softened
¾	cup granulated sugar
1	teaspoon baking powder
½	teaspoon salt
1	egg
1	teaspoon finely shredded lime peel (set aside)
2	tablespoons lime juice
1	teaspoon vanilla
2	cups all-purpose flour
½	cup ground pistachio nuts
1	tablespoon finely snipped fresh basil
1	recipe Lime-and-Cream Cheese Frosting
	Fresh basil leaves (optional)

1 In a large mixing bowl beat butter with an electric mixer on medium to high speed for 30 seconds. Add granulated sugar, baking powder, and salt. Beat until combined, scraping sides of bowl occasionally. Beat in egg, lime juice, and vanilla until combined. Beat in as much of the flour as you can with the mixer. Stir in any remaining flour, the pistachio nuts, the snipped basil, and the lime peel. Divide dough in half. Cover and chill dough about 1 hour or until easy to handle.

2 Preheat oven to 375°F. On a lightly floured surface, roll half of the dough at a time into a 12×6-inch rectangle. Using a fluted pastry wheel or a sharp knife, cut dough in half lengthwise, then crosswise into 3×1½-inch rectangles. Place rectangles 1 inch apart on an ungreased cookie sheet.

3 Bake for 7 to 8 minutes or until edges are firm and bottoms are very light brown. Transfer to a wire rack and let cool. Frost cooled cookies with Lime-and-Cream Cheese Frosting. If desired, garnish with basil leaves.

lime-and-cream cheese frosting: *In a bowl combine half of a 3-ounce package softened cream cheese, 2 tablespoons softened butter, and 2 teaspoons lime juice. Beat until fluffy. Beat in ¾ to 1 cup powdered sugar until frosting reaches spreading consistency. Stir in ½ teaspoon finely shredded lime peel.*

Pulverized or ground hazelnuts are the star ingredient in these shortbread cutouts. A drizzle of white chocolate makes them extra special.

hazelnut shortbread cookies

prep: 35 min. chill: 30 min. bake: 12 min. per batch oven: 350°F
makes: about 30 cookies

1 cup chopped
   hazelnuts (filberts)
   or pecan halves
2 cups all-purpose flour
½ cup sugar
⅓ cup cornstarch
1 cup cold butter, cut
   into small pieces
½ teaspoon vanilla
4 ounces white
   baking bar, melted
   (optional)

1 Preheat oven to 350°F. Place nuts in a shallow baking pan. Bake about 8 minutes or until lightly toasted; cool.

2 Place flour, sugar, and cornstarch in a food processor. Add butter and vanilla; process with several on/off turns until mixture is crumbly. Add nuts and process until mixture is combined but slightly crumbly. (Mixture should not be a ball of dough.)

3 Place dough on a lightly floured surface and form into a ball. Knead dough until smooth. Divide dough in half. Wrap in plastic wrap and chill dough about 30 minutes or until easy to handle.

4 On a lightly floured surface, roll half of the dough at a time until ¼ to ½ inch thick. Using 2½- to 3-inch star-shape or round cookie cutters, cut out dough. Place cutouts 1 inch apart on an ungreased cookie sheet. Using a fork, pierce each cutout three times, going all the way through to the cookie sheet.

5 Bake about 12 minutes or until edges and bottoms just start to brown. Transfer to a wire rack and let cool. If desired, drizzle cooled cookies with melted white baking bar.

This cookie version of chocolate-covered cherries is as delicious as the real thing.

chocolate-cherry pockets

prep: 45 min. chill: 2 hr. bake: 8 min. per batch oven: 375°F
makes: about 30 cookies

½	cup butter, softened
1	3-ounce package cream cheese, softened
1½	cups powdered sugar
⅓	cup unsweetened cocoa powder
½	teaspoon baking powder
¼	teaspoon baking soda
¼	teaspoon salt
1	egg
½	teaspoon vanilla
1¾	cups all-purpose flour
½	cup cherry preserves
2	tablespoons snipped dried cherries
1	teaspoon brandy (optional)
4	ounces bittersweet or semisweet chocolate, chopped
2	teaspoons shortening Sliced almonds, toasted (see tip, page 19)

1 In a large mixing bowl beat butter and cream cheese with an electric mixer on medium to high speed for 30 seconds. Add powdered sugar, cocoa powder, baking powder, baking soda, and salt. Beat until combined, scraping sides of bowl occasionally. Beat in egg and vanilla until combined. Beat in as much of the flour as you can with the mixer. Stir in any remaining flour. Divide dough in half. Cover and chill dough about 2 hours or until easy to handle.

2 Meanwhile, for cherry filling, in a small bowl stir together cherry preserves, dried cherries, and, if desired, the brandy. Set aside.

3 Preheat oven to 375°F. Line two cookie sheets with foil; set aside. On a lightly floured surface, roll half of the dough at a time until ⅛ inch thick. Using a 3-inch scalloped or plain round cutter, cut out dough. Place cutouts ½ inch apart on the prepared cookie sheets. Spoon a scant 1 teaspoon of the cherry filling onto the center of each cutout. Brush edges of the cutouts with water. Fold cutouts in half over filling, gently pressing edges to seal. Bake for 8 to 9 minutes or until edges are firm. Transfer cookies to a wire rack; cool.

4 In a small heavy saucepan heat and stir chocolate and shortening over low heat until smooth. Let stand until cool enough to handle. Transfer the warm chocolate mixture to a resealable plastic bag. Cut a small hole in one corner of the bag. Squeezing gently, drizzle chocolate mixture over cookies. Sprinkle with almonds. If desired, drizzle cookies again. Let stand until chocolate sets.

The combination of vanilla, ground nutmeg, and lemon extract gives this classic cookie its signature flavor.

old-fashioned sugar cookies

prep: 20 min. chill: 3 hr. bake: 10 min. per batch oven: 375°F
makes: 32 cookies

1¼	cups shortening
2	cups granulated sugar
2	teaspoons baking powder
1	teaspoon baking soda
½	teaspoon ground nutmeg
¼	teaspoon salt
2	eggs
1	teaspoon vanilla
½	teaspoon lemon extract
4½	cups all-purpose flour
1	cup buttermilk or sour milk*
	Granulated sugar, fine sanding sugar, coarse sugar, or colored coarse sugar

1 In a large mixing bowl beat shortening with an electric mixer on medium to high speed for 30 seconds. Add the 2 cups sugar, the baking powder, baking soda, nutmeg, and salt. Beat until combined, scraping sides of bowl occasionally. Beat in eggs, vanilla, and lemon extract until combined. Alternately add flour and buttermilk, beating until combined after each addition. Divide dough in half. Cover and chill dough about 3 hours or until it is easy to handle.

2 Preheat oven to 375°F. On a lightly floured surface, roll half of the dough at a time until ½ inch thick. Using a 2½-inch round cookie cutter, cut out dough. Place cutouts 2½ inches apart on an ungreased cookie sheet. Sprinkle with desired sugar. Bake about 10 minutes or until set and edges just begin to brown. Transfer to a wire rack and let cool.

* To make sour milk, in a glass measuring cup stir together 1 tablespoon lemon juice or vinegar and enough milk to make 1 cup. Let stand for 5 minutes.

Tangy with a hint of spice, these classic cookies are sure to evoke memories of your childhood.

Great for your next adult get-together, these nut-filled, lime-scented cookies get a lively kick from tangy cream cheese frosting.

lime zingers

prep: 40 min. bake: 8 min. per batch oven: 350°F makes: 72 cookies

1	cup butter, softened
½	cup sugar
2	teaspoons finely shredded lime peel
¼	cup lime juice (about 2 limes)
1	teaspoon vanilla
2¼	cups all-purpose flour
¾	cup finely chopped Brazil nuts or hazelnuts (filberts)
1	recipe Cream Cheese Frosting

1 Preheat oven to 350°F. In a large mixing bowl beat butter with an electric mixer on medium to high speed for 30 seconds. Add sugar. Beat until combined, scraping sides of bowl occasionally. Beat in lime peel, lime juice, and vanilla until combined. Beat in as much of the flour as you can with the mixer. Stir in nuts and any remaining flour. Divide dough in half.

2 On a lightly floured surface, roll half of the dough at a time until ¼ inch thick. Using 1- or 2-inch desired-shape cookie cutters, cut out dough. Place cutouts on an ungreased cookie sheet. Bake for 8 to 10 minutes or until edges are light brown. Transfer to a wire rack and let cool. Decorate cooled cookies with Cream Cheese Frosting.

cream cheese frosting: *In a medium mixing bowl beat half of an 8-ounce package softened cream cheese, 1 cup powdered sugar, 1 tablespoon lemon or lime juice, and 1 teaspoon vanilla with an electric mixer on medium speed until smooth. Tint with green food coloring. Pipe or spread frosting on cookies.*

"Gossamer" refers to something light and delicate, which perfectly describes these crisp, inviting cookies.

gossamer spice cookies

prep: 35 min. chill: 1 hr. bake: 5 min. per batch oven: 375°F
makes: about 66 cookies

1⅓ cups all-purpose flour
½ teaspoon ground ginger
½ teaspoon apple pie spice
¼ teaspoon ground cloves
¼ teaspoon ground cardamom
⅛ teaspoon cayenne pepper
⅓ cup butter, softened
⅓ cup molasses
¼ cup packed dark brown sugar

1 In a medium bowl stir together flour, ginger, apple pie spice, cloves, cardamom, and cayenne pepper; set aside. In a large mixing bowl beat butter with an electric mixer on medium to high speed for 30 seconds. Add molasses and brown sugar. Beat until combined, scraping sides of bowl occasionally. Beat in flour mixture until just combined. Divide dough in half. Cover and chill dough about 1 hour or until easy to handle.

2 Preheat oven to 375°F. On a lightly floured surface, roll half of the dough at a time until ¹⁄₁₆ inch thick. Using a 2-inch scalloped round cookie cutter, cut out dough. Place cutouts on an ungreased cookie sheet. Bake for 5 to 6 minutes or until edges are brown. Transfer to a wire rack and let cool.

Bring happy faces to the cookie lovers in your life with these jam-filled gems.

happy faces

prep: 45 min. chill: 1 hr. bake: 7 min. per batch oven: 375°F
makes: 36 sandwich cookies

1½ cups all-purpose flour
1 cup ground pecans
½ cup sugar
⅔ cup butter
3 tablespoons cold water
½ teaspoon vanilla
Pink colored coarse sugar (optional)
¾ cup raspberry or strawberry jam

1 In a large bowl stir together the flour, pecans, and sugar. Using a pastry blender, cut in butter until the mixture resembles coarse crumbs. Combine the water and vanilla. Sprinkle over flour mixture a little at a time while mixing with a fork until dough forms a ball. Wrap in plastic wrap. Chill dough for 1 to 2 hours or until easy to handle.

2 Preheat oven to 375°F. On a lightly floured surface, roll dough until ⅛ inch thick. Using a 2-inch scalloped or plain round cookie cutter, cut out dough. Place cutouts on an ungreased cookie sheet. Using a crescent-shape hors d'oeuvre cutter, cut out eyes and mouths from half the rounds. If desired, sprinkle "cheeks" with pink colored sugar. Bake for 7 to 10 minutes or until edges begin to brown. Transfer to a wire rack and let cool.

3 Up to 1 hour before serving, spread bottom of each whole cookie with about 1 teaspoon jam. Top with cutout cookies, bottom sides down.

note: *Store unfilled cookies as directed on page 16. Freeze for up to 1 month.*

Piped-on colored candy coating gives these cutouts a fun, cheerful look, while chocolate gives them a more rustic appearance.

coconut cutouts

prep: 35 min. chill: 1 hr. bake: 8 min. per batch oven: 375°F
makes: about 48 cookies

1¼ cups flaked coconut
¾ cup butter, softened
¾ cup sugar
1½ teaspoons baking powder
2 eggs
1 teaspoon vanilla
2 cups all-purpose flour
6 ounces colored candy coating disks and/or semisweet chocolate
1 tablespoon shortening (optional)

1 Finely chop coconut by hand or in a food processor. Set aside.

2 In a large mixing bowl beat butter with an electric mixer on medium to high speed for 30 seconds. Add sugar and baking powder. Beat until combined, scraping sides of bowl occasionally. Beat in eggs and vanilla until combined. Beat in as much of the flour as you can with the mixer. Stir in any remaining flour and the coconut. Divide dough in half. Cover and chill about 1 hour or until dough is easy to handle.

3 Preheat oven to 375°F. On a lightly floured surface, roll half of the dough at a time until ⅛ inch thick. Using 2½-inch desired-shape cookie cutters, cut out dough. Place cutouts 1 inch apart on an ungreased cookie sheet. Bake about 8 minutes or until edges are light brown. Transfer to a wire rack and let cool.

4 In a small saucepan heat and stir candy coating disks (or chocolate and shortening*) over low heat until smooth. Cool slightly. Place the melted candy coating in a resealable plastic bag. Cut a small hole in one corner of the bag. Pipe a decorative pattern on cookies. Let stand until candy coating sets.

✳ If desired, use one or more colors of candy coating and the chocolate. Melt candy coatings and the chocolate and shortening separately. Place in separate plastic bags to decorate cookies.

If you crave even more chocolate, top these filled cookies with a drizzle of melted chocolate instead of powdered sugar.

double-fudge pockets

prep: 30 min. chill: 1 hr. bake: 10 min. per batch stand: 1 min. per batch
oven: 350°F makes: about 30 cookies

1	cup butter, softened
1	cup granulated sugar
1	teaspoon baking powder
1	egg
1	egg yolk
1	teaspoon vanilla
½	cup unsweetened cocoa powder
2½	cups all-purpose flour
1	recipe Sour Cream-Fudge Filling
	Sifted powdered sugar

1 In a large mixing bowl beat butter with an electric mixer on medium to high speed for 30 seconds. Add granulated sugar and baking powder. Beat until combined, scraping sides of bowl occasionally. Beat in whole egg, egg yolk, and vanilla until combined. Beat in cocoa powder and as much of the flour as you can with the mixer. Stir in any remaining flour. Divide dough in half. Cover and chill dough about 1 hour or until easy to handle.

2 Preheat oven to 350°F. On a lightly floured surface, roll half of the dough at a time until ⅛ inch thick. Using a scalloped 2½-inch round cookie cutter, cut out dough. Place half of the cutouts 1 inch apart on an ungreased cookie sheet. Spoon a rounded teaspoon of Sour Cream-Fudge Filling into the center of each round. Place remaining rounds over the filled cookies on cookie sheet. Press edges together to seal.

3 Bake for 10 to 12 minutes or until edges are firm. Let stand for 1 minute on cookie sheet. Transfer to a wire rack and let cool. Before serving, sprinkle with powdered sugar.

note: *Store cookies as directed on page 16. Refrigerate up to 2 days. Do not freeze.*

sour cream-fudge filling: *In a small heavy saucepan heat and stir 4 ounces semisweet chocolate over low heat until smooth. Remove from heat. Stir in ½ cup dairy sour cream and ¼ cup finely chopped walnuts. Mixture will stiffen as it cools.*

These luscious two-bite tarts combine chocolate-and-cream cheese pastry and a rich coconut-and-pecan filling.

chocolate coconut tassies

prep: 30 min. bake: 20 min. per batch stand: 10 min. per batch oven: 325°F
makes: 30 tassies

2   ounces sweet baking chocolate, cut up
2   3-ounce packages cream cheese, softened
⅓   cup butter, softened
1   cup all-purpose flour
⅓   cup sugar
2   teaspoons vanilla
1   cup flaked coconut
½   cup chopped toasted pecans
2   ounces sweet baking chocolate, cut up (optional)

1 In a small saucepan heat and stir the 2 ounces chocolate over low heat until smooth. Cool slightly (10 to 15 minutes). In a medium mixing bowl beat melted chocolate, 3 ounces of the cream cheese, and the butter with an electric mixer on medium speed until combined. Beat in flour until combined. If necessary, cover and chill dough about 1 hour or until easy to handle.

2 Preheat oven to 325°F. On a lightly floured surface, roll the dough until ⅛ inch thick. Using a 2½-inch scalloped cutter, cut out dough. Place cutouts in ungreased 1¾-inch muffin pans, pressing dough against bottom and sides of each cup. Set aside.

3 For filling, in a medium mixing bowl beat remaining 3 ounces cream cheese, the sugar, and vanilla with an electric mixer on medium speed until smooth. Stir in coconut and pecans. Spoon filling evenly into prepared muffin cups.

4 Bake about 20 minutes or until filling begins to brown on top. Let stand for 10 minutes in muffin cups. Remove from pans. Cool completely on a wire rack.

5 If desired, in a small saucepan heat and stir additional 2 ounces chocolate until smooth. Cool slightly. Drizzle melted chocolate over tassies. Chill in the refrigerator until chocolate is set.

note: *Store cookies as directed on page 16. Refrigerate for up to 3 days or freeze up to 2 weeks.*

These **chai-scented** cookies taste like **heaven** with a steamy cup of **honey-sweetened** tea.

India's beloved spices—ginger and cardamom—give warmth and depth to these pretty moon-shape cookies.

chai crescents

prep: 45 min. chill: 1 hr. bake: 8 min. per batch oven: 375°F
makes: 48 cookies

1 cup butter, softened
1 cup packed brown sugar
1 tablespoon leaf chai tea, finely ground*
1 teaspoon vanilla
½ teaspoon baking soda
⅛ teaspoon salt
2¼ cups all-purpose flour
1 recipe Buttercream Frosting (page 96)
Finely chopped crystallized ginger**

1 In a large mixing bowl beat butter with an electric mixer on medium to high speed for 30 seconds. Add brown sugar, chai tea, vanilla, baking soda, and salt. Beat until light and fluffy, scraping sides of bowl occasionally. Beat in as much of the flour as you can with the mixer. Stir in any remaining flour. Divide dough in half. Cover and chill dough about 1 hour or until easy to handle.

2 Preheat oven to 375°F. On a lightly floured surface, roll half of dough at a time until ¼ inch thick. Using a 3-inch crescent-shape cutter, cut out dough. Place cutouts 1 inch apart on an ungreased cookie sheet.

3 Bake for 8 to 10 minutes or until edges are firm and light brown. Transfer to a wire rack and let cool. Frost cooled cookies with Buttercream Frosting. Immediately sprinkle with crystallized ginger.

*Use a spice or coffee grinder to grind the chai tea.

** Crystallized or candied ginger is gingerroot that has been cooked in a sugar syrup and coated with coarse sugar. Look for it in the produce section or spice aisle of larger supermarkets.

The high-sparkle sanding sugar that dresses up these cookies is a little coarser than granulated sugar. Find it where cake-decorating supplies are sold.

pastel cream wafers

prep: 30 min. bake: 8 min. per batch oven: 375°F
makes: about 20 sandwich cookies

½ cup all-purpose flour
½ cup cold butter
3 to 4 tablespoons light
    cream or
    half-and-half
    Sanding sugar or
    granulated sugar
1 recipe Powdered
    Sugar Frosting

1 Heat oven to 375°F. Place flour in a medium bowl. Using a pastry blender, cut in butter until pieces are the size of small peas. Sprinkle 1 tablespoon of the cream over part of mixture. Gently toss with a fork and push to sides of bowl. Repeat until all is moistened. Form dough into a ball.

2 On a lightly floured surface, roll dough until slightly less than ⅛ inch thick. Using a 1¾-inch scalloped round cookie cutter, cut out dough. Dip one side of each cutout in sugar. Place cutouts, sugared sides up, 1 inch apart on an ungreased cookie sheet. Using a fork, prick four parallel rows in each cutout. Bake for 8 to 10 minutes or until edges just begin to brown. Transfer to a wire rack and let cool.

3 Spread a scant 1 teaspoon Powdered Sugar Frosting on each of the bottoms of half of the cookies. Top with the remaining cookies, bottom sides down.

note: *Store unfilled cookies as directed on page 16. Fill before serving.*

powdered sugar frosting: *In a small bowl stir together 1 cup powdered sugar, 1 tablespoon softened butter, ½ teaspoon vanilla, 1 drop food coloring, and enough light cream or half-and-half (about 1 tablespoon) to make a frosting of spreading consistency.*

Perfect for a special gift, these cottage-style cookies boast a scrumptious cherry filling.

quilt-block cookies

prep: 35 min. chill: 2 hr. bake: 6 min. per batch oven: 375°F
makes: 24 cookies

½ cup butter, softened
½ cup packed brown sugar
½ teaspoon baking soda
½ teaspoon ground cardamom or 1 teaspoon ground cinnamon
1 egg
⅓ cup honey
1 teaspoon vanilla
1 cup all-purpose flour
1 cup whole wheat flour
1 recipe Cherry Filling
1 recipe Royal Icing (page 128)

1 In a large mixing bowl beat butter with an electric mixer on medium to high speed for 30 seconds. Add brown sugar, baking soda, and cardamom. Beat until combined, scraping sides of bowl occasionally. Beat in egg, honey, and vanilla until combined. Beat in all-purpose flour. Stir in whole wheat flour. Divide dough in half. Cover and chill dough about 2 hours or until easy to handle.

2 Preheat oven to 375°F. On a lightly floured surface, roll half of the dough at a time into a 13×11-inch rectangle. Using a fluted pastry wheel, trim to a 12½×10-inch rectangle. Cut rectangle into twenty 2½-inch squares. Place half of the squares 1 inch apart on an ungreased cookie sheet. Spread about 1 teaspoon Cherry Filling over the center of each square.

3 Using 1-inch desired-shape cookie cutters, cut out and remove a shape from the center of each of the remaining squares. Place a cutout square on top of each filled square; press edges to seal. Reroll scraps.

4 Bake for 6 to 8 minutes or until edges are light brown. Transfer to a wire rack and let cool. Pipe Royal Icing in lines around the edges of the cooled cookies to look like stitching.

cherry filling: *In a small saucepan stir together 1 cup dried tart red cherries, ½ cup cherry blend drink or apple juice, and 1 tablespoon lemon juice. Bring just to boiling; reduce heat. Simmer, uncovered, about 10 minutes or until cherries are tender and most of the liquid is absorbed, stirring occasionally. Remove from heat. Stir in 2 tablespoons granulated sugar. Cool slightly. Transfer mixture to a food processor or blender. Cover and process or blend until a paste forms. Cool completely.*

creative **cutouts**

Serve these minty, ganache-filled beauties at your next shindig. Guests will eat them up in no time.

chocolate-mint star cookies

prep: 45 min. chill: 30 min. bake: 8 min. per batch oven: 350°F
makes: 36 sandwich cookies

1 cup butter
⅔ cup packed brown sugar
1 teaspoon vanilla
2½ cups all-purpose flour
¼ cup unsweetened cocoa powder
1 egg, lightly beaten
6 ounces semisweet chocolate, finely chopped
¾ cup whipping cream
¼ teaspoon peppermint extract

1 In a medium saucepan heat and stir butter and brown sugar over low heat until butter is melted. Remove from heat; stir in vanilla. Let stand for 15 minutes to cool slightly. Meanwhile, in a medium bowl stir together flour and cocoa powder; set aside. When butter mixture has cooled, stir in egg and flour mixture until combined. Divide dough in half. Cover and chill dough about 30 minutes or until easy to handle.

2 Preheat oven to 350°F. On a lightly floured surface, roll half of the dough at a time until ¼ inch thick. Using a 2-inch star-shape cookie cutter, cut out dough. Place cutouts 1 inch apart on an ungreased cookie sheet. Bake for 8 to 9 minutes or until edges are firm. Transfer to a wire rack and let cool.

3 Meanwhile, place chocolate in a heatproof bowl. In a small saucepan heat cream over medium heat just until boiling. Remove from heat. Immediately pour hot cream over chocolate. Let stand for 5 minutes. Stir gently until smooth. Stir in peppermint extract. Cool chocolate mixture to room temperature (about 20 minutes).

4 To assemble, spread ½ teaspoon chocolate mixture each on the bottoms of half of the cookies. Top with remaining cookies, bottom sides down. If desired, place some of the chocolate mixture in a resealable plastic bag. Cut a small hole in one corner of the bag. Pipe patterns on top of the filled cookies.

Pipe a squiggle of Powdered Sugar Icing onto each cookie, followed by a sprinkle of nonpareils for a fun and attractive finish.

pineapple ribbons

prep: 30 min. bake: 7 min. per batch stand: 1 min. per batch oven: 375°F
makes: about 96 ribbons

1　cup butter, softened
1　3-ounce package
　　cream cheese,
　　softened
¾　cup sugar
1　teaspoon baking
　　powder
1　egg
¼　cup pineapple
　　preserves or
　　apricot-pineapple
　　preserves
3½　cups all-purpose flour
1　recipe Powdered
　　Sugar Icing
　　(optional)
　　Nonpareils (optional)

1 Preheat oven to 375°F. In a large mixing bowl beat butter and cream cheese with an electric mixer on medium to high speed for 30 seconds. Add sugar and baking powder. Beat until combined, scraping sides of bowl occasionally. Beat in egg and preserves until combined. Beat in as much of the flour as you can with the mixer. Stir in any remaining flour. Divide dough in half.

2 On a lightly floured surface, roll half of the dough at a time into a 16×10-inch rectangle. Using a fluted pastry wheel, cut rectangle crosswise into 1¼-inch-wide strips. Cut strips into 4-inch lengths. Place cutouts 1 inch apart on an ungreased cookie sheet. If desired, curve cutouts slightly.

3 Bake for 7 to 8 minutes or until edges are firm and bottoms are light brown. Let stand for 1 minute on cookie sheet. Transfer to a wire rack and let cool. If desired, drizzle cooled cookies with Powdered Sugar Icing and sprinkle with nonpareils.

powdered sugar icing: *In a small bowl stir together 2 cups powdered sugar and 2 tablespoons milk. Stir in additional milk, 1 teaspoon at a time, to make an icing of drizzling consistency.*

Baked onto wooden crafts sticks or frozen-pop sticks, these fun-shape cookies are a big hit with kids.

peppermint pinwheels

prep: 45 min. chill: 3 hr. bake: 7 min. per batch stand: 1 min. per batch
oven: 350°F makes: 24 cookies

⅓ cup butter, softened
⅓ cup shortening
¾ cup sugar
1½ teaspoons baking
   powder
¾ teaspoon salt
1 egg
4 teaspoons milk
1 teaspoon vanilla
2 cups all-purpose flour
½ cup crushed
   peppermint candies
   (about 20)
⅓ cup red colored
   coarse sugar
24 wooden crafts sticks

1 In a large mixing bowl beat butter and shortening with an electric mixer on medium to high speed for 30 seconds. Add sugar, baking powder, and salt. Beat until combined, scraping sides of bowl occasionally. Beat in egg, milk, and vanilla until combined. Beat in as much flour as you can with the mixer. Stir in any remaining flour. Divide dough in half. Cover and chill dough about 3 hours or until easy to handle.

2 Preheat oven to 350°F. On a lightly floured surface, roll half of the dough at a time into a 12×9-inch rectangle. Using a sharp knife or a fluted pastry wheel, cut rectangle into twelve 3-inch squares. Place cutouts 2 inches apart on an ungreased cookie sheet. Sprinkle each with about 1 teaspoon crushed candy and about ½ teaspoon red colored sugar; gently press into dough.

3 Cut 1-inch slits from each corner toward the center of each square. Fold every other tip to the center of the square to form pinwheels, pressing lightly to seal the tips. Tuck a crafts stick into each pinwheel, pressing dough around stick. Sprinkle with additional crushed candy and red colored sugar.

4 Bake for 7 to 8 minutes or until edges begin to brown. Let stand for 1 minute on cookie sheet. Transfer cookies to a wire rack and let cool. (Do not lift by sticks until completely cooled.)

note: *Store cookies as directed on page 16. Refrigerate for up to 3 days.*

Sage is more than an ingredient in stuffing and savory foods; it adds subtle and pleasing flavor to cookies too.

sage cookies

prep: 30 min. bake: 7 min. per batch oven: 375°F makes: 32 cookies

1¾ cups all-purpose flour
⅓   cup sugar
¼   cup yellow cornmeal
½   cup butter
2   tablespoons snipped
    fresh sage, lemon
    thyme, or rosemary
    or 2 teaspoons dried
    sage or rosemary,
    crushed
3   tablespoons milk
1   egg white, beaten
1   tablespoon water
32 fresh sage leaves or
    lemon thyme leaves
    (optional)
    Sugar

1 Preheat oven to 375°F. In a medium bowl stir together flour, sugar, and cornmeal. Using a pastry blender, cut in butter until mixture resembles fine crumbs and starts to cling. Stir in sage. Add milk and stir with a fork to combine. Form mixture into a ball; knead until smooth. Divide dough in half.

2 On a lightly floured surface, roll half of the dough at a time until ⅛ inch thick. Using a 2½-inch round or oval cookie cutter, cut out dough. Place cutouts onto an ungreased cookie sheet.

3 In a small bowl stir together egg white and water. Brush cutouts with egg white mixture. If desired, place one or two small sage leaves on each cutout; brush leaves with egg white mixture. Sprinkle cutouts with sugar. Bake about 7 minutes or until edges are firm and bottoms are very light brown. Transfer to a wire rack and let cool.

These fun-to-shape cookies burst with flecks of coconut and buttery macadamia nuts. A drizzle of pineapple icing tops them off.

tropical pinwheels

prep: 40 min. chill: 3 hr. bake: 8 min. per batch stand: 1 min. per batch
oven: 350°F makes: 32 cookies

⅓ cup butter, softened
⅓ cup shortening
¾ cup sugar
1½ teaspoons baking powder
¼ teaspoon salt
1 egg
4 teaspoons milk
1 teaspoon vanilla
2 cups all-purpose flour
1 3-ounce package cream cheese, softened
2 tablespoons sugar
¼ cup shredded coconut
¼ cup finely chopped macadamia nuts or almonds
Colored sugar (optional)
1 recipe Tropical Icing (optional)

1 In a large mixing bowl beat butter and shortening with an electric mixer on medium to high speed for 30 seconds. Add the ¾ cup sugar, the baking powder, and salt. Beat until combined, scraping sides of bowl occasionally. Beat in egg, milk, and vanilla until combined. Beat in as much of the flour as you can with the mixer. Stir in any remaining flour. Divide dough in half. Cover and chill dough about 3 hours or until easy to handle.

2 Preheat oven to 350°F. For filling, in a small bowl stir together cream cheese and the 2 tablespoons sugar. Stir in coconut. Set aside.

3 On a lightly floured surface, roll half of the dough at a time into a 10-inch square. Using a fluted pastry wheel or a sharp knife, cut square into sixteen 2½-inch squares. Place squares 2 inches apart on an ungreased cookie sheet. Cut 1-inch slits from each corner toward the center of each square. Spoon a level teaspoon of the filling in each center. Fold every other tip to centers of squares to form a pinwheel, pressing the tips lightly. Carefully sprinkle the chopped nuts onto the centers of pinwheels; press nuts lightly into the dough. If desired, sprinkle cookies with colored sugar.

4 Bake for 8 to 10 minutes or until edges are light brown. Let stand for 1 minute on cookie sheet. Transfer to a wire rack and let cool. If desired, drizzle cooled cookies with Tropical Icing.

tropical icing: *In a small bowl stir together ¾ cup powdered sugar and enough pineapple juice (about 1 tablespoon) to make an icing of drizzling consistency.*

Cut these crisp cookies into simple shapes and embellish them with rich melted chocolate.

pistachio sugar cookies

prep: 30 min. chill: 3 hr. bake: 7 min. per batch oven: 375°F
makes: 54 to 72 cookies

1 cup butter, softened
1 cup granulated sugar
1½ teaspoons baking powder
Dash salt
1 egg
3 tablespoons light cream or milk
¼ teaspoon almond extract
3 cups all-purpose flour
½ cup ground pistachio nuts
Granulated sugar
6 ounces semisweet chocolate, cut up
2 teaspoons shortening
1 ounce green or white candy coating, melted

1 In a large mixing bowl beat butter with an electric mixer on medium to high speed for 30 seconds. Add the 1 cup sugar, the baking powder, and salt. Beat until combined, scraping sides of bowl occasionally. Beat in egg, light cream, and almond extract until combined. Beat in as much of the flour as you can with the mixer. Stir in any remaining flour and the ground nuts. Divide dough into thirds. Cover and chill dough about 3 hours or until easy to handle.

2 Preheat oven to 375°F. On a lightly floured surface, roll one-third of the dough at a time until ⅛ inch thick. Using a 2½- to 3-inch desired-shape cookie cutter, cut out dough. Place cutouts on an ungreased cookie sheet. Sprinkle with additional sugar. Bake for 7 to 8 minutes or until edges are firm and bottoms are very light brown. Transfer to a wire rack and let cool.

3 In a small saucepan heat and stir chocolate and shortening over low heat until smooth. Dip half of each cookie into the chocolate mixture. Let stand until chocolate sets. Place melted candy coating in a heavy resealable plastic bag. Snip off a small corner of the bag. Drizzle coating in a loop design over chocolate-coated cookies. Let stand until coating sets.

note: *Store cookies as directed on page 16. Freeze for up to 1 month.*

Orange-scented fig filling and cinnamon-flavor dough make these cookies special and sophisticated.

orange-fig pillows

prep: 40 min. chill: 1 hr. bake: 8 min. per batch oven: 375°F
makes: 24 cookies

⅔ cup butter, softened
½ cup packed brown
   sugar
½ teaspoon baking
   powder
½ teaspoon ground
   cinnamon
¼ teaspoon baking soda
¼ teaspoon salt
1 egg
1 teaspoon vanilla
2 cups all-purpose flour
¼ cup fig preserves or
   jam
½ teaspoon finely
   shredded orange
   peel or lemon peel
Milk (optional)
Coarse white and/
   or colored sugar
   (optional)

1 In a large mixing bowl beat butter with an electric mixer on medium to high speed for 30 seconds. Add brown sugar, baking powder, cinnamon, baking soda, and salt. Beat until combined, scraping sides of bowl occasionally. Beat in egg and vanilla until combined. Beat in as much of the flour as you can with the mixer. Stir in any remaining flour. Divide dough in half. Cover and chill dough about 1 hour or until easy to handle.

2 Preheat oven to 375°F. Grease two large cookie sheets; set aside. For filling, in a small bowl stir together fig preserves and orange peel; set aside.

3 On a lightly floured surface, roll half of the dough at a time into a 12×8-inch rectangle. Using a fluted pastry wheel, trim the edges of rectangle. Using the pastry wheel, cut rectangle into twenty-four 2-inch squares. Place half of the squares 1 inch apart on the prepared cookie sheets. Spoon ½ teaspoon filling onto the center of each square on the cookie sheets. Top each with a second dough square. Using a fork, gently press edges to seal. If desired, lightly brush tops of cookies with milk and sprinkle with coarse sugar. Bake for 8 to 10 minutes or until edges are light brown. Transfer to a wire rack and let cool.

*If you prefer not to use alcohol,
substitute strongly brewed coffee
for the coffee liqueur.*

mocha cutouts

prep: 35 min. bake: 12 min. per batch stand: 1 min. per batch oven: 350°F
makes: 18 to 24 cookies

½ cup butter, softened
½ cup packed light
    brown sugar
2 teaspoons instant
    espresso powder
2 teaspoons cocoa
    powder
    Dash salt
1 egg yolk
1 tablespoon coffee
    liqueur or
    strong coffee
1½ cups all-purpose flour
¾ cup semisweet
    chocolate pieces
1 tablespoon
    shortening

1 In a medium mixing bowl beat butter with
an electric mixer on medium to high speed
for 30 seconds. Add brown sugar, espresso
powder, cocoa powder, and salt. Beat until
combined, scraping sides of bowl occasionally.
Beat in egg yolk and coffee liqueur until
combined. Beat in as much of the flour as you
can with the mixer. Stir in any remaining flour.
Divide dough in half. If necessary, cover and
chill dough until easy to handle.

2 Preheat oven to 350°F. On a lightly floured
surface, roll half of the dough at a time
until ¼ inch thick. Using 2½- to 3-inch desired-
shape cookie cutters, cut out dough. Place
cutouts 1 inch apart on an ungreased cookie
sheet. Bake about 12 minutes or until bottoms
are light brown. Let stand for 1 minute on
cookie sheet. Transfer to a wire rack; cool.

3 In a small heavy saucepan heat and stir
chocolate pieces and shortening over
medium-low heat until smooth. Dip cooled
cookies partway into chocolate mixture. Let
stand until chocolate sets.

Dress up these tender ribbons with Lemon Glaze and,
if you wish, a sprinkling of sugar.

cornmeal ribbons

prep: 30 min. chill: 3 hr. bake: 7 min. per batch oven: 375°F
makes: about 32 cookies

⅔ cup butter, softened
⅔ cup granulated sugar
1 teaspoon baking
   powder
¼ teaspoon salt
1 egg
1½ teaspoons finely
   shredded lemon
   peel
1 teaspoon vanilla
½ cup yellow cornmeal
1½ cups all-purpose flour
1 recipe Lemon Glaze
   Yellow colored sugar
   (optional)

1 In a large mixing bowl beat butter with an electric mixer on medium to high speed for 30 seconds. Add granulated sugar, baking powder, and salt. Beat until combined, scraping sides of bowl occasionally. Beat in egg, lemon peel, and vanilla until combined. Beat in cornmeal and as much of the flour as you can with the mixer. Stir in any remaining flour. Divide dough in half. Cover and chill dough about 3 hours or until easy to handle.

2 Preheat oven to 375°F. On a lightly floured surface, roll half of the dough into a 10×8-inch rectangle. Using a fluted pastry wheel, trim edges of rectangle. Cut rectangle in half lengthwise. Cut crosswise into 1¼-inch-wide strips. Place strips 1 inch apart on an ungreased cookie sheet. Repeat with remaining dough.

3 Bake for 7 to 8 minutes or until edges are light brown. Transfer to a wire rack and let cool. Frost cooled cookies with Lemon Glaze and, if desired, sprinkle with yellow sugar. Let stand until glaze sets.

lemon glaze: *In a small bowl stir together 1½ cups powdered sugar, 2 teaspoons lemon juice, and enough milk (1 to 2 tablespoons) to make a glaze of spreading consistency.*

The whole wheat flour called for in this recipe gives the cookies a pleasantly chewy texture and wholesome goodness.

date and orange pockets

prep: 25 min. chill: 1 hr. bake: 7 min. per batch oven: 375°F
makes: about 48 cookies

½ cup butter, softened
⅔ cup packed brown
   sugar
1 teaspoon baking
   powder
½ teaspoon ground
   cinnamon
⅛ teaspoon salt
1 egg
½ teaspoon vanilla
1 cup all-purpose flour
⅔ cup whole wheat
   flour
1 8-ounce package
   sugar-coated
   chopped pitted
   dates
⅓ cup orange juice
¼ cup granulated sugar
¼ cup chopped walnuts
   or pecans
1 recipe Golden Icing

1 In a large mixing bowl beat butter with an electric mixer on medium to high speed for 30 seconds. Add the brown sugar, baking powder, cinnamon, and salt. Beat until combined, scraping sides of bowl occasionally. Beat in egg and vanilla until combined. Beat in the all-purpose flour and the whole wheat flour. Cover and chill dough about 1 hour or until easy to handle.

2 Meanwhile, for filling, in a food processor combine dates, orange juice, granulated sugar, and nuts. Cover and process until smooth, stopping to scrape sides of bowl occasionally. Set aside.

3 Preheat oven to 375°F. On a lightly floured surface, roll dough until ⅛ inch thick. Using a 2½-inch round cookie cutter, cut out dough. Place cutouts ½ inch apart on an ungreased cookie sheet. Spoon 1 level teaspoon of filling into the center of each round. Fold the rounds in half over filling, making half-moons. Using the tines of a fork, seal edges.

4 Bake for 7 to 9 minutes or until edges are firm and bottoms are light brown. Transfer to a wire rack and let cool. Drizzle cooled cookies with Golden Icing. Let stand until the icing is set.

golden icing: *In a small saucepan heat 2 tablespoons butter over medium-low heat for 10 to 12 minutes or until light brown. Remove from heat. Stir in ¾ cup powdered sugar and ¼ teaspoon vanilla (mixture will be crumbly). Gradually stir in enough milk (2 to 3 teaspoons) to make an icing of drizzling consistency.*

These fudge-filled sandwiches freeze well even after assembly. Be sure to let the cookies come to room temperature before serving.

dark chocolate stars

prep: 30 min. chill: 1 hr. bake: 7 min. per batch oven: 375°F
makes: about 36 large and 18 small sandwich cookies

1	cup butter, softened
1¼	cups sugar
½	cup dark chocolate pieces or 2 ounces dark chocolate bar, melted and cooled
½	teaspoon baking powder
½	teaspoon salt
2	eggs
1	tablespoon milk
1½	teaspoons vanilla
3	cups all-purpose flour
1	recipe Fudge Filling or about 1 cup purchased hot fudge or chocolate fudge ice cream topping
¾	cup dark chocolate pieces or 3 ounces dark chocolate bar, melted (optional) Unsweetened cocoa powder (optional)

1 In a large mixing bowl beat butter with an electric mixer on medium to high speed for 30 seconds. Add sugar, the melted ½ cup chocolate pieces, the baking powder, and salt. Beat until combined, scraping sides of bowl occasionally. Beat in eggs, milk, and vanilla until combined. Beat in as much of the flour as you can with the mixer. Stir in any remaining flour. Divide dough in half. Cover and chill dough about 1 hour or until easy to handle.

2 Preheat oven to 375°F. On a lightly floured surface, roll half of the dough at a time until ⅛ inch thick. Using a 2½- or 3-inch star-shape cookie cutter, cut out dough. Using a 1-inch star shape cutter, cut out the centers of half of the large star cutouts. Place large and small cutouts 2 inches apart on an ungreased cookie sheet. Bake for 7 to 8 minutes or until edges are firm. Transfer to a wire rack; cool.

3 To assemble cookies, spread a small amount of Fudge Filling on bottoms of large whole stars. Top with cutout large stars, bottom sides down. Spread filling on bottoms of half of the small whole stars. Top with remaining small stars, bottom sides down. If desired, drizzle sandwiched stars with additional melted chocolate or sprinkle with cocoa powder.

note: *Freeze sandwiches as directed on page 16 or refrigerate up to 3 days.*

fudge filling: *In a small saucepan heat and stir ½ cup dark chocolate pieces over low heat until smooth. Remove from heat; cool slightly. In a bowl combine one 3-ounce package softened cream cheese and ⅓ cup powdered sugar. Stir in melted chocolate and ¼ teaspoon vanilla. If necessary, stir in 1 to 2 tablespoons hot water for a filling of spreading consistency.*

Finely shredded lemon peel gives these gingery cookies a tangy citrus twist.

ginger stars

prep: 25 min. chill: 3 hr. bake: 6 min. per batch stand: 1 min. per batch
oven: 350°F makes: 84 to 96 cookies

½	cup butter, softened
½	cup sugar
1	tablespoon grated fresh ginger
¾	teaspoon baking soda
½	teaspoon ground cinnamon
¼	teaspoon ground cloves
½	cup molasses
1	egg
½	cup whole wheat flour
1¾	cups all-purpose flour
2	teaspoons finely shredded lemon peel
1	recipe Creamy White Frosting

1 In a large mixing bowl beat butter with an electric mixer on medium to high speed for 30 seconds. Add the sugar, ginger, baking soda, cinnamon, and cloves. Beat until combined, scraping sides of bowl occasionally. Beat in molasses and egg until combined. Beat in the whole wheat flour and as much of the all-purpose flour as you can with the mixer. Stir in lemon peel and any remaining all-purpose flour. Divide dough in half. Cover and chill dough about 3 hours or until easy to handle.

2 Preheat oven to 350°F. On a well-floured surface, roll half of the dough at a time until ⅛ inch thick. Using 1½- to 2½-inch star-shape cookie cutters, cut out dough. Place cutouts 1 inch apart on an ungreased cookie sheet. Bake for 6 to 8 minutes or until edges are firm. Let stand for 1 minute on cookie sheet. Transfer to a wire rack; cool. Decorate cooled cookies with Creamy White Frosting.

creamy white frosting: *In a medium bowl beat 1 cup shortening, 1½ teaspoons vanilla, and ½ teaspoon almond extract with an electric mixer on medium speed for 30 seconds. Slowly add 2¼ cups powdered sugar, beating well. Beat in 2 tablespoons milk. Gradually beat in 2¼ cups additional powdered sugar and enough milk (1 to 2 tablespoons) to make an icing of piping consistency.*

Pure maple syrup and toasty pecans are a masterpiece combination. These cookies exhibit that fact deliciously.

maple-nut diamonds

prep: 30 min. bake: 7 min. per batch oven: 350°F makes: 72 cookies

½	cup butter, softened
½	cup shortening
1	cup granulated sugar
1	teaspoon baking powder
¼	teaspoon salt
1	egg
1	teaspoon vanilla
2¼	cups all-purpose flour
½	cup finely chopped pecans, toasted (see tip, page 19)
3	tablespoons maple syrup
	Maple sugar* or raw sugar
	Finely chopped pecans (optional)

1 In a large mixing bowl beat butter and shortening with an electric mixer on medium to high speed for 30 seconds. Add granulated sugar, baking powder, and salt. Beat until combined, scraping sides of bowl occasionally. Beat in egg and the vanilla until combined. Beat in as much of the flour as you can with the mixer. Stir in any remaining flour. Knead in the ½ cup pecans and the maple syrup. If necessary, cover and chill dough for 1 to 2 hours or until easy to handle.

2 Preheat oven to 350°F. On a lightly floured surface, roll half of the dough at a time until ¼ inch thick. Using a 2½×1¾-inch diamond-shape cookie cutter, cut out dough. Place cutouts 1 inch apart on an ungreased cookie sheet. Sprinkle with maple sugar and, if desired, additional nuts. Bake for 7 to 9 minutes or until edges are firm and bottoms are light brown. Transfer to a wire rack; cool.

✱ Look for maple sugar at specialty food stores and through mail order catalogs.

creative **cutouts**

Sesame seeds and pecans, favorite ingredients in Southern cooking,
come together in these sweet and nutty cookies.

sesame-pecan wafers

prep: 30 min. bake: 7 min. per batch oven: 375°F makes: 56 cookies

1 cup butter, softened
⅔ cup sugar
1 teaspoon vanilla
1¾ cups all-purpose flour
½ cup sesame seeds
½ cup ground pecans or
    almonds
4 ounces semisweet
    chocolate or white
    baking bar
1 teaspoon shortening
    Ground pecans or
    toasted sesame
    seeds

1 In a large mixing bowl beat butter with an electric mixer on medium to high speed for 30 seconds. Add the sugar and vanilla. Beat until combined, scraping sides of bowl occasionally. Beat in as much of the flour as you can with the mixer. Stir in any remaining flour, the ½ cup sesame seeds, and the ½ cup nuts. Divide dough in half. If necessary, cover and chill about 1 hour or until easy to handle.

2 Preheat oven to 375°F. On a lightly floured surface, roll half of the dough at a time until ⅛ inch thick. Using 2-inch desired-shape cookie cutters, cut out dough. Place cutouts 1 inch apart on an ungreased cookie sheet. Bake for 7 to 8 minutes or until edges are light brown. Transfer to a wire rack; let cool.

3 In a small saucepan combine chocolate* and shortening. Heat and stir over low heat until smooth. Dip half of each cookie into melted chocolate mixture. Sprinkle ground pecans or toasted sesame seeds over melted chocolate. Let stand until chocolate sets.

✱ To use both types of chocolate for coating, melt 2 ounces chocolate and ½ teaspoon shortening in one small saucepan; melt 2 ounces white baking bar and ½ teaspoon shortening in another small saucepan.

If you don't have teacup and teapot cookie cutters, these sugar cookies are just as pretty in flower or heart shapes.

teatime sugar cookies

prep: 30 min. bake: 7 min. per batch oven: 375°F makes: 36 to 48 cookies

⅓ cup butter, softened
⅓ cup shortening
¾ cup sugar
1 teaspoon baking powder
Dash salt
1 egg
1 teaspoon vanilla
2 cups all-purpose flour
1 recipe Decorating Frosting

1 In a medium mixing bowl beat butter and shortening with an electric mixer on medium to high speed for 30 seconds. Add sugar, baking powder, and salt. Beat until combined, scraping sides of bowl occasionally. Beat in egg and the 1 teaspoon vanilla until combined. Beat in as much of the flour as you can with the mixer. Stir in any remaining flour. Divide dough in half. If necessary, cover and chill dough about 3 hours or until it is easy to handle.

2 Preheat oven to 375°F. On a lightly floured surface, roll half of the dough at a time until ⅛ inch thick. Using 2½-inch teapot- and teacup-shape cookie cutters or other desired cutters, cut out dough. Place cutouts on an ungreased cookie sheet

3 Bake for 7 to 8 minutes or until edges are firm and bottoms are very light brown. Transfer to a wire rack and let cool. Pipe Decorating Frosting on cooled cookies.

decorating frosting: *In a medium mixing bowl beat ½ cup shortening and ½ teaspoon vanilla with an electric mixer on medium speed for 30 seconds. Gradually beat in 1⅓ cups powdered sugar, mixing well. Beat in 1 tablespoon milk. Gradually beat in 1 cup additional powdered sugar and enough milk (3 to 4 teaspoons) to make a frosting of piping consistency. Tint as desired with pastel paste food coloring.*

If you're looking for an all-out dazzler for a party, these painted beauties are sure to fit the bill. See page 22 for decorating tips.

painted sour-cream
sugar cookies

prep: 40 min. chill: 1 hr. bake: 7 min. per batch oven: 375°F
makes: 48 cookies

½ cup butter, softened
1 cup sugar
1 teaspoon baking
   powder
¼ teaspoon baking soda
   Dash salt
½ cup dairy sour cream
1 egg
1 teaspoon vanilla
1 teaspoon finely
   shredded lemon
   peel
2½ cups all-purpose flour
1 recipe Royal Icing
   (below)
   Food coloring

1 In a large mixing bowl beat butter for 30 seconds. Add sugar, baking powder, baking soda, and salt. Beat until combined; scrape sides of bowl. Beat in sour cream, egg, vanilla, and lemon peel until combined. Beat in as much of the flour as you can with the mixer. Stir in any remaining flour. Divide dough in half. Cover and chill dough for 1 to 2 hours or until easy to handle.

2 Preheat oven to 375°F. On a well-floured surface, roll half of the dough at a time until ⅛ to ¼ inch thick. Using desired cookie cutters, cut out dough; place 1 inch apart on an ungreased cookie sheet. Bake for 7 to 8 minutes or until edges are firm. Transfer cookies to a wire rack; cool.

3 Spread tops of cooled cookies with Royal Icing. Allow icing to dry completely. Using a small paintbrush, paint designs on each cookie with food coloring.

royal icing

start to finish: 15 min. makes: about 5 cups

1 16-ounce package
   powdered sugar
   (3¼ cups)
3 tablespoons
   meringue powder
½ teaspoon cream of
   tartar
½ cup warm water
1 teaspoon vanilla

1 In a large mixing bowl stir together powdered sugar, meringue powder, and cream of tartar. Add the water and vanilla. Beat with an electric mixer on low speed until combined. Beat on high speed for 7 to 10 minutes or until mixture is very stiff.* Cover bowl with a damp paper towel and plastic wrap; refrigerate for up to 2 days.

*This icing offers the perfect consistency for piping. For a thinner consistency, add more water, 1 tablespoon at a time.

These classic sugar cookies cut into fanciful star shapes are sure to delight hungry children and adults alike.

sugar cookie star cutouts

prep: 30 min. chill: 1 hr. bake: 8 min. per batch stand: 1 min. per batch
oven: 375°F makes: about 48 (2½-inch) cookies or about 16 (5-inch) cookies

⅓ cup butter, softened
⅓ cup shortening
¾ cup granulated sugar
1 teaspoon baking powder
Dash salt
1 egg
1 teaspoon vanilla
2 cups all-purpose flour
1 recipe Royal Icing (recipe, page 128)
Sanding sugar (optional)
1 recipe Luster Dust (optional)
Jam or preserves (optional)
Powdered sugar (optional)

1 In a medium mixing bowl beat butter and shortening with an electric mixer on medium to high speed for 30 seconds. Add the ¾ cup sugar, baking powder, and salt. Beat until combined, scraping sides of bowl occasionally. Beat in egg and vanilla until combined. Beat in as much of the flour as you can with the mixer. Stir in any remaining flour. Cover and chill dough about 1 hour or until easy to handle.

2 Preheat oven to 375°F. On a lightly floured surface, roll half of the dough at a time until ¼ inch thick. Using 2½- to 5-inch star-shape cookie cutters, cut out dough. For sandwich cookies, using a ½-inch to 1-inch star-shape cutter, cut out the centers of half the big cutouts. (Reroll the small cutouts to make more cookies or bake the smaller shapes separately.) Place cutouts on an ungreased cookie sheet. Bake for 8 to 10 minutes or until edges are firm and bottoms are very light brown. Let stand for 1 minute on cookie sheet. Transfer to a wire rack and let cool.

3 Spread or pipe Royal Icing on cooled cookies. If desired, sprinkle with sanding sugar or, using a tiny clean paintbrush, paint the piped designs with Luster Dust.

luster dust: *In a custard cup place ½ teaspoon gold, silver, or pearl luster dust. Stir in 2 teaspoons vodka. (The vodka will evaporate, leaving a dry mixture.)*

sandwich cookies: *Prepare as above, except spread each of the whole stars with jam (use about ½ teaspoon for 2-inch cookies and 1 teaspoon for 3-inch cookies). Sift powdered sugar over "windowed" cookies and place on top of whole cookies. Assemble cookies just before serving.*

In today's world of megasize cookies, these cute-as-a-button little gems work their charm on any cookie tray.

chocolate buttons

prep: 25 min. bake: 4 min. per batch stand: 1 min. per batch oven: 375°F
makes: about 144 cookies

¼ cup butter, softened
½ cup packed dark
   brown sugar
¼ cup unsweetened
   cocoa powder
1 tablespoon milk
1 teaspoon vanilla
¼ teaspoon baking soda
⅔ cup all-purpose flour
4 ounces bittersweet
   chocolate, chopped
1½ teaspoons shortening
½ teaspoon mint extract

1 Preheat oven to 375°F. In a large mixing bowl beat butter, brown sugar, cocoa powder, milk, and vanilla with an electric mixer on low to medium speed until combined. Beat in baking soda and as much of the flour as you can with the mixer. Stir in any remaining flour. Divide dough in half.

2 On a lightly floured surface, roll half of the dough at a time until ¹⁄₁₆ inch thick. Using a 1- to 1½-inch round cookie cutter, cut out dough. Place cutouts on an ungreased cookie sheet. Bake for 4 to 5 minutes or until edges are firm. Let stand for 1 minute on cookie sheet. Transfer to a wire rack and let cool.

3 In a small heavy saucepan heat and stir chocolate and shortening over low heat until smooth. Remove from heat. Stir in mint extract. Let stand until just cool enough to handle. Transfer the warm chocolate mixture to a resealable plastic bag. Cut a small hole in one corner of the bag. Squeezing gently, drizzle chocolate mixture over cookies. Let stand until chocolate sets.

*A dusting of powdered sugar and cocoa makes for an elegant finish.
If you prefer, drizzle melted chocolate onto the sandwiches instead.*

coffee-and-cream
sandwich cookies

prep: 20 min. chill: 2 hr. bake: 8 min. per batch oven: 375°F
makes: about 40 sandwich cookies

½ cup butter, softened
½ cup shortening
1 cup granulated sugar
1 teaspoon baking
   powder
¼ teaspoon salt
1 egg
1 teaspoon vanilla
2¼ cups all-purpose flour
1 recipe Coffee Filling
1 tablespoon
   unsweetened cocoa
   powder
1 tablespoon powdered
   sugar

1 In a large mixing bowl beat butter and shortening with an electric mixer on medium to high speed for 30 seconds. Add granulated sugar, baking powder, and salt. Beat until combined, scraping sides of bowl occasionally. Beat in egg and the vanilla until combined. Beat in as much of the flour as you can with the mixer. Stir in any remaining flour. Divide dough in half. Cover and chill dough about 2 hours or until easy to handle.

2 Preheat oven to 375°F. On a lightly floured surface, roll half of the dough at a time until ⅛ inch thick. Using a 1½-inch desired-shape cookie cutter, cut out dough. Place cutouts 2 inches apart on an ungreased cookie sheet. Bake for 8 to 10 minutes or until edges are light brown. Transfer to a wire rack; cool.

3 Spread 1 teaspoon Coffee Filling each on the bottoms of half of the cookies. Top with remaining cookies, bottom sides down. In a small bowl stir together cocoa powder and powdered sugar. Place mixture in a fine-mesh sieve and sift over filled cookies.

coffee filling: *In a bowl stir together
2 cups powdered sugar, 2 tablespoons
softened butter, 2 teaspoons espresso
powder, 1 teaspoon vanilla, and
enough milk to make a filling of
spreading consistency.*

Cocoa in the dough, as well as in the frosting, makes for a double dose of rich chocolate in every bite.

rolled cocoa cookies

prep: 50 min. chill: 1 hr. bake: 7 min. per batch oven: 375°F
makes: about 48 cookies

3 cups all-purpose flour
1 cup unsweetened cocoa powder
1 tablespoon baking powder
½ teaspoon salt
2 cups sugar
1 cup shortening
2 eggs
¼ cup milk
1 recipe Cocoa-Butter Frosting

1. In a large bowl stir together flour, cocoa powder, baking powder, and salt; set aside.

2. In a large mixing bowl beat sugar and shortening with an electric mixer on medium to high speed until combined. Beat in eggs and milk until combined. Beat in as much of the flour mixture as you can with the mixer. Stir in any remaining flour mixture. Divide dough in half. Cover and chill dough for 1 to 2 hours or until easy to handle.

3. Preheat oven to 375°F. On a lightly floured surface, roll half of the dough at a time until ¼ inch thick. Using a 2½-inch round cookie cutter, cut out dough. Place cutouts 1 inch apart on an ungreased cookie sheet. Bake about 7 minutes or until firm. Transfer to a wire rack and let cool. Frost cooled cookies with Cocoa-Butter Frosting.

note: *Store unfrosted cookies as directed on page 16. Freeze for up to 1 month. Frost cookies before serving.*

cocoa butter frosting: *In a medium mixing bowl beat ¼ cup softened butter with an electric mixer on medium to high speed until fluffy. Gradually beat in 1½ cups powdered sugar and 2 tablespoons unsweetened cocoa powder; combine well. Beat in 3 tablespoons milk and 1 teaspoon vanilla. Gradually beat in 1¼ cups additional powdered sugar. If necessary, beat in enough additional milk to make frosting of spreading consistency.*

Every bite of this simple shortbread is full of rich, buttery macadamia nuts and sweet, chewy candied pineapple.

pineapple
and macadamia nut shortbread

2½	cups all-purpose flour
⅓	cup packed brown sugar
1	cup cold butter
¼	cup finely chopped macadamia nuts
¼	cup finely chopped candied pineapple
1	recipe Pineapple Icing

1 Preheat oven to 325°F. In a large bowl stir together flour and brown sugar. Using a pastry blender, cut in butter until mixture resembles fine crumbs and starts to cling. Stir in macadamia nuts and candied pineapple. Carefully form mixture into a ball and knead until nearly smooth.

2 On a lightly floured surface, roll dough until ¼ inch thick. Using a 2-inch desired-shape cookie cutter, cut out dough. (Reroll scraps no more than once.) Place cutouts 1 inch apart on an ungreased cookie sheet.

3 Bake for 15 to 20 minutes or until bottoms just start to brown. Transfer to a wire rack and let cool. Using a decorating bag, pipe Pineapple Icing on cooled cookies, as desired. Let stand until icing sets.

pineapple icing: *In a small bowl stir together 1 cup powdered sugar and ½ teaspoon vanilla. Stir in enough unsweetened pineapple juice (about 3 to 4 teaspoons) to make an icing of piping consistency.*

*These dainty tarts brimming with homemade orange curd
are the perfect addition to an afternoon coffee break.*

orange curd tarts

prep: 45 min. bake: 18 min. stand: 20 min. oven: 350°F makes: 32 tarts

1	package piecrust mix (for 2 crusts)
¼	cup finely chopped pecans
⅓	cup cold water
1	cup granulated sugar
2	teaspoons cornstarch
1	tablespoon finely shredded orange peel (set aside)
⅓	cup orange juice
1	tablespoon butter, cut up
3	eggs, beaten
	Small orange peel curls (optional)

1 Lightly grease thirty-two 1¾-inch muffin pan cups; set aside. In a small mixing bowl stir together piecrust mix and the pecans. Add cold water; stir until moistened. Divide dough in half.

2 On a lightly floured surface, roll half of the dough at a time into a 10½-inch square; trim to a 10-inch square. Cut square into sixteen 2½-inch squares. Fit squares into prepared muffin cups, pleating sides and leaving corners standing up slightly.

3 Preheat oven to 350°F. For filling, in a medium saucepan stir together sugar and cornstarch. Add orange juice and butter. Cook and stir over medium heat until thickened and bubbly. Cook and stir for 2 minutes more. Stir about half of the juice mixture into beaten eggs. Return egg mixture to saucepan. Remove from heat. Stir in orange peel. Spoon about 2 teaspoons filling into each pastry-lined muffin cup.

4 Bake for 18 to 20 minutes or until filling is set and crust is light brown. Let stand in pans on a wire rack for 20 minutes. Carefully transfer tarts from pans to a wire rack and let cool completely. If desired, garnish each tart with an orange peel curl just before serving.

note: *Store cookies as directed on page 16. Do not store at room temperature. Refrigerate up to 3 days. Do not freeze.*

creative **cutouts**

Shortbread dough takes beautifully to fancy fluted edges. If you don't have a crinkle cutter, a fluted pastry wheel creates the same effect.

pistachio shortbread

prep: 30 min. bake: 15 min. chill: 15 min. oven: 325°F
makes: about 24 to 30 cookies

1¾ cups all-purpose flour
1 cup finely ground
     pistachio nuts
⅓ cup sugar
1 cup butter
1½ cups white baking
     pieces
1 tablespoon
     shortening
1 cup finely chopped
     pistachio nuts

1 Preheat oven to 325°F. In a medium bowl stir together the flour, ground nuts, and sugar. Using a pastry blender, cut in butter until mixture resembles fine crumbs and starts to cling. Form mixture into a ball; knead until smooth. Divide dough in half.

2 On a lightly floured surface, roll half of the dough at a time into an 8×4-inch rectangle. Using a crinkle cutter or fluted pastry wheel, cut dough into 2×¾-inch rectangles and/or 1-inch squares. Place cutouts about 2 inches apart on an ungreased cookie sheet. Bake for 15 to 18 minutes or until edges are firm and bottoms are very light brown. Transfer cookies to a wire rack and let cool.

3 Line cookie sheets with waxed paper; set aside. In a small saucepan heat and stir white baking pieces and shortening over low heat until smooth. Dip one end or corner of cooled cookies into melted mixture. Place dipped cookies on prepared cookie sheets. Sprinkle with some of the chopped nuts. Chill about 15 minutes or until set.

note: *Store cookies as directed on page 16. Freeze for up to 1 month.*

Big and thick with soft centers, these old-fashioned cookies are perfect with a tall glass of ice cold milk.

nutmeg softies

prep: 30 min. chill: 2 hr. bake: 10 min. per batch oven: 350°F

makes: about 32 cookies

½	cup butter, softened
½	cup shortening
1½	cups granulated sugar
1	teaspoon baking soda
1	teaspoon ground nutmeg
½	teaspoon salt
1	cup dairy sour cream
1	egg
1	teaspoon vanilla
4	cups all-purpose flour
	Colored coarse sugar

1 In a large mixing bowl beat butter and shortening with an electric mixer on medium to high speed for 30 seconds. Add granulated sugar, baking soda, nutmeg, and salt. Beat until combined, scraping sides of bowl occasionally. Beat in sour cream, egg, and vanilla until combined. Beat in as much of the flour as you can with the mixer. Stir in any remaining flour. (Dough will be sticky.) Divide dough into thirds. Cover and chill dough about 2 hours or until easy to handle.

2 Preheat oven to 350°F. On a lightly floured surface, roll one-third of the dough at a time until ¼ inch thick. Using a floured 3-inch desired-shape cookie cutter, cut out dough. Place cutouts on an ungreased cookie sheet. Sprinkle with colored sugar. Bake about 10 minutes or until edges of cookies are firm and bottoms are golden. Transfer to a wire rack and let cool.

These cutouts stay true to their name with luscious, moist texture that's hard to beat.

From eyecatching swirl cookies to elegant biscotti, these impressive treats will have your friends and family raving. They're actually quite simple to make—but that can be your secret.

slice & bake

swe

4

ets

Cardamom is the key spice in these cookies. Its warm, slightly spicy essence rounds out the sweetness of the dried apricots.

chocolate almond-apricot cookies

prep: 40 min. chill: 4 hr. bake: 8 min. per batch stand: 1 min. per batch oven: 375°F makes: about 80 cookies

1	cup butter, softened
1	cup granulated sugar
½	cup packed brown sugar
½	teaspoon baking powder
½	teaspoon salt
¼	teaspoon ground cardamom
2	eggs
1	teaspoon vanilla
3	cups all-purpose flour
1	cup coarsely grated semisweet chocolate (about 5 ounces)
½	cup finely snipped dried apricots
⅓	cup almonds, ground
1½	cups semisweet chocolate pieces (9 ounces)
1	tablespoon butter
¼	teaspoon almond extract

1 In a large mixing bowl beat the 1 cup butter with an electric mixer on medium to high speed for 30 seconds. Add granulated sugar, brown sugar, baking powder, salt, and cardamom. Beat until combined, scraping sides of bowl occasionally. Beat in eggs and vanilla until combined. Beat in as much of the flour as you can with the mixer. Stir in any remaining flour, the grated chocolate, the apricots, and almonds. Divide dough in half. If necessary, cover and chill dough about 30 minutes or until easy to handle.

2 Meanwhile, for filling, in a small saucepan heat and stir the 1½ cups chocolate pieces and the 1 tablespoon butter over low heat until smooth. Stir in almond extract. Set aside.

3 On a lightly floured surface, roll half of the dough into a 10-inch square. Spread half of the filling over square, leaving a ½-inch border around edges. (If filling becomes too thick to spread, add hot water, 1 teaspoon at a time, until filling is spreadable.) Roll up square. (If dough cracks slightly, allow it to stand at room temperature for a few minutes.) Pinch to seal. Wrap roll in plastic wrap or waxed paper. Repeat with remaining dough and filling. Chill about 4 hours or until firm.

4 Preheat oven to 375°F. Using a sharp knife, cut rolls into ¼-inch slices. Place slices 2 inches apart on an ungreased cookie sheet. Bake for 8 to 10 minutes or until edges are light brown. Let stand for 1 minute on cookie sheet. Transfer to a wire rack and let cool.

The addition of cornstarch gives these buttery rounds a light, delicate texture that accentuates the evocative perfume of jasmine tea.

jasmine-orange meltaways

prep: 35 min. chill: 2 hr. bake: 8 min. per batch stand: 1 day (dredging sugar)
oven: 375°F makes: about 40 cookies

¾ cup butter, softened
2 tablespoons jasmine tea dragon pearls*
½ cup powdered sugar
½ teaspoon vanilla
1 cup all-purpose flour
½ cup cornstarch
2 teaspoons finely shredded orange peel
1 recipe Jasmine Dredging Sugar

1 In a small saucepan heat ¼ cup of the butter over medium heat until butter is melted and bubbly. Remove from heat. Stir in tea. Allow tea to steep in butter for 4 minutes. Strain butter through a fine-mesh sieve.

2 In a large mixing bowl combine the strained butter, the remaining ½ cup butter, and the powdered sugar. Beat with an electric mixer on medium to high speed until light and fluffy. Beat in vanilla until combined. Beat in flour and cornstarch until combined. Stir in orange peel.

3 On waxed paper, shape dough into a 10-inch-long log. Lift and smooth the waxed paper to help shape the log. Wrap in plastic wrap. Chill about 2 hours or until firm.

4 Preheat oven to 375°F. Using a serrated knife, cut roll into ¼-inch slices. Place slices 1 inch apart on an ungreased cookie sheet. Bake for 8 to 10 minutes or until edges are lightly golden. Transfer to a wire rack and let cool for 10 minutes.

5 Gently shake warm cookies in Jasmine Dredging Sugar. Return coated cookies to wire rack. Cool completely.

✳ Look for jasmine tea dragon pearls at a shop that features specialty teas.

jasmine dredging sugar: *Place ¼ cup jasmine tea dragon pearls in the center of a double-thick, 6-inch square of 100-percent-cotton cheesecloth. Tie closed with a clean string. Place 1 cup powdered sugar in a 1-quart resealable plastic bag. Add tea in cheesecloth to powdered sugar; seal bag. Let stand in a cool, dry place for 1 day. Remove tea-filled cheesecloth.*

Use either canned frosting or your favorite homemade frosting to stuff these warm, spicy cookie sandwiches.

molasses slices

prep: 25 min. **chill:** 6 hr. **bake:** 8 min. per batch **stand:** 2 min. per batch
oven: 375°F **makes:** about 72 cookies (36 sandwich cookies)

½   cup butter, softened
½   cup shortening
¾   cup sugar
1½   teaspoons baking
      soda
½   teaspoon ground
      cinnamon
¼   teaspoon ground
      nutmeg
¼   teaspoon ground
      ginger
¼   teaspoon ground
      cloves
1   egg
½   cup molasses
2¼   cups all-purpose flour
      Canned frosting
      (optional)

1 In a large mixing bowl beat butter and shortening with an electric mixer on medium to high speed for 30 seconds. Add sugar, baking soda, cinnamon, nutmeg, ginger, and cloves. Beat until combined, scraping sides of bowl occasionally. Beat in egg and molasses until combined. Beat in as much of the flour as you can with the mixer. Stir in any remaining flour. Divide dough in half. Cover and chill dough about 2 hours or until easy to handle.

2 Shape each half of dough into a 9-inch-long log. Wrap each log in plastic wrap or waxed paper. Chill about 4 hours or until firm.

3 Preheat oven to 375°F. Using a sharp knife, cut logs into ¼-inch slices. Place slices 2 inches apart on an ungreased cookie sheet. Bake 8 minutes or until edges are firm. Let stand for 2 minutes on cookie sheet. Transfer to a wire rack and let cool.

4 If desired, just before serving spread the flat sides of half the cookies with frosting. Top with remaining cookies, flat sides down.

The tantalizing aroma of molasses and spice will awaken your senses as it wafts from the hot oven.

A coating of graham crackers before slicing and baking likens these cream cheese gems to the popular cheesecake dessert.

cheesecake slices

prep: 30 min. chill: 2 hr. bake: 8 min. per batch stand: 1 min. per batch
oven: 375°F makes: about 64 cookies

¾ cup butter, softened
1 3-ounce package
   cream cheese,
   softened
¾ cup sugar
2 teaspoons finely
   shredded lemon
   peel
2 tablespoons lemon
   juice
2 teaspoons finely
   shredded orange
   peel
1 teaspoon vanilla
2 cups all-purpose flour
¼ cup finely chopped
   pecans
¼ cup finely crushed
   graham crackers

1 In a large mixing bowl beat butter and cream cheese with an electric mixer on medium to high speed for 30 seconds. Add sugar, lemon peel, lemon juice, orange peel, and vanilla. Beat until combined, scraping sides of bowl occasionally. Beat in as much of the flour as you can with the mixer. Stir in any remaining flour. If necessary, cover and chill dough 30 minutes or until easy to handle.

2 Shape each half of dough into an 8-inch-long log. In a small bowl stir together pecans and crushed crackers; transfer to waxed paper. Roll logs in nut mixture to coat. If necessary, press mixture lightly into dough. Wrap in plastic wrap or waxed paper. Chill about 2 hours or until firm.

3 Preheat oven to 375°F. Using a serrated knife, cut logs into ¼-inch slices. Place slices 2 inches apart on an ungreased cookie sheet. Bake for 8 to 10 minutes or until bottoms are light brown. Let stand for 1 minute on cookie sheet. Transfer to a wire rack and let cool.

Surprise friends with the flavor of luscious cheesecake packaged into a cookie-size treat.

Just slice and stack flavored doughs twice to make these knockout plaid cookies. Coconut and chopped nuts add flavor and texture.

tropical checkerboards

prep: 40 min. chill: 2½ hr. bake: 10 min. per batch oven: 375°F
makes: about 48 cookies

¾   cup butter, softened
1   cup sugar
½   teaspoon baking powder
¼   teaspoon salt
1   egg
1   teaspoon vanilla
2   cups all-purpose flour
½   teaspoon rum extract
    Orange paste food coloring
½   teaspoon coconut extract
    Yellow paste food coloring
⅓   cup flaked coconut
⅓   cup finely chopped macadamia nuts

1 In a medium mixing bowl beat butter with an electric mixer on medium to high speed for 30 seconds. Add sugar, baking powder, and salt. Beat until combined, scraping sides of bowl occasionally. Beat in egg and vanilla until combined. Beat in as much of the flour as you can with the mixer. Stir in any remaining flour.

2 Divide dough in half. Knead rum extract and orange food coloring into one half of dough. Knead coconut extract and yellow food coloring into the other half of dough.

3 Shape each dough portion into a rectangular log that is about 6 inches long and 2 inches wide. Wrap logs in plastic wrap or waxed paper. Chill for 1 hour. Using a sharp knife, cut each log lengthwise into four slices. Alternating colors, stack the slices to form two four-layer logs. Press together to seal layers. Wrap logs in plastic wrap or waxed paper. Chill about 30 minutes or until firm.

4 Place logs on a cutting board with a solid color facing up. Using a sharp knife, cut logs lengthwise into four slices. (Each will have four layers in alternating colors.) Stack four slices of dough, alternating color placement for a checkerboard effect. Repeat with remaining slices. Trim edges to straighten. In a shallow dish stir together coconut and macadamia nut. Roll logs in coconut mixture to coat. Wrap and chill 1 hour or until firm.

5 Preheat oven to 375°F. Cut logs crosswise into ¼-inch slices. Place slices 2 inches apart on an ungreased cookie sheet. Bake for 10 to 12 minutes or until edges are light brown. Transfer to a wire rack and let cool.

Nutmeg and rum extract give these cookies the flavor of creamy eggnog. Tangy cranberries provide the perfect flavor complement.

cranberry-eggnog twirls

prep: 25 min. chill: 5 hr. bake: 10 min. per batch stand: 1 min. per batch
oven: 375°F makes: about 80 cookies

1 cup butter, softened
1½ cups sugar
½ teaspoon baking
powder
½ teaspoon salt
½ teaspoon ground
nutmeg
2 eggs
1 teaspoon rum extract
3¼ cups all-purpose flour
½ cup cranberry
preserves or jam
1½ teaspoons cornstarch
½ cup finely chopped
pecans, toasted
(see tip, page 19)

1 In a large mixing bowl beat butter with an electric mixer on medium to high speed for 30 seconds. Add sugar, baking powder, salt, and nutmeg. Beat until combined, scraping sides of bowl occasionally. Beat in eggs and rum extract until combined. Beat in as much of the flour as you can with the mixer. Stir in any remaining flour. Divide dough in half. Cover and chill dough 1 hour or until easy to handle.

2 Meanwhile, for filling, in a small saucepan heat and stir preserves and cornstarch over medium heat until thickened and bubbly. Remove from heat. Stir in pecans. Cover and set aside to cool.

3 Roll half of the dough between two pieces of waxed paper into a 10-inch square. Spread half of the filling over square, leaving a ½-inch border along the edges. Roll up dough. Moisten edges and pinch to seal. Wrap log in plastic wrap or waxed paper. Repeat with remaining dough and filling. Chill about 4 hours or until firm.

4 Preheat oven to 375°F. Line a large cookie sheet with parchment paper. Using a sharp knife, cut rolls into ¼-inch slices. Place slices 2 inches apart on the prepared cookie sheet.

5 Bake for 10 to 12 minutes or until edges are firm and bottoms are light brown. Let stand for 1 minute on cookie sheet. Transfer to a wire rack and let cool.

These attractive cookies are simple to shape—just be sure to thoroughly chill the dough before rolling it out.

chocolate palmiers

prep: 35 min. chill: 4 hr. bake: 8 min. per batch oven: 375°F
makes: about 80 cookies

1	8-ounce package cream cheese, softened
½	cup powdered sugar
¼	cup unsweetened cocoa powder
2	tablespoons all-purpose flour
2	tablespoons coffee liqueur, hazelnut liqueur, or strong coffee
½	cup finely chopped pecans or hazelnuts, toasted (optional) (see tip, page 19)
½	cup butter, softened
½	cup granulated sugar
½	cup packed brown sugar
½	teaspoon baking powder
½	teaspoon ground cinnamon
¼	teaspoon salt
1	egg
3	tablespoons milk
½	teaspoon vanilla
2¾	cups all-purpose flour

1 For filling, in a medium mixing bowl combine cream cheese, powdered sugar, cocoa powder, the 2 tablespoons flour, and the liqueur. Beat with an electric mixer on low to medium speed until smooth. If desired, stir in nuts. Cover and set aside.

2 For dough, in a large mixing bowl beat the butter with an electric mixer on medium to high speed for 30 seconds. Add granulated sugar, brown sugar, baking powder, cinnamon, and salt. Beat until combined, scraping sides of bowl occasionally. Beat in egg, milk, and vanilla until combined. Beat in as much of the 2¾ cups flour as you can with the mixer. Stir in any remaining flour. Divide dough in half. If necessary, cover and chill 30 minutes or until easy to handle.

3 On a lightly floured surface, roll half of the dough into a 12×8-inch rectangle. Spread half of the filling over rectangle, leaving a ½-inch border along each long side. Roll both long sides, scroll style, to meet in the center. Brush the seam where the dough spirals meet with water; lightly press together. Repeat with remaining dough and filling. Wrap each roll in plastic wrap or waxed paper. Chill about 4 hours or until firm.

4 Preheat oven to 375°F. Grease a cookie sheet; set aside. Using a sharp knife, cut rolls into ¼-inch slices. Place slices 2 inches apart on the prepared cookie sheet. Bake 8 minutes or until edges are firm and bottoms are light brown. Transfer to a wire rack; cool.

note: *Store cookies as directed on page 16. Refrigerate up to 3 days. Do not freeze.*

Great for party treats, these little cookie sandwiches give a big jolt of chocolate flavor in a tiny bite.

mini milk-chocolate cookie sandwiches

prep: 45 min. freeze: 30 min. bake: 9 min. per batch stand: 2 min. per batch
oven: 350°F makes: about 72 tiny sandwich cookies

¾ cup all-purpose flour
¾ teaspoon baking
    powder
⅛ teaspoon salt
6 ounces milk chocolate
3 tablespoons butter,
    softened
½ cup sugar
1 egg
¾ teaspoon vanilla
1 recipe Milk Chocolate
    and Sour Cream
    Frosting

1 In a medium bowl stir together flour, baking powder, and salt; set aside. In a small saucepan heat and stir milk chocolate over low heat until smooth; set aside. In a medium mixing bowl beat butter with electric mixer on medium to high speed for 30 seconds. Add sugar. Beat until combined, scraping sides of bowl occasionally. Beat in melted chocolate, the egg, and vanilla until combined. Beat in flour mixture.

2 Divide dough into four equal portions. Wrap each portion in plastic wrap. Freeze about 30 minutes or until easy to handle. (Or chill in the refrigerator about 1 hour.)

3 Preheat oven to 350°F. On waxed paper, shape one portion of dough at a time into a 10-inch-long log. Lift and smooth the waxed paper to help shape the logs. Using a sharp knife, cut logs crosswise into ¼-inch slices. Place slices 1 inch apart on ungreased cookie sheets. Bake for 9 to 10 minutes or until edges are set. Let stand for 2 minutes on cookie sheet. Carefully transfer to a wire rack; cool.

4 Spread ½ teaspoon of the Milk Chocolate and Sour Cream Frosting on each of the flat sides of half of the cookies. Top with remaining cookies, flat sides down. Serve the same day.

milk chocolate and sour cream frosting: *In a saucepan heat and stir 3 ounces chopped milk chocolate and 2 tablespoons butter over low heat until smooth. Cool for 5 minutes. Stir in ¼ cup dairy sour cream. Gradually stir in 1 to 1¼ cups powdered sugar to make a frosting of spreading consistency.*

While these petite sandwiches may appear modest, they boast immense chocolate flavor.

These melt-in-your-mouth cookies take on different looks, depending on the color of chip you use.

buttery mint slices

prep: 25 min. chill: 2 hr. bake: 10 min. per batch oven: 350°F
makes: about 72 cookies

½ cup butter, softened
⅔ cup sugar
1 teaspoon baking powder
½ teaspoon salt
1 egg
1 tablespoon milk
1 teaspoon vanilla
2 cups all-purpose flour
⅓ cup green mint or chocolate-mint baking pieces, melted and slightly cooled
⅓ cup white baking pieces, melted and slightly cooled

1 In a large mixing bowl beat butter with an electric mixer on medium to high speed for 30 seconds. Add sugar, baking powder, and salt. Beat until combined, scraping sides of bowl occasionally. Beat in egg, milk, and vanilla until combined. Beat in as much of the flour as you can with the mixer. Stir in any remaining flour. Divide dough in half.

2 In a medium bowl stir or knead together half of the dough and the melted mint baking pieces. Divide mint dough into thirds. In a second bowl stir or knead together the remaining half dough and the melted white baking pieces; divide white dough in half.

3 Line an 8×4×2-inch loaf pan with plastic wrap. Press one-third of the mint dough evenly into pan. Press half of the white dough evenly on top of mint layer. Repeat the layers, finishing with mint dough on top. Cover with plastic wrap. Chill about 2 hours or until firm.

4 Preheat oven to 350°F. Remove dough brick from pan and unwrap; place on cutting board. Using a sharp knife, cut brick crosswise into ⅛-inch slices. Cut each slice in half; place 2 inches apart on an ungreased cookie sheet. Bake about 10 minutes or until edges are set. Transfer to a wire rack; cool.

A mascarpone cheese and apple butter filling makes these cakelike cookies taste like an elegant dessert.

cashew torte cookies

prep: 50 min. chill: 4 hr. bake: 8 min. per batch stand: 30 min. oven: 375°F
makes: about 24 cookies

½ cup shortening
½ cup butter, softened
1 cup granulated sugar
¼ cup packed brown
   sugar
½ teaspoon baking soda
¼ teaspoon baking
   powder
¼ teaspoon salt
2 eggs
1 teaspoon vanilla
2½ cups all-purpose flour
¾ cup lightly salted
   cashews, ground
   Cashew halves
1 recipe Apple Butter
   Filling
   Powdered sugar
   (optional)
   Ground mace or
   ground nutmeg
   (optional)

1 In a large mixing bowl beat shortening and butter with an electric mixer on medium to high speed for 30 seconds. Add granulated sugar, brown sugar, baking soda, baking powder, and salt. Beat until combined, scraping sides of bowl occasionally. Beat in eggs and vanilla until combined. Beat in as much of the flour as you can with the mixer. Stir in any remaining flour and ground nuts.

2 Divide the dough into four equal portions. Shape each portion into a 6-inch-long log. Wrap logs in plastic wrap or waxed paper. Chill about 4 hours or until firm.

3 Preheat oven to 375°F. Using a sharp knife, cut logs into ¼-inch slices. Place slices 1 inch apart on an ungreased cookie sheet. Press cashew halves into the tops of 24 of the cookies. Bake 8 minutes or until edges are firm and golden. Transfer to a wire rack and let cool.

4 About 30 minutes before serving, spread about 1 teaspoon Apple Butter Filling on a plain cookie. Top with a second plain cookie. Spread about 1 teaspoon filling on the second cookie. Top with a nut-topped cookie. Repeat with remaining cookies and filling. If desired, sift powdered sugar and additional ground mace over cookies. Let stacked cookies stand about 30 minutes before serving to soften.

note: *Store unfilled cookies as directed on page 16. Refrigerate up to 3 days. Fill the cookie layers before serving.*

apple butter filling: *In a bowl stir together one 8-ounce container mascarpone cheese or one 8-ounce package softened cream cheese, ¼ cup apple butter, 2 tablespoons brown sugar, and ¼ teaspoon ground mace until smooth.*

These salty-sweet cookies, attractive as well as tasty, are great additions to an hors d'oeuvres table at a party.

savory cheese swirls

prep: 45 min. chill: 5 hr. bake: 10 min. per batch stand: 1 min. per batch
oven: 375°F makes: 72 cookies

2   5.2-ounce packages
    semisoft cheese
    with garlic and
    herbs
2   tablespoons grated
    Romano cheese
¼   cup pine nuts,
    toasted (see tip,
    page 19)
½   cup butter, softened
½   cup shortening
½   cup sugar
½   teaspoon baking
    powder
½   teaspoon salt
2   eggs
3   cups all-purpose flour
    Several drops green
    food coloring
¼   cup snipped fresh
    chives

1 For filling, in a small bowl stir together semisoft cheese and Romano cheese. Stir in pine nuts. Cover and chill until needed.

2 In a large mixing bowl beat butter and shortening with an electric mixer on medium to high speed for 30 seconds. Add sugar, baking powder, and salt. Beat until combined, scraping sides of bowl occasionally. Beat in eggs until combined. Beat in as much of the flour as you can with the mixer. Add green food coloring, 1 drop at a time, beating until dough is a pale green color. Stir in any remaining flour and the chives. Divide dough in half. Cover and chill about 1 hour or until easy to handle.

3 Roll half of the dough between two pieces of waxed paper into a 10-inch square. Spread half of the filling over square, leaving a ½-inch border along the edges. Roll up dough. Moisten edges and pinch to seal. Wrap log in plastic wrap or waxed paper. Repeat with remaining dough and filling. Chill about 4 hours or until firm.

4 Preheat oven to 375°F. Line a cookie sheet with parchment paper; set aside. Using a sharp knife, cut logs into ¼-inch slices. Place slices 2 inches apart on the prepared cookie sheet. Bake about 10 minutes or until edges and bottoms are light brown. Let stand for 1 minute on cookie sheet. Transfer to a wire rack and let cool.

note: *Store cookies as directed on page 16. Refrigerate for up to 3 days or freeze for up to 3 months. Let stand at room temperature 15 minutes before serving.*

Brown sugar adds richness to these classic cookies. A drizzle of melted milk chocolate gives them a fancy finish.

brown sugar icebox cookies

prep: 30 min. chill: 4 hr. bake: 10 min. per batch oven: 375°F
makes: about 80 cookies

½ cup shortening
½ cup butter, softened
1¼ cups packed brown sugar
½ teaspoon baking soda
¼ teaspoon salt
1 egg
1 teaspoon vanilla
2½ cups all-purpose flour
¾ cup toasted ground hazelnuts (filberts) or pecans (see tip, page 19)
⅔ cup finely chopped toasted hazelnuts (filberts) or pecans (optional)
Milk chocolate, melted (optional)

1 In a large mixing bowl beat shortening and butter with an electric mixer on medium to high speed for 30 seconds. Add the brown sugar, baking soda, and salt. Beat until combined, scraping sides of bowl occasionally. Beat in egg and vanilla until combined. Beat in as much of the flour as you can. Stir in remaining flour and the ¾ cup ground nuts.

2 Divide dough in half. On waxed paper, shape each half of dough into a 10-inch-long loaf. Lift and smooth the waxed paper to help shape the loaves. If desired, roll loaves in the ⅔ cup chopped nuts. Wrap each loaf in plastic wrap. Chill 4 hours or until firm. (Or wrap dough in foil and freeze up to 3 months; thaw in the refrigerator before slicing.)

3 Preheat oven to 375°F. Cut loaves into ¼-inch slices. Place slices 1 inch apart on an ungreased cookie sheet. Bake 10 minutes or until edges are firm. Transfer to a wire rack; cool. If desired, drizzle cooled cookies with melted chocolate. Let stand until set.

Add surprising flavor to these slice-and-bake cookies by rolling the loaves in chopped toasted nuts.

A bit of lemon juice adds a tangy accent to the luscious dates in these attractive cookies.

date pinwheels

prep: 40 min. chill: 1 hr. freeze: 2 hr. bake: 8 min. per batch
stand: 1 min. per batch oven: 375°F makes: about 80 cookies

1	8-ounce package (1⅓ cups) pitted whole dates, finely snipped
½	cup water
⅓	cup granulated sugar
2	tablespoons lemon juice
1½	teaspoons vanilla
½	cup shortening
½	cup butter, softened
½	cup granulated sugar
½	cup packed brown sugar
½	teaspoon baking soda
¼	teaspoon salt
1	egg
2	tablespoons milk
3	cups all-purpose flour

1 For filling, in a medium saucepan combine dates, the water, and the ⅓ cup granulated sugar. Bring to boiling; reduce heat. Cook and stir about 2 minutes or until thick. Stir in lemon juice and ½ teaspoon of the vanilla; cool.

2 In a large mixing bowl beat shortening and butter with an electric mixer on medium to high speed for 30 seconds. Add the ½ cup granulated sugar, the brown sugar, baking soda, and salt. Beat until combined, scraping sides of bowl occasionally. Beat in egg, milk, and the remaining 1 teaspoon vanilla until combined. Beat in as much of the flour as you can with the mixer. Stir in any remaining flour. Divide dough in half. Cover and chill dough about 1 hour or until easy to handle.

3 Roll half of the dough between two pieces of waxed paper into a 12×10-inch rectangle. Spread half of the filling over the rectangle. Roll up dough, starting from a short side. Moisten edges and pinch to seal. Wrap log in plastic wrap or waxed paper. Repeat with remaining dough and filling. Freeze about 2 hours or until firm.

4 Preheat oven to 375°F. Grease a cookie sheet; set aside. Using a serrated knife, cut rolls into ¼-inch slices. Place slices 1 inch apart on the prepared cookie sheet. Bake for 8 to 10 minutes or until edges are light brown. Let stand for 1 minute on cookie sheet. Transfer to a wire rack and let cool.

Fresh cranberries and shredded orange peel give these pleasingly soft cookies a tangy taste and bright color.

cranberry-orange pinwheels

prep: 25 min. chill: 5 hr. bake: 8 min. per batch stand: 1 min. per batch
oven: 375°F makes: about 60 cookies

1 cup cranberries
1 cup pecans
¼ cup packed brown
    sugar
1 cup butter, softened
1½ cups granulated
    sugar
½ teaspoon baking
    powder
½ teaspoon salt
2 eggs
2 teaspoons finely
    shredded orange
    peel
3 cups all-purpose flour

1 For filling, in a blender or food processor combine cranberries, pecans, and brown sugar. Cover and blend or process until cranberries and nuts are very finely chopped; set aside.

2 In a large mixing bowl beat butter with an electric mixer on medium to high speed for 30 seconds. Add granulated sugar, baking powder, and salt. Beat until combined, scraping sides of bowl occasionally. Beat in eggs and orange peel until combined. Beat in as much of the flour as you can. Stir in any remaining flour. Divide dough in half. Cover and chill dough 1 hour or until easy to handle.

3 Roll half of the dough between two pieces of waxed paper into a 10-inch square. Spread half of the filling over square, leaving a ½-inch border along the edges. Roll up dough. Moisten edges and pinch to seal. Wrap log in plastic wrap or waxed paper. Repeat with remaining dough and filling. Chill about 4 hours or until firm.

4 Preheat oven to 375°F. Using a sharp knife, cut rolls into ¼-inch slices. Place slices 2 inches apart on an ungreased cookie sheet. Bake for 8 to 10 minutes or until edges are firm and bottoms are light brown. Let stand for 1 minute on cookie sheet. Transfer to a wire rack and let cool.

Be sure to use white (clear) crème de menthe instead of green to avoid adding color to your cookies.

peppermint palmiers

prep: 45 min. chill: 5 hr. freeze: 4 hr. bake: 10 min. per batch oven: 350°F
makes: about 80 cookies

½ cup butter, softened
½ cup granulated sugar
½ cup packed brown sugar
½ teaspoon baking powder
¼ teaspoon salt
1 egg
3 tablespoons white crème de menthe
1 tablespoon milk
½ teaspoon vanilla
2¾ cups all-purpose flour
1 8-ounce package cream cheese, softened
½ cup powdered sugar
¼ cup all-purpose flour
Few drops liquid red food coloring
½ cup finely crushed peppermint candies

1 For dough, in a large mixing bowl beat the butter with an electric mixer on medium to high speed for 30 seconds. Add granulated sugar, brown sugar, baking powder, and salt. Beat until combined, scraping sides of bowl occasionally. Beat in egg, 2 tablespoons of the crème de menthe, the milk, and vanilla until combined. Beat in as much of the 2¾ cups flour as you can with the mixer. Stir in any of the remaining 2¾ cups flour. Divide dough in half. Cover and chill dough about 3 hours or until dough is easy to handle.

2 Meanwhile, for filling, in a medium mixing bowl combine cream cheese, powdered sugar, the ¼ cup flour, and the remaining 1 tablespoon crème de menthe. Beat on low to medium speed until smooth. Stir in a few drops red food coloring until pale pink. Gently fold in crushed candies. Cover and chill for up to 2 hours. (Do not chill longer than 2 hours or the candies will bleed into the filling and the filling will become too soft and sticky.)

3 On a lightly floured surface, roll half of the dough into a 12×8-inch rectangle. Spread half of the filling over rectangle, leaving a ½ inch border along each long side. Roll both long sides, scroll fashion, to meet in the center. Brush the seam where the dough spirals meet with water; lightly press together. Repeat with remaining dough and filling. Wrap each roll in plastic wrap or waxed paper. Freeze for 4 to 24 hours or until firm.

4 Preheat oven to 350°F. Line a cookie sheet with parchment paper; set aside. Using a serrated knife, cut rolls into ¼-inch slices. Place slices 2 inches apart on the prepared cookie sheet. Bake 10 minutes or until edges are firm and bottoms are light brown. Transfer to a wire rack and let cool.

You'll have visions of purple fields swaying in the breeze when you take in the aroma of the lavender buds.

lemon-lavender cookies

prep: 40 min. chill: 2 hr. bake: 10 min. per batch oven: 350°F
makes: 36 cookies

1½ cups all-purpose flour
1 teaspoon dried lavender buds, ground with mortar and pestle
1 teaspoon finely shredded lemon peel
¼ teaspoon salt
1 cup butter, softened
2 cups powdered sugar
1 tablespoon milk
Dried lavender buds (optional)
Thin strips of lemon peel (optional)

1 In a medium bowl stir together the flour, ground lavender buds, finely shredded lemon peel, and salt; set aside. In a large mixing bowl beat ¾ cup of the butter with an electric mixer on medium to high speed for 30 seconds. Add 1 cup of the powdered sugar. Beat until combined, scraping sides of bowl occasionally. Beat in as much of the flour mixture as you can with the mixer. Stir in any remaining flour mixture.

2 On a lightly floured surface, shape dough into a 10-inch-long log. Wrap log in plastic wrap. Chill 2 hours or until firm.

3 Preheat oven to 350°F. Using a sharp knife, cut roll into ¼-inch slices. Place slices 2 inches apart on ungreased cookie sheet. Bake 10 minutes or until edges are light brown. Transfer to a wire rack and let cool.

4 For frosting, in a small bowl combine the remaining ¼ cup butter, the remaining 1 cup powdered sugar, and the milk. Beat with a wooden spoon until smooth. If necessary, stir in additional milk, 1 teaspoon at a time, to make a frosting of spreading consistency. Spread frosting on cooled cookies and, if desired, garnish with additional lavender buds and thin strips of lemon peel.

If the dough logs start to break as you work with them,
gently reroll the pieces together.

two-tone peanut butter slices

prep: 40 min. chill: 2 hr. bake: 8 min per batch oven: 375°F
makes: about 120 cookies

¾ cup creamy peanut
   butter
½ cup butter, softened
½ cup granulated sugar
½ cup packed brown
   sugar
½ teaspoon baking
   powder
½ teaspoon baking soda
1 egg
1 teaspoon vanilla
1½ cups all-purpose flour
1½ ounces unsweetened
   chocolate, melted
   and slightly cooled

1 In a large mixing bowl beat peanut butter and butter with an electric mixer on medium to high speed for 30 seconds. Add granulated sugar, brown sugar, baking powder, and baking soda. Beat until combined, scraping sides of bowl occasionally. Beat in egg and vanilla until combined. Beat in as much of the flour as you can with the mixer. Stir in any remaining flour.

2 Divide dough in half. Stir melted chocolate into one half of the dough. Divide each dough portion in half. On a lightly floured surface, roll each portion of dough into a 10-inch-long log. Wrap logs in plastic wrap or waxed paper. Chill about 1 hour or until firm.

3 Cut logs in half lengthwise. Place the cut side of one peanut butter log and the cut side of one chocolate log together; press to seal. Roll the log lightly to smooth seams. Repeat with remaining log halves. Wrap and chill logs about 1 hour or until firm.

4 Preheat oven to 375°F. Cut two-tone logs into ¼-inch slices. Place slices 1 inch apart on an ungreased cookie sheet. Bake 8 minutes or until edges are light brown and slightly firm. Transfer to a wire rack and let cool.

Peanut butter and chocolate make a winning
combination in these mini cookie rounds.

The flavors that make a margarita so enticing—tequila, lime, and orange—do the same for these crisp cookies.

margarita slices

prep: 30 min. chill: 4 hr. bake: 8 min. per batch oven: 350°F
makes: about 48 cookies

½ cup butter, softened
½ cup granulated sugar
⅛ teaspoon baking soda
4 teaspoons tequila
2 teaspoons orange-
   flavor liqueur
½ teaspoon vanilla
1½ cups all-purpose flour
¾ cup finely chopped
   walnuts
1 tablespoon finely
   shredded lime peel
Few drops green food
   coloring
Coarse green colored
   sugar

1 In a large mixing bowl beat butter with an electric mixer on medium to high speed for 30 seconds. Add granulated sugar and baking soda. Beat until combined, scraping sides of bowl occasionally. Beat in tequila, liqueur, and vanilla until combined. Beat in as much of the flour as you can with the mixer. Stir in any remaining flour, the walnuts, and lime peel. Stir in enough food coloring to create desired shade.

2 Shape dough into a 6-inch-long log. Roll log in coarse colored sugar to coat. Wrap log in plastic wrap or waxed paper. Chill about 4 hours or until firm.

3 Preheat oven to 350°F. Using a sharp knife, cut log into ¼-inch slices; cut each slice in half crosswise. Place slices 1 inch apart on an ungreased cookie sheet. Bake for 8 to 10 minutes or until edges are light brown. Transfer to a wire rack and let cool.

These tequila-spiked cookies are just right for nibbling with a glass of lemonade on a hot summer day.

For make-ahead convenience, chill the dough loaves up to three days or freeze them up to a week before slicing and baking.

sugar-and-spice coffee slices

prep: 25 min. **chill:** 2 hr. **bake:** 9 min. per batch **stand:** 1 min. per batch
oven: 375°F **makes:** about 36 cookies

½ cup butter, softened
¼ cup shortening
1 cup granulated sugar
½ cup packed brown sugar
1 teaspoon baking powder
1 teaspoon ground cinnamon
¼ teaspoon salt
2 tablespoons instant espresso powder
1 tablespoon hot water
1 egg
2 cups all-purpose flour
1 recipe Coffee Topping
   Coffee beans (optional)

1 In a large bowl beat butter and shortening with an electric mixer on medium to high speed for 30 seconds. Add the granulated sugar, brown sugar, baking powder, cinnamon, and salt. Beat until combined, scraping sides of bowl occasionally. In a small bowl stir together the espresso powder and hot water until dissolved. Add to butter mixture along with egg; beat until combined. Beat in as much of the flour as you can with the mixer. Stir in any remaining flour.

2 Divide dough into thirds. Shape each portion into a 7-inch-long log. Wrap each log with plastic wrap. Chill about 2 hours or until firm.

3 Preheat oven to 375°F. Using a sharp knife, cut logs into ⅜-inch slices. Place slices 2 inches apart on an ungreased cookie sheet. Sprinkle with Coffee Topping. If desired, gently press a few coffee beans onto each slice. Bake for 9 to 10 minutes or until edges are light brown. Let stand for 1 minute on cookie sheet. Transfer to a wire rack and let cool

coffee topping: *In a small bowl stir together ¼ cup granulated sugar and 1 teaspoon instant espresso powder.*

*Hickory nuts boast
extremely rich and buttery
flavor. If you can't find
them, pecans taste
equally delicious.*

hickory nut cookies

prep: 30 min. chill: 4 hr. bake: 6 min. per batch oven: 375°F
makes: about 60 cookies

¾ cup shortening
½ cup granulated sugar
½ cup packed brown
   sugar
¼ teaspoon baking soda
¼ teaspoon salt
2 eggs
1 teaspoon vanilla
2½ cups all-purpose flour
1 cup finely chopped
   hickory nuts* or
   pecans, toasted
   (see tip, page 19)
   Pecan halves
   (optional)
   Powdered sugar
   (optional)

1 In a large mixing bowl beat shortening with an electric mixer on medium to high speed for 30 seconds. Add granulated sugar, brown sugar, baking soda, and salt. Beat until combined, scraping sides of bowl occasionally. Beat in eggs and vanilla until combined. Beat in as much of the flour as you can with the mixer. Stir in any remaining flour and the nuts.

2 Divide dough in half. Shape each half of dough into an 8-inch-long log. Wrap in plastic wrap or waxed paper. Chill about 4 hours or until firm.

3 Preheat oven to 375°F. Using a sharp knife, cut logs into ¼-inch slices. Place slices 2 inches apart on an ungreased cookie sheet. If desired, gently press a pecan half into each slice. Bake for 6 to 8 minutes or until edges are light brown. Transfer to a wire rack; cool. If desired, sift powdered sugar over cookies.

✳ Look for hickory nuts at your local farmer's market or at specialty food stores.

Twisted ropes of dough create these tricolor treats. Be sure to finely chop the pistachios for the green dough so it will slice with ease.

chocolate-pistachio swirls

prep: 45 min. chill: 30 min. bake: 8 min. per batch oven: 375°F
makes: about 48 cookies

¾ cup butter, softened
1 cup sugar
½ teaspoon baking
  powder
¼ teaspoon salt
1 egg
1 teaspoon vanilla
2 cups all-purpose flour
1 ounce bittersweet
  chocolate, melted
¼ cup finely chopped
  pistachios
  Green food coloring
  Sugar

1 In a medium mixing bowl beat butter with an electric mixer on medium to high speed for 30 seconds. Add the 1 cup sugar, baking powder, and salt. Beat until combined, scraping sides of bowl occasionally. Beat in egg and vanilla until combined. Beat in as much of the flour as you can with the mixer. Stir in any remaining flour.

2 Divide dough into thirds. Stir melted chocolate into one portion of dough. Stir pistachios and several drops of green food coloring into another portion of dough. Leave the remaining portion of dough plain.

3 Divide each dough portion into fourths. On a lightly floured surface, roll each portion into a ½-inch-thick rope about 8 inches long. Place a chocolate, plain, and pistachio rope side by side; twist together. Repeat with remaining ropes. Cover and chill the four twisted ropes for 30 minutes.

4 Preheat oven to 375°F. Using a sharp knife, cut ropes into ½-inch slices. Carefully roll slices into balls, blending colors as little as possible. Place balls about 2 inches apart on an ungreased cookie sheet. Using the bottom of a glass dipped in sugar, flatten each ball until ¼ inch thick. Bake for 8 to 10 minutes or until edges are light brown. Transfer to a wire rack and let cool.

Paste food coloring, rather than liquid, is the secret to obtaining a deep red color in these easy swirl cookies.

cherry-almond pinwheels

prep: 30 min. chill: 2 hr. bake: 8 min. per batch oven: 375°F
makes: about 65 cookies

¾ cup butter, softened
1 cup sugar
½ teaspoon baking powder
¼ teaspoon salt
1 egg
1 teaspoon vanilla
2 cups all-purpose flour
Red paste food coloring
¼ cup ground almonds
Candied cherries or maraschino cherries, quartered

1 In a medium mixing bowl beat butter with an electric mixer on medium to high speed for 30 seconds. Add sugar, baking powder, and salt. Beat until combined, scraping sides of bowl occasionally. Beat in egg and vanilla until combined. Beat in as much of the flour as you can with the mixer. Stir in any remaining flour.

2 Divide dough in half. Tint half of the dough with the red food coloring. Stir or knead the ground almonds into the remaining half of the dough. Cover and chill dough portions about 1 hour or until firm. Divide each portion in half.

3 On a lightly floured pastry cloth, roll one red dough portion into a 12×8-inch rectangle. On a piece of waxed paper, roll one almond dough portion into a 12×8-inch rectangle. Invert almond dough rectangle over red dough rectangle; peel off waxed paper. Roll up dough, starting from a long side. Pinch to seal. Wrap in plastic wrap or waxed paper. Repeat with remaining dough portions. Chill about 1 hour or until firm.

4 Preheat oven to 375°F. Lightly grease a cookie sheet; set aside. Remove one roll from the refrigerator. Unwrap and reshape, if necessary. Using a sharp knife, cut roll into ¼-inch slices. Place slices 2 inches apart on the prepared cookie sheet. Place a cherry piece in the center of each slice. Bake for 8 to 10 minutes or until tops are set. Transfer to a wire rack and let cool. Repeat with remaining dough roll.

Brown sugar makes these cookies soft and moist, while almond toffee pieces give them a good crunch.

brown sugar toffee rounds

prep: 30 min. chill: 4 hr. bake: 9 min. per batch oven: 350°F
makes: about 80 cookies

½	cup butter, softened
½	cup shortening
1	cup packed brown sugar
½	teaspoon baking powder
½	teaspoon baking soda
¼	teaspoon salt
1	egg
2	tablespoons milk
½	teaspoon almond extract
3	cups all-purpose flour
1	7½-ounce package (1⅓ cups) almond toffee pieces

1 In a large mixing bowl beat butter and shortening with an electric mixer on medium to high speed for 30 seconds. Add brown sugar, baking powder, baking soda, and salt. Beat until combined, scraping sides of bowl occasionally. Beat in egg, milk, and almond extract until combined. Beat in as much of the flour as you can with the mixer. Stir in any remaining flour and the almond toffee pieces.

2 Divide dough in half. Shape each half of dough into a 10-inch-long log. Wrap each log in plastic wrap. Chill about 4 hours or until logs are firm.

3 Preheat oven to 350°F. Using a serrated knife, cut logs into ¼-inch slices. Place slices 2 inches apart on an ungreased cookie sheet. Bake about 9 minutes or until edges are firm. Transfer to a wire rack and let cool.

*For perfectly round cookies, be sure to thoroughly chill
the dough after you complete each step.*

molasses-spice rounds

prep: 30 min. chill: 4 hr. bake: 7 min. per batch oven: 375°F
makes: about 60 cookies

¾ cup butter, softened
1 cup sugar
½ teaspoon baking
    powder
¼ teaspoon salt
1 egg
1 teaspoon vanilla
2 cups all-purpose flour
2 tablespoons molasses
½ teaspoon ground
    cinnamon
½ teaspoon ground
    ginger
⅛ teaspoon ground
    cloves

1 In a medium mixing bowl beat butter with an electric mixer on medium to high speed for 30 seconds. Add sugar, baking powder, and salt. Beat until combined, scraping sides of bowl occasionally. Beat in egg and vanilla until combined. Beat in as much of the flour as you can with the mixer. Stir in any remaining flour.

2 Divide dough in half. Knead the molasses, cinnamon, ginger, and cloves into one half of the dough; leave the other half plain. Divide each dough half into thirds. Cover and chill the 6 portions about 1 hour or until dough is easy to handle.

3 On a lightly floured surface, roll one portion of each dough into a 1-inch-thick rope about 8 inches long. (Keep remaining dough chilled.) Wrap and chill the two ropes for 1 hour.

4 On the floured surface, roll the remaining two portions of plain dough into one 8×4-inch rectangle about ½ inch thick. Place the rope of molasses dough lengthwise on the plain dough rectangle. Roll up; pinch edges to seal. Roll the remaining two portions of molasses dough into one 8×4-inch rectangle. Place the rope of plain dough lengthwise on the molasses dough rectangle. Roll up; pinch edges to seal. Wrap and chill rolls about 2 hours or until firm.

5 Preheat oven to 375°F. Using a sharp knife, cut rolls into ¼-inch slices. Place slices 2 inches apart on an ungreased cookie sheet. Bake about 7 minutes or until edges are light brown. Transfer to a wire rack and let cool.

A citrus bite comes through the poppy seed and vanilla flavors in these dainty, refreshing teatime cookies.

lemon and poppy seed slices

prep: 25 min. chill: 3 hr. bake: 11 min. per batch oven: 375°F
makes: 60 cookies

¾ cup butter, softened
1 cup granulated sugar
1 egg
1 tablespoon milk
2 teaspoons finely shredded lemon peel
½ teaspoon vanilla
½ teaspoon lemon extract (optional)
2¼ cups all-purpose flour
2 tablespoons poppy seeds
Sanding sugar

1 In a medium mixing bowl beat butter with an electric mixer on medium to high speed for 30 seconds. Add granulated sugar. Beat until combined, scraping sides of bowl occasionally. Beat in egg, milk, lemon peel, vanilla, and, if desired, lemon extract until combined. Beat in as much of the flour as you can with the mixer. With a wooden spoon, stir in any remaining flour and the poppy seeds.

2 Divide dough in half. Shape each half of dough into an 8-inch-long log. Wrap each log in plastic wrap or waxed paper. Chill about 3 hours or until firm.

3 Preheat oven to 375°F. Using a sharp knife, cut logs into ¼-inch slices. Sprinkle with sanding sugar. Place slices on an ungreased cookie sheet. Bake for 11 to 12 minutes or until edges are golden. Transfer to a wire rack and let cool.

Tangy, aromatic lemon zest enlivens these poppy seed-flecked cookies.

Warm spices and orange marmalade team up to give these cookies a sweet-spicy twist.

spice mingles

prep: 45 min. chill: 2 hr. bake: 8 min. per batch oven: 375°F
makes: 36 sandwich cookies

½   cup butter, softened
½   cup packed brown
     sugar
1   egg yolk
1   tablespoon milk
½   teaspoon ground
     ginger
¼   teaspoon baking soda
¼   teaspoon ground
     cinnamon
⅛   teaspoon salt
⅛   teaspoon ground
     cloves
1½ cups all-purpose flour
¼   cup orange
     marmalade, fruit
     pieces snipped
2   ounces white
     chocolate baking
     squares (with
     cocoa butter)
½   teaspoon shortening

1 In a large mixing bowl beat butter with an electric mixer on medium to high speed for 30 seconds. Add brown sugar. Beat until combined, scraping sides of bowl occasionally. Beat in egg yolk, milk, ginger, baking soda, cinnamon, salt, and cloves until combined. Beat in as much of the flour as you can with the mixer. Stir in any remaining flour.

2 Divide dough in half. Shape each half of dough into a 9-inch-long log. Wrap log in waxed paper or plastic wrap. Chill about 2 hours or until firm.

3 Preheat oven to 375°F. Using a sharp knife, cut logs into ¼-inch slices. Place slices 1 inch apart on an ungreased cookie sheet. Bake for 8 to 10 minutes or until bottoms are light brown. Transfer to a wire rack; cool.

4 Just before serving, spread ¼ teaspoon of the marmalade on each of the flat sides of half of the cookies. Top with remaining cookies, flat sides down. In a small saucepan heat and stir white chocolate and shortening over low heat until melted and smooth. Drizzle cookies with melted chocolate mixture. Let stand until set.

note: *Store unfilled cookies as directed on page 16. Fill before serving.*

*For perfect squares,
use a small metal spatula
to smooth and square off
the sides of the dough log.*

mocha squares

prep: 30 min. **chill:** 5 hr. **bake:** 9 min. per batch **stand:** 1 min. per batch
oven: 375°F **makes:** 20 sandwich cookies

1	tablespoon coffee liqueur or milk
2	teaspoons instant espresso powder or instant coffee crystals
½	cup butter, softened
¾	cup sugar
½	teaspoon baking powder
1	egg
1	ounce semisweet chocolate, melted and cooled
1¾	cups all-purpose flour
1	recipe Coffee Liqueur Icing

1 In a small bowl stir together coffee liqueur and espresso powder; set aside for a few minutes or until coffee is dissolved.

2 In a large mixing bowl beat butter with an electric mixer on medium to high speed for 30 seconds. Add sugar and baking powder. Beat until combined, scraping sides of bowl occasionally. Beat in liqueur mixture, the egg, and melted chocolate until well combined. Beat in as much of the flour as you can with the mixer. Stir in any remaining flour. Cover and chill dough about 1 hour or until easy to handle.

3 Shape dough into a square-shape log that is 10 inches long and 1¾ inches wide. Wrap log in plastic wrap or waxed paper. Chill about 4 hours or until firm.

4 Preheat oven to 375°F. Using a sharp knife, cut log into ¼-inch slices. Place slices 2 inches apart on an ungreased cookie sheet. Bake for 9 to 11 minutes or until edges are firm. Let stand for 1 minute on cookie sheet. Transfer to a wire rack and let cool.

5 Up to 1 hour before serving, spread about 1 teaspoon Coffee Liqueur Icing on each of the flat sides of half of the cookies. Top with remaining cookies, flat sides down. Store in the refrigerator until serving time.

coffee liqueur icing: *In a small bowl stir together ¼ teaspoon instant coffee crystals and 2 tablespoons whipping cream until coffee is dissolved. In a medium bowl stir together the coffee mixture, 2 cups powdered sugar, and 1 tablespoon coffee liqueur. Add enough whipping cream (1 to 2 tablespoons) to make icing of spreading consistency.*

The popular snickerdoodle reinvents itself with a new shape and even more cinnamon in these swirly cookies.

snickerdoodle pinwheels

prep: 25 min. chill: 4 hr. bake: 8 min. per batch stand: 1 min. per batch
oven: 375°F makes: about 60 cookies

1⅓	cups sugar
1	tablespoon ground cinnamon
½	cup butter, softened
1	3-ounce package cream cheese, softened
½	teaspoon baking powder
1	egg
1	teaspoon vanilla
2⅔	cups all-purpose flour
1	tablespoon butter, melted

1 In a small bowl stir together ⅓ cup of the sugar and the cinnamon; set aside.

2 In a large mixing bowl beat the ½ cup butter and the cream cheese with an electric mixer on medium to high speed for 30 seconds. Add the remaining 1 cup sugar and the baking powder. Beat until combined, scraping sides of bowl occasionally. Beat in egg and vanilla until combined. Beat in as much of the flour as you can with the mixer. Stir in any remaining flour. If necessary, cover and chill about 1 hour or until easy to handle.

3 Divide dough in half. Roll half of the dough between two pieces of waxed paper into a 12x8-inch rectangle. Remove top sheet of waxed paper. Brush dough with half of the melted butter. Sprinkle with 2 tablespoons of the cinnamon-sugar mixture. Starting at a short side, carefully roll up dough, using the waxed paper to lift and guide the roll. Moisten the edges of the log and pinch to seal. Repeat with remaining dough, remaining melted butter, and 2 tablespoons of the cinnamon-sugar mixture.

4 Roll logs in the remaining cinnamon-sugar mixture to coat. Wrap logs in plastic wrap or waxed paper. Chill about 4 hours or until dough is firm.

5 Preheat oven to 375°F. Using a sharp knife, cut rolls into ¼-inch slices. Place slices 1 inch apart on an ungreased cookie sheet. Bake for 8 to 10 minutes or until edges are firm. Let stand for 1 minute on cookie sheet. Transfer to a wire rack and let cool.

Crystallized ginger gives these sweet but tangy cookies a pleasantly spicy bite and chewy texture.

cranberry-orange biscotti

prep: 45 min. **bake:** 25 min./15 min. **stand:** 20 min. **oven:** 350°F/300°F
makes: about 40 cookies

1½ cups dried cranberries
⅔ cup orange juice
½ cup butter, softened
¾ cup sugar
1½ teaspoons baking powder
2 eggs
4 teaspoons finely shredded orange peel
2¼ cups all-purpose flour
⅓ cup chopped crystallized ginger

1 Preheat oven to 350°F. In a small saucepan combine cranberries and orange juice. Heat over medium heat until warm; remove from heat. Let stand for 10 to 15 minutes or until cranberries are soft. Drain well, pressing berries to remove excess liquid. Discard juice; set cranberries aside.

2 In a large mixing bowl beat butter with an electric mixer on medium speed for 30 seconds. Add sugar and baking powder. Beat until combined, scraping sides of bowl occasionally. Beat in eggs and orange peel. Beat in as much of the flour as you can with the mixer. Stir in any remaining flour, the cranberries, and ginger.

3 Divide dough into thirds. With lightly floured hands, shape each portion into a 9×2-inch loaf. Place loaves 3 inches apart on an ungreased cookie sheet. Bake 25 minutes or until tops are light brown. Let stand on cookie sheet on a wire rack for 20 minutes. Reduce oven temperature to 300°F.

4 Transfer loaves to a cutting board. Using a serrated knife, cut loaves diagonally into ½-inch slices. Place slices upright on cookie sheet, leaving ½ inch between slices. Bake about 15 minutes or until dry and crisp. Transfer to a wire rack and let cool.

Melted chocolate chips in a dough accented with golden cappuccino chips make these biscotti perfect with a cup of nut-flavored coffee.

mocha-hazelnut biscotti

prep: 1 hr. bake: 30 min./30 min. cool: 1 hr. oven: 350°F/300°F
makes: about 36 cookies

2¾ cups all-purpose flour
2½ teaspoons baking
    powder
½ teaspoon salt
⅔ cup butter, softened
1 cup sugar
2 cups bittersweet
    or semisweet
    chocolate pieces,
    melted and cooled
3 eggs
1 teaspoon vanilla
¾ cup cappuccino-flavor
    baking pieces
½ cup finely chopped
    toasted hazelnuts
    (see tip, page 19)
1 recipe Chocolate and
    Cappuccino Glazes

1 Preheat oven to 350°F. Grease a large cookie sheet; set aside. In a medium bowl stir together the flour, baking powder, and salt; set aside. In a large mixing bowl beat butter on medium to high speed for 30 seconds. Add sugar. Beat until combined, scraping sides of bowl occasionally. Beat in melted chocolate, eggs, and vanilla until combined. Beat in as much of the flour mixture as you can with the mixer. Stir in any remaining flour mixture, the cappuccino baking pieces, and hazelnuts. (Dough will be soft.)

2 With lightly floured hands, shape dough into two 9×3-inch loaves. Place loaves 4 inches apart on the prepared cookie sheet; flatten slightly. Bake about 30 minutes or until a wooden toothpick inserted near the centers comes out clean. Cool completely on cookie sheet on a wire rack.

3 Reduce oven temperature to 300°F. Transfer loaves to a cutting board. Using a serrated knife, cut into ½-inch slices. Carefully place slices, cut sides down, on the cookie sheet. Bake for 15 minutes. Gently turn slices over. Bake about 15 minutes more or until dry and crisp. Transfer to a wire rack and let cool. Drizzle cooled cookies with Chocolate and Cappuccino Glazes. Let stand until set.

chocolate and cappuccino glazes: *In a small saucepan heat and stir ½ cup bittersweet or semisweet chocolate pieces and 2 teaspoons shortening over low heat until smooth. Set aside. Repeat with ½ cup cappuccino-flavor baking pieces and 2 teaspoons shortening in a second saucepan.*

Rum-soaked cherries and a drizzling of sweet, rum-spiked icing bring spicy depth and richness to these pecan-flecked biscotti.

cherry-rum biscotti

prep: 45 min. bake: 20 min./20 min. cool: 1 hr. oven: 350°F/300°F
makes: 48 cookies

1¼ cups dried tart red cherries, coarsely chopped
½ cup light rum or spiced rum
½ cup butter, softened
1 cup sugar
1 tablespoon baking powder
¼ teaspoon salt
3 eggs
½ teaspoon vanilla
3¼ cups all-purpose flour
¾ cup chopped pecans, toasted (see tip, page 19)
1 recipe Rum Icing

1 In a saucepan combine cherries and rum. Bring just to simmering over medium heat. Remove from heat; let stand 15 minutes. Drain well, reserving rum for the icing and pressing cherries to remove liquid. Set cherries aside.

2 Preheat oven to 350°F. Lightly grease a very large cookie sheet; set aside. In a large mixing bowl beat butter for 30 seconds. Add sugar, baking powder, and salt. Beat until combined, scraping sides of bowl occasionally. Beat in eggs and vanilla until combined. Beat in as much of the flour as you can with the mixer. Stir in any remaining flour, the drained cherries, and the pecans.

3 Divide dough into thirds. Shape each portion into a 9-inch-long loaf. Place loaves 3 inches apart onto the prepared cookie sheet. Flatten each loaf until about 2½ inches wide.

4 Bake for 20 to 25 minutes or until golden brown and tops are cracked. Cool completely on cookie sheet on a wire rack. Reduce oven temperature to 300°F.

5 Transfer loaves to a cutting board. Using a serrated knife, cut loaves diagonally into ½-inch slices. Place slices, cut sides down, on cookie sheet. Bake 10 minutes. Turn cookies over. Bake 10 to 15 minutes more or until dry. Transfer to a wire rack; cool. Drizzle cooled cookies with Rum Icing. Let stand until set.

rum icing: *In a small bowl stir together 1½ cups powdered sugar and 1 tablespoon of the reserved rum. Add enough additional rum (1 to 2 tablespoons) to make an icing of drizzling consistency.*

These cookies, based on an Italian dessert, sing tiramisu's signature notes—coffee and chocolate—in biscotti form.

tiramisu biscotti

prep: 40 min. chill: 1 hr. bake: 25 min./18 min. oven: 350°F/325°F
makes: about 30 cookies

2	tablespoons whipping cream
1	tablespoon instant espresso powder or 2 tablespoons instant coffee crystals
⅓	cup butter, softened
1	cup sugar
1½	teaspoons baking powder
¼	teaspoon salt
2	eggs
1	teaspoon vanilla
2¼	cups all-purpose flour
3	ounces semisweet chocolate, finely chopped
1½	teaspoons finely shredded orange peel (optional)
6	ounces semisweet chocolate, coarsely chopped
1	tablespoon shortening
2	ounces white chocolate baking squares (with cocoa butter), coarsely chopped
2	teaspoons shortening

1 Lightly grease two cookie sheets; set aside. In a small bowl stir together whipping cream and the espresso powder until dissolved; set aside.

2 In a large mixing bowl beat butter with an electric mixer on medium to high speed for 30 seconds. Add sugar, baking powder, and salt. Beat until combined, scraping sides of bowl occasionally. Beat in espresso mixture, eggs, and vanilla until combined. Beat in as much of the flour as you can with the mixer. Stir in any remaining flour, the 3 ounces semisweet chocolate, and, if desired, the orange peel. Divide dough in half. Cover and chill dough 1 hour or until easy to handle.

3 Preheat oven to 350°F. Shape each half of dough into a 9-inch-long loaf. Place loaves on the prepared cookie sheets; flatten each loaf until about 2 inches wide. Bake about 25 minutes or until a toothpick inserted near the centers comes out clean. Cool completely on cookie sheet on a wire rack. (If desired, wrap loaves in plastic wrap and let stand overnight at room temperature.) Reduce oven temperature to 325°F.

4 Transfer loaves to a cutting board. Using a serrated knife, cut loaves diagonally into ½-inch slices; place on an ungreased cookie sheet. Bake for 10 minutes. Turn slices over. Bake for 8 to 10 minutes more or until dry and crisp. Transfer to a wire rack and let cool.

5 In a small saucepan heat and stir the 6 ounces semisweet chocolate and the 1 tablespoon shortening over low heat until smooth. Dip bottom edge of each cookie into the melted chocolate. Let stand until set. In another small saucepan heat and stir white chocolate and the 2 teaspoons shortening over low heat until smooth; drizzle over cookies. Let stand until set.

Double baking gives these cookie slices their distinctive crunchy texture, which makes them ideal for dipping.

almond biscotti

prep: 25 min. bake: 25 min./20 min. stand: 15 min. oven: 325°F
makes: about 84 cookies

2¾ cups all-purpose flour
1½ teaspoons baking powder
1 teaspoon salt
1½ cups sugar
2 eggs
2 egg yolks
6 tablespoons butter, melted
1½ teaspoons finely shredded orange or lemon peel (optional)
1 cup coarsely chopped almonds

1 Preheat oven to 325°F. Lightly grease two cookie sheets; set aside. In a large bowl stir together flour, baking powder, salt, and sugar. Make a well in the center of the flour mixture. Place eggs and egg yolks in the well and stir into the flour mixture. Add butter and, if desired, orange peel; stir until dough starts to form a ball. Stir in almonds.

2 Divide dough into three equal portions. On a lightly floured surface, shape each portion of dough into a 14-inch-long loaf. Place the loaves about 3 inches apart on the prepared cookie sheets. Flatten the loaves until about 1½ inches wide. Bake for 25 to 30 minutes or until firm and light brown. Let stand on cookie sheets on a wire rack for 15 minutes.

3 Transfer logs to a cutting board. Using a serrated knife, cut loaves diagonally into ½-inch slices. Place slices, cut sides down, on cookie sheets. Bake for 10 minutes. Turn cookies over; bake for 10 to 15 minutes more or until crisp and golden brown. Transfer to a wire rack and let cool.

Serve these nut-filled biscotti with your favorite pairing (see page 177) for a special afternoon snack.

almond biscotti variations

hazelnut biscotti: *Prepare as on page 176, except use the option of orange peel and substitute 1 cup chopped hazelnuts for the almonds.*

pistachio biscotti: *Prepare as on page 176, except use the option of lemon peel and substitute 1 cup chopped pistachios for the almonds.*

cashew-chocolate biscotti: *Prepare as on page 176, except omit the peel and substitute ½ cup chopped cashews and ½ cup finely chopped bittersweet chocolate for the almonds.*

biscotti pairings

* Hot chocolate
* Coffee
* Hot tea
* Gelato
* Ice cream shake
* Pudding
* Yogurt

These crisp Italian cookie sticks dotted with nuggets of chocolate will delight any chocolate lover.

triple chocolate biscotti

prep: 30 min. **bake:** 20 min/15 min. **oven:** 375°F/325°F
makes: about 36 cookies

½	cup butter, softened
⅔	cup sugar
¼	cup unsweetened cocoa powder
2	teaspoons baking powder
2	eggs
1¾	cups all-purpose flour
¾	cup white baking pieces
½	cup semisweet chocolate pieces

1 Preheat oven to 375°F. Grease a large cookie sheet; set aside. In a large mixing bowl beat butter on medium to high speed for 30 seconds. Add sugar, cocoa powder, and baking powder. Beat until combined, scraping sides of bowl occasionally. Beat in eggs until combined. Beat in as much of the flour as you can with the mixer. Stir in any remaining flour, the white baking pieces, and semisweet chocolate pieces.

2 Divide dough in half. Shape each half of dough into a 9-inch-long loaf. Place loaves on the prepared cookie sheet; flatten each loaf until about 2 inches wide.

3 Bake for 20 to 25 minutes or until a toothpick inserted near centers comes out clean. Cool completely on cookie sheet on a wire rack. Reduce oven temperature to 325°F.

4 Transfer loaves to a cutting board. Using a serrated knife, cut loaves diagonally into ½-inch slices. Place slices, cut sides down, on an ungreased cookie sheet. Bake for 8 minutes. Turn slices over. Bake for 7 to 9 minutes more or until dry and crisp. Transfer cookies to a wire rack and let cool.

The unexpected flavor combination of fresh ginger and cocoa is refreshingly delicious in these twice-baked cookies.

ginger-cocoa biscotti

prep: 30 min. bake: 25 min./16 min. stand: 10 min. oven: 350°F/300°F
makes: about 30 cookies

2½	cups all-purpose flour
1	cup sugar
2	tablespoons unsweetened cocoa powder
½	teaspoon baking soda
½	teaspoon salt
¼	teaspoon ground cinnamon
¼	teaspoon ground cloves
2	eggs, beaten
¼	cup milk
2	tablespoons grated fresh ginger
1	cup chopped, toasted almonds (see tip, page 19)
2	ounces semisweet chocolate, coarsely chopped
2	tablespoons shortening

1 Preheat oven to 350°F. Grease and flour a large cookie sheet; set aside. In a large bowl stir together flour, sugar, cocoa powder, baking soda, salt, cinnamon, and cloves. In a small bowl combine eggs, milk, and ginger. Add egg mixture to flour mixture; stir until well combined. Stir in almonds.

2 Turn dough onto a well-floured surface. Knead dough several times until smooth. Divide dough in half. Shape each half of dough into a 12-inch-long loaf. Place loaves 3 inches apart on the prepared cookie sheet. Flatten each loaf until 2 inches wide.

3 Bake about 25 minutes or until a wooden toothpick inserted in centers comes out clean. Let stand on cookie sheet on a wire rack for 10 minutes. Reduce the oven temperature to 300°F.

4 Transfer loaves to a cutting board. Using a serrated knife, cut loaves diagonally into ¾-inch slices. Place slices, cut sides down, on the cookie sheet. Bake for 8 minutes. Turn slices over. Bake for 8 minutes more. Transfer to a wire rack and let cool.

5 In a small saucepan heat and stir chocolate and shortening over low heat until smooth. Drizzle cooled cookies with melted chocolate. Let stand until set.

Dunk these twice-baked cookies into a cup of steaming-hot spiced apple cider for a special treat.

spicy golden biscotti

prep: 20 min. bake: 20 min./16 min. oven: 375°F/325°F
makes: about 36 cookies

¾ cup butter, softened
½ cup sugar
1 teaspoon baking
    powder
¼ teaspoon cayenne
    pepper
1 egg
1 teaspoon vanilla
1 cup cornmeal
1½ cups all-purpose flour
½ cup toasted chopped
    pecans (see tip,
    page 19)

1 Preheat oven to 375°F. In a large mixing bowl beat butter with an electric mixer on medium to high speed for 30 seconds. Add sugar, baking powder, and cayenne pepper. Beat until combined, scraping sides of bowl occasionally. Beat in egg and vanilla until combined. Beat in cornmeal and as much of the flour as you can with the mixer. Stir in remaining flour and the pecans.

2 Divide dough in half. Shape each half of dough into a 9×1½-inch loaf. Place loaves 4 inches apart on an ungreased cookie sheet; flatten slightly. Bake about 20 minutes or until a wooden toothpick inserted near the centers comes out clean. Cool completely on cookie sheet on a wire rack.

3 Reduce oven temperature to 325°F. Transfer loaves to a cutting board. Using a serrated knife, cut loaves into ½-inch slices. Carefully place slices, cut sides down, on the cookie sheet. Bake for 8 minutes. Gently turn slices over. Bake for 8 to 10 minutes more or until light brown. Transfer to a wire rack and let cool.

Cayenne pepper and chopped pecans create a sweet-spicy combination that will make your mouth water.

Destined for dipping, these toasty oblongs—kissed with warm spices and zesty citrus—are just the thing to get the day started.

tea-scented breakfast biscotti

prep: 35 min. **chill:** 1 hr. **bake:** 20 min./16 min. **oven:** 375°F/325°F
makes: about 36 cookies

4   orange-spiced tea
      bags
⅓   cup butter, softened
⅔   cup sugar
2   teaspoons baking
      powder
½   teaspoon salt
2   eggs
1   teaspoon vanilla
2   cups all-purpose flour
⅓   cup sliced almonds

1 Remove tea from tea bags (about 1 tablespoon loose tea) and place it in a blender or coffee grinder; grind until fine. Set ground tea aside. Lightly grease a very large cookie sheet; set aside.

2 In a large mixing bowl beat butter with an electric mixer on medium to high speed for 30 seconds. Add sugar, baking powder, and salt. Beat until combined, scraping sides of bowl occasionally. Beat in eggs and vanilla until combined. Beat in the ground tea and as much of the flour as you can with the mixer. Stir in any remaining flour and the almonds. Cover and chill dough about 1 hour or until easy to handle.

3 Preheat oven to 375°F. Divide dough into thirds. Shape each portion into an 8-inch-long loaf. Place loaves at least 3 inches apart on the prepared cookie sheet; flatten each loaf until about 2 inches wide.

4 Bake 20 minutes or just until bottoms and edges are golden (loaves will spread slightly). Cool completely on cookie sheet on a wire rack. Reduce oven temperature to 325°F.

5 Transfer loaves to a cutting board. Using a serrated knife, cut loaves diagonally into ½-inch slices. Place slices, cut sides down, on an ungreased cookie sheet. Bake for 8 minutes. Turn slices over. Bake for 8 to 10 minutes more or until slices are dry and crisp. Transfer to a wire rack and let cool.

Studded with tiny chocolate pieces and almond toffee pieces, then dipped into melted chocolate, these cookies burst with great flavor.

chocolate-toffee biscotti

prep: 30 min. bake: 25 min./16 min. stand: 1 hr. oven: 350°/325°F
makes: about 30 cookies

¼	cup butter, softened
½	cup granulated sugar
½	cup packed brown sugar
2½	teaspoons baking powder
⅛	teaspoon salt
3	eggs
1	teaspoon vanilla
2¾	cups all-purpose flour
½	cup almond toffee pieces
⅓	cup miniature semisweet chocolate pieces
6	ounces semisweet chocolate, chopped
4	teaspoons shortening Almond toffee pieces (optional)

1 Preheat oven to 350°F. Grease a cookie sheet; set aside. In a large mixing bowl beat butter with an electric mixer on medium to high speed for 30 seconds. Add granulated sugar, brown sugar, baking powder, and salt. Beat until combined, scraping sides of bowl occasionally. Beat in eggs and vanilla until combined. Beat in as much of the flour as you can with the mixer. Stir in any remaining flour. Stir in the ½ cup toffee pieces and the chocolate pieces.

2 Divide dough in half (dough will be sticky). Using floured hands, on a lightly floured surface, shape each half of dough into an 8-inch-long loaf. Place loaves about 5 inches apart on the prepared cookie sheet.

3 Bake about 25 minutes or until golden brown and firm to the touch in the center. Transfer to a wire rack and let stand for 1 hour.

4 Reduce oven temperature to 325°F. Transfer loaves to a cutting board. Using a serrated knife, cut loaves diagonally into ½-inch slices. (Or cool completely; wrap and store overnight at room temperature before slicing.) Place slices, cut sides down, on the cookie sheet. Bake for 8 minutes. Turn slices over. Bake for 8 to 10 minutes more or until dry. Transfer to a wire rack and let cool.

5 In a small saucepan heat and stir the chocolate and shortening over low heat until smooth. Dip one end of each cookie into melted chocolate mixture. Place on a sheet of waxed paper. If desired, sprinkle with additional almond toffee pieces. Let stand until chocolate is set.

These twice-baked cookies get a spicy kick from a dash of crushed red pepper. For a more mellow flavor, add a dash of paprika instead.

dried tomato biscotti

prep: 45 min. bake: 18 min./15 min. stand: 6 hr. oven: 375°F/325°F
makes: 32 cookies

½ cup butter, softened
½ cup packed brown sugar
¼ cup grated Parmesan cheese
2 teaspoons baking powder
½ teaspoon salt
¼ teaspoon crushed red pepper
¼ teaspoon black pepper
2 eggs
2 cups all-purpose flour
¼ cup snipped dried tomatoes
1 egg, lightly beaten
1 recipe Biscotti Dipping Oil

biscotti dipping oil:
In a small bowl stir together ½ cup olive oil, 2 tablespoons grated Parmesan cheese, ⅛ teaspoon black pepper, and a dash of salt.

1 Preheat oven to 375°F. Lightly grease a cookie sheet; set aside. In a large mixing bowl beat butter with an electric mixer on medium to high speed for 30 seconds. Add brown sugar, Parmesan cheese, baking powder, salt, crushed red pepper, and black pepper. Beat until combined, scraping sides of bowl occasionally. Beat in the 2 eggs until combined. Beat in as much of the flour as you can with the mixer. Stir in any remaining flour and the dried tomatoes.

2 Divide dough in half. Shape each half of dough into a 9-inch-long loaf. Place loaves 5 inches apart on the prepared cookie sheet. Flatten each loaf until 2 inches wide. Brush lightly beaten egg on loaves.

3 Bake for 18 to 20 minutes or until a wooden toothpick inserted in centers comes out clean. Cool completely on cookie sheet on a wire rack. Wrap loaves and let stand at room temperature for 6 to 24 hours.

4 Preheat oven to 325°F. Transfer loaves to a cutting board. Using a serrated knife, cut loaves diagonally into ½-inch slices. Place slices, cut sides down, on an ungreased cookie sheet. Bake for 8 minutes. Turn slices over. Bake for 7 to 9 minutes more or until slices are dry and crisp. Transfer to a wire rack and let cool. Serve with Biscotti Dipping Oil.

scrumptious

sha

Press, pipe, stamp, and hand-shape your way to delicious and beautiful cookies. In this assortment of recipes, creative cookie-shaping techniques and fantastic flavors are the secrets to extraordinary treats your family will love.

5

pes

With just the right amount of spices— including a bit of black pepper—these bold and flavorful cookies taste similar to gingersnaps.

spicy molasses cookies

prep: 35 min. **chill:** 1 hr. **bake:** 8 min. per batch **stand:** 1 min. per batch
oven: 375°F **makes:** 42 cookies

1¾ cups all-purpose flour
½ cup whole wheat flour
1½ teaspoons ground cinnamon
1 teaspoon baking soda
1 teaspoon ground ginger
¼ teaspoon ground allspice
¼ teaspoon ground cloves
¼ teaspoon salt
¼ teaspoon black pepper
½ cup butter, softened
¼ cup shortening
⅓ cup granulated sugar
⅓ cup packed brown sugar
1 egg yolk
½ cup dark molasses
1 teaspoon vanilla
⅓ cup coarse sugar

1 In a medium bowl stir together all-purpose flour, whole wheat flour, cinnamon, baking soda, ginger, allspice, cloves, salt, and pepper; set aside.

2 In a large mixing bowl beat butter and shortening with an electric mixer on medium to high speed for 30 seconds. Add granulated sugar and brown sugar. Beat until combined, scraping sides of bowl occasionally. Beat in egg yolk, molasses, and vanilla until combined. Gradually beat in flour mixture. Cover and chill dough about 1 hour or until easy to handle.

3 Preheat oven to 375°F. Shape dough into 1-inch balls. Roll balls in coarse sugar to coat. Place balls 2 inches apart on an ungreased cookie sheet. Bake for 8 to 10 minutes or until bottoms are light brown. Let stand for 1 minute on cookie sheet. Transfer to a wire rack and let cool.

Crystallized ginger, also called candied ginger, consists of bits of fresh ginger cooked in sugar syrup, then coated with sugar.

candied ginger cookies

prep: 35 min. **chill:** 1 hr. **bake:** 8 min. per batch **oven:** 375°F
makes: about 48 cookies

1 cup unsalted butter, softened
¾ cup granulated sugar
¾ cup packed brown sugar
1 teaspoon cream of tartar
1 teaspoon baking soda
½ teaspoon salt
½ teaspoon ground ginger
2 eggs
1 teaspoon vanilla
2¾ cups all-purpose flour
½ cup finely chopped crystallized ginger
Granulated sugar

1 In a large mixing bowl beat butter with an electric mixer on medium to high speed for 30 seconds. Add the ¾ cup granulated sugar, the brown sugar, cream of tartar, baking soda, salt, and ground ginger. Beat until combined, scraping sides of bowl occasionally. Beat in eggs and vanilla until combined. Beat in as much of the flour as you can with the mixer. Stir in any remaining flour and the crystallized ginger. Cover and chill dough about 1 hour or until easy to handle.

2 Preheat oven to 375°F. Shape dough into 1¼-inch balls. Roll balls in granulated sugar to coat. Place balls 3 inches apart on an ungreased cookie sheet. Bake for 8 to 10 minutes or until edges are light brown. Transfer to a wire rack and let cool.

Chewy crystallized ginger adds a sweet-spicy touch to these soft cookies.

A hint of spice accentuates the citrus flavor from the lime juice and shredded lime peel in these sugar-topped cookie rounds.

lime cookies

prep: 30 min. bake: 10 min. per batch oven: 350°F makes: about 48 cookies

1 cup butter, softened
1 cup sugar
1 teaspoon baking powder
¼ teaspoon salt
¼ teaspoon ground cinnamon
¼ teaspoon ground nutmeg
1 tablespoon finely shredded lime peel
2 tablespoons lime juice
2 cups all-purpose flour
1 recipe Sugar Topping

1 In a large mixing bowl beat butter with an electric mixer on medium to high speed for 30 seconds. Add sugar, baking powder, salt, cinnamon, and nutmeg. Beat until combined, scraping sides of bowl occasionally. Beat in lime peel and lime juice until combined. Beat in as much of the flour as you can with the mixer. Stir in any remaining flour.

2 Preheat oven to 350°F. Shape dough into 1-inch balls. Place balls 2 inches apart on an ungreased cookie sheet. Using the bottom of a glass dipped into Sugar Topping, flatten balls until ¼ inch thick. Bake about 10 minutes or until edges are golden. Transfer to a wire rack and let cool.

sugar topping: *In a small bowl stir together ⅓ cup granulated sugar, 2 tablespoons green colored coarse sugar, ¼ teaspoon ground cinnamon, and ¼ teaspoon ground nutmeg.*

In this buttery, nut-studded cookie, the cornstarch mixed with flour gives the product its tender, melt-in-your-mouth texture.

orange-macadamia cookies

prep: 25 min. **bake:** 12 min. per batch **oven:** 350°F **makes:** about 36 cookies

2 cups all-purpose flour
1 cup powdered sugar
½ cup cornstarch
1 cup butter
½ cup chopped
   macadamia nuts
   or toasted walnuts
   (see tip, page 19)
1 egg yolk
1½ teaspoons finely
   shredded orange
   peel
2 tablespoons orange
   juice
   Granulated sugar
1 recipe Orange
   Frosting
   Finely chopped
   macadamia nuts
   (optional)

1 Preheat oven to 350°F. In a large bowl stir together flour, powdered sugar, and cornstarch. Using a pastry blender, cut in butter until mixture resembles coarse crumbs. Stir in the ½ cup nuts. In a small bowl combine the egg yolk, orange peel, and orange juice. Add egg yolk mixture to flour mixture, stirring until moistened. Knead dough in bowl until it forms a ball.

2 Shape dough into 1¼-inch balls. Place balls 2 inches apart on an ungreased cookie sheet. Using the bottom of a glass dipped in granulated sugar, flatten balls until ¼ inch thick.

3 Bake for 12 to 15 minutes or until edges are set and surfaces are dry. Transfer to a wire rack and let cool. Frost cooled cookies with Orange Frosting. If desired, sprinkle with finely chopped macadamia nuts.

orange frosting: *In a medium bowl stir together 1 cup powdered sugar, 2 tablespoons softened butter, and ½ teaspoon finely shredded orange peel. Stir in 1 to 2 tablespoons orange juice to make a frosting of spreading consistency.*

Apricot jam and preserves tend to be somewhat chunky.
Use kitchen shears to cut up any large pieces of fruit.

mocha and apricot jam bites

prep: 30 min. **bake:** 8 min. per batch **oven:** 375°F **makes:** about 84 cookies

1½ cups butter, softened
½ of an 8-ounce
   package cream
   cheese, softened
1 cup granulated sugar
¼ cup unsweetened
   cocoa powder
4 teaspoons instant
   espresso powder
1 teaspoon baking
   powder
¼ teaspoon salt
1 egg
1 teaspoon vanilla
3½ cups all-purpose flour
½ cup apricot jam or
   preserves
   Powdered sugar

1 Preheat oven to 375°F. In a large mixing bowl beat butter and cream cheese with an electric mixer on medium to high speed for 30 seconds. Add sugar, cocoa powder, espresso powder, baking powder, and salt. Beat until combined, scraping sides of bowl occasionally. Beat in egg and vanilla until combined. Beat in as much of the flour as you can with the mixer. Stir in any remaining flour.

2 Force unchilled dough through a cookie press fitted with a star or flower plate onto an ungreased cookie sheet. Place cookies 1 inch apart. Bake for 8 to 10 minutes or until edges are firm. Transfer to a wire rack; cool.

3 Just before serving, spoon about ¼ teaspoon of the apricot jam into the center of each cookie. Sift powdered sugar over tops.

note: *Store unfilled cookies as directed on page 16. Fill before serving.*

Who would guess that the flavors of mocha and apricot mesh so magnificently?

For the most tender cookies, be sure to process the pecans until they form a butterlike consistency.

pecan rounds

prep: 35 min. **chill:** 1 hr. **bake:** 7 min. per batch **oven:** 350°F/375°F
makes: about 48 rounds

1½   cups pecan pieces
½   cup butter, cut up
½   cup granulated sugar
½   cup packed brown
     sugar
½   teaspoon baking soda
½   teaspoon baking
     powder
1   egg
1   teaspoon vanilla
1⅓   cups all-purpose flour
     Granulated sugar

1 Preheat oven to 350°F. Spread pecan pieces in a single layer in a shallow baking pan. Bake for 5 to 10 minutes or until light golden brown, stirring once or twice. Let cool slightly. Place toasted nuts in a food processor. Cover and process until a paste forms, stopping to scrape sides of bowl occasionally (mixture will appear grainy).

2 Add butter, the ½ cup granulated sugar, brown sugar, baking soda, and baking powder. Process just until combined. Add egg and vanilla; process just until combined. Add flour; pulse two or three times just until flour is combined. Transfer dough to a bowl. Cover and chill the dough about 1 hour or until easy to handle.

3 Preheat oven to 375°F. Shape dough into 1-inch balls. Roll balls in additional granulated sugar to coat. Place balls 2 inches apart on an ungreased cookie sheet. Using the bottom of a glass, flatten balls slightly. Bake for 7 to 9 minutes or until light brown. Transfer to a wire rack and let cool.

The heavenly flavor of pecans enriches these smooth, nutty cookies.

Rolled in powdered sugar before they're baked, these cookies look as if they are covered with freshly fallen snow.

chocolate-mint
snow-top cookies

prep: 35 min. **freeze:** 30 min. **bake:** 10 min. per batch **stand:** 2 min. per batch **oven:** 350°F **makes:** 42 cookies

1½ cups all-purpose flour
1½ teaspoons baking powder
¼ teaspoon salt
1½ cups semisweet chocolate pieces
6 tablespoons butter, softened
1 cup granulated sugar
2 eggs
1½ teaspoons vanilla
¼ teaspoon mint flavoring
Powdered sugar

1 In a medium bowl stir together flour, baking powder, and salt; set aside. In a small saucepan heat and stir 1 cup of the chocolate pieces over low heat until smooth; set aside.

2 In a large mixing bowl beat butter with an electric mixer on medium to high speed for 30 seconds. Add granulated sugar. Beat until combined, scraping sides of bowl occasionally. Beat in melted chocolate, the eggs, vanilla, and mint flavoring. Beat in flour mixture. Stir in the remaining ½ cup chocolate pieces. Cover and chill dough in freezer about 30 minutes or until easy to handle.

3 Preheat oven to 350°F. Shape dough into 1-inch balls. Roll balls in powdered sugar to coat. Place balls 2 inches apart on an ungreased cookie sheet. Bake for 10 to 12 minutes or until tops are crackled. Let stand for 2 minutes on cookie sheet. Transfer to a wire rack and let cool.

The pretty pink color in these cookies comes from the cherries and the cherry liquid; no food coloring is necessary.

cherry chocolate kisses

prep: 20 min. **bake:** 14 min. per batch **oven:** 325°F **makes:** 48 cookies

1 cup butter, softened
1 cup powdered sugar
⅛ teaspoon salt
2 teaspoons maraschino cherry liquid
¼ teaspoon almond extract
2¼ cups all-purpose flour
½ cup chopped maraschino cherries
Granulated sugar
48 milk chocolate kisses

1 Preheat oven to 325°F. In a large mixing bowl beat butter with an electric mixer on medium to high speed for 30 seconds. Add powdered sugar and salt. Beat until combined, scraping sides of bowl occasionally. Beat in cherry liquid and almond extract until combined. Beat in as much of the flour as you can with the mixer. Stir in any remaining flour and the cherries.

2 Shape dough into 1-inch balls. Place balls 2 inches apart on an ungreased cookie sheet. Using the bottom of a glass dipped in granulated sugar, flatten balls until ½ inch thick. Bake 14 minutes or until bottoms are light brown. Immediately press a chocolate kiss into each cookie's center. Transfer to a wire rack and let cool.

*Egg white is the glue that holds the chopped nuts on the cookie dough.
Purchased lemon or raspberry curd serves as a quick filling.*

fruity almond thumbprints

prep: 30 min. **bake:** 8 min. per batch **oven:** 375°F **makes:** about 42 cookies

½ cup butter, softened
½ cup shortening
1 cup sugar
1 teaspoon baking powder
¼ teaspoon salt
1 egg
1 teaspoon vanilla
2¼ cups all-purpose flour
1 egg white, lightly beaten
1 cup finely chopped almonds
1 cup purchased lemon or raspberry curd

1 Preheat oven to 375°F. Lightly grease a cookie sheet; set aside. In a large mixing bowl beat butter and shortening with an electric mixer on medium to high speed for 30 seconds. Add the sugar, the baking powder, and salt. Beat until combined, scraping sides of bowl occasionally. Beat in egg and vanilla until combined. Beat in as much of the flour as you can with the mixer. Stir in any remaining flour.

2 Shape dough into 1-inch balls. Roll balls in egg white, then in almonds to coat. Place balls 2 inches apart on the prepared cookie sheet. Using your thumb, make an indentation in the center of each ball of dough.

3 Bake for 8 to 10 minutes or until edges are light brown. If the cookie centers have puffed up during baking, repress with the bowl of a measuring teaspoon. Transfer to a wire rack and let cool. Just before serving, fill cookie centers with about 1 teaspoon lemon or raspberry curd.

note: *Store unfilled cookies as directed on page 16. Fill before serving.*

Don't be fooled by the simple, homey look of these crackled cookies. They are full of ground almonds and flavored with coffee liqueur, making them perfect for any party.

mocha-almond cookies

prep: 45 min. **chill:** 1 hr. **bake:** 13 min. per batch **oven:** 325°F
makes: 60 cookies

½ cup unsalted butter
4 ounces unsweetened chocolate, cut up
6 tablespoons coffee-flavor liqueur
¾ cup granulated sugar
4 eggs
1⅓ cups all-purpose flour
¾ teaspoon baking powder
1 cup blanched almonds, finely ground
Powdered sugar

1 In a small saucepan heat and stir butter and chocolate over low heat until smooth. Remove from heat; stir in coffee liqueur. Set aside to cool slightly.

2 In a large mixing bowl combine granulated sugar and eggs. Beat with an electric mixer on medium speed until combined. Stir in chocolate mixture. In a small bowl stir together flour and baking powder. Add flour mixture to the chocolate mixture, stirring until combined. Stir in almonds. Divide dough in half. Cover and chill the dough about 1 hour or until it is easy to handle.

3 Preheat oven to 325°F. Shape dough into 1-inch balls. Roll balls in powdered sugar to coat. Place balls 2 inches apart on an ungreased cookie sheet. Bake 13 minutes or until firm. Transfer to a wire rack and let cool.

The classic combination of coffee and chocolate is made extra decadent with the addition of buttery ground almonds.

Pumpkin pie spice gives these cookies paramount flavor. Try these youngster-friendly treats the next time you are baking for children.

spice doodles

prep: 40 min. **bake:** 10 min. per batch **stand:** 1 min. per batch **oven:** 375°F
makes: about 40 cookies

½ cup butter, softened
½ cup shortening
1 cup sugar
1 teaspoon baking
    powder
¼ teaspoon salt
1 egg
1 teaspoon vanilla
2¼ cups all-purpose flour
2 tablespoons sugar
1 teaspoon pumpkin
    pie spice

1 Lightly grease a cookie sheet; set aside. In a large mixing bowl beat butter and shortening with an electric mixer on medium to high speed for 30 seconds. Add the 1 cup sugar, the baking powder, and salt. Beat until combined, scraping sides of bowl occasionally. Beat in egg and vanilla until combined. Beat in as much of the flour as you can with the mixer. Stir in any remaining flour. If necessary, cover and chill the dough about 1 hour or until it is easy to handle.

2 Preheat oven to 375°F. In a small bowl stir together the 2 tablespoons sugar and the pumpkin pie spice. Shape dough into 1-inch balls. Roll balls in sugar mixture to coat. Place balls 2 inches apart on an ungreased cookie sheet. Bake for 10 to 11 minutes or until edges are golden. Let stand for 1 minute on cookie sheet. Transfer to a wire rack and let cool.

The dough for these chocolaty cookies is rolled in powdered sugar before baking, giving the tops of the cookies a crackled appearance.

chocolate crinkles

prep: 25 min. **chill:** 2 hr. **bake:** 8 min. per batch **oven:** 375°F
makes: about 60 cookies

4 eggs
1¾ cups granulated sugar
4 ounces unsweetened chocolate, melted and cooled
½ cup cooking oil
2 teaspoons baking powder
2 teaspoons vanilla
2 cups all-purpose flour
Powdered sugar (optional)

1 In a large mixing bowl beat eggs, granulated sugar, chocolate, oil, baking powder, and vanilla with an electric mixer until combined. Gradually beat in as much of the flour as you can with the mixer. Stir in any remaining flour. Cover and chill dough about 2 hours or until easy to handle.

2 Preheat oven to 375°F. Lightly grease a cookie sheet; set aside. Shape dough into 1-inch balls. Roll balls in powdered sugar to coat. Place balls 1 inch apart on the prepared cookie sheet. Bake for 8 to 10 minutes or until edges are set and tops are dry (do not overbake). Transfer to a wire rack and let cool. (Cookies will deflate slightly upon cooling.) If desired, sift powdered sugar over the tops of cookies.

With beautifully crackled tops, these sugar-coated chocolate goodies look as good as they taste.

In each of these bite-size morsels, a simple vanilla-flavor dough covers a chunk of chocolate.

chocolate surprise bites

prep: 45 min. bake: 12 min. per batch oven: 350°F
makes: about 36 cookies

½   cup butter, softened
¾   cup powdered sugar
1   teaspoon vanilla
1¼ cups all-purpose flour
    Semisweet chocolate
      chunks or miniature
      milk chocolate
      kisses (about 36)
1   recipe Powdered
      Sugar Icing
    Decorative sprinkles
      (optional)

1 Preheat oven to 350°F. In a large mixing bowl beat butter with an electric mixer on medium to high speed for 30 seconds. Add powdered sugar and vanilla. Beat until combined, scraping sides of bowl occasionally. Beat in as much of the flour as you can with the mixer. Stir in any remaining flour; knead dough together, if necessary.

2 Shape 1 teaspoon of the dough into a ball. Press a chocolate chunk into the ball and reshape the dough into a ball, enclosing the chocolate. Repeat with remaining dough and chocolate. Place balls 1 inch apart on an ungreased cookie sheet.

3 Bake for 12 to 14 minutes or until bottoms are light brown. Transfer to a wire rack and let cool. Dip cooled cookies in Powdered Sugar Icing. If desired, sprinkle wet icing with decorative sprinkles.

powdered sugar icing: *In a bowl stir together 1 cup powdered sugar, 1 tablespoon milk, and ¼ teaspoon vanilla. Stir in enough additional milk (1 to 3 teaspoons) to make an icing of drizzling consistency. If desired, tint icing with food coloring.*

Serve these cookies at your next party or get-together. Bright red maraschino cherries buried in a chocolaty dough form the sweet surprise for guests.

chocolate-cherry cookies

prep: 30 min. **bake:** 10 min. per batch **stand:** 1 min. per batch **oven:** 350°F
makes: 42 to 48 cookies

1   10-ounce jar maraschino cherries (42 to 48)
½   cup butter, softened
1   cup sugar
¼   teaspoon baking powder
¼   teaspoon baking soda
¼   teaspoon salt
1   egg
1½   teaspoons vanilla
½   cup unsweetened cocoa powder
1½   cups all-purpose flour
1   cup semisweet chocolate pieces
½   cup sweetened condensed milk or low-fat sweetened condensed milk

1 Preheat oven to 350°F. Drain cherries, reserving juice. Halve any large cherries. In a medium mixing bowl beat butter with an electric mixer on medium to high speed for 30 seconds. Add the sugar, baking powder, baking soda, and salt. Beat until combined, scraping sides of bowl occasionally. Beat in egg and vanilla until combined. Beat in cocoa powder and as much of the flour as you can with the mixer. Stir in any remaining flour.

2 Shape dough into 1-inch balls. Place balls about 2 inches apart on an ungreased cookie sheet. Press your thumb into the center of each ball. Place a cherry in each center.

3 For frosting, in a small saucepan heat and stir chocolate pieces and sweetened condensed milk over low heat until smooth. Stir in 4 teaspoons reserved cherry juice. (If necessary, thin frosting with additional cherry juice.) Spoon 1 teaspoon frosting over each cherry, spreading to cover the cherry completely. Bake 10 minutes or until edges are firm. Let stand for 1 minute on cookie sheet.

White crème de cacao is a clear, chocolate-flavor liqueur with a hint of vanilla. It adds unbeatable flavor to these cookies.

white chocolate,
apricot, and nut balls

start to finish: 30 min. **makes:** 48 balls

3 ounces white chocolate baking squares (with cocoa butter), cut up
¼ cup light-color corn syrup
2 to 3 tablespoons white crème de cacao
2 cups shortbread cookie crumbs (about 20 cookies)
1 cup finely chopped macadamia nuts or almonds, toasted (see tip, page 19)
⅓ cup snipped dried apricots
Powdered sugar

1 In a small saucepan heat and stir white chocolate over low heat until smooth; remove from heat. Add the corn syrup and crème de cacao; stir until combined.

2 In a large bowl stir together cookie crumbs, nuts, and dried apricots. Stir in chocolate mixture until combined. Shape mixture into 1¼-inch balls. Roll balls in powdered sugar to coat. Place on a sheet of waxed paper and let stand until dry. Before serving, roll cookies again in powdered sugar.

note: *Store cookies as directed on page 16. Do not freeze.*

These soft yet crispy cookie balls are totally irresistible—no oven required.

Fruit-flavor drink mix provides the bright color and intense fruity taste in this kid favorite.

fruit dream cookies

prep: 45 min. **chill:** 30 min. **bake:** 9 min. per batch **stand:** 2 min. per batch
oven: 375°F **makes:** about 60 cookies

½ cup butter, softened
½ cup shortening
1 cup granulated sugar
½ cup sugar-sweetened orange-, lemon-, or cherry-flavor drink mix
½ teaspoon baking powder
¼ teaspoon baking soda
2 eggs
1 teaspoon vanilla
2½ cups all-purpose flour
1½ cups white baking pieces
   Colored or coarse sugar

1 Preheat oven to 375°F. In a large mixing bowl beat butter and shortening with an electric mixer on medium to high speed for 30 seconds. Add granulated sugar, drink mix, baking powder, and baking soda. Beat until combined, scraping sides of bowl occasionally. Beat in eggs and vanilla until combined. Beat in as much of the flour as you can with the mixer. Stir in any remaining flour and the baking pieces. Cover and chill dough about 30 minutes or until easy to handle.

2 Shape dough into 1-inch balls. Roll balls in colored or coarse sugar to coat. Place balls 2 inches apart on an ungreased cookie sheet. Bake for 9 to 11 minutes or until edges are just set (centers will still be soft). Let stand for 2 minutes on cookie sheet. Transfer to a wire rack and let cool.

Cranberry-Pecan Tassies and **Fruit Balls**

scrumptious **shapes**

A filling made with tangy cranberries, brown sugar, and toasty pecans tastes delightful in the cream cheese dough.

cranberry-pecan tassies

prep: 25 min. bake: 30 min. oven: 325°F makes: 24 tassies

1   3-ounce package cream cheese, softened
½   cup butter, softened
1   cup all-purpose flour
1   egg
¾   cup packed brown sugar
1   teaspoon vanilla
    Dash salt
⅓   cup finely chopped cranberries
3   tablespoons chopped pecans

1 Preheat oven to 325°F. In a medium mixing bowl beat cream cheese and butter with an electric mixer on medium speed until combined. Stir in flour. Divide dough into 24 equal pieces. Press pieces evenly into bottoms and up the sides of 24 ungreased 1¾-inch muffin cups.

2 For filling, in a small mixing bowl beat egg, brown sugar, vanilla, and salt with an electric mixer just until smooth. Stir in cranberries and pecans. Spoon filling into pastry-lined cups. Bake for 30 to 35 minutes or until pastry is golden brown. Cool in pan on a wire rack. Remove tassies from pan.

Candied fruit, chopped nuts, and marshmallows make for outstanding flavor in these delicious no-bake morsels.

fruit balls

start to finish: 45 min. chill: 4 hr. makes: about 60 balls

3   cups assorted chopped nuts
¾   cup chopped candied pineapple
¾   cup chopped candied cherries
¾   cup raisins
⅔   cup graham cracker crumbs
2   tablespoons butter
¼   cup evaporated milk
2½   cups tiny marshmallows
2   cups flaked coconut, chopped

1 In a large bowl combine chopped nuts, candied fruits, raisins, and graham cracker crumbs.

2 In a medium saucepan heat and stir butter, evaporated milk, and marshmallows over medium-low heat until smooth. Stir marshmallow mixture into the nut mixture until well coated. With wet hands, shape nut mixture into 1-inch balls. Roll balls in coconut to coat. Place balls in a single layer in an airtight container; cover. Chill at least 4 hours before serving.

scrumptious **shapes**

These sophisticated treats boast a cashew shortbread base, a luscious caramel filling, and a glistening chocolate drizzle.

caramel-cashew cookies

prep: 1 hr. **bake:** 15 min. per batch **stand:** 1 hr. **oven:** 325°F
makes: 48 cookies

1	cup butter, softened
½	cup sifted powdered sugar
1	tablespoon water
1	teaspoon vanilla
2	cups all-purpose flour
1½	cups finely chopped cashews
16	vanilla caramels
3	tablespoons whipping cream
¼	cup coarsely chopped cashews
¾	cup semisweet chocolate pieces
2	teaspoons shortening

1 Preheat oven to 325°F. In a large mixing bowl beat butter with an electric mixer on medium to high speed for 30 seconds. Add powdered sugar. Beat until combined, scraping sides of bowl occasionally. Beat in water and vanilla until combined. Beat in as much of the flour as you can with the mixer. Stir in any remaining flour and the finely chopped cashews.

2 Shape dough into 1-inch balls. Place balls 1½ inches apart on an ungreased cookie sheet. Using your thumb, make an indentation in the center of each cookie. Bake 15 minutes or until bottoms are light brown. Transfer to a wire rack and let cool.

3 In a small saucepan heat and stir caramels and whipping cream over low heat until smooth. Stir in the coarsely chopped cashews. Spoon the melted caramel mixture into cookie centers. (If necessary, reheat caramel mixture to keep it spoonable.)

4 In another small saucepan heat and stir chocolate pieces and shortening over low heat until smooth. Drizzle chocolate mixture over tops of cookies. Let stand 1 hour or until set.

note: *Store unfilled cookies as directed on page 16. Refrigerate for up to 3 days. Fill cookies before serving.*

If you want to go the healthful route with these cookies, try using only 1 cup all-purpose flour and adding ¾ cup whole wheat flour.

peanut butter
blossoms

prep: 25 min. **bake:** 10 min. per batch **oven:** 350°F **makes:** about 54 cookies

½ cup shortening
½ cup peanut butter
½ cup granulated sugar
½ cup packed brown sugar
1 teaspoon baking powder
⅛ teaspoon baking soda
1 egg
2 tablespoons milk
1 teaspoon vanilla
1¾ cups all-purpose flour
Granulated sugar
Milk chocolate kisses or stars (about 54)

1 Preheat oven to 350°F. In a large mixing bowl beat shortening and peanut butter with an electric mixer on medium to high speed for 30 seconds. Add the ½ cup granulated sugar, the brown sugar, baking powder, and baking soda. Beat until combined, scraping sides of bowl occasionally. Beat in egg, milk, and vanilla until combined. Beat in as much of the flour as you can with the mixer. Stir in any remaining flour.

2 Shape dough into 1-inch balls. Roll balls in additional granulated sugar to coat. Place balls 2 inches apart on an ungreased cookie sheet. Bake for 10 to 12 minutes or until edges are firm and bottoms are light brown. Immediately press a chocolate kiss into each cookie's center. Transfer to a wire rack; cool.

Instant espresso powder makes these cookies taste extra rich.
Look for it near the instant coffee crystals at larger supermarkets.

espresso delights

prep: 25 min. **bake:** 12 min. per batch **oven:** 325°F **makes:** about 36 cookies

1 cup butter, softened
⅔ cup powdered sugar
1 tablespoon instant
espresso powder
or regular instant
coffee crystals
1 teaspoon vanilla
½ teaspoon ground
cinnamon
2 cups all-purpose flour
1 ounce semisweet
chocolate, finely
chopped
Powdered sugar and/
or unsweetened
cocoa powder

1 Preheat oven to 325°F. In a large mixing bowl beat butter with an electric mixer on medium to high speed for 30 seconds. Add the ⅔ cup powdered sugar, the espresso powder, vanilla, and cinnamon. Beat until combined, scraping sides of bowl occasionally. Beat in as much of the flour as you can with the mixer. Stir in any remaining flour and the chocolate. If necessary, knead dough slightly to blend.

2 Shape dough into 1-inch balls. Place balls 2 inches apart on an ungreased cookie sheet. Press to flatten slightly. Bake 12 minutes or until cookie edges are set and bottoms are golden. Transfer to a wire rack and let cool. Sift additional powdered sugar and/or cocoa powder over cooled cookies.

It's the sugar that makes these cookies irresistible. Vary the flavor by using light brown sugar or maple sugar.

melt-in-your-mouth
sugar cookies

prep: 30 min. **bake**: 12 min. per batch **stand**: 1 min. per batch **oven**: 300°F
makes: about 48 cookies

½ cup butter, softened
½ cup shortening
2 cups sugar
1 teaspoon baking soda
1 teaspoon cream of
   tartar
⅛ teaspoon salt
3 egg yolks
½ teaspoon vanilla
1¾ cups all-purpose flour

1 Preheat oven to 300°F. In a large mixing bowl beat butter and shortening on medium to high speed for 30 seconds. Add sugar, baking soda, cream of tartar, and salt. Beat until combined, scraping sides of bowl occasionally. Beat in egg yolks and vanilla until combined. Beat in as much of the flour as you can with the mixer. Stir in any remaining flour.

2 Shape dough into 1-inch balls. Place balls 2 inches apart on an ungreased cookie sheet. Bake for 12 to 14 minutes or until edges are set. (Do not let edges brown.) Let stand 1 minute on cookie sheet. Transfer to a wire rack and let cool.

Soft, moist, and oh-so-tender, these extra special sugar cookies live up to their name.

Throughout the years these buttery cookies have been called many different names, from pecan sandies to Mexican wedding cookies.

pecan balls

prep: 40 min. **bake:** 12 min. per batch **oven:** 350°F **makes:** about 72 cookies

1 cup butter, softened
½ cup granulated sugar
¼ teaspoon salt
2 teaspoons vanilla
2 cups all-purpose flour
1 cup finely chopped
   pecans
   Powdered sugar
   Edible glitter
   (optional)

1 Preheat oven to 350°F. In a large mixing bowl beat butter with an electric mixer on medium to high speed for 30 seconds. Add granulated sugar and salt. Beat until combined, scraping sides of bowl occasionally. Beat in vanilla until combined. Beat in as much of the flour as you can with the mixer. Stir in any remaining flour and the pecans.
2 Shape slightly rounded teaspoons of dough into balls. Place balls 1 inch apart on an ungreased cookie sheet. Bake 12 minutes or until bottoms just begin to brown. Transfer to wire rack and let cool. Sift powdered sugar over cooled cookies. If desired, sprinkle with edible glitter.

Youngsters will want to be in on the fun of shaping and rolling the nut-flecked dough.

If miniature cherry chips are not available, chop up regular-size cherry chips. Or try semisweet or white chocolate chips for a different flavor twist.

cherry chip and coconut tartlets

prep: 45 min. bake: 18 min. oven: 350°F/325°F makes: 36 tartlets

¾ cup butter, softened
1 8-ounce package cream cheese, softened
2 tablespoons sugar
1 teaspoon finely shredded lemon peel
⅛ teaspoon salt
1½ cups all-purpose flour
½ cup flaked coconut
½ cup white baking pieces, melted and cooled
⅓ cup lemon curd
¼ cup miniature cherry baking pieces

1 In a large mixing bowl beat butter and half of the cream cheese with an electric mixer on medium to high speed for 30 seconds. Add sugar, lemon peel, and salt. Beat until combined, scraping sides of bowl occasionally. Beat in as much of the flour as you can with the mixer. Stir in any remaining flour. Shape dough into a ball. If necessary, cover and chill dough about 30 minutes or until easy to handle.

2 Meanwhile, preheat oven to 350°F. Spread coconut in a single layer in a shallow baking pan. Toast for 5 to 10 minutes or until light golden brown, stirring occasionally. Let cool. Set aside.

3 Reduce oven to 325°F. Divide dough into 36 equal pieces. Press pieces evenly into bottoms and up the sides of 36 ungreased 1¾-inch muffin cups. Bake for 18 to 20 minutes or until light brown. Transfer pastry cups to a wire rack and let cool.

4 For filling, in a medium mixing bowl beat remaining cream cheese with an electric mixer at medium to high speed for 30 seconds. Beat in melted white baking pieces until smooth. Spoon about ½ teaspoon of the lemon curd into each pastry cup. Spoon cream cheese mixture on top of lemon curd. (Or transfer cream cheese mixture to a decorating bag fitted with a large star tip; pipe on top of lemon curd.) Sprinkle with toasted coconut and cherry baking pieces.

note: *Store in a single layer as directed on page 16. Refrigerate for up to 3 days. Do not freeze.*

Vanilla, which is featured in the frosting and in the dough, is one of the world's most loved and tantalizing flavors. Crown the cookie with a light sprinkling of cardamom.

macadamia nut cookies
with vanilla cream frosting

prep: 25 min. **chill:** 1 hr. **bake:** 10 min. per batch **oven:** 375°F
makes: about 60 cookies

3 eggs
1 cup butter, softened
¾ cup sugar
2 teaspoons vanilla
2¼ cups all-purpose flour
2 cups finely chopped
   macadamia nuts
1 recipe Vanilla Cream
   Frosting
   Ground cardamom
   (optional)

1 Separate eggs; place yolks and whites in separate bowls. Cover and chill egg whites until needed. In a large mixing bowl beat butter with an electric mixer on medium to high speed for 30 seconds. Add sugar. Beat until combined, scraping sides of bowl occasionally. Beat in egg yolks and vanilla until combined. Beat in as much of the flour as you can with the mixer. Stir in any remaining flour. Cover and chill dough about 1 hour or until easy to handle.

2 Preheat oven to 375°F. Line a cookie sheet with parchment paper; set aside. Shape dough into 1-inch balls. Lightly beat egg whites. Roll balls in egg whites, then in nuts to coat. Place balls 1 inch apart on the prepared cookie sheet.

3 Bake 10 minutes or until bottoms are light brown. Transfer to a wire rack and let cool. Frost cooled cookies with Vanilla Cream Frosting. If desired, sprinkle with cardamom.

note: *Store frosted cookies in a single layer as directed on page 16. Refrigerate up to 3 days.*

vanilla cream frosting: *In a medium mixing bowl beat ¼ cup softened butter, one 3-ounce package softened cream cheese, and ½ teaspoon vanilla with an electric mixer on medium speed until smooth. Gradually beat in 2 cups powdered sugar until smooth and frosting is of spreading consistency.*

Curly chocolate shavings make a great presentation on these decadent tarts. To make them, warm the chocolate bar by rubbing it between your hands for 30 seconds; then carefully use a vegetable peeler to make the shavings.

chocolate cheesecake tarts

prep: 30 min. **bake:** 18 min. **stand:** 10 min. **oven:** 350°F **makes:** 36 tarts

½	cup butter, softened
½	cup shortening
1½	cups sugar
1	teaspoon baking powder
¼	teaspoon salt
1	egg
1½	teaspoons vanilla
2¼	cups all-purpose flour
1	8-ounce package cream cheese, softened
3	ounces bittersweet chocolate, melted and cooled
2	egg yolks
3	tablespoons chocolate liqueur or milk
1	tablespoon milk
	Whipped cream
	Bittersweet chocolate shavings
	Fresh raspberries (optional)

1 Preheat oven to 350°F. Grease and flour thirty-six 1¾-inch muffin cups; set aside. In a large mixing bowl beat butter and shortening with an electric mixer on medium to high speed for 30 seconds. Add 1 cup of the sugar, the baking powder, and salt. Beat until combined, scraping sides of bowl occasionally. Beat in egg and 1 teaspoon of the vanilla until combined. Beat in as much of the flour as you can with the mixer. Stir in any remaining flour. Shape dough into thirty-six 1-inch balls. Press balls into the bottoms and up the sides of the prepared cups; set aside.

2 For filling, in a medium mixing bowl beat cream cheese and chocolate with an electric mixer on medium speed until combined. Beat in the remaining ½ cup sugar, the egg yolks, liqueur, milk, and the remaining ½ teaspoon vanilla until combined. Spoon a rounded teaspoon of the filling into each dough-lined cup.

3 Bake 18 minutes or until crusts are golden and filling is set. Let stand for 10 minutes in pan. Remove tarts from pan. Transfer to a wire rack and let cool. (Centers may dip slightly as they cool.) To serve, top each tart with a mound of whipped cream and a pinch of chocolate shavings. If desired, garnish serving plate with fresh raspberries.

note: *Store tarts in a single layer as directed on page 16. Refrigerate up to 3 days.*

Perfectly spiced and flecked with soft, chewy raisins, these cookies will disappear from your cookie jar in no time.

big soft ginger cookies

prep: 20 min. **bake:** 10 min. per batch **stand:** 2 min. per batch **oven:** 350°F
makes: 24 cookies

¾ cup butter, softened,
   or shortening
1 cup granulated sugar
2 teaspoons ground
   ginger
1 teaspoon baking soda
¾ teaspoon ground
   cinnamon
½ teaspoon ground
   cloves
1 egg
¼ cup molasses
2¼ cups all-purpose flour
½ cup raisins (optional)
¼ cup coarse or
   granulated sugar

1 Preheat oven to 350°F. In a large mixing bowl beat butter with an electric mixer on medium to high speed for 30 seconds. Add the 1 cup sugar, ginger, baking soda, cinnamon, and cloves. Beat until combined, scraping sides of bowl occasionally. Beat in the egg and molasses until combined. Beat in as much flour as you can with the mixer. Stir in any remaining flour and, if desired, the raisins.

2 Shape dough into 1½-inch balls. Roll balls in the coarse sugar to coat. Place balls about 2½ inches apart on an ungreased cookie sheet. Bake about 10 minutes or until light brown but still puffed. (Do not overbake.) Let stand for 2 minutes on cookie sheet. Transfer to a wire rack and let cool.

A coating of coarse sugar gives these cookies
a sweet crunch and pretty sparkle.

If you haven't tried using chestnuts in cookies, give this recipe a try. The maple syrup accentuates the nuts wonderfully.

maple-and-chestnut
mincemeat tarts

prep: 30 min. bake: 25 min. per batch oven: 325°F makes: 48 tarts

1 cup butter, softened
1 8-ounce package
    cream cheese,
    softened
2¼ cups all-purpose flour
¼ teaspoon ground
    allspice or ground
    cinnamon
2 eggs
¾ cup packed brown
    sugar
¼ cup pure maple syrup
    or maple-flavor
    syrup
¾ cup purchased
    mincemeat
½ cup canned whole,
    peeled chestnuts,
    drained and
    chopped, or canned
    candied chestnuts,
    drained and
    chopped
  Powdered sugar
    (optional)
  Cut-up candied
    cherries and dried
    apricots (optional)

1 Preheat oven to 325°F. For pastry, in a large mixing bowl beat butter and cream cheese on medium to high speed for 30 seconds. Stir in flour and allspice. Divide dough in half. Using one half of the dough, press a rounded teaspoon of dough evenly into bottom and up the sides of 24 ungreased 1¾-inch muffin cups. Wrap remaining dough in plastic wrap; chill until needed.

2 For filling, in a bowl beat eggs, brown sugar, and maple syrup until combined. Stir in mincemeat and chopped chestnuts. Spoon about 1 heaping teaspoon filling into each pastry-lined muffin cup. Cover remaining filling with plastic wrap; chill until needed.

3 Bake for 25 to 30 minutes or until pastry is golden and filling puffs. Cool slightly in pan. Carefully remove from pan. Transfer to a wire rack and let cool. Repeat with remaining pastry and filling

4 If desired, hold a fork over each cooled tart and sift powdered sugar through fork, making a stenciled design. If desired, top with pieces of candied cherry and dried apricot.

These soft, spicy cookies contain plenty of molasses,
which is the key to their dark color and intense flavor.

lumberjacks

prep: 25 min. bake: 12 min. per batch oven: 350°F makes: about 64 cookies

4	cups all-purpose flour
2	teaspoons ground cinnamon
1	teaspoon baking soda
1	teaspoon ground ginger
1	teaspoon salt
1	cup shortening
1	cup granulated sugar
1	cup dark molasses
2	eggs
¼	cup coarse sugar or granulated sugar

1 Preheat oven to 350°F. Lightly grease a cookie sheet; set aside. In a medium bowl stir together flour, cinnamon, baking soda, ginger, and salt; set aside.

2 In a large mixing bowl beat shortening with an electric mixer on medium to high speed for 30 seconds. Add the 1 cup granulated sugar. Beat until combined, scraping sides of bowl occasionally. Beat in molasses and eggs until combined. Beat in as much of the flour mixture as you can with the mixer. Stir in any remaining flour mixture.

3 Place the ¼ cup coarse sugar in a small bowl. Dip your fingers into the sugar, then pinch off pieces of dough and roll them into walnut-size balls. Roll balls in sugar to coat. Place balls about 3 inches apart on the prepared cookie sheet. Bake 12 minutes or until edges are firm and tops are slightly cracked. Transfer to a wire rack and let cool.

This New England favorite features megaflavor with lots of cinnamon, ginger, and molasses.

Bake these pecan- and chocolate-studded goodies in large rounds, then cut into charming little wedges.

pecan crispies

prep: 45 min. **bake:** 20 min. per batch **stand:** 2 min. per batch **oven:** 350°F
makes: 48 wedges

½	cup butter, softened
½	cup shortening
2½	cups packed brown sugar
½	teaspoon baking soda
¼	teaspoon salt
2	eggs
2½	cups all-purpose flour
1	cup chopped pecans
½	cup semisweet chocolate pieces (optional)

1 Preheat oven to 350°F. Lightly grease a large cookie sheet; set aside. In a large mixing bowl beat butter and shortening with an electric mixer on medium to high speed for 30 seconds. Add brown sugar, baking soda, and salt. Beat until combined, scraping sides of bowl occasionally. Beat in eggs until combined. Beat in as much of the flour as you can with the mixer. Stir in any remaining flour, the pecans, and, if desired, chocolate pieces.

2 Divide dough into 8 equal portions; shape into balls. Place balls 7 inches apart on the prepared cookie sheet. Flatten balls until ½ inch thick.

3 Bake 20 minutes or until tops are golden brown. (Do not underbake.) Let stand for 2 minutes on cookie sheet. Using a knife or pizza cutter, cut each cookie round into 6 wedges. Transfer wedges to wire racks and let cool.

The delicate but distinct flavors of pistachios and poppy seeds fill these orange-glazed shortbread cookies.

pistachio and poppy seed
shortbread

prep: 30 min. bake: 25 min. stand: 5 min. oven: 325°F makes: 16 wedges

1¼ cups all-purpose flour
⅓ cup sugar
3 tablespoons finely chopped pistachio nuts
2 teaspoons poppy seeds
⅔ cup cold butter
1 recipe Orange Glaze
 Diced candied orange or lemon peel (optional)

1 Preheat oven to 325°F. In a large mixing bowl stir together flour, sugar, pistachios, and poppy seeds. Using a pastry blender, cut in butter until mixture resembles fine crumbs and starts to cling. Form mixture into a ball and knead until smooth.

2 Place dough on an ungreased cookie sheet. Pat dough into an 8-inch circle. Use your fingers to crimp the edges of the circle to make scalloped edges. Cut circle into 16 wedges. Do not separate wedges. Bake 25 minutes or until edges are light brown and center is set. Recut circle into wedges while warm. Let stand for 5 minutes on cookie sheet. Transfer to a wire rack and let cool.

3 Drizzle cooled wedges with Orange Glaze and, if desired, sprinkle with candied orange peel.

orange glaze: *In a small bowl stir together ¾ cup powdered sugar and enough orange juice (about 1 to 2 tablespoons) to make a mixture of drizzling consistency.*

scrumptious **shapes**

Give these cookies a colorful frill with a dip in melted white chocolate and a roll in nonpareils and edible glitter.

white-chocolate cherry shortbread

prep: 40 min. **bake:** 10 min. per batch **stand:** 1 min. per batch **oven:** 325°F
makes: about 60 cookies

½ cup maraschino
cherries, drained
and finely chopped
2½ cups all-purpose flour
½ cup sugar
1 cup cold butter
12 ounces white
chocolate baking
squares (with
cocoa butter),
finely chopped
½ teaspoon almond
extract
2 drops red food
coloring (optional)
Sugar
2 teaspoons shortening
White nonpareils
and/or red edible
glitter (optional)

1 Preheat oven to 325°F. Spread cherries on paper towels to drain well.

2 In a large mixing bowl stir together flour and sugar. Using a pastry blender, cut in the butter until mixture resembles fine crumbs. Stir in drained cherries and 4 ounces (⅔ cup) of the chopped white chocolate. Stir in almond extract and, if desired, red food coloring. Form mixture into a ball and gently knead until smooth.

3 Shape dough into ¾-inch balls. Place balls 2 inches apart on an ungreased cookie sheet. Using the bottom of a drinking glass dipped in sugar, flatten balls to 1½-inch rounds. Bake for 10 to 12 minutes or until centers are set. Let stand for 1 minute on cookie sheet. Transfer cookies to a wire rack and let cool.

4 In a small saucepan heat and stir remaining 8 ounces white chocolate and the shortening over low heat until smooth. Dip half of each cookie into chocolate mixture, allowing excess to drip off. If desired, roll dipped edge in nonpareils and/or edible glitter. Place cookies on waxed paper. Let stand until set.

These cookies get their signature flavor from the simple melding of savory peanut butter into a sweet, buttery dough.

classic peanut butter cookies

prep: 25 min. **bake:** 7 min. per batch **oven:** 375°F **makes:** about 36 cookies

½   cup butter, softened
½   cup peanut butter
½   cup granulated sugar
½   cup packed brown
     sugar or ¼ cup
     honey
½   teaspoon baking soda
½   teaspoon baking
     powder
 1   egg
½   teaspoon vanilla
1¼ cups all-purpose flour
     Granulated sugar

1 In a large mixing bowl beat butter and peanut butter with an electric mixer on medium to high speed for 30 seconds. Add the granulated sugar, brown sugar, baking soda, and baking powder. Beat until combined, scraping sides of bowl occasionally. Beat in the egg and vanilla until combined. Beat in as much of the flour as you can with the mixer. Stir in any remaining flour. If necessary, cover and chill dough 1 hour or until easy to handle.

2 Preheat oven to 375°F. Shape dough into 1-inch balls. Roll balls in additional granulated sugar to coat. Place balls 2 inches apart on an ungreased cookie sheet. Using the tines of a fork, flatten balls by making crisscross marks on top. Bake for 7 to 9 minutes or until bottoms are light brown. Transfer to a wire rack and let cool.

Peanuts have been ground into a paste (aka peanut butter) to be used in cooking for centuries—no wonder this recipe is an all-time classic!

Potato chips in cookies? Yes, indeed! A coating of crushed potato chips adds a pleasant crunch and a salty-sweet flavor.

chocolate-fruit crispies

prep: 40 min. **bake:** 14 min. per batch **oven:** 350°F **makes:** 18 cookies

¾ cup butter, softened
½ cup sugar
¼ teaspoon salt
1 egg
1 teaspoon vanilla
2 cups all-purpose flour
½ cup miniature semisweet chocolate pieces
⅓ cup finely chopped candied cherries or candied fruits and peels
1 teaspoon finely shredded orange peel
1 cup crushed potato chips (about 3 cups uncrushed)

1 Preheat oven to 350°F. In a large mixing bowl beat butter with an electric mixer on medium to high speed for 30 seconds. Add sugar and salt. Beat until combined, scraping sides of bowl occasionally. Beat in egg and vanilla until combined. Beat in as much flour as you can with the mixer. Stir in any remaining flour, the chocolate pieces, candied fruits, and orange peel.

2 Shape dough into 1½-inch balls. Roll balls in crushed potato chips to coat. Place balls 2 inches apart on an ungreased cookie sheet. Using the bottom of a glass, flatten balls until they are about 2½ inches in diameter. Bake for 14 to 16 minutes or until golden. Transfer to a wire rack and let cool.

Try a variety of jam flavors for these little thumbprints, such as strawberry, cherry, black currant, or apricot.

jam thumbprints

prep: 25 min. **chill:** 1 hr. **bake:** 10 min. per batch **oven:** 375°F
makes: about 42 cookies

2 eggs
⅔ cup butter, softened
½ cup sugar
1 teaspoon vanilla
1½ cups all-purpose flour
1 cup finely chopped walnuts
⅓ to ½ cup jam or preserves

1 Separate eggs; place yolks and whites in separate bowls. Cover and chill egg whites until needed. In a large mixing bowl beat butter with an electric mixer on medium to high speed for 30 seconds. Add sugar. Beat until combined, scraping sides of bowl occasionally. Beat in egg yolks and vanilla until combined. Beat in as much of the flour as you can with the mixer. Stir in any remaining flour. Cover and chill dough about 1 hour or until easy to handle.

2 Preheat oven to 375°F. Grease a cookie sheet; set aside. Shape dough into 1-inch balls. Lightly beat egg whites. Roll balls in egg whites, then in walnuts to coat. Place balls 1 inch apart on the prepared cookie sheet. Using your thumb, make an indentation in the center of each ball. Bake for 10 to 12 minutes or until edges are light brown. If the cookie centers have puffed up during baking, repress with the bowl of a measuring teaspoon. Transfer to a wire rack and let cool. Just before serving, fill cookie centers with jam.

note: *Store unfilled cookies as directed on page 16. Fill just before serving.*

A delectable chocolate and hazelnut filling makes these oatmeal sandwich cookies a hit with chocolate and nut lovers alike.

hazelnut-filled
sandwich cookies

prep: 45 min. **bake:** 5 min. per batch **oven:** 375°F **makes:** about 48 sandwich cookies

½ cup shortening
⅓ cup granulated sugar
⅓ cup packed brown
   sugar
½ teaspoon baking
   powder
¼ teaspoon baking soda
⅛ teaspoon salt
1 egg
1 teaspoon vanilla
1½ cups all-purpose flour
¾ cup quick-cooking
   rolled oats
½ cup chocolate-
   hazelnut spread

1 Heat oven to 375°F. In a large mixing bowl beat shortening with an electric mixer on medium to high speed for 30 seconds. Add the granulated sugar, brown sugar, baking powder, baking soda, and salt. Beat until combined, scraping sides of bowl occasionally. Beat in egg and vanilla until combined. Beat in as much of the flour as you can with the mixer. Stir in any remaining flour and the oats.

2 Shape dough into ¾-inch balls. Place balls 1½ inches apart on an ungreased cookie sheet. Using the bottom of a drinking glass, press balls into 1-inch circles. Bake for 5 to 7 minutes or until edges are firm and bottoms are light brown. Transfer to a wire rack; cool.

3 Spread a scant ½ teaspoon chocolate-hazelnut spread each on the flat sides of half of the cookies. Top with the remaining cookies, flat sides down.

note: *Store as directed on page 16. Refrigerate for up to 3 days.*

A nest of buttery dough covered in finely chopped nuts houses a mound of sweet jam in these mouthwatering gems.

birds' nests

prep: 25 min. **bake:** 10 min. per batch **oven:** 375°F **makes:** 36 nests

1	cup butter, softened
½	cup packed brown sugar
2	egg yolks
2	cups all-purpose flour
2	egg whites, lightly beaten
2	cups finely chopped walnuts or pecans
½	cup seedless raspberry jam or preserves
1	recipe Powdered Sugar Drizzle (optional)

1 Heat oven to 375°F. Lightly grease a cookie sheet; set aside. In a large mixing bowl beat butter with an electric mixer on medium to high speed for 30 seconds. Add the brown sugar. Beat until combined, scraping sides of bowl occasionally. Beat in egg yolks until combined. Beat in as much of the flour as you can with the mixer. Stir in any remaining flour.

2 Shape dough into 1¼-inch balls. Roll the balls in egg whites, then in chopped nuts to coat. Place balls 1 inch apart on the prepared cookie sheet. Using your thumb, make an indentation in the center of each cookie. Bake for 10 to 12 minutes or until edges are light brown. Transfer to a wire rack and let cool. Fill cookie centers with jam (about ½ teaspoon each). If desired, drizzle with Powdered Sugar Drizzle.

powdered sugar drizzle:
In a small bowl stir together 1 cup sifted powdered sugar and enough milk (1 to 2 tablespoons) to make an icing of drizzling consistency.

For a no-mess method of crushing the wheat cereal flakes, place the cereal in a resealable plastic bag, seal, and crush it with a rolling pin.

coconut-wheat cookies

prep: 40 min. bake: 10 min. per batch stand: 1 min. per batch oven: 350°F
makes: 54 cookies

2	cups all-purpose flour
1	teaspoon baking powder
½	teaspoon baking soda
½	teaspoon salt
1	cup shortening
1	cup granulated sugar
1	cup packed brown sugar
2	eggs
1	teaspoon vanilla
2	cups wheat cereal flakes, crushed (1 cup crushed)
1	cup flaked coconut

1 Preheat oven to 350°F. In a small bowl stir together flour, baking powder, baking soda, and salt; set aside. In a large mixing bowl beat shortening with an electric mixer on medium to high speed for 30 seconds. Add granulated sugar and brown sugar. Beat until combined, scraping sides of bowl occasionally. Beat in eggs and vanilla until combined. Beat in flour mixture. Stir in cereal and coconut.

2 Shape dough into 1-inch balls. Place balls 2 inches apart on an ungreased cookie sheet. Bake for 10 to 11 minutes or until golden. Let stand for 1 minute on cookie sheet. Transfer to a wire rack and let cool.

Flakes of coconut, along with crushed wheat cereal, make for an extra chewy, extra delicious cookie.

Mulling spice, a combination of spices such as cinnamon, allspice, cloves, and nutmeg, perfectly offsets the sweetness of coconut.

mulling spice
and coconut cookies

prep: 35 min. **chill:** 2 hr. **bake:** 8 min. per batch **oven:** 375°F
makes: 60 cookies

½ cup canned coconut milk
2 tablespoons mulling spice
½ cup chopped, pitted dates
½ cup butter, softened
½ cup shortening
1½ cups granulated sugar
2 teaspoons cream of tartar
1 teaspoon baking soda
¼ teaspoon salt
2 eggs
3 cups all-purpose flour
1½ cups sifted powdered sugar
Milk
1¼ cups flaked coconut (optional)

1 In a small saucepan combine coconut milk and mulling spice. Bring just to boiling; reduce heat to low. Simmer, covered, for 5 minutes. Strain through a fine-mesh sieve; discard mulling spice. Reserve 2 tablespoons of the spiced coconut milk; cover and chill for use in frosting. Add dates to remaining spiced coconut milk. Cover; set aside.

2 For cookie dough, in a large mixing bowl beat butter and shortening on medium to high speed for 30 seconds. Add granulated sugar, cream of tartar, baking soda, and salt. Beat until combined, scraping sides of bowl occasionally. Beat in eggs until combined. Beat in as much flour as you can with the mixer. Stir in any remaining flour. Stir in the coconut milk and date mixture. Cover and chill dough for 2 to 4 hours or until easy to handle.

3 Preheat oven to 375°F. Shape dough into 1-inch balls. Place balls 2 inches apart on an ungreased cookie sheet. Bake for 8 to 10 minutes or until light brown. Transfer to a wire rack and let cool.

4 For frosting, in a small bowl stir together powdered sugar and reserved spiced coconut milk. Stir in enough milk (1 to 2 teaspoons) until desired consistency. Spread or drizzle cooled cookies with frosting and, if desired, sprinkle with flaked coconut.

While the whimsical name of this cookie has no actual definition, over time the word "snickerdoodle" has come to describe this crackle-topped, cinnamon-flavor classic.

snickerdoodles

prep: 25 min. **chill:** 1 hr. **bake:** 10 min. per batch **oven:** 375°F
makes: about 36 cookies

½ cup butter, softened
1 cup sugar
¼ teaspoon baking soda
¼ teaspoon cream of
   tartar
1 egg
½ teaspoon vanilla
1½ cups all-purpose flour
2 tablespoons sugar
1 teaspoon ground
   cinnamon

1 In a medium mixing bowl beat butter with an electric mixer on medium to high speed for 30 seconds. Add the 1 cup sugar, baking soda, and cream of tartar. Beat until combined, scraping sides of bowl occasionally. Beat in egg and vanilla until combined. Beat in as much of the flour as you can with the mixer. Stir in any remaining flour. Cover and chill dough about 1 hour or until easy to handle.

2 Preheat oven to 375°F. In a small bowl stir together the 2 tablespoons sugar and the cinnamon. Shape dough into 1-inch balls. Roll balls in sugar-cinnamon mixture to coat. Place balls 2 inches apart on an ungreased cookie sheet. Bake for 10 to 11 minutes or until edges are golden. Transfer to a wire rack and let cool.

Coated with glistening sugar and spicy cinnamon, these twinkling classics are the perfect addition to any cookie tray.

Look for mini madeleine cookie molds at specialty cookware stores and through mail order catalogs.

mini **madeleines** with candied orange

prep: 35 min. **chill:** 1 hr. **bake:** 7 min. per batch **oven:** 375°F
makes: about 60 miniature madeleine sandwich cookies

1⅔	cups powdered sugar
½	cup all-purpose flour
½	cup yellow cornmeal
4	eggs
½	cup butter, melted
1	tablespoon honey
¼	cup candied orange peel, finely chopped
1	recipe Orange-Butter Frosting
	Powdered sugar

1 In a medium bowl stir together the 1⅔ cups powdered sugar, the flour, and cornmeal; set aside.

2 In a large mixing bowl beat eggs with an electric mixer on high speed about 4 minutes or until eggs are thick and lemon colored. Beat in flour mixture on low speed just until combined. Beat in butter and honey until combined. Stir in candied orange peel. Cover and chill batter for 1 hour.

3 Preheat oven to 375°F. Grease and flour miniature (1¾-inch) madeleine molds. Stir chilled batter; spoon 1 teaspoon batter into each mold. Bake for 7 to 8 minutes or until golden. Immediately invert pan and gently tap on counter to unmold madeleines. Loosen cookies with a small spatula, if necessary. Transfer to a wire rack and let cool. Cool molds; wash, dry, and grease and flour them to bake remaining cookies.

4 Pipe or spread flat sides of half of the madeleines with Orange-Butter Frosting. Top with remaining madeleines, flat sides down. Sift powdered sugar over tops. If desired, serve in paper or foil candy cups.

orange-butter frosting: *In a medium mixing bowl beat 3 tablespoons softened butter until fluffy. Gradually beat in 1 cup sifted powdered sugar. Slowly beat in 3 tablespoons orange juice and 1¾ cups powdered sugar. Beat in additional orange juice, 1 teaspoon at a time, to make a frosting of piping consistency.*

If using a cookie mold, you need only to coat the mold with cooking spray for the first cookie. Use a brush to flour the mold for the second use, then tap out the excess flour.

gingersnap shortbread

prep: 30 min. **bake:** 18 min. **oven:** 325°F **makes:** 16 to 18 cookies

2 cups all-purpose flour
½ cup powdered sugar
¼ teaspoon ground ginger
¼ teaspoon ground cinnamon
⅛ teaspoon ground cloves
1 cup cold butter
2 tablespoons molasses
Granulated sugar (optional)
Luster dust* (optional)

1 Preheat oven to 325°F. In a large mixing bowl stir together flour, powdered sugar, ginger, cinnamon, and cloves. Using a pastry blender, cut in the butter and molasses until mixture resembles fine crumbs. Knead until dough forms a ball. Divide dough in half.

2 Lightly coat a 7½- to 8-inch shortbread mold with cooking spray; dust with flour. Press half of the dough at a time into the prepared mold, flouring the mold between uses. (It is not necessary to spray the mold again.) Unmold dough onto a very large ungreased cookie sheet; trim edges if necessary. Do not sprinkle molded cookies with sugar. (If you do not have a shortbread mold, on a very large ungreased cookie sheet pat dough into two 8-inch rounds. Use your fingers to crimp the edges of the circles to make scalloped edges. Sprinkle rounds with granulated sugar.)

3 Bake for 18 to 20 minutes until bottoms just start to turn golden brown and centers are set. Remove from oven and, while warm, cut molded shortbread into nine pieces. (Or cut each round into eight wedges.) Transfer to a wire rack and let cool. If desired, use a small brush to brush luster dust over designs on molded cookies.

*Look for luster dust in the cake- and cookie-decorating section of a crafts store. See page 25 for tips on how to use luster dust.

These rich sandwiches are adapted from an Italian cookie called bocca di dama—or lady's kisses. This tea-scented version is called bocca di nonna—or grandmother's kisses.

earl grey bocca di nonna

prep: 40 min. **chill:** 1 hr. **bake:** 12 min. per batch **stand:** 15 min. (ganache)
oven: 350°F **makes:** 28 sandwich cookies

⅔ cup all-purpose flour
2 tablespoons Dutch-process unsweetened cocoa powder
¾ cup butter, softened
1 cup sugar
¾ teaspoon vanilla
1½ cups finely ground blanched almonds
1 recipe Earl Grey Ganache

1 In a small bowl stir together flour and cocoa powder; set aside. In a large mixing bowl beat butter with an electric mixer on medium to high speed for 30 seconds. Add sugar and vanilla. Beat until combined, scraping sides of bowl occasionally. Beat in almonds. Beat in flour mixture just until combined. Cover and chill dough about 1 hour or until easy to handle.

2 Preheat oven to 350°F. Line a cookie sheet with parchment paper or foil; set aside. Shape dough into 1-inch balls. Place balls 2 inches apart on the prepared cookie sheet. Press to flatten slightly.

3 Bake for 12 to 15 minutes or until firm. Cool on cookie sheet on a wire rack. Remove cooled cookies from sheet. Spread about 1 teaspoon Earl Grey Ganache each on the flat sides of half of the cookies. Top with the remaining cookies, flat sides down.

note: *Store as directed on page 16. Refrigerate up to 3 days. Do not freeze.*

earl grey ganache: *In a small saucepan bring ⅓ cup whipping cream to boiling. Remove from heat. Add four Earl Grey tea bags. Cover and let stand for 15 minutes. Remove tea bags from cream. Squeeze tea bags well or press tea leaves in tea ball with the back of a spoon to release any liquid. Return cream to boiling. Remove from heat. Immediately add 4 ounces finely chopped milk chocolate. Stir until chocolate melts and mixture is shiny and smooth. Cool to room temperature.*

These fun, colorful cookies make great treats at kids' parties. Little hands will make them disappear before your eyes.

chocolate thumbprints

prep: 25 min. **chill:** 1 hr. **bake:** 7 min. per batch **oven:** 375°F
makes: 36 cookies

⅔	cup butter, softened
½	cup sugar
¼	cup unsweetened cocoa powder
¼	teaspoon baking soda
⅛	teaspoon salt
1	egg
1	teaspoon vanilla
1¼	cups all-purpose flour
¾	cup chocolate-flavor or multicolor sprinkles
36	milk chocolate kisses, unwrapped

1 In a large mixing bowl beat butter with an electric mixer on medium to high speed for 30 seconds. Add sugar, cocoa powder, baking soda, and salt. Beat until combined, scraping sides of bowl occasionally. Beat in egg and vanilla until combined. Beat in as much of the flour as you can with the mixer. Stir in any remaining flour. Cover and chill dough about 1 hour or until easy to handle.

2 Preheat oven to 375°F. Shape dough into 1-inch balls. Roll balls in sprinkles to coat. Place balls 2 inches apart on a greased cookie sheet. Using your thumb, make an indentation in the center of each cookie.

3 Bake for 7 to 8 minutes or until edges are firm. Immediately press a chocolate kiss into each cookie's center. Transfer to a wire rack and let cool.

Even though you add the orange juice before the peel, it's easier to shred and measure the peel first, then squeeze the orange for juice.

orange snowballs

prep: 25 min. **bake:** 15 min. per batch **stand:** 5 min. per batch **oven:** 325°F
makes: 48 cookies

1 cup butter, softened
¾ cup powdered sugar
1 tablespoon finely
shredded orange
peel
2 teaspoons finely
shredded orange
peel (set aside)
1 tablespoon orange
juice
2⅔ cups all-purpose flour
Granulated sugar
¾ cup granulated sugar

1 Preheat oven to 325°F. In a large mixing bowl beat butter with an electric mixer on medium to high speed for 30 seconds. Add powdered sugar. Beat until combined, scraping sides of bowl occasionally. Beat in orange juice until combined. Beat in as much of the flour as you can with mixer. Stir in the 1 tablespoon orange peel and any remaining flour.

2 Shape dough into 1¼-inch balls. Roll balls in granulated sugar to coat. Place balls 2 inches apart on an ungreased cookie sheet. Bake 15 minutes or until bottoms are light brown. Let cookies stand for 5 minutes on cookie sheet.

3 Meanwhile, in a food processor or a blender combine the ¾ cup granulated sugar and the 2 teaspoons orange peel. Cover and process or blend until mixture is combined. Roll the warm baked cookies in the sugar mixture. Transfer to a wire rack; let cool.

These cookies, still warm from the oven, are rolled in a mixture of sugar and orange zest. The heat from the cookies releases the aromatic oils in the zest.

Organically grown edible flowers are available year-round in most supermarkets.

viola shortbread

prep: 30 min. **bake:** 30 min. **oven:** 325°F **makes:** 12 or 16 cookies

1¼ cups all-purpose flour
3 tablespoons
granulated sugar
½ cup cold butter
1 tablespoon dried egg
whites*
2 tablespoons water
12 or 16 edible violas or
other edible flowers
Fine sanding sugar

1 Preheat oven to 325°F. In a medium mixing bowl stir together the flour and granulated sugar. Using a pastry blender, cut in butter until mixture resembles fine crumbs and starts to cling. Form mixture into a ball and knead until smooth.

2 Place dough on an ungreased cookie sheet. Pat dough into an 8-inch circle. Use your fingers to crimp the edges of the circle to make scalloped edges. Cut circle into 12 or 16 wedges. Do not separate wedges. Bake for 25 to 30 minutes or until edges are light brown and center is set. Recut circle into wedges while warm. Cool on cookie sheet on a wire rack.

3 In a small bowl stir together dried egg whites and water. Brush tops of wedges with egg white mixture. Place flowers on top; brush with more egg white mixture. Sprinkle with fine sanding sugar. Bake in the 325 F oven for 5 minutes. Transfer to a wire rack; cool.

*Dried egg whites are available in the baking products section of larger supermarkets

Perfect for afternoon tea or brunch with friends, these darling shortbread wedges are elegantly embellished with edible flowers and fine sugar.

You may want to make more than one batch of these tasty jewel-toned cookies to give to friends.

pecan shortbread logs

prep: 20 min. **bake:** 30 min. **oven:** 325°F **makes:** about 14 cookies

1¼ cups all-purpose flour
3 tablespoons packed brown sugar
½ cup cold butter
¼ cup pecans, finely chopped
4 teaspoons seedless raspberry jam or apricot preserves
½ cup powdered sugar
1 tablespoon rum, brandy, or milk

1 Preheat oven to 325°F. In a large bowl stir together flour and brown sugar. Using a pastry blender, cut in the butter until mixture resembles fine crumbs. Stir in pecans. Gently knead mixture until it forms a ball. Divide dough in half.

2 On a lightly floured surface, roll each portion of dough into a 7-inch-long log. Place logs four inches apart on an ungreased cookie sheet. Make a ¼-inch-deep groove down the center of each log, leaving a ½-inch edge on the ends. Stir jam until nearly smooth (snip any large pieces of fruit if using apricot preserves). Spoon jam into grooves.

3 Bake 30 minutes or until logs are light brown. Cool logs completely on cookie sheet on a wire rack. Cut cooled logs into 1-inch slices. In a small bowl stir together powdered sugar and rum until smooth. Drizzle over cookies.

Chocolate pastry and a spiked chocolate filling make these treats great for the dessert tray at your next adult party.

fudgy liqueur cups

prep: 30 min. **bake:** 18 min. **stand:** 10 min. **oven:** 325°F **makes:** 24 cups

¾ cup all-purpose flour
¼ cup unsweetened
    cocoa powder
⅓ cup butter, softened
⅓ cup sugar
1 3-ounce package
    cream cheese,
    softened
¼ cup butter
½ cup sugar
⅓ cup unsweetened
    cocoa powder
1 egg
2 tablespoons orange
    liqueur, cherry
    liqueur, or milk
1 teaspoon vanilla
1 recipe White
    Chocolate Shapes
    (optional)
  Chopped candied
    fruit (optional)

1 For pastry, in a small bowl stir together flour and the ¼ cup cocoa powder; set aside. In a medium mixing bowl beat the ⅓ cup butter, the ⅓ cup sugar, and the cream cheese with an electric mixer on medium speed until combined. Gradually beat in the flour mixture. If necessary, cover and chill dough 30 minutes or until easy to handle.

2 Preheat oven to 325°F. Lightly grease twenty-four 1¾-inch muffin cups. Divide dough into 24 equal pieces. Place each piece into a muffin cup; press evenly into bottoms and up the sides. Set aside.

3 For filling, in a small saucepan melt the ¼ cup butter over low heat. Remove from heat. Stir in the ½ cup sugar, the ⅓ cup cocoa powder, the egg, liqueur, and vanilla. Spoon about 1 tablespoon of filling into each pastry-lined cup.

4 Bake 18 minutes or until filling is set. Let stand for 10 minutes in pans. Remove cups from pans. Transfer to a wire rack and let cool. If desired, top with White Chocolate Shapes and chopped candied fruit.

white chocolate shapes: *In a small saucepan heat and stir ¼ cup white baking pieces until smooth. Transfer to a small resealable plastic bag; snip a tiny hole in the corner of the bag. On a sheet of waxed paper, pipe melted chocolate into small leaf designs or other shapes. Let stand until set.*

Dried pears lend a subtle sweetness to these spiced cookies. Look for them near other dried fruits in the produce section of larger supermarkets.

gingery pear-pecan cookies

prep: 40 min. **bake:** 8 min. per batch **stand:** 1 min. per batch **oven:** 350°F
makes: 60 cookies

3½ cups all-purpose flour
1 tablespoon
    finely chopped
    crystallized ginger
2 teaspoons ground
    ginger
1½ teaspoons baking
    soda
1 teaspoon ground
    cinnamon
¼ teaspoon salt
¼ teaspoon ground
    cloves
¼ teaspoon ground
    nutmeg
½ cup shortening
½ cup butter, softened
¾ cup granulated sugar
¾ cup packed brown
    sugar
2 eggs
⅓ cup molasses
½ cup chopped pecans,
    toasted (see tip,
    page 19)
½ cup snipped dried
    pears
½ cup coarse or
    granulated sugar

1 Preheat oven to 350°F. In a medium bowl stir together flour, crystallized ginger, ground ginger, baking soda, cinnamon, salt, cloves, and nutmeg; set aside.

2 In a large mixing bowl beat shortening and butter with an electric mixer on medium to high speed for 30 seconds. Add the granulated sugar and the brown sugar. Beat until combined, scraping sides of bowl occasionally. Beat in eggs and molasses until combined. Beat in as much of the flour mixture as you can with the mixer. Stir in any remaining flour mixture. Stir in pecans and dried pears.

3 Shape dough into 1-inch balls. Roll balls in the coarse sugar to coat. Place balls 2 inches apart on an ungreased cookie sheet. Bake for 8 to 10 minutes or until tops are puffed and edges are set. (Do not overbake.) Let stand for 1 minute on cookie sheet. Transfer to a wire rack and let cool.

These goodies offer the best of everything—tender cookie, buttery caramel, chewy nuts, and satiny chocolate.

chocolate-caramel
thumbprints

prep: 30 min. **chill:** 2 hr. **bake:** 10 min. per batch **oven:** 350°F
makes: 36 cookies

1 egg
1 cup all-purpose flour
⅓ cup unsweetened
  cocoa powder
¼ teaspoon salt
½ cup butter, softened
⅔ cup sugar
2 tablespoons milk
1 teaspoon vanilla
16 vanilla caramels,
  unwrapped
3 tablespoons
  whipping cream
1¼ cups finely chopped
  pecans
½ cup semisweet
  chocolate pieces
1 teaspoon shortening

1 Separate egg; place yolk and white in separate bowls. Cover and chill egg white until needed. In a medium bowl stir together the flour, cocoa powder, and salt; set aside.

2 In a large mixing bowl beat butter with an electric mixer on medium to high speed for 30 seconds. Add sugar. Beat until combined, scraping sides of bowl occasionally. Beat in the egg yolk, milk, and vanilla until combined. Beat in the flour mixture. Cover and chill dough 2 hours or until easy to handle.

3 Preheat oven to 350°F. Lightly grease a cookie sheet; set aside. In a small saucepan heat and stir caramels and whipping cream over low heat until smooth. Set aside.

4 Lightly beat reserved egg white. Shape dough into 1-inch balls. Roll balls in egg white, then in pecans to coat. Place balls 1 inch apart on the prepared cookie sheet. Using your thumb, make an indentation in the center of each cookie.

5 Bake 10 minutes or until edges are firm. Spoon melted caramel mixture into cookie centers. (If necessary, reheat caramel mixture to keep it spoonable.) Transfer to a wire rack and let cool.

6 In another small saucepan heat and stir chocolate pieces and shortening over low heat until smooth. Let cool slightly. Drizzle chocolate mixture over tops of cookies. Let stand until set.

A mocha—a coffee shop drink that combines espresso, chocolate, and milk—is the inspiration for these chocolate-dipped, coffee-flavor cookies.

mocha wands

prep: 25 min. **bake:** 10 min. per batch **oven:** 375°F **makes:** 72 cookies

1	cup butter, softened
¾	cup sugar
4	teaspoons instant espresso powder
½	teaspoons salt
¼	teaspoon baking powder
1	egg
1	teaspoon vanilla
2⅓	cups all-purpose flour
8	ounces semisweet chocolate, melted and cooled
1½	cups finely chopped pecans

1 Preheat oven to 375°F. In medium bowl beat butter with electric mixer on medium to high speed for 30 seconds. Add sugar, espresso powder, salt, and baking powder. Beat until combined, scraping sides of bowl occasionally. Beat in egg and vanilla until combined. Beat in as much of the flour as you can with the mixer. Stir in any remaining flour.

2 Force unchilled dough through a cookie press with a star plate into 3-inch-long strips onto an ungreased cookie sheet. Space strips 1 inch apart. Bake for 10 to 12 minutes or until edges of cookies are firm. Transfer to a wire rack and let cool.

3 Dip ends of cooled cookies into melted chocolate. Sprinkle with pecans. Let stand until set.

The lively combination of tangy lemon and earthy sage makes this cookie's flavor slightly sweet and refreshing to the palate.

lemon-sage cookies

prep: 45 min. **bake:** 10 min. per batch **stand:** 1 min. per batch **oven:** 350°F
makes: about 36 cookies

1 cup butter, softened
¾ cup powdered sugar
¼ teaspoon ground ginger
1 tablespoon finely shredded lemon peel
1 tablespoon lemon juice
2⅔ cups all-purpose flour
2 teaspoons finely snipped fresh sage or ½ teaspoon dried sage, crushed

1 Preheat oven to 350°F. In a large mixing bowl beat butter with an electric mixer on medium to high speed for 30 seconds. Add sugar, ginger, lemon peel, and lemon juice. Beat until combined, scraping sides of bowl occasionally. Beat in as much of the flour as you can with the mixer. Stir in any remaining flour and the sage.

2 For molded cookies: Lightly grease two cookie sheets; set aside. Lightly oil ceramic or wooden cookie molds. Wipe off excess oil with a paper towel. Lightly coat mold with flour, then tap mold to remove excess flour. (Flour the molds between each use but do not oil them again.) Evenly press dough into prepared mold. If necessary, trim off excess dough with a serrated knife. Unmold dough onto a lightly floured board by tapping the mold lightly on a cutting board until dough starts to release. Trim edges as necessary. Using a metal spatula, transfer cookies to the prepared cookie sheets; place cookies 1 inch apart. Bake for 10 to 12 minutes or until edges are golden. Let stand for 1 minute on cookie sheets. Transfer to wire racks and let cool. The yield depends on size of molds used.

3 For stamped cookies: Shape dough into 1- to 1½-inch balls. Place balls 2 inches apart on an ungreased cookie sheet. Using a floured cookie stamp or the floured patterned bottom of a glass or dish, flatten balls until ¼ inch thick. Bake for 10 to 12 minutes or until edges are golden. Let stand for 1 minute on cookie sheet. Transfer to a wire rack; cool.

note: *Store as directed on page 16. Store at room temperature up to 2 days.*

This golden cookie's texture is similar to that of a shortbread cookie. Ground almonds and pumpkin pie spices add unbeatable flavor.

almond-spice cookies

prep: 20 min. **chill:** 1 hr. **bake:** 12 min./10 min. per batch
stand: 5 min./1 min. per batch **oven:** 350°F **makes:** about 28 cookies

½ cup butter, softened
¾ cup packed brown sugar
1 teaspoon ground cinnamon
½ teaspoon ground nutmeg
¼ teaspoon baking powder
¼ teaspoon ground ginger
⅛ teaspoon salt
⅛ teaspoon ground cloves
1 egg yolk
1 tablespoon milk
1⅓ cups all-purpose flour
3 tablespoons finely ground almonds

1 In a large mixing bowl beat butter with an electric mixer on medium to high speed for 30 seconds. Add brown sugar, cinnamon, nutmeg, baking powder, ginger, salt, and cloves. Beat until combined, scraping sides of bowl occasionally. Beat in egg yolk and milk until combined. Beat in as much of the flour as you can with the mixer. Stir in any remaining flour and the nuts. Cover and chill dough about 1 hour or until easy to handle.

2 For molded cookies: Preheat oven to 350°F. Lightly grease two cookie sheets; set aside. Lightly oil ceramic or wooden cookie molds. Wipe off excess oil with a paper towel. Lightly coat mold with flour, then tap mold to remove excess flour. (Flour the molds between each use but do not oil them again.) Evenly press dough into prepared mold. If necessary, trim off excess dough with a serrated knife. Unmold dough onto a lightly floured board by tapping the mold lightly on a cutting board until dough starts to release. Trim edges as necessary. Using a metal spatula, transfer cookies to the prepared cookie sheets; place cookies 1 inch apart. Bake for 12 to 15 minutes or until edges are firm. Let stand for 5 minutes on cookie sheets. Transfer to wire racks and let cool. The yield depends on size of molds used.

3 For stamped cookies: Preheat oven to 350°F. Shape dough into 1- to 1½-inch balls. Place balls 2 inches apart on an ungreased cookie sheet. Using a floured cookie stamp or the floured patterned bottom of a glass or dish, flatten balls until ¼ inch thick. Bake for 10 to 12 minutes or until edges are firm. Let stand for 1 minute on cookie sheet. Transfer to a wire rack and let cool.

An orange-scented glaze tops these cranberry-studded cornmeal shortbread cookies. Garnish with a sprig of fresh rosemary for an elegant presentation.

rosemary shortbread

prep: 25 min. **bake:** 25 min. **stand:** 5 min. **oven:** 325°F **makes:** 16 wedges

1 cup all-purpose flour
¼ cup yellow cornmeal
3 tablespoons granulated sugar
1 teaspoon snipped fresh rosemary or ¼ teaspoon dried rosemary, crushed
Dash cayenne pepper
½ cup cold butter
2 tablespoons finely snipped dried cranberries
⅓ cup powdered sugar
⅛ teaspoon finely shredded orange peel
2 to 4 teaspoons orange juice

1 Preheat oven to 325°F. In a medium bowl stir together flour, cornmeal, granulated sugar, rosemary, and cayenne pepper. Using a pastry blender, cut in butter until mixture resembles fine crumbs and starts to cling. Add dried cranberries. Form mixture into a ball and knead until smooth. (Mixture may appear crumbly at first, but it will come together as you work it with your hands.)

2 Place dough on an ungreased cookie sheet. Pat dough into an 8-inch circle. Use your fingers to crimp the edges of the circle to make scalloped edges.* Cut circle into 16 wedges. Do not separate wedges. Bake for 25 to 30 minutes or until edges are light brown and center is set. Recut circle into wedges while warm. Let stand for 5 minutes on the cookie sheet.

3 Meanwhile, in a small bowl stir together the powdered sugar, orange peel, and 1 teaspoon of the orange juice. Stir in enough of the remaining orange juice, 1 teaspoon at a time, to make a glaze of drizzling consistency. Spread or brush glaze over warm wedges on cookie sheet. Transfer glazed wedges to a wire rack and let cool.

✱To make a scalloped edge on your shortbread, pinch the upper edge of the dough with your thumb and forefinger. At the same time, press into the pinched dough with your other thumb, creating a raised indentation on the dough edge. Repeat all around the circle.

scrumptious **shapes**

Finely shredded lime peel adds a fresh citrus bite to these rich, golden cookies.

cornmeal and
lime butter cookies

prep: 25 min. chill: 1 hr. bake: 8 min. per batch stand: 5 min./1 min. per batch oven: 350°F makes: 26 cookies

¾ cup butter, softened
⅔ cup sifted powdered
   sugar
⅛ teaspoon salt
1 cup all-purpose flour
½ cup yellow cornmeal
2 teaspoons finely
   shredded lime peel
½ teaspoon vanilla

1 In a large mixing bowl beat butter with an electric mixer on medium to high speed for 30 seconds. Add powdered sugar and salt. Beat until combined, scraping sides of bowl occasionally. Beat in as much of the flour as you can with the mixer. Stir in any remaining flour, the cornmeal, lime peel, and vanilla with a wooden spoon. Cover and chill dough about 1 hour or until easy to handle.

2 For molded cookies: Preheat oven to 350°F. Lightly grease two cookie sheets; set aside. Lightly oil ceramic or wooden cookie molds. Wipe off excess oil with a paper towel. Lightly coat mold with flour, then tap mold to remove excess flour. (Flour the molds between each use but do not oil them again.) Evenly press dough into prepared mold. If necessary, trim off excess dough with a serrated knife. Unmold dough onto a lightly floured board by tapping the mold lightly on a cutting board until dough starts to release. Trim edges as necessary. Using a metal spatula, transfer cookies to the prepared cookie sheets; place cookies 1 inch apart. Bake for 8 to 12 minutes or until edges are golden and center is set. Let stand for 5 minutes on cookie sheets. Transfer to wire racks and let cool. The yield depends on size of molds used.

3 For stamped cookies: Preheat oven to 350°F. Shape dough into 1- to 1½-inch balls. Place balls 2 inches apart on an ungreased cookie sheet. Using a floured cookie stamp or the floured patterned bottom of a glass or dish, flatten balls until ¼ inch thick. Bake for 8 to 10 minutes or until edges are golden. Let stand for 1 minute on cookie sheets. Transfer to a wire rack and let cool.

A double rolling in granulated sugar makes these crackled, coffee-flavor confections extra sparkly.

cappuccino crinkles

prep: 15 minutes **bake:** 8 minutes per batch **oven:** 350°F **makes:** about 32 cookies

⅓ cup butter, softened

1 cup packed brown sugar

⅔ cup unsweetened cocoa powder

1 tablespoon instant coffee crystals

1 teaspoon baking soda

1 teaspoon ground cinnamon

2 egg whites

⅓ cup vanilla yogurt

1½ cups all-purpose flour

¼ cup granulated sugar

1 Heat oven to 350°F. In a large mixing bowl beat butter with an electric mixer on medium to high speed for 30 seconds. Add the brown sugar, cocoa powder, coffee crystals, baking soda, and cinnamon. Beat until combined, scraping sides of bowl occasionally. Beat in egg whites and yogurt until combined. Beat in as much of the flour as you can with the mixer. Stir in any remaining flour.

2 Place granulated sugar in a small bowl. Drop dough by heaping teaspoons into sugar and roll into balls. Roll again in sugar. Place balls 2 inches apart on an ungreased cookie sheet. Bake for 8 to 10 minutes or until edges are firm. Transfer to a wire rack; cool.

Prized by coffee lovers, these sugar-coated gems make a great after-dinner treat.

scrumptious **shapes**

The high concentration of antioxidants in matcha, or Japanese green tea powder, makes these beautiful cookies healthful as well as tasty.

green tea shortbread wedges

prep: 20 min. **bake:** 25 min. **stand:** 5 min. **oven:** 325°F
makes: 8 to 12 wedges

1¼   cups all-purpose flour
3   tablespoons sugar
1½   teaspoons matcha
     (green tea powder)
1   teaspoon finely
     shredded lemon
     peel
½   cup cold butter
     Green luster dust*
     (optional)

1 Preheat oven to 325°F. In a medium bowl stir together flour, sugar, matcha, and lemon peel. Using a pastry blender, cut in butter until mixture resembles fine crumbs and starts to cling. Form mixture into a ball; knead until smooth.

2 To make shortbread wedges, place dough on an ungreased cookie sheet. Pat dough into an 8-inch circle. Use your fingers to crimp the edges of the circle to make scalloped edges. Cut circle into 8 to 12 wedges. Do not separate wedges. If desired, using the rounded edge of a candy mold, make a leaf imprint in each wedge.

3 Bake for 25 to 30 minutes or just until bottom starts to brown and center is set. Remove from oven and, while warm, recut circle into wedges. Let stand for 5 minutes on cookie sheet. Transfer to a wire rack and let cool. If desired, lightly brush luster dust on the leaf designs.

✱Look for luster dust in the cake- and cookie-decorating section of a crafts store. See page 25 for tips on how to use luster dust.

Use a mortar and pestle to crush fennel seeds for these cookies. If you don't have this tool, place the seeds on a cutting board and gently crush them with the side of a chef's knife.

sugared **lemon-fennel** cookies

prep: 30 min. **chill:** 4 hr. **bake:** 10 min. per batch **oven:** 375°F
makes: 42 cookies

1	lemon
⅔	cup butter, softened
½	cup granulated sugar
2	eggs
1	teaspoon vanilla
1	teaspoon fennel seeds, crushed
2	cups all-purpose flour
	Coarse sugar
	Purchased lemon curd (optional)
	Finely crushed fennel seeds (optional)

1 Finely shred peel from the lemon; measure 2 teaspoons shredded peel. Squeeze juice from the lemon; measure 2 tablespoons juice. Set measured lemon peel and juice aside.

2 In a large mixing bowl beat butter with an electric mixer on medium to high speed for 30 seconds. Add the ½ cup sugar. Beat until combined, scraping sides of bowl occasionally. Beat in the 2 tablespoons lemon juice, the 2 teaspoons lemon peel, eggs, vanilla, and the 1 teaspoon fennel seeds until combined. Beat in as much of the flour as you can with the mixer. Stir in any remaining flour. Cover dough; chill about 4 hours or until easy to handle.

3 Preheat oven to 375°F. Shape dough into 1-inch balls. Roll balls in coarse sugar to coat. Place balls 1 inch apart on an ungreased cookie sheet. Using your thumb, make an indentation in the center of each cookie. Bake for 10 to 12 minutes or until edges are very light brown. Transfer to a wire rack; cool.

4 Fill cookie centers with lemon curd just before serving. If desired, sprinkle with additional crushed fennel seeds.

For a fun way to pretty up these candy-coated gems, drizzle them with white- or pink-tinted icing or sprinkle on chopped cherries or nuts before the candy coating sets up.

cherry-nut rum balls

prep: 1 hr. **stand:** 2 hr. **chill:** 15 min. **makes:** about 45 balls

¾ cup chopped dried tart cherries

¼ cup dark rum

2 cups finely crushed vanilla wafers (about 54)

¾ cup ground pecans, almonds, or walnuts

¼ cup powdered sugar

¼ cup butter, melted

2 tablespoons frozen orange juice concentrate, thawed

1⅔ cups white baking pieces

2 tablespoons shortening

1 In a small mixing bowl stir together cherries and rum; cover and let stand for 1 hour. Line two baking sheets with waxed paper; set aside.

2 In a large mixing bowl stir together crushed vanilla wafers, ground pecans, and powdered sugar. Add undrained cherry mixture, the melted butter, and orange juice concentrate; stir until combined. Shape wafer mixture into 1-inch balls. Place balls on the prepared baking sheets; let stand until dry (about 1 hour).

3 In a small heavy saucepan heat and stir baking pieces and shortening over medium-low heat until smooth. Remove from heat. Dip rum balls in mixture, turning to coat completely. Remove balls with fork, letting excess drip off; return to baking sheets. Drizzle with any remaining coating. Chill 15 minutes or until coating is set.

note: *Store as directed on page 16. Refrigerate for up to 1 month. Do not freeze.*

Dried cherries soaked in dark rum provide these no-bake confections with their signature rich yet tangy flavor.

Looking to make a good impression? Nothing works better than this buttery, citrus-scented shortbread.

shortbread with a citrus twist

prep: 30 min. bake: 15 min. per batch oven: 325°F makes: about 20 cookies

1¼ cups all-purpose flour
3 tablespoons sugar
1 tablespoon finely shredded orange peel
½ cup cold butter
Luster dust (optional)

1 Preheat oven to 325°F. In a medium bowl stir together flour, sugar, and orange peel. Using a pastry blender, cut in butter until mixture resembles fine crumbs. Form mixture into a ball and knead until smooth.

2 Shape dough into 1-inch balls. Place balls 1 inch apart on an ungreased cookie sheet. Using a floured cookie stamp, flatten balls until ¼ inch thick. Bake for 15 to 18 minutes or just until bottoms start to brown and centers are set. Transfer to a wire rack and let cool. If desired, use a small brush to brush designs on cookies with luster dust.

Halved pistachio nuts create an attractive garnish on these nut-filled cookies. To remove the unsightly brown skins, simply rub the shelled pistachios between your hands. Most of the skins should fall off, exposing the pretty bright green flesh.

pistachio balls

prep: 25 min. bake: 16 min. per batch oven: 325°F makes: about 48 cookies

½ cup blanched
   almonds, toasted
   (see tip, page 19)
¾ cup butter, softened
⅓ cup granulated sugar
1 tablespoon water
1 teaspoon vanilla
½ cups all-purpose flour
½ cup finely chopped
   pistachio nuts
   Halved pistachio nuts
   (optional)
   Powdered sugar

1 Place toasted almonds in a blender or food processor. Cover and blend or process until finely ground; set aside.

2 Preheat oven to 325°F. In a medium mixing bowl beat butter with an electric mixer on medium to high speed for 30 seconds. Add granulated sugar. Beat until combined, scraping sides of bowl occasionally. Beat in the water and vanilla until combined. Beat in as much of the flour as you can with the mixer. Stir in any remaining flour, the ground almonds, and chopped pistachios.

3 Roll dough into 1-inch balls. Place balls 1 inch apart on an ungreased cookie sheet. If desired, place a pistachio nut half on top of each ball.

4 Bake for 16 to 18 minutes or until bottoms are light brown. Transfer cookies to a wire rack and let cool. Sift powdered sugar over cooled cookies.

Spoonfuls of a rich, fluffy mascarpone cheese mixture fill these spiced cookie cones.

cardamom cream-filled snaps

prep: 40 min. **bake:** 5 min. per batch **stand:** 1 min. per batch **oven:** 350°F
makes: about 26 cookies

¼ cup packed brown
  sugar
3 tablespoons butter,
  melted
1 tablespoon light-color
  corn syrup
2 teaspoons rum,
  bourbon, or rum
  extract
⅓ cup all-purpose flour
¼ teaspoon ground
  cinnamon
¼ teaspoon ground
  nutmeg
½ of an 8-ounce
  container
  mascarpone cheese
  or ½ of an 8-ounce
  package cream
  cheese, softened
½ cup powdered sugar
1 teaspoon vanilla
¼ teaspoon ground
  cardamom
  Freshly grated
  nutmeg (optional)

1 Preheat oven to 350°F. Line a cookie sheet with foil. Grease foil; set aside. In a small bowl stir together brown sugar, butter, corn syrup, and rum. Stir in flour, cinnamon, and nutmeg until combined.

2 Drop batter by scant teaspoons 4 inches apart onto the prepared cookie sheet (do not bake more than four at a time); spread each mound of batter evenly until 1½ inches in diameter.

3 Bake for 5 to 6 minutes or until bubbly and golden. Let stand for 1 minute on cookie sheet. Using the end of a metal cone,* quickly shape cookies, one at a time, into small cone shapes. (If cookies harden before you can shape them, return them to the hot oven about 1 minute or until softened.) Cool on a wire rack.

4 For filling, in a small mixing bowl beat mascarpone cheese, powdered sugar, vanilla, and cardamom with an electric mixer on medium speed until mixture thickens slightly. Pipe or spoon a slightly rounded teaspoon of the cheese mixture into each cookie cone. If desired, dust cheese mixture with freshly grated nutmeg.

*The metal cones used to shape these cookies are available in kitchen specialty shops and by mail from baking supply catalogs.

note: *Store cookies in a single layer as directed on page 16. Refrigerate for up to 1 hour. Do not freeze.*

These deeply ridged shell-shape cookies look like a pastry-shop specialty, making them a real attention grabber on a party tray.

spiced chocolate tea cakes

prep: 25 min. bake: 10 min. per batch oven: 350°F makes: about 48 cookies

1½ cups all-purpose flour
¼ cup unsweetened cocoa powder
¼ teaspoon baking powder
¼ teaspoon ground nutmeg or ground cardamom
½ cup butter, softened
¾ cup sugar
1 egg yolk
⅓ cup milk
 Powdered sugar

1 Preheat oven to 350°F. In a small bowl stir together the flour, cocoa powder, baking powder, and nutmeg. Set aside.

2 In a large mixing bowl beat butter with an electric mixer on medium to high speed for 30 seconds. Add sugar. Beat until combined, scraping sides of bowl occasionally. Beat in egg yolk until combined. Add about half of the flour mixture and the milk; beat until combined. Beat or stir in the remaining flour mixture.

3 Place dough in a decorating bag fitted with a large (½ inch) open star tip. Pipe dough into 1½-inch shell shapes 2 inches apart on an ungreased cookie sheet, pulling the pastry bag toward you as you pipe. Bake for 10 to 12 minutes or until firm and bottoms are light brown. Transfer to a wire rack and let cool. Sift powdered sugar over cooled cookies before serving.

Top: **Cardamom Cream-Filled Snaps**
Bottom: **Spiced Chocolate Tea Cakes**

The flavors of lemon and ginger give these light, airy cookies a tangy yet spicy flavor that you'll love.

lemon-ginger meringues

prep: 1 hr. **bake:** 10 min. **stand:** 40 min. **oven:** 325°F
makes: about 32 cookies

2	egg whites
1	teaspoon lemon extract
⅛	teaspoon cream of tartar
⅛	teaspoon ground ginger
⅓	cup sugar

1 Place egg whites in a medium mixing bowl; let stand at room temperature for 30 minutes. Preheat oven to 325°F. Line two large cookie sheets with foil or parchment paper; set aside.

2 Add lemon extract, cream of tartar, and ginger to egg whites. Beat with an electric mixer on medium speed until soft peaks form (tips curl). Add the sugar, 1 tablespoon at a time, beating on high speed until stiff peaks form (tips stand straight).

3 Spoon egg white mixture into a decorating bag fitted with a large open star or round tip. Pipe 1-inch-diameter drops 1½ inches apart onto the prepared cookie sheets. (Or drop egg white mixture by rounded measuring teaspoons 1½ inches apart onto the prepared cookie sheets.)

4 Place both sheets on separate racks in the preheated oven. Bake for 10 minutes. Turn oven off. Let cookies dry in closed oven for 40 minutes. Transfer to a wire rack and let cool.

note: *Store cookies as directed on page 16. Do not freeze.*

Narrow drizzles of melted semisweet chocolate dress up these nutty spritz sticks.

hazelnut spritz

prep: 35 min. **bake:** 15 min./10 min. per batch **oven:** 325°F/350°F
makes: about 40 cookies

¾ cup hazelnuts (filberts)
¾ cup butter, softened
½ cup sugar
1 egg
1½ teaspoons vanilla
1½ cups all-purpose flour
2 ounces semisweet chocolate, cut up
¼ teaspoon shortening

1 Preheat oven to 325°F. Spread hazelnuts in a shallow baking pan. Bake about 15 minutes or until lightly toasted; cool. Rub hazelnuts in a kitchen towel to remove skins. Place nuts in a food processor. Cover and process until finely ground; set aside. Increase oven temperature to 350°F.

2 In a large mixing bowl beat butter with an electric mixer on medium to high speed for 30 seconds. Add sugar. Beat until combined, scraping sides of bowl occasionally. Beat in egg and vanilla until combined. Stir in flour and ground nuts.

3 Place dough in a decorating bag fitted with a large star tip. Pipe dough in 2½-inch strips onto an ungreased cookie sheet. Bake about 10 minutes or until edges begin to brown. Transfer to wire rack and let cool.

4 In a small saucepan heat and stir chocolate and shortening over low heat until smooth. Drizzle cooled cookies with melted chocolate. Let stand until set.

Finely ground toasted hazelnuts give these spritz cookies a delicious nutty flavor and moist texture.

Ground nutmeg, which is warm, sweet, and spicy, works delightfully as the star flavor in these elegant pressed cookies.

nutmeg spritz

prep: 25 min. **bake:** 8 min. per batch **oven:** 375°F **makes:** 84 cookies

1½ cups butter, softened
 1 cup granulated sugar
 1 teaspoon baking
    powder
 ¼ teaspoon ground
    nutmeg
 1 egg
 1 teaspoon vanilla
3½ cups all-purpose flour
 1 tablespoon fine
    sanding sugar or
    granulated sugar
    Dash ground nutmeg

1 Preheat oven to 375°F. In a large mixing bowl beat butter with an electric mixer on medium to high speed for 30 seconds. Add the 1 cup of sugar, baking powder, and the ¼ teaspoon nutmeg. Beat until combined, scraping sides of bowl occasionally. Beat in egg and vanilla until combined. Beat in as much flour as you can with the mixer. Stir in any remaining flour.

2 Force unchilled dough through a cookie press onto an ungreased cookie sheet. Space cookies 1 inch apart. In a small bowl stir together the 1 tablespoon sugar and dash nutmeg; sprinkle over cookies. Bake about 8 minutes or until edges are light brown. Transfer to a wire rack and let cool.

These simple tart-shape cookies incorporate cream cheese into the pastry, giving the finished product a hint of tartness.

pecan tassies

prep: 30 min. **bake:** 25 min. **oven:** 325°F **makes:** 24 tassies

½ cup butter, softened
 1 3-ounce package
    cream cheese,
    softened
 1 cup all-purpose flour
 1 egg
 ¾ cup packed brown
    sugar
 1 tablespoon butter,
    melted
 ⅔ cup coarsely chopped
    pecans

1 Preheat oven to 325°F. For pastry, in a mixing bowl beat the ½ cup butter and the cream cheese until combined. Stir in the flour. Press a rounded teaspoon of dough evenly into the bottom and up the sides of 24 ungreased 1¾-inch muffin cups. Set aside.

2 For filling, in a small bowl beat egg, brown sugar, and the melted butter until combined. Stir in pecans. Spoon about 1 heaping teaspoon of filling into each pastry-lined muffin cup. Bake for 25 to 30 minutes or until pastry is golden and filling is puffed. Cool slightly in pan. Carefully transfer to a wire rack and let cool.

Dried dates and apricots add a nice, chewy texture to the preserve filling in these tarts. The meringue topping creates a showstopping finish.

meringue-topped fruit tarts

prep: 35 min. **bake:** 25 min. **oven:** 350°F **makes:** 24 tarts

1¼	cups all-purpose flour
2	tablespoons packed brown sugar
⅓	cup butter
2	egg yolks
¼	cup dairy sour cream
½	teaspoon vanilla
½	cup snipped pitted dates
½	cup snipped dried apricots
⅓	cup apricot preserves or orange marmalade
2	tablespoons candied orange peel
⅓	cup dairy sour cream
1	egg white
¼	cup granulated sugar
¼	cup chopped walnuts

1 Preheat oven to 350°F. Grease twenty-four 1¾ inch muffin cups; set aside.

2 For pastry, in a medium mixing bowl stir together flour and brown sugar. Using a pastry blender, cut in butter until mixture resembles coarse crumbs. In a small bowl stir together egg yolks, the ¼ cup sour cream, and the vanilla; stir into flour mixture. Press a scant tablespoon of dough into the bottom and sides of each prepared muffin cup; set aside.

3 For fruit filling, stir together dates, apricots, preserves, orange peel, and the ⅓ cup sour cream. Spoon about 1 heaping teaspoon of filling into each pastry-lined muffin cup. Bake for 10 minutes.

4 Meanwhile, for meringue topping, in a small mixing bowl beat egg white on medium speed until soft peaks form (tips curl). Add sugar, 1 tablespoon at a time, beating until stiff peaks form (tips stand straight). Carefully spoon or pipe a small mound of meringue over partially baked fruit mixture in each muffin cup; sprinkle with walnuts. Bake 15 minutes more or until light brown. Cool slightly in pan. Transfer to a wire rack; cool.

note: *Store as directed on page 16. Refrigerate up to 3 days or freeze up to 1 month.*

These cookies get a cool, refreshing burst of flavor with peppermint extract. You can use spearmint extract, if you prefer.

peppermint stars

prep: 30 min. **bake:** 15 min. **stand:** 30 min. **oven:** 300°F **makes:** 45 cookies

2 egg whites
½ teaspoon vanilla
¼ teaspoon cream of tartar
¼ teaspoon peppermint extract
 Few drops red food coloring (optional)
½ cup sugar

1 Place egg whites in a medium mixing bowl; let stand at room temperature for 30 minutes. Preheat oven to 300°F. Line two large cookie sheets with parchment paper or foil; set aside.

2 Add vanilla and cream of tartar to egg whites. Beat with an electric mixer on medium speed until soft peaks form (tips curl). Beat in peppermint extract and, if desired, red food coloring. Add sugar, 2 tablespoons at a time, beating on medium speed until stiff peaks form (tips stand straight).

3 Spoon egg white mixture into a decorating bag fitted with a large star tip. Pipe 1½-inch-diameter mounds about 2 inches apart onto prepared cookie sheet. Bake for 15 minutes. Turn off oven. Let cookies dry in closed oven about 30 minutes. Transfer to a wire rack and let cool.

note: *Store as directed on page 16. Do not freeze.*

Crisp and minty, these piped meringue cookies are cool and refreshing to the palate.

If you don't have a pastry bag with a star tip, simply spoon the meringue mixture onto the cookie sheet. Make the freeform kisses as uniform in size as possible so they will fit together nicely.

meringue kiss sandwiches

prep: 50 min. **bake:** 15 min. per batch **oven:** 300°F **makes:** about 30 sandwich cookies

2 egg whites
½ teaspoon vanilla
⅛ teaspoon cream of tartar
Few drops red food coloring
⅔ cup sugar
2 ounces semisweet chocolate, melted

1 Place egg whites in a medium mixing bowl; let stand at room temperature for 30 minutes. Preheat oven to 300°F. Lightly grease a cookie sheet; set aside.

2 Add vanilla and cream of tartar to egg whites. Beat with an electric mixer on medium speed until soft peaks form (tips curl). Beat in food coloring. Add sugar, 1 tablespoon at a time, beating until stiff peaks form (tips stand straight).

3 Spoon egg white mixture into a decorating bag fitted with a large star tip. Pipe 1½-inch-diameter mounds about 2 inches apart onto prepared cookie sheet. Bake 15 minutes or until firm and bottoms are very light brown. Transfer to wire rack and let cool.

4 Spread about 1 teaspoon melted chocolate each on the flat sides of half of the meringues. Top with remaining meringues, flat sides down.

Chocolate-hazelnut spread is the key to the rich, nutty filling in these heavenly meringue desserts. You'll find the specialty ingredient near the peanut butter in larger supermarkets.

double chocolate-hazelnut meringues

prep: 50 min. **bake:** 20 min. **stand:** 1 hr. **oven:** 300°F
makes: 20 to 24 cookies

3	egg whites
⅓	cup powdered sugar
2	tablespoons unsweetened cocoa powder
¼	cup granulated sugar
¼	cup semisweet chocolate pieces (optional)
1	teaspoon shortening (optional)
20	to 24 whole hazelnuts (filberts)
⅓	to ½ cup purchased chocolate-hazelnut spread

1 Place egg whites in a medium mixing bowl; let stand at room temperature for 30 minutes. Preheat oven to 300°F. Line a large baking sheet with parchment paper; set aside. In a small bowl stir together powdered sugar and cocoa powder; set aside.

2 Beat egg whites with an electric mixer on high speed until soft peaks form (tips curl). Add granulated sugar, 1 tablespoon at a time, beating on high speed until stiff peaks form (tips stand straight). Gently fold in cocoa mixture. Spoon egg white mixture into a decorating bag fitted with a ¼-inch round tip. Pipe a 1- to 1¼-inch spiral onto prepared baking sheet; continue piping upward on outside edge to make spiral about 1 inch high. Repeat with remaining meringue mixture to make 20 to 24 cookies. Bake for 20 minutes. Turn off oven. Let cookies dry in the closed oven for 1 hour.

3 If desired, in a small saucepan heat and stir chocolate pieces and shortening over low heat until smooth. Dip each hazelnut halfway into melted chocolate; let excess drip off. Set nuts on waxed paper; let stand until set.

4 To serve, spoon about 1 teaspoon chocolate-hazelnut spread into each cooled meringue. Top each with a chocolate-dipped or plain hazelnut.

note: *Store unfilled cookies as directed on page 16. Store at room temperature up to a day or freeze up to a month. Fill meringues before serving.*

The subtle sweetness of unblanched almonds is a delightful contrast to the tart lime filling in these airy cookies.

almond-lime macaroons

prep: 50 min. **bake:** 10 min. **stand:** 30 min. **oven:** 300°F
makes: about 20 sandwich cookies

2	egg whites
1	tablespoon amaretto or ¼ teaspoon almond extract
½	teaspoon vanilla
¼	teaspoon cream of tartar
½	cup sugar
2	tablespoons all-purpose flour
1½	cups ground almonds
1	3-ounce package cream cheese, softened
¼	cup lime curd or lemon curd

1 Place egg whites in a medium mixing bowl; let stand at room temperature for 30 minutes. Preheat oven to 300°F. Line two large cookie sheets with parchment paper or foil; set aside.

2 Add amaretto, vanilla, and cream of tartar to egg whites. Beat with an electric mixer on high speed until soft peaks form (tips curl). Add the sugar, 1 tablespoon at a time, beating on high speed until stiff peaks form (tips stand straight). Beat in flour just until combined. Gently fold in almonds.

3 Spoon egg white mixture into a decorating bag fitted with a ½-inch round tip. Pipe 1-inch mounds 1½ inches apart on prepared cookie sheets.

4 Bake both sheets on separate racks 10 minutes or until set. Turn off oven; let cookies dry in closed oven for 30 minutes. Transfer to wire racks and let cool.

5 Up to 2 hours before serving, in a medium mixing bowl beat cream cheese with an electric mixer on medium speed for 30 seconds. Beat in curd until smooth. Spread on flat sides of half of the macaroons. Top with remaining macaroons, flat sides down.

The flavors of lemon and raspberry—always fast friends—play happily together in these tiny French sponge cakes. Savor their flavor with a steaming cup of raspberry tea.

lemony madeleines
with raspberry ganache

prep: 30 min. **bake:** 10 min. **stand:** 1 min. **oven:** 375°F **makes:** 24 cookies

2 eggs
½ cup sugar
½ cup butter, melted and cooled
½ teaspoon finely shredded lemon peel
1 tablespoon lemon juice
½ teaspoon vanilla
½ cup all-purpose flour
½ teaspoon baking powder
⅛ teaspoon baking soda
⅛ teaspoon salt
¼ cup finely chopped pecans, toasted (see tip, page 19)
1 recipe Raspberry Ganache

1 Preheat oven to 375°F. Grease and flour twenty-four 3-inch madeleine molds. Set aside. Separate eggs; place yolks and whites in separate bowls. Cover and chill egg whites until needed.

2 In a medium mixing bowl combine egg yolks and sugar. Beat with an electric mixer on medium to high speed for 30 seconds. Add butter, lemon peel, lemon juice, and vanilla. Beat on low speed until combined.

3 In a small bowl stir together flour, baking powder, baking soda, and salt. Sprinkle flour mixture over the egg yolk mixture; gently stir in. Stir in pecans. Lightly beat egg whites; gently fold into batter. Spoon batter into the prepared molds, filling each about half full.

4 Bake for 10 to 12 minutes or until edges are golden and tops spring back when lightly touched. Let stand for 1 minute in molds. Using the tip of a knife, loosen cookies from molds; invert onto a wire rack. Remove molds; cool cookies on wire rack.

5 When cookies are completely cool, use a soft brush to remove excess crumbs from cookies. Holding each cookie at an angle, dip halfway into Raspberry Ganache; place on waxed paper. Let stand until set.

raspberry ganache: *In a small saucepan heat ⅓ cup whipping cream over low heat just until boiling. Remove from heat. Add four raspberry-flavor tea bags. Let stand for 15 minutes. Remove tea bags from cream. Return cream to boiling. Remove from heat. Immediately add 4 ounces white chocolate baking squares (with cocoa butter), finely chopped. Stir until melted. Tint with red paste food coloring to desired color. Cool slightly before dipping cookies.*

Crisp meringues take a dip in melted chocolate for a flavor and texture combination that's truly spectacular.

hazelnut meringues

prep: 40 min. **bake:** 3 min. per batch **stand:** 45 min. **oven:** 300°F
makes: about 36 cookies

2   egg whites
½   teaspoon vanilla
¼   teaspoon cream of tartar
⅔   cup sugar
2   teaspoons hazelnut liqueur, crème de cacao, or your desired liqueur
    Whole hazelnuts (filberts)
½   cup milk chocolate pieces
2   teaspoons shortening

1 Place egg whites in a large bowl; let stand at room temperature for 30 minutes. Preheat oven to 300°F. Line a very large cookie sheet with parchment paper; set aside.

2 Add vanilla and cream of tartar to egg whites. Beat with an electric mixer on medium speed until soft peaks form (tips curl). Add sugar, 1 tablespoon at a time, beating on high speed until stiff peaks form (tips stand straight). Gently fold in liqueur.

3 Spoon egg white mixture into a decorating bag fitted with a large open star tip. Pipe 1½-inch-diameter stars about 1½ inches apart onto prepared cookie sheet. Press a hazelnut into the center of each star.

4 Bake for 3 minutes. Turn off oven. Let cookies dry in closed oven about 45 minutes or until crisp. Peel cookies from parchment paper.

5 In a small saucepan heat and stir chocolate pieces and shortening over low heat until smooth. Gently dip the bottom of each cookie into chocolate mixture; wipe off excess. Place dipped cookies, chocolate sides down,* on waxed paper. Let stand until set.

*If hazelnut falls out of cookie, use a small dab of chocolate to stick it back in place.

express

6

tre

These cookies live life in the fast lane, using store-bought mixes, ready-made dough, and quick techniques to get you in and out of the kitchen fast. And no one will guess you took shortcuts—these cookies are every bit as flavorful and attractive as those made from scratch.

ats

You can cut the chilling step in half by stashing the dough logs in the freezer for 30 minutes or until firm enough to slice.

peanut butter and chocolate
pinwheels

prep: 25 min. **chill:** 1 hr. **bake:** 8 min. per batch **oven:** 375°F **makes:** 60 cookies

1 18-ounce package refrigerated peanut butter cookie dough
¼ cup all-purpose flour
1 18-ounce package refrigerated sugar cookie dough
¼ cup unsweetened cocoa powder
½ cup finely chopped peanuts (optional)

1 In a large resealable bag knead together peanut butter cookie dough and flour until combined. Divide dough in half; set aside. In another large resealable bag knead together sugar cookie dough and cocoa powder until combined. Divide dough in half; set aside.

2 Between pieces of waxed paper roll out half of the peanut butter dough into a 12×6-inch rectangle. Repeat with half of the sugar cookie dough. Remove the top pieces of waxed paper from both doughs. Invert one rectangle on top of the other; press down gently to seal. Remove top piece of waxed paper. Tightly roll up from a long side. Repeat with remaining dough portions.

3 If desired, sprinkle half of the peanuts onto a piece of waxed paper. Roll one log in the peanuts. Wrap log in waxed paper or plastic wrap. Repeat with remaining dough and peanuts. Chill logs about 1 hour or until firm enough to slice.

4 Preheat oven to 375°F. Using a sharp knife, cut logs into ¼-inch slices. Place slices 2 inches apart on an ungreased cookie sheet. Bake for 8 to 10 minutes or until edges are firm. Transfer to a wire rack and let cool.

Peanut butter and chocolate complement each other in flavor and contrast each other in color. For this reason they're the perfect duo in these pretty swirl cookies.

A creamy, two-ingredient filling and purchased cookie dough are all that make up these peanut butter and chocolate delights.

simple fudge tarts

prep: 20 min. **bake:** 11 min. **stand:** 15 min. **oven:** 350°F **makes:** 24 tarts

½ of an 18-ounce package refrigerated peanut butter cookie dough

½ cup semisweet chocolate pieces

¼ cup sweetened condensed milk

1 Preheat oven to 350°F. Lightly grease twenty-four 1¾-inch muffin cups; set aside. For tart shells, cut cookie dough into six equal pieces. Cut each piece into four equal slices. Place each slice of dough in a prepared cup.

2 Bake about 9 minutes or until edges are light brown and dough is slightly firm but not set. Remove tart shells from oven. Gently press a shallow indentation into each tart shell with the back of a round ½-teaspoon measuring spoon. Bake about 2 minutes more or until the edges of tart shells are firm and light golden brown. Let stand in cups on a wire rack for 15 minutes. Carefully remove tart shells from cups. Cool completely on wire rack.

3 For filling, in a small saucepan heat and stir chocolate pieces and sweetened condensed milk over medium heat until smooth. Spoon a generous teaspoon of filling into each cooled tart shell. Let stand until filling is set.

Purchased sugar cookies work as well as freshly baked ones in this recipe. Orange liqueur lends a wonderful citrus flavor.

no-bake orange balls

prep: 20 min. **stand:** 2 hr. **makes:** 40 balls

2   cups finely crushed
    crisp unfrosted
    sugar cookies
    (about 8 ounces)
1   cup toasted
    hazelnuts* (filberts),
    almonds, or pecans,
    finely chopped
    (see tip, page 19)
1⅓ cups powdered sugar
¼   cup light-color corn
    syrup
2   tablespoons orange
    liqueur
2   tablespoons butter,
    melted
2   teaspoons orange
    edible glitter
    (optional)

1 In a large bowl combine crushed cookies, nuts, 1 cup of the powdered sugar, the corn syrup, liqueur, and butter. Stir with a wooden spoon until well mixed. Shape dough into 1-inch balls.

2 In a shallow dish stir together the remaining ⅓ cup powdered sugar and, if desired, the edible glitter. Roll balls in powdered sugar mixture; cover. Let stand for 2 hours. Roll balls again in powdered sugar mixture to coat.

*After toasting hazelnuts, place the warm nuts in a clean kitchen towel. Rub nuts with the towel to remove loose skins

*Once you have tried the chocolate
and peppermint combination, try
substituting crushed cherry-flavor
hard candies for the peppermints.*

chocolate-
peppermint
sandwiches

start to finish: 15 min. makes: 22 sandwich cookies

½ cup canned vanilla or
    chocolate frosting
3 tablespoons finely
    crushed striped
    peppermint candies
44 chocolate wafers

1 In a small mixing bowl stir together
frosting and crushed candy. Spread
1 level teaspoon frosting mixture on flat sides
of half of the chocolate wafers. Top with the
remaining chocolate wafers, flat sides down.

note: *Store cookies as directed on page 10.
Refrigerate for up to 3 days. Do not freeze.*

Cranberry juice icing accentuates the flavor of the dried cranberries in these peanutty drop cookies.

peanut butter cranberry drops

prep: 25 min. **bake:** 10 min. per batch **stand:** 1 min. per batch **oven:** 375°F
makes: about 36 cookies

1   18-ounce package
    refrigerated peanut
    butter cookie dough
1   cup chopped peanuts
½   cup dried cranberries
2   tablespoons all-
    purpose flour
2   cups powdered sugar
3   tablespoons
    cranberry juice

1 Preheat oven to 375°F. In a large resealable plastic bag combine cookie dough, peanuts, cranberries, and flour; seal bag. Using your hands, squeeze and knead dough mixture together in the bag until combined. Remove dough from bag. Drop dough by rounded teaspoons 2 inches apart onto an ungreased cookie sheet. Bake for 10 to 12 minutes or until cookies are golden brown around edges. Let stand for 1 minute on cookie sheet. Transfer to a wire rack and let cool slightly.

2 For icing, in a small bowl stir together powdered sugar and cranberry juice until smooth. Spoon icing over warm cookies. Cool cookies completely on wire rack.

Gingerbread cookie dough is available only during the holidays.
Sugar cookie dough makes a tasty alternative.

cherry-almond chews

prep: 10 min. bake: 8 min. per batch oven: 375°F makes: about 36 cookies

1   18-ounce package
       refrigerated
       gingerbread cookie
       dough or sugar
       cookie dough
¾   cup dried tart red
       cherries
½   cup chopped toasted
       almonds (see tip,
       page 19)

1 Preheat oven to 375°F. In a large resealable
plastic bag combine cookie dough,
cherries, and almonds; seal bag. Using your
hands, squeeze and knead dough mixture
together in the bag until combined. Remove
dough from bag. Drop by teaspoons 2 inches
apart onto an ungreased cookie sheet. Bake
for 8 to 10 minutes or until light brown around
edges. Transfer to a wire rack and let cool.

Celebrate the last day of school by munching down the alphabet.
Filled with strawberry preserves and cream cheese, the sandwich
cookies disappear almost as fast as schoolbooks.

abc sandwich cookies

start to finish: 15 min. makes: 16 sandwich cookies

2   ounces cream cheese
       (tub-style)
1   tablespoon
       strawberry
       preserves
       Red food coloring
       (optional)
32 plain and/or chocolate
       shortbread alphabet
       cookies*

1 In a small bowl stir together the cream
cheese and strawberry preserves. If
desired, stir in one drop of red food coloring.
Spread cream cheese mixture onto the flat
sides of half of the cookies. Top with the
remaining cookies, flat sides down.

✻ If desired, substitute purchased regular
shortbread cookies, vanilla wafers, or soft sugar
cookies for the alphabet cookies.

note: *Store cookies as directed on page 16.*
Refrigerate for up to 3 days. Do not freeze.

Toasty almonds and tangy cherries bring
out-of-this-world flavor to these quick treats.

Cherry-Almond Chews

express **treats**

Cinnamon, cardamom, and nutmeg give these chocolate-kissed cookies a warm, spicy bite.

chocolate chip kisses

prep: 15 min. **bake:** 8 min. per batch **oven:** 375°F **makes:** 32 cookies

1   18-ounce package
     refrigerated
     chocolate chip
     cookie dough
1   teaspoon ground
     cinnamon
¼   teaspoon ground
     cardamom
¼   teaspoon ground
     nutmeg
32 milk chocolate kisses,
     unwrapped
     Powdered sugar

1 Preheat oven to 375°F. In a large resealable plastic bag combine cookie dough, cinnamon, cardamom, and nutmeg; seal bag. Using your hands, squeeze and knead dough mixture together in the bag until combined. Remove dough from bag.

2 Shape dough into 1-inch balls. Place 2 inches apart on an ungreased cookie sheet. Bake for 8 to 10 minutes or until edges are light brown. Immediately press a kiss into the center of each cookie. Transfer to a wire rack and let cool. Sift powdered sugar over cooled cookies.

These fun-to-eat cookies are baked onto crafts sticks (also called frozen-pop sticks). Purchase the wooden sticks at crafts stores.

easy flower cookies on sticks

prep: 40 min. **bake:** 8 min. per batch **stand:** 1 min. per batch **oven:** 375°F
makes: 20 cookies

1   18-ounce package refrigerated sugar cookie dough
¼   cup all-purpose flour
¼   cup fine or coarse colored sugar(s)
20   4½-inch crafts sticks
20   milk chocolate stars

1 Preheat oven to 375°F. Knead together cookie dough and flour until combined. Shape dough into one hundred ¾-inch balls. Roll balls in colored sugar(s) to coat. For each flower cookie, place a crafts stick on an ungreased cookie sheet. Place five balls in a circle around the tip of the stick so their sides are just touching. Leave 2 inches between flower cookies on cookie sheet.

2 Bake for 8 to 10 minutes or until edges are light brown. Immediately press a chocolate star into the center of each flower shape. Let stand for 1 minute on cookie sheet. Transfer to a wire rack and let cool.

Enlist the help of kids for these fun-to-make goodies.
A bit of dough play and chocolate stars result in a colorful bouquet of flower cookies.

These chubby rounds are a textural delight—chunky, chewy, smooth, and creamy all at once. When the kids aren't looking, pop one of the plump morsels into your mouth for breakfast!

oatmeal-apricot cookies

prep: 25 min. **bake:** 10 min. per batch **stand:** 1 min. per batch **oven:** 375°F
makes: about 36 cookies

½ cup butter, softened
2 eggs
1 tablespoon water
1 17.5- to 22-ounce package oatmeal-raisin cookie mix
½ cup snipped dried apricots
⅓ cup flaked coconut
1 recipe Cream Cheese Frosting
Snipped dried apricots

1 Preheat oven to 375°F. Line a cookie sheet with parchment paper; set aside. In a large bowl stir together butter, eggs, and the water. Stir in dry cookie mix until mixture is combined. Gently stir in the ½ cup apricots and the coconut.

2 Drop dough by rounded teaspoons 2 inches apart onto the prepared cookie sheet. Bake for 10 to 12 minutes or until edges are golden brown. Let stand for 1 minute on cookie sheet. Transfer cookies to a wire rack and let cool.

3 Frost cooled cookies with Cream Cheese Frosting. Sprinkle with additional apricots.

note: *Store cookies in a single layer as directed on page 16. Refrigerate for up to 3 days. Do not freeze.*

cream cheese frosting: *In a medium mixing bowl combine two 3-ounce packages softened cream cheese, ¼ cup softened butter, and 2 teaspoons vanilla. Beat with an electric mixer on medium speed until combined. Gradually add 4 cups powdered sugar, beating until smooth and frosting is of spreading consistency.*

Creamy eggnog—the silky smooth, decadently delicious wintertime drink—becomes a picture-perfect sandwich cookie.

hazelnut and eggnog
cookie sandwiches

prep: 50 min. **bake:** 10 min. per batch **oven:** 350°F **makes:** about 36 sandwich cookies

1   cup butter, softened
1   egg
1   19-ounce package
    sugar cookie mix
¼   teaspoon ground
    nutmeg
½   cup finely chopped
    hazelnuts (filberts)
1   teaspoon finely
    shredded orange
    peel
    Colored sugar or
    granulated sugar
1   recipe Eggnog Filling

1 Preheat oven to 350°F. In a large mixing bowl beat the butter with an electric mixer on medium to high speed for 30 seconds. Beat in egg and 1 cup of the dry cookie mix just until combined. Gradually beat in as much of the remaining cookie mix as you can with the mixer. Stir in nutmeg, hazelnuts, orange peel, and any remaining cookie mix. If necessary, knead gently to combine. Divide dough in half.

2 On a lightly floured surface, roll half of the dough at a time until ⅛ to ¼ inch thick. Using a 1¾-inch scalloped cookie cutter, cut out dough. Place cutouts 1 inch apart on an ungreased cookie sheet. Sprinkle with colored sugar. Bake about 10 minutes or just until edges begin to brown. Transfer to a wire rack and let cool.

3 Spread about 1 teaspoon of the Eggnog Filling each on flat sides of half of the cookies. Top with remaining cookies, placing the flat sides down.

note: *Store filled cookies as directed on page 16. Store at room temperature for up to 2 days or freeze for up to 1 month.*

eggnog filling: *In a small bowl stir together 2 cups powdered sugar, 2 tablespoons softened butter, and enough eggnog (2 to 3 tablespoons) to make a mixture of spreading consistency.*

Finely shredded lemon peel gives these delicate, chewy cookies a delightful citrus flavor.

lemon and poppy seed
cornmeal cookies

prep: 20 min. bake: 7 min. per batch oven: 375°F makes: 60 cookies

1 8.5-ounce package
   corn muffin mix
½ cup quick-cooking
   rolled oats
¼ cup sugar
2 tablespoons butter,
   softened
2 teaspoons milk
1 egg, lightly beaten
1 teaspoon finely
   shredded lemon
   peel
1 teaspoon poppy
   seeds

1 Preheat oven to 375°F. Line a cookie sheet with parchment paper; set aside. In a medium bowl stir together muffin mix, oats, sugar, butter, milk, egg, lemon peel, and poppy seeds until combined.

2 Drop dough by level measuring teaspoons 2 inches apart onto the prepared cookie sheet. Bake for 7 to 9 minutes or until light brown. Transfer to a wire rack and let cool.

Start with packaged cookies—your favorite crunchy or soft variety of spicy bites—and top them with a buttery lemon curd mixture.

lemon snaps

start to finish: 25 min. makes: 30 cookies

¼ cup lemon curd or
   orange curd
2 tablespoons butter,
   softened
¾ cup powdered sugar
30 purchased
   gingersnap cookies
Toasted coconut
   (see tip, page 19) or
   finely chopped nuts

1 In a medium mixing bowl beat curd and butter with an electric mixer on medium to high speed for 30 seconds. Add powdered sugar. Beat until smooth and fluffy. Spread mixture on top of cookies. Sprinkle with coconut or nuts.

note: *Store cookies in a single layer as directed on page 16. Do not freeze.*

Chili powder, an unexpected but delicious match with chocolate, is the surprise ingredient that transforms devil's food cake mix into flavorful cookies with a nut-crunch texture.

chili powder and
pecan crackles

prep: 25 min. bake: 8 min. per batch stand: 1 min. per batch oven: 375°F
makes: about 20 cookies

1	9-ounce package devil's food cake mix
2	tablespoons unsweetened cocoa powder
¼	to ½ teaspoon ground chipotle chili powder
1	egg, lightly beaten
1	tablespoon butter, softened
2	tablespoons milk
½	cup finely chopped pecans

1 Preheat oven to 375°F. In a medium bowl stir together cake mix, cocoa powder, chipotle chili powder, egg, and butter until moistened (dough will be stiff).

2 Shape dough into 1-inch balls. Place milk in a shallow dish. Place nuts in another shallow dish. Dip balls in milk, then roll in nuts to coat. Place 2 inches apart on an ungreased cookie sheet. Bake for 8 to 9 minutes or until tops are crackled. Let stand for 1 minute on cookie sheet. Transfer cookies to a wire rack and let cool.

Showy and oozing with cherry-flecked marshmallow crème, these candy-dipped cookie sandwiches are a hit with kids.

easy'mallow cookies

start to finish: 30 min. **makes:** 16 sandwich cookies

16 maraschino cherries
  with stems
⅓ cup marshmallow
  crème
1 tablespoon
  finely chopped
  maraschino cherries
32 vanilla wafer cookies
4 ounces vanilla-flavor
  candy coating

1 Place cherries with stems on paper towels; drain well. Line a cookie sheet with waxed paper; set aside. In a small bowl stir together marshmallow crème and chopped cherries. Spread 1 level teaspoon marshmallow mixture each on flat sides of half of the vanilla wafers. Top with the remaining vanilla wafers, flat sides down. Place on prepared baking sheet.

2 In a small saucepan heat and stir candy coating over medium-low heat until smooth. Cool slightly.

3 Dip cookies halfway into the melted candy coating. Return to baking sheet. Holding a cherry by the stem, dip bottom of cherry into the melted candy coating. Place cherry on top of candy-coated side of one cookie. Hold for several seconds or just until set. Repeat with remaining cherries and cookies. Let stand until coating is completely set.

note: *Store cookies in a single layer as directed on page 16. Refrigerate for up to 2 days. Do not freeze.*

These no-bake cookies get a pleasant crunch with crisp rice cereal. If the mixture is sticky, coat the scoop with nonstick cooking spray.

fry-pan cookies

start to finish: 20 min. **makes:** 48 cookies

1	tablespoon butter
½	cup sugar
2	eggs, beaten
1½	cups chopped pitted dates
1	teaspoon vanilla
2½	cups crisp rice cereal
½	cup chopped nuts
3	cups flaked coconut

1 In a large skillet melt the butter over low heat. In a small bowl stir together the sugar and eggs. Add to skillet along with the dates and vanilla. Cook and stir over low heat about 5 minutes or until thick. Remove from heat; stir in cereal and nuts.

2 Place coconut in a shallow dish. Using a cookie scoop or small ice cream scoop (about 1¼-inch diameter), drop dough into coconut. Roll to coat. Refrigerate until firm.

note: *Store cookies as directed on page 16. Refrigerate for up to 1 week. Serve at room temperature. Do not freeze.*

With their fancy two-chocolate coating, these cherry-filled cookies look like yummy bonbons.

chocolate-cherry dips

prep: 30 min. chill: 30 min. stand: 30 min. makes: 30 cookies

½	of an 8-ounce package cream cheese, softened
½	cup powdered sugar
½	cup finely chopped, drained maraschino cherries
¼	teaspoon almond extract
60	vanilla wafers
12	ounces chocolate-flavor candy coating, coarsely chopped
2	teaspoons shortening
2	ounces vanilla-flavor candy coating, coarsely chopped
½	teaspoon shortening

1 For filling, in a medium mixing bowl beat cream cheese and powdered sugar with an electric mixer on medium speed until combined. Stir in cherries and almond extract. Spread filling on the flat sides of half of the vanilla wafers. Top with remaining wafers, flat sides down. Cover and chill about 30 minutes or until filling is firm.

2 In a small saucepan heat and stir chocolate-flavor candy coating and the 2 teaspoons shortening over low heat until smooth. Remove from heat. Using a fork, dip cookies into the chocolate to completely cover. Allow excess to drip off. Place cookies on waxed paper until chocolate sets.

3 In another small saucepan heat and stir vanilla-flavor candy coating and the ½ teaspoon shortening over low heat until smooth. Drizzle over dipped cookies. Let stand 30 minutes or until set.

note: *Store coated cookies as directed on page 16. Refrigerate for up to 3 days. Do not freeze.*

Whip up a batch of these beauties for a party and guests will think you've spent hours in the kitchen.

If you have time, toast the macadamia nuts to enhance the flavor of these no-bake treats.

cranberry-vanilla
cereal drops

prep: 25 min. **stand:** 1 hr. **makes:** 60 drops

3 cups cranberry-vanilla crunch cereal

1½ cups tiny marshmallows

1½ cups macadamia nuts, toasted, if desired (see tip, page 19) or mixed nuts, chopped

½ cup dried cranberries

1¼ pounds vanilla-flavor candy coating, chopped

1 Line two cookie sheets with waxed paper; set aside. In a large microwave-safe bowl stir together cereal, marshmallows, nuts, and cranberries; set aside.

2 In a medium saucepan heat and stir candy coating over low heat until smooth. Pour melted candy coating over cereal mixture; stir gently to coat. Quickly drop cereal mixture by rounded teaspoons onto the prepared cookie sheets. (If mixture sets up in the bowl, microwave on 100 percent power [high] about 30 seconds or just until mixture is soft enough to drop by rounded teaspoons; stir.) Let cookies stand about 1 hour or until set.

note: *Store cookies as directed on page 16. Do not freeze.*

Browned Butter Icing—the luscious, caramelized frosting so popular in the 1950s—makes a stellar comeback on top of these spicy cutouts.

pumpkin-spiced star cookies

prep: 30 min. **bake:** 8 min. per batch **stand:** 1 min. per batch **oven:** 375°F
makes: 36 large stars or 72 small stars

1 17.5-ounce package
sugar cookie mix
⅓ cup butter, melted
1 egg
2 teaspoons pumpkin
pie spice
½ teaspoon ground
nutmeg
1 recipe Browned
Butter Icing

1 Preheat oven to 375°F. In a large bowl combine dry cookie mix, butter, egg, pumpkin pie spice, and nutmeg. Stir with a wooden spoon until a stiff dough forms. If necessary, gently knead to combine.

2 On a lightly floured surface, roll dough until ¼ inch thick. Using a 1½- to 2½-inch star-shape cookie cutter, cut out dough. Place cutouts 1 inch apart on an ungreased cookie sheet. Bake about 8 minutes or until bottoms are light brown. Let stand for 1 minute on cookie sheet. Transfer to a wire rack and let cool. Drizzle cooled cookies with Browned Butter Icing.

note: *Store cookies in a single layer as directed on page 16. Refrigerate for up to 3 days. Do not freeze.*

browned butter icing: *In a small saucepan heat and stir 2 tablespoons butter over medium-low heat about 15 minutes or until butter turns golden brown. (Do not scorch.) Remove from heat. Whisk in 2 cups powdered sugar, 2 tablespoons milk, and 1 teaspoon vanilla. Immediately drizzle over cooled cookies (icing will harden quickly).*

Lovers of German chocolate cake adore this quick and easy rendition, created in its honor.

crispy chocolate chewies

prep: 20 min. bake: 10 min. per batch stand: 1 min. per batch oven: 350°F
makes: about 40 cookies

1   18.25-ounce package
    German chocolate
    cake mix
½   cup butter, melted
¼   cup milk
1   egg, lightly beaten
¾   cup crisp rice cereal
¼   cup flaked coconut
1   cup purchased
    coconut-pecan
    frosting
    Flaked coconut,
    toasted (see tip,
    page 19)

1 Preheat oven to 350°F. In a large mixing bowl combine cake mix, melted butter, milk, and egg. Beat with an electric mixer on low speed until well mixed. Stir in cereal and the ¼ cup coconut. Drop dough by rounded teaspoons 2 inches apart onto an ungreased cookie sheet.

2 Bake for 10 to 12 minutes or until bottoms are light brown. Let stand for 1 minute on cookie sheet. Transfer to a wire rack and let cool. Frost cooled cookies with the coconut-pecan frosting. Sprinkle with toasted coconut.

Chocolate-hazelnut spread serves as the frosting on these thumbprint cookies. Look for it near the peanut butter in larger supermarkets.

chocolate chip thumbprints

prep: 25 min. **bake:** 10 min. per batch **oven:** 375°F **makes:** about 30 cookies

1   18-ounce package refrigerated chocolate chip cookie dough
⅓   cup all-purpose flour
¾   cup finely chopped hazelnuts (filberts) or almonds
¼   cup milk
½   cup purchased chocolate-hazelnut spread
     Candy sprinkles

1 Preheat oven to 375°F. Knead together cookie dough and flour until combined. Shape 1-tablespoon pieces of dough into balls. Place nuts in a shallow dish. Place milk in another shallow dish. Roll balls in milk, then in nuts to coat. Place balls 2 inches apart on an ungreased cookie sheet. Using your thumb, make an indentation in the center of each cookie. Bake for 10 to 12 minutes or until light brown. Transfer to a wire rack and let cool.

2 Just before serving, fill cookie centers with chocolate-hazelnut spread. Sprinkle with candy sprinkles.

note: *Store cookies as directed on page 16. Refrigerate for up to 3 days.*

These pretty fix-ups begin with ready-made dough, get rolled in chopped nuts, and finish with a flourish of colorful sprinkles.

Cut these extra-rich, fudgy bars into 64 bite-size pieces—8 horizontal and 8 vertical cuts—to satisfy lots of chocolate lovers.

peanut butter **brownie** bites

prep: 15 min. **bake:** 30 min. **stand:** 1 hr. **oven:** 350°F **makes:** 64 bars

1 18- to 21-ounce package fudge brownie mix

½ cup chopped peanuts (optional)

1 3-ounce package cream cheese, softened

1 cup creamy peanut butter

2 tablespoons milk

1 egg yolk

1 16-ounce can chocolate frosting Chopped peanuts (optional)

1 Preheat oven to 350°F. Lightly grease a 13×9×2-inch baking pan; set aside. Prepare brownie mix according to package directions. If desired, stir in the ½ cup peanuts. Spread batter in prepared pan.

2 In a medium mixing bowl beat cream cheese, ½ cup of the peanut butter, the milk, and egg yolk with an electric mixer on medium speed until smooth. Spoon mixture into a decorating bag fitted with a small round tip (or spoon it into a resealable plastic bag and snip off one corner of the bag). Pipe mixture over brownie batter in pan. Bake for 30 minutes. Cool in pan on wire rack for 1 hour.

3 In a medium mixing bowl stir together the frosting and the remaining ½ cup peanut butter. Spread over cooled brownies. If desired, sprinkle with additional peanuts. Cut bars into small squares.

Purchased piecrust, in place of the traditional phyllo dough, provides the flaky layers in these nut-filled wedge cookies.

shortcut **baklava**

prep: 15 min. **bake:** 25 min. **cool:** 10 min. **oven:** 375°F **makes:** 16 wedges

1   15-ounce package rolled refrigerated unbaked piecrust (2 crusts)
1   cup finely chopped walnuts
⅓   cup sugar
3   tablespoons honey
1   teaspoon ground cinnamon
1   teaspoon lemon juice
1   teaspoon water
Cinnamon-sugar*

1 Preheat oven to 375°F. Let piecrusts stand according to package directions. Unroll; place one crust on an ungreased cookie sheet. For filling, in a bowl stir together walnuts, sugar, 2 tablespoons of the honey, the cinnamon, and lemon juice. Spread over piecrust on cookie sheet, leaving about a ½-inch border. Top with remaining piecrust. Press edges with the tines of a fork to seal. Prick top of piecrust all over. In a bowl stir together the remaining 1 tablespoon honey and the water; brush over top crust. Sprinkle with cinnamon-sugar.

2 Bake 25 minutes or until golden. Cool on cookie sheet on a wire rack for 10 minutes. Cut into 16 wedges. Cool completely.

* If you don't have cinnamon-sugar, in a small bowl stir together 2 teaspoons sugar and ¼ teaspoon ground cinnamon.

Packaged biscuit mix, which supplies the flour, shortening, leavening, and salt for this recipe, is the secret to its quick prep.

blonde brownies

prep: 15 min. **bake:** 25 min. **oven:** 350°F **makes:** 16 brownies

2   cup packaged biscuit mix
¾   cup packed brown sugar
½   cup white baking pieces
½   cup chopped almonds, toasted (see tip, page 19)
½   cup butter, melted
1   egg, beaten
1   teaspoon vanilla

1 Preheat oven to 350°F. Grease an 8×8×2-inch baking pan; set aside. In a large bowl stir together biscuit mix, brown sugar, white baking pieces, and almonds. Add melted butter, egg, and vanilla. Stir until combined. Spread batter into prepared pan.

2 Bake about 25 minutes or until golden brown around edges and center is almost set. Cool in pan on a wire rack. Cut into bars.

Chocolate chip cookie dough provides the base for a luscious topping of caramel, coconut, and honey-roasted nuts.

caramel-nut chocolate chip bars

prep: 15 min. **bake:** 35 min. **oven:** 350°F **makes:** 36 bars

1   18-ounce package refrigerated chocolate chip cookie dough

2   cups quick-cooking rolled oats

1½   cups chopped honey-roasted peanuts or cashews

1   14-ounce can sweetened condensed milk (1¼ cups)

¼   cup caramel ice cream topping

½   cup flaked coconut

1 Preheat oven to 350°F. Line a 13×9×2-inch baking pan with foil, extending the foil over the edges of pan. Grease foil; set aside. In a large resealable plastic bag combine cookie dough, oats, and ½ cup of the nuts; seal bag. Using your hands, squeeze and knead dough mixture together in the bag until combined. Remove dough from bag and pat evenly into prepared pan. Bake for 15 minutes.

2 Meanwhile, in a small bowl stir together sweetened condensed milk and ice cream topping. Drizzle mixture over partially baked bars. Sprinkle bars evenly with the remaining 1 cup nuts and the coconut. Bake for 20 to 25 minutes more or until the top is golden. Cool in pan on a wire rack. Use the foil to lift bars from pan. Cut bars into squares.

Bananas, peanut butter, and chocolate make an outstanding flavor combo. Purchased frosting gives the bars a fabulous finish.

banana chocolate chip bars

prep: 20 min. **bake:** 25 min. **oven:** 350°F **makes:** 36 bars

1 18-ounce package refrigerated peanut butter cookie dough
1 cup rolled oats
½ cup mashed banana
½ cup miniature semisweet chocolate pieces
½ cup chopped peanuts
1 16-ounce can chocolate and/or vanilla frosting

1 Preheat oven to 350°F. Lightly grease a 13×9×2-inch baking pan; set aside. In a large resealable plastic bag combine cookie dough, oats, banana, chocolate pieces, and peanuts; seal bag. Using your hands, squeeze and knead dough mixture together in the bag until combined. Remove dough from bag and pat evenly into prepared pan.

2 Bake about 25 minutes or until bars are golden brown. Cool completely in pan on a wire rack. Frost bars with desired frosting or use one-half can chocolate frosting and one-half can of vanilla frosting and swirl frostings together on bars.

Panforte, a fruitcake-like pastry dense with nuts and candied fruit, becomes an easy bar cookie with the help of ready-made sugar cookie dough.

quick **panforte** bars

prep: 15 min. **bake:** 30 min. **oven:** 350°F **makes:** 32 bars

1   18-ounce package refrigerated sugar cookie dough

1   10- to 12-ounce can unsalted mixed nuts, coarsely chopped

½   cup butterscotch-flavor pieces or semisweet chocolate pieces

½   cup mixed dried fruit bits, coarsely chopped dried apricots, or golden raisins (optional)

½   cup flaked coconut

1 Preheat oven to 350°F. Lightly grease a 9×9×2-inch baking pan; set aside.

2 In a large resealable plastic bag combine cookie dough, nuts, butterscotch pieces, and, if desired, dried fruit; seal bag. Using your hands, squeeze and knead dough mixture together in the bag until combined. Remove dough from bag and pat evenly into the prepared pan. Sprinkle with coconut; lightly press into dough.

3 Bake about 30 minutes or until a wooden toothpick inserted near the center comes out clean. Cool completely in pan on a wire rack. Cut into bars.

A tasty combo of crunchy nuts, rich butterscotch pieces, and chewy dried fruits tops a sugar cookie crust for flavorful fruitcake-like bars.

Two always-popular desserts—chocolate chip cookies and cheesecake—combine with a hint of coffee in these irresistible bar cookies.

mocha-chocolate chip
cheesecake bars

prep: 20 min. **bake:** 20 min. **oven:** 350°F **makes:** 36 bars

1   18-ounce package
    refrigerated
    chocolate chip
    cookie dough
1   8-ounce package
    cream cheese or
    reduced-fat cream
    cheese (Neufchatel),
    softened
⅓   cup sugar
1   egg
1   tablespoon instant
    coffee crystals
1   teaspoon vanilla
1   teaspoon water
½   cup miniature
    semisweet
    chocolate pieces

1 Preheat oven to 350°F. Crumble the cookie dough into a 13×9×2-inch baking pan. Press evenly over bottom of pan; set aside.

2 In a medium bowl combine the cream cheese, sugar, and egg. Beat by hand until smooth. In a small bowl stir together the coffee crystals, vanilla, and water until crystals are dissolved. Stir coffee mixture into cream cheese mixture. Spread evenly over dough; sprinkle with chocolate pieces.

3 Bake about 20 minutes or until mixture is completely set. Cool in pan on a wire rack. Cut into bars.

In India cardamom is known as the grain of paradise. Sample its woodsy, sweet flavor in these moist, fruit-flecked bars.

cranberry-date bars

prep: 15 min. bake: 25 min. oven: 350°F makes: 20 bars

1⅔ cups packaged
biscuit mix
¼ teaspoon ground
cardamom
½ cup chopped dates
½ cup dried cranberries
½ cup chopped pecans
½ cup butter, softened
¾ cup granulated sugar
1 egg
1 teaspoon vanilla
Powdered sugar

1 Preheat oven to 350°F. Line an 8×8×2-inch square baking pan with foil, extending the foil over the edges of pan. Grease the foil; set aside.

2 In a medium bowl stir together biscuit mix and cardamom. Stir in dates, cranberries, and pecans. Set aside. In a large mixing bowl beat butter with an electric mixer on medium to high speed for 30 seconds. Add granulated sugar and beat until combined, scraping sides of bowl occasionally. Beat in egg and vanilla until combined. Beat in biscuit mix mixture just until combined. Spread dough evenly in the prepared pan.

3 Bake for 25 to 30 minutes or until top is lightly browned and a wooden toothpick inserted in center comes out clean. Cool in pan on a wire rack. Use the foil to lift bars from pan. Cut bars into squares. Dust with powdered sugar.

*If you could bake your favorite coffeehouse beverage in a pan,
it might taste like these treats. Take a plateful to work and you'll
become known as the barista of baking!*

toffee-coffee brownies

prep: 25 min. **bake:** 35 min. **oven:** 350°F **makes:** 20 brownies

1   19.8- or 21-ounce
     package brownie
     mix
½   cup toffee pieces
2   to 3 tablespoons
     instant espresso
     powder or instant
     coffee crystals
¾   cup canned vanilla
     frosting
1   tablespoon Irish
     cream liqueur or
     coffee liqueur
¼   cup toffee pieces

1 Preheat oven to 350°F. Line a 9×9×2-inch baking pan with foil, extending the foil over the edges of the pan. Grease foil; set aside. Prepare brownie mix according to package directions. Stir in the ½ cup toffee pieces and the espresso powder. Spread batter in prepared pan.

2 Bake for 35 minutes. Cool in pan on a wire rack. Use the foil to lift brownies from pan. In a small bowl stir together vanilla frosting and liqueur. Spread frosting mixture over cooled brownies. Sprinkle with the ¼ cup toffee pieces. Cut into squares.

note: *Store frosted brownies in a single layer as directed on page 16. Refrigerate for up to 3 days. Do not freeze.*

*With five layers and five ingredients, these bars are as easy
to make as they are delicious.*

five-layer bars

prep: 10 min. **bake:** 37 min. **oven:** 350°F **makes:** 30 bars

2   13-ounce packages
     soft coconut
     macaroon cookies
     (32 cookies)
¾   cup sweetened
     condensed milk
¾   cup semisweet
     chocolate pieces
¾   cup raisins or dried
     cranberries
1   cup chopped peanuts

1 Preheat oven to 350°F. Arrange cookies in the bottom of a greased 13×9×2-inch baking pan. Press cookies together to form a crust. Bake for 12 minutes. Drizzle crust evenly with condensed milk. Sprinkle with chocolate pieces, raisins, and peanuts. Bake about 25 minutes more or until edges are light brown. Cool in pan on wire rack. Cut into bars.

note: *Store bars as directed on page 16. Do not freeze.*

This treasure trove of recipes from around the world boasts exciting flavors that stem from time-honored heritage. Spanning the globe from Europe to Mexico, these cookies turn everyday ingredients into international delicacies.

worldly bit

Orange peel and almond extract are the secret ingredients that make these bars incredibly flavorful.

italian cheese bars

prep: 20 min. bake: 25 min. stand: 1 hr. chill: 2 hr. oven: 350°F
makes: 20 bars

½ cup butter
1¼ cups finely crushed graham crackers (about 18)
1 15-ounce container low-fat ricotta cheese
1 egg
¼ cup sugar
2 tablespoons all-purpose flour
2 teaspoons finely shredded orange peel
1 teaspoon almond extract
½ cup sliced almonds or chopped hazelnuts
⅓ cup chopped candied cherries
⅓ cup golden raisins

1 Preheat oven to 350°F. Melt butter in a 9×9×2-inch baking pan in the oven (about 6 minutes). Remove from oven. Stir crushed crackers into melted butter; press mixture firmly and evenly onto bottom of pan using a wooden spoon. Set aside.

2 In a food processor or blender combine the ricotta cheese, egg, sugar, flour, orange peel, and almond extract; process or blend until smooth. Carefully spread cheese mixture over crumb mixture in pan. In a small bowl stir together the almonds, cherries, and raisins; sprinkle over cheese layer. Bake for 25 to 30 minutes or until edges are puffed and golden. Let stand in pan on a wire rack for 1 hour. Cover; chill for 2 hours. Cut into bars.

Cookies unite the world in celebration.
No other food embraces family customs so
endearingly, so simply, and so completely.

Serve these brandy-flavored cookies, which are Welsh in origin, with a steaming cup of English tea.

brandy snaps

prep: 40 min. bake: 9 min. per batch stand: 2 min. per batch oven: 350°F
makes: about 30 cookies

½ cup sugar
½ cup butter
⅓ cup golden syrup*
   or dark-color corn
   syrup
¾ cup all-purpose flour
½ teaspoon ground
   ginger
1 tablespoon brandy
   Whipped cream
   (optional)

1 Preheat oven to 350°F. Line a cookie sheet with foil. Lightly grease the foil; set aside.

2 In a medium saucepan heat and stir sugar, butter, and golden syrup over low heat until butter melts; remove from heat. In a small bowl stir together flour and ginger; add to butter mixture, mixing well. Stir in brandy.

3 Drop batter by rounded teaspoons 3 to 4 inches apart onto the prepared cookie sheet. (Bake only three cookies at a time.)

4 Bake for 9 to 10 minutes or until bubbly and golden brown. Let stand 2 minutes on cookie sheet. Quickly invert cookies onto another cookie sheet; wrap each cookie around the greased handle of a wooden spoon or a metal cone. When cookie is set, transfer to a wire rack and let cool. If desired, fill cooled cookies with whipped cream.

✱Golden syrup is available in specialty stores and larger supermarkets.

*Spicy, bite-size cookies have been a favorite of German cooks
to serve at special occasions for centuries.*

pfeffernuesse

prep: 30 min. chill: 1 hr. bake: 10 min. per batch oven: 350°F
makes: 240 small cookies

⅓ cup molasses
¼ cup butter
2 cups all-purpose flour
¼ cup packed brown
   sugar
¾ teaspoon ground
   cinnamon
½ teaspoon baking soda
¼ teaspoon ground
   cardamom
¼ teaspoon ground
   allspice
⅛ teaspoon black
   pepper
1 egg, beaten

1 In a large saucepan combine molasses and butter. Heat and stir over low heat until butter melts. Remove from heat. Pour into a large bowl and cool to room temperature. In medium bowl stir together the flour, brown sugar, cinnamon, baking soda, cardamom, allspice, and pepper; set aside.

2 Stir egg into cooled molasses mixture. Gradually stir in flour mixture until combined, kneading in the last of the flour mixture by hand, if necessary. Cover and chill dough about 1 hour or until easy to handle.

3 Preheat oven to 350°F. Divide dough into 12 portions. On a lightly floured surface, roll each portion of the dough into a 10-inch-long rope. Cut ropes into ½-inch pieces. Place pieces ½ inch apart in an ungreased shallow baking pan. Bake about 10 minutes or until edges are firm and bottoms are light brown. Transfer to paper towels and let cool.

These Italian gems are not as overly sweet as their name suggests. They're a great treat to serve to company or simply to have around the house.

almond sweets

prep: 35 min. bake: 12 min. per batch oven: 350°F makes: about 60 cookies

3 cups all-purpose flour
1 tablespoon baking powder
½ teaspoon salt
3 eggs
½ cup granulated sugar
½ cup cooking oil
1 teaspoon vanilla
1 recipe Almond Icing
  Colored sugar (optional)

1 Preheat oven to 350°F. Lightly grease a cookie sheet; set aside. In a medium bowl stir together flour, baking powder, and salt; set aside. In a large mixing bowl beat eggs, granulated sugar, oil, and vanilla with an electric mixer on medium speed until combined. Beat in as much of the flour mixture as you can with the mixer. Stir in any remaining flour mixture.

2 Shape dough into 1-inch balls. Place balls 2 inches apart on the prepared cookie sheet. Bake for 12 to 15 minutes or until bottoms are light brown. Transfer to a wire rack and let cool. Frost cooled cookies with Almond Icing. If desired, sprinkle wet icing with colored sugar. Let stand until set.

almond icing: *In a medium bowl stir together 1 cup powdered sugar, ½ teaspoon almond extract, and enough milk (1 to 2 tablespoons) to make an icing of spreading consistency.*

These tender pastries originated in Eastern European Jewish communities but have become even more popular in America. The fruit-nut filling makes them anything but ordinary.

cherry-nut rugalach

prep: 30 min. bake: 15 min. per batch oven: 350°F makes: 36 cookies

1 cup dried tart cherries and/or dried apricots, finely snipped
¼ cup sugar
¼ cup water
2 teaspoons kirsch (optional)
½ cup finely chopped walnuts
1 cup butter, softened
1 3-ounce package cream cheese, softened
2 cups all-purpose flour
2 tablespoons sugar
Milk
Sugar (optional)

1 Preheat oven to 350°F. Grease a cookie sheet; set aside. For filling, in a small saucepan stir together dried fruit, the ¼ cup sugar, and the water. Bring to boiling. Reduce heat and simmer, uncovered, for 5 minutes or until thickened, stirring occasionally. Remove from heat. If desired, stir in kirsch; let cool. Stir in walnuts.

2 For pastry, in a medium mixing bowl beat butter and cream cheese with an electric mixer on medium speed for 30 seconds. Add flour and the 2 tablespoons sugar; beat on low speed until crumbly; knead until dough forms a ball. Divide dough into thirds.

3 On a lightly floured surface, roll one-third of the dough into a 9-inch circle. Spread the dough with one-third of the cooled filling. Cut circle into 12 wedges. Beginning at the wide end of each wedge, roll up dough. Place cookies, tip sides down, about 2 inches apart on the prepared cookie sheet. Repeat with remaining dough and filling. Brush cookies with milk and, if desired, sprinkle with additional sugar. Bake 15 minutes or until golden brown. Transfer to a wire rack; cool.

Using a rosette iron is simple—just place the thin batter in a shallow dish, gently dip the preheated iron into the batter, and fry until golden.

swedish cardamom rosettes

start to finish: 40 min. makes: about 60 rosettes

1 tablespoon powdered
   sugar
1½ teaspoons ground
   cardamom
2 eggs, beaten
1 cup all-purpose flour
1 cup milk
1 tablespoon
   granulated sugar
1 teaspoon vanilla
¼ teaspoon salt
   Cooking oil for deep-
   fat frying

1 In a small bowl stir together powdered sugar and ½ teaspoon of the cardamom; set aside. In a medium mixing bowl combine eggs, flour, milk, granulated sugar, the remaining 1 teaspoon cardamom, the vanilla, and salt. Beat with an electric mixer on medium speed until mixture is smooth. Transfer batter to a shallow bowl or platter.

2 Heat a rosette iron in deep hot oil (365°F). Dip hot iron into batter for 2 to 3 seconds. (Batter should come only three-fourths of the way up the sides of the iron.) Dip iron into hot oil for 30 to 45 seconds or until cookie is golden. Lift out iron and tip slightly to drain. With a fork, push rosette off iron onto a wire rack set over paper towels. Repeat with remaining batter, reheating rosette iron in oil each time before dipping into the batter. Sift powdered sugar mixture over cooled rosettes.

note: *Store cookies as directed on page 16. Store at room temperature for up to 1 day.*

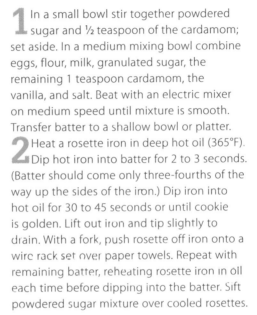

The combination of ground almonds and amaretto boosts the intense almond flavor of these chewy, Italian-style morsels.

amaretti

prep: 1 hr. bake: 10 min. stand: 30 min. oven: 300°F
makes: about 20 sandwich cookies

2   egg whites
1   tablespoon amaretto
      or ¼ teaspoon
      almond extract
½   teaspoon vanilla
¼   teaspoon cream of
      tartar
½   cup sugar
2   tablespoons all-
      purpose flour
1½   cups ground almonds
½   cup semisweet
      chocolate pieces
1   teaspoon shortening

1 Place egg whites in a large mixing bowl; let stand at room temperature for 30 minutes. Preheat oven to 300°F. Line two cookie sheets with parchment paper or foil; set aside.

2 Add amaretto, vanilla, and cream of tartar to egg whites. Beat with an electric mixer on medium speed until soft peaks form (tips curl). Add sugar, 1 tablespoon at a time, beating on high speed until stiff peaks form (tips stand straight) and sugar is almost dissolved. Beat in flour just until combined. Fold in almonds.

3 Spoon egg white mixture into a decorating bag fitted with a ½-inch round tip. Pipe into 1-inch mounds 1½ inches apart onto the prepared cookie sheets. (Or place the egg white mixture in a resealable plastic bag; snip off a corner of bag and pipe as above.)

4 Bake about 10 minutes or until set. Turn off oven. Let cookies stand in closed oven for 30 minutes. Peel cookies from paper. Transfer to a wire rack and let cool.

5 In a small saucepan heat and stir chocolate pieces and shortening over low heat until smooth. Spread the flat sides of half of the cookies with ¼ teaspoon each chocolate mixture. Top with remaining cookies, flat sides down. Let stand until set.

Filled with maple flavor and whole wheat goodness, this dough is a little sticky, so use damp hands to roll the chilled dough into balls.

canadian maple-date cookies

prep: 40 min. chill: 2 hr. bake: 10 min. per batch oven: 350°F makes: 60 cookies

3½ cups whole wheat flour
1 teaspoon baking powder
1 teaspoon baking soda
1 teaspoon ground cinnamon
¼ teaspoon salt
1 cup butter, softened
½ cup packed brown sugar
1 cup pure maple syrup
3 eggs
1 teaspoon vanilla
1 cup coarsely chopped pecans
1 cup chopped pitted dates
Raw sugar

1 In a medium bowl stir together flour, baking powder, baking soda, cinnamon, and salt; set aside. In a large mixing bowl beat butter with an electric mixer on medium to high speed for 30 seconds. Add brown sugar. Beat until combined, scraping sides of bowl occasionally. Beat in maple syrup, eggs, and vanilla until combined (mixture will appear curdled). Beat in as much of the flour mixture as you can with the mixer. Stir in any remaining flour mixture, the pecans, and dates. Cover and chill dough about 2 hours or until easy to handle.

2 Preheat oven to 350°F. Line a cookie sheet with foil or parchment paper; set aside. Shape dough into 1-inch balls. Roll balls in raw sugar to coat. Place balls 1 inch apart on the prepared cookie sheet. Bake about 10 minutes or until edges are firm. Transfer to a wire rack and let cool.

Before transferring these diamond-shape cookies to a cooling rack, let them sit on the cookie sheet for a couple of minutes to prevent the delicate layers from sliding.

german biberli

prep: 45 min. chill: 2 hr. bake: 8 min. per batch stand: 2 min. per batch
oven: 350°F makes: about 30 cookies

½ cup packed brown
sugar
⅓ cup honey
2 cups all-purpose flour
1½ teaspoons ground
cinnamon
½ teaspoon baking
powder
½ teaspoon ground
nutmeg
1 egg
¼ cup butter, softened
½ cup mixed candied
fruits and peels,
finely chopped
½ cup chopped slivered
almonds
1 7- to 8-ounce package
marzipan
Powdered sugar
1 recipe Lemon Glaze
Chopped almonds
(optional)
Maraschino cherries
(optional)

1 In a small saucepan heat and stir brown sugar and honey over low heat until sugar is dissolved. Remove from heat; cool slightly. In a medium bowl stir together flour, cinnamon, baking powder, and nutmeg; set aside. In a large mixing bowl combine honey mixture, egg, and butter. Beat on low speed until combined. Stir in candied fruits and peels and the ½ cup almonds. Stir in flour mixture. Cover dough; chill for 2 hours or until easy to handle.

2 In a bowl knead marzipan with your hands until softened; shape into a ball and flatten slightly. Sprinkle with powdered sugar. Roll ball between two sheets of waxed paper into an 8-inch square; set aside.

3 Preheat oven to 350°F. Lightly grease a cookie sheet; set aside. On a lightly floured surface, roll dough into a 16×8-inch rectangle. Place marzipan square on half of rectangle; carefully lift the unlayered dough portion and fold it over the marzipan. Using a rolling pin, roll layered dough until ½ inch thick (about a 9-inch square). Using a long, sharp knife, cut square into diamonds about 3 inches long and 1½ inches wide. Place diamonds 1 inch apart on the prepared cookie sheet.

4 Bake 8 minutes or until golden. Let stand 2 minutes on cookie sheet. Transfer to a wire rack. While still warm, brush cookies with Lemon Glaze. If desired, sprinkle with chopped almonds and top with a maraschino cherry. Let stand until set.

lemon glaze: *Stir together ½ cup powdered sugar, 1 teaspoon melted butter, ¼ teaspoon finely shredded lemon peel, and 1 teaspoon lemon juice. Stir in water, 1 teaspoon at a time, until glaze is of brushing consistency.*

These festive cookie sandwiches hail from New Zealand. Candied cherries in the dough and in the frosting make them fruity and sweet.

yo-yos

prep: 25 min. bake: 8 min. per batch oven: 375°F
makes: 24 sandwich cookies

½	cup butter, softened
½	cup sugar
1	egg
1	teaspoon vanilla
1¾	cups all-purpose flour
¾	cup finely chopped red and/or green candied cherries
	Sugar (optional)
1	recipe Cherry Frosting

1 Preheat oven to 375°F. In a large mixing bowl beat butter with an electric mixer on medium to high speed for 30 seconds. Add the ½ cup sugar. Beat until combined, scraping sides of bowl occasionally. Beat in egg and vanilla until combined. Beat in as much flour as you can with the mixer. Stir in any remaining flour and the candied cherries.

2 Shape dough into 1-inch balls. Place balls 2 inches apart on an ungreased cookie sheet. Using the tines of a fork, flatten balls slightly in a crisscross pattern. If desired, sprinkle cookies with sugar. Bake about 8 minutes or until edges are golden. Transfer to a wire rack and let cool.

3 Spread Cherry Frosting on flat sides of half of the cookies. Top with remaining cookies, flat sides down.

cherry frosting: *In a medium mixing bowl beat a 3-ounce package of softened cream cheese with an electric mixer on medium speed until fluffy. Gradually beat in 1 cup powdered sugar. Beat in ¼ teaspoon vanilla. Beat in 1 cup additional powdered sugar to make a frosting of spreading consistency. Stir in ¼ cup finely chopped red or green candied cherries.*

Generously topped with powdered sugar, these buttery confections look as if they have been dusted with snow. Remember to remove the spicy cloves before eating.

greek kourabiedes

prep: 45 min. bake: 12 min. per batch oven: 325°F makes: about 75 cookies

1 cup butter, softened
⅔ cup powdered sugar
½ teaspoon baking powder
1 egg yolk
2 tablespoons brandy or orange juice
½ teaspoon vanilla
2¼ cups all-purpose flour
⅔ cup finely chopped almonds or walnuts, toasted (see tip, page 19)
Whole cloves
Powdered sugar

1 Preheat oven to 325°F. In a large mixing bowl beat butter with an electric mixer on medium to high speed for 30 seconds. Add the ⅔ cup powdered sugar and the baking powder. Beat until combined, scraping sides of bowl occasionally. Beat in egg yolk, brandy, and vanilla until combined. Beat in as much of the flour as you can with the mixer. Stir in any remaining flour and the nuts.

2 Shape dough into 1-inch balls. Place balls 1 inch apart on an ungreased cookie sheet. Insert the stem end of a whole clove into the center of each cookie.

3 Bake about 12 minutes or until bottoms are light brown. Transfer to a wire rack and let cool. Sift powdered sugar over tops of cooled cookies. Remove and discard cloves before eating cookies.

Peek into the cookie jars of other cultures and you'll discover favorites that have been around for centuries.

You may have seen these spice cookies in the shape of windmills; in Germany, the Netherlands, and Denmark they come in many other shapes. Look for cookie molds in specialty cooking shops or mail order catalogs.

speculaas

prep: 45 min. chill: 1 hr. bake: 8 min. per batch stand: 1 min. per batch
oven: 350°F makes: about 8 (6-inch) or 48 (2- to 2½-inch) cookies

½ cup butter, softened
¾ cup packed brown sugar
¾ teaspoon ground cinnamon
½ teaspoon baking powder
¼ teaspoon ground nutmeg
¼ teaspoon ground cloves
⅛ teaspoon salt
1 egg yolk
1 tablespoon milk
1⅓ cups all-purpose flour
3 tablespoons finely chopped blanched almonds (optional)
1 recipe Powdered Sugar Glaze (optional)

powdered sugar glaze: In a bowl stir together 1½ cups powdered sugar and 4 teaspoons milk. Stir in additional milk, 1 teaspoon at a time, to make a glaze of piping consistency.

1 In a large mixing bowl beat butter with an electric mixer on medium to high speed for 30 seconds. Add brown sugar, cinnamon, baking powder, nutmeg, cloves, and salt. Beat until combined, scraping sides of bowl occasionally. Beat in egg yolk and milk until combined. Beat in as much of the flour as you can with the mixer. Stir in any remaining flour and, if desired, the almonds. Divide dough in half. Cover and chill dough about 1 hour or until easy to handle.

2 Preheat oven to 350°F. Lightly grease a cookie sheet; set aside. Lightly oil a cookie mold. Press a small amount of dough into the prepared cookie mold. Unmold dough onto the prepared cookie sheet. If cookie does not unmold easily, tap the mold on the counter to release the dough. (Or on a lightly floured surface, roll one half of the dough at a time until ⅛ inch thick. Using desired cookie cutters, cut out dough.) Place cookies 1 inch apart on the prepared cookie sheet.

3 Bake for 8 to 10 minutes or until edges are golden. Let stand for 1 minute on cookie sheet. Transfer to a wire rack and let cool. If desired, decorate cooled cookies with Powdered Sugar Glaze.

Don't strive for a perfect appearance in these south-of-the-border treats—the more handcrafted they look, the better.

mexican sugar cookies

prep: 30 min. chill: 1 hr. bake: 14 min. per batch oven: 350°F
makes: 24 cookies

3 cups all-purpose flour
2 teaspoons baking
   powder
1 teaspoon anise seeds,
   crushed
¾ teaspoon ground
   cinnamon
¼ teaspoon salt
1 cup lard or
   shortening
1 cup granulated sugar
1 egg
4 tablespoons milk
3 tablespoons brandy
   or apple juice
   Yellow food coloring
⅓ cup granulated or
   coarse sugar

1 In a medium bowl stir together flour, baking powder, anise seeds, ¼ teaspoon of the cinnamon, and the salt; set aside. In a large mixing bowl beat lard with an electric mixer on medium to high speed for 30 seconds. Gradually beat in the 1 cup granulated sugar; beat until fluffy. Beat in egg and 2 tablespoons of the milk until combined. Alternately add the flour mixture and brandy, beating well after each addition.

2 In a small bowl stir together one-fourth of the dough and a few drops yellow food coloring until combined. Cover and chill doughs about 1 hour or until easy to handle.

3 Preheat oven to 350°F. On a lightly floured surface, roll white dough until ¼ inch thick. Using a 2½-inch snowflake- or flower-shape cookie cutter, cut out dough. Place cutouts 1 inch apart on an ungreased cookie sheet. On a lightly floured surface, roll yellow dough until ¼ inch thick. Using a 1½-inch star-shape cookie cutter, cut out dough. Place yellow stars in centers of snowflakes or flowers. Brush cookies with the remaining 2 tablespoons milk. In a small bowl stir together the ⅓ cup granulated sugar and the remaining ½ teaspoon cinnamon; sprinkle over cookies. Bake about 14 minutes or until edges are light golden brown. Transfer to a wire rack; cool.

If you choose to drizzle white chocolate onto these cookies, be sure to use baking squares that contain cocoa butter for the best flavor.

french pistachio buttercreams

prep: 35 min. chill: 1 hr./40 min. bake: 8 min. per batch oven: 350°F
makes: about 30 sandwich cookies

1½ cups all-purpose flour
½ teaspoon salt
1 cup unsalted butter, softened
1 cup powdered sugar
1 egg
Granulated sugar
1 teaspoon rum, cognac, or milk
6 ounces semisweet chocolate pieces or white baking squares, melted
½ cup pistachio nuts, chopped

1 In a small bowl stir together flour and salt; set aside. In a medium mixing bowl beat ¾ cup of the butter and ½ cup of the powdered sugar with an electric mixer on medium to high speed until combined. Beat in egg until combined. Beat in flour mixture on low speed just until combined. Cover and chill dough about 1 hour or until easy to handle.

2 Preheat oven to 350°F. Shape dough into ¾-inch balls. Place balls 2 inches apart on an ungreased cookie sheet. Using the bottom of a glass dipped in granulated sugar, flatten balls to 1½-inch circles. Bake about 8 minutes or until bottoms are light brown. Transfer to a wire rack and let cool.

3 Meanwhile, for filling, in a small mixing bowl beat the remaining ½ cup powdered sugar, the remaining ¼ cup butter, and the rum with an electric mixer on medium to high speed until combined.

4 To assemble cookies, spread filling on the flat sides of half of the cookies. Top with the remaining cookies, flat sides down. Chill cookies about 30 minutes or until filling sets. Drizzle or spread melted chocolate on tops of cookies and sprinkle with pistachio nuts. Chill about 10 minutes or until chocolate sets.

In Switzerland honey serves as a popular sweetener for baked goods. Cookies made with honey, such as these Swiss treats, tend to be chewier than those made with all sugar.

leckerle

prep: 30 min. bake: 10 min. per batch oven: 350°F makes: about 60 cookies

2½	cups all-purpose flour
1	cup sugar
1	cup unblanched almonds, finely chopped
¼	cup candied orange peel, finely chopped
¼	cup candied lemon peel, finely chopped
1	teaspoon baking powder
1	teaspoon ground cinnamon
½	teaspoon ground nutmeg
¼	teaspoon ground cloves
¾	cup honey
2	tablespoons kirsch or brandy
1	egg, beaten
1	recipe Citrus Glaze

1 Preheat oven to 350°F. Grease a cookie sheet; set aside. In a large mixing bowl stir together flour, sugar, almonds, candied peels, baking powder, cinnamon, nutmeg, and cloves. Make a well in the center of the flour mixture. Add honey, kirsch, and the beaten egg. Stir and knead the dough until it forms a ball. Divide dough in half.

2 On a lightly floured surface, roll half of the dough at a time until ¼ inch thick. Cut dough into 2½×1-inch strips. Place strips 1 inch apart on the prepared cookie sheet. Bake about 10 minutes or until golden brown. Transfer to a wire rack and let cool. While still warm, brush cookies with Citrus Glaze.

citrus glaze: *In a small bowl stir together 1 cup powdered sugar, ½ teaspoon finely shredded lemon or orange peel, and 2 teaspoons lemon or orange juice. Add enough water (2 to 3 teaspoons) to make a glaze of brushing consistency.*

Inspired by ischler krapferl—an Austrian sandwich cookie made with two different nut doughs—these cookies made with a spice dough and a plain dough get more delicious with a few days' aging.

ischl tarts

prep: 1½ hr. chill: 1 hr. bake: 8 min. per batch oven: 375°F
makes: 18 to 20 sandwich cookies

½	cup butter
1	cup powdered sugar
2	egg yolks
2	teaspoons vanilla
¼	teaspoon ground cinnamon
¼	teaspoon salt
⅛	teaspoon ground cloves
1	cup all-purpose flour
½	cup butter, softened
1¼	cups all-purpose flour
½	cup seedless red raspberry and/or apricot preserves
	Powdered sugar

1 For the spice dough, in a small saucepan heat the ½ cup butter over medium heat until butter turns golden brown (about 12 minutes). Remove from heat. Pour into a mixing bowl; chill until butter just resolidifies but is still soft. Beat on medium to high speed 30 seconds. Add ½ cup of the powdered sugar, 1 of the egg yolks, 1 teaspoon of the vanilla, the cinnamon, ⅛ teaspoon of the salt, and the cloves. Beat until combined, scraping sides of bowl occasionally. Beat in as much of the 1 cup flour as you can with the mixer. Stir in any remaining flour. Cover and chill dough about 1 hour or until easy to handle.

2 Meanwhile, for plain dough, in a mixing bowl beat softened butter on medium to high speed for 30 seconds. Add remaining ½ cup powdered sugar, remaining egg yolk, vanilla, and salt. Beat until combined, scraping sides of bowl occasionally. Beat in as much of the 1¼ cups flour as you can with the mixer. Stir in any remaining flour. Cover and chill dough about 1 hour or until easy to handle.

3 Preheat oven to 375°F. On a lightly floured surface, roll spice dough to ⅛ inch thick. Using 2½- to 3-inch scalloped cookie cutters, cut out dough. Repeat with plain dough to make matching shapes. Using ½-inch cookie cutters, cut 3 to 5 shapes in a pattern from each plain-dough cutout (do not cut pattern shapes in spice dough). Discard or reroll small cutouts. Place cutouts 1 inch apart on an ungreased cookie sheet.

4 Bake about 8 minutes or until edges are light brown. Transfer to a wire rack and let cool. Up to 4 hours before serving, spread about 1 teaspoon preserves on the bottom of each spice cookie. Top with plain cookies, bottom sides down. Just before serving, sift powdered sugar over tops.

Orange-flower water, which is used to flavor these cookies, is a distillation of bitter orange blossoms used in Middle Eastern cooking.

middle eastern ghraybeh

prep: 30 min. bake: 12 min. per batch oven: 325°F makes: 24 cookies

1   cup butter
2   cups all-purpose flour
1   cup sifted powdered
     sugar
2   tablespoons milk
1   tablespoon orange-
     flower water* or
     rose water or
     1 teaspoon vanilla
12 blanched almonds,
     halved lengthwise
     and/or chopped
     pistachios

1 Preheat oven to 325°F. To clarify butter, in a small saucepan melt butter over low heat without stirring. Skim off solids that float to the surface; discard. Pour the clear layer into a measuring cup; discard the milky bottom layer. You should have about ¾ cup clarified butter.

2 In a medium mixing bowl stir together clarified butter, the flour, powdered sugar, milk, and orange-flower water.

3 Divide dough in half. Divide each half into 12 portions. Roll each portion into a ½-inch-thick rope about 5 inches long. Place ropes on an ungreased cookie sheet. Form ropes into S and/or O shapes. Place an almond half and/or chopped pistachios on top of each shape. Bake for 12 minutes or until bottoms are light brown. Transfer to a wire rack; cool.

*Look for orange-flower water in the liquor department of larger supermarkets or in specialty food stores.

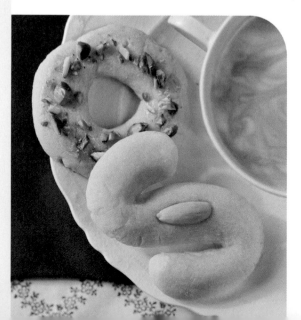

A pizza cutter makes quick work of cutting the long ropes of dough into bite-size pieces.

danish pebbernodder

prep: 1 hr. **chill:** 2 hr. **bake:** 10 min. per batch **oven:** 375°F **makes:** 6 cups of bite-size cookies

½ cup granulated sugar
½ cup mild-flavor molasses
2 tablespoons butter
1 egg, lightly beaten
¼ teaspoon baking powder
¼ teaspoon baking soda
¼ teaspoon ground ginger
¼ teaspoon vanilla
⅛ teaspoon salt
⅛ teaspoon ground cinnamon
⅛ teaspoon ground cardamom
⅛ teaspoon ground cloves
Several drops anise extract or ⅛ teaspoon crushed anise seeds
Dash black pepper
2 cups all-purpose flour
Powdered sugar

1 In a large saucepan combine granulated sugar, molasses, and butter. Heat and stir over medium-high heat until mixture boils. Remove from heat; let stand at room temperature for 30 minutes.

2 Stir the egg, baking powder, baking soda, ginger, vanilla, salt, cinnamon, cardamom, cloves, anise extract, and pepper into the sugar mixture. Stir in flour until combined. Cover and chill dough about 2 hours or until easy to handle.

3 Preheat oven to 375°F. Lightly grease cookie sheet; set aside. Divide dough into 12 equal portions. On a surface lightly coated with powdered sugar, roll each portion of the dough into a ½-inch-thick rope about 10 inches long. Cut ropes into ½-inch pieces. Place pieces 1 inch apart on the prepared cookie sheet.

4 Bake about 10 minutes or until bottoms are light brown. Transfer to paper towels and let cool.

The dough for this traditional favorite is stiff and sticky,
but it readily rolls out into ropes on a well-floured surface.

norwegian **kringla**

prep: 40 min. bake: 8 min. per batch oven: 350°F
makes: about 48 cookies

3¾ cups all-purpose flour
2 teaspoons baking powder
½ teaspoon baking soda
½ teaspoon salt
3 egg yolks, lightly beaten
1¼ cups granulated sugar
½ cup milk
¼ cup dairy sour cream
1 tablespoon butter, melted
¼ teaspoon anise extract or ½ teaspoon vanilla
1 egg white (optional)
1 tablespoon water (optional)
Raw sugar or sifted powdered sugar (optional)

1 Preheat oven to 350°F. Lightly grease a cookie sheet; set aside. In a medium bowl stir together flour, baking powder, baking soda, and salt; set aside.

2 In a large mixing bowl stir together egg yolks, granulated sugar, milk, sour cream, butter, and anise extract until combined. Using a wooden spoon, stir in flour mixture until combined (dough will be stiff and sticky).

3 On a well-floured surface, drop 1 rounded tablespoon of dough. Roll dough into a 5-inch-long rope. On the prepared cookie sheet, shape rope into a ring, crossing it over itself about 1 inch from ends. Repeat with remaining dough, placing rings 2 inches apart on cookie sheet. If desired, in a small bowl beat together egg white and the water. Brush over rings and sprinkle with raw sugar.

4 Bake about 8 minutes or until light golden. Transfer to a wire rack and let cool.

A Canadian specialty, these no-bake bars include a heavenly mixture of graham crackers, nuts, coconut, and chocolate.

nanaimo bars

prep: 30 min. chill: 1 hr./2 hr. makes: 25 bars

½ cup butter
¼ cup granulated sugar
¼ cup unsweetened
   cocoa powder
1 egg, beaten
1 teaspoon vanilla
2 cups graham
   cracker crumbs
   (36 crackers)
1 cup flaked coconut
½ cup chopped nuts
¼ cup butter, softened
¼ cup half-and-half,
   light cream, or milk
3 tablespoons vanilla
   custard mix (half
   of a 2.9-ounce
   package)
2 cups powdered sugar
6 ounces semisweet
   chocolate, cut up
4 teaspoons butter

1 For crust, in a saucepan combine the ½ cup butter, granulated sugar, cocoa powder, egg, and vanilla. Cook and stir over medium-low heat until butter melts and mixture just starts to bubble. Remove from heat. Stir in graham cracker crumbs, coconut, and nuts. Press crumb mixture onto the bottom of a 9×9×2-inch baking pan. Set aside.

2 For filling, in a medium mixing bowl beat the ¼ cup softened butter, half-and-half, and vanilla custard mix with an electric mixer on medium speed until combined. Beat in powdered sugar until light in texture. Carefully spread filling evenly over crust. Cover and chill bars about 1 hour or until firm.

3 For topping, heat and stir chocolate and the 4 teaspoons butter in a small saucepan over low heat until smooth. Spread over filling. Cover and chill bars about 2 hours or until firm. Cut into squares.

Fruits, nuts, and cherished traditional flavors create a taste-filled sampling that's out of this world.

Small cookie cutters with sharply defined edges work perfectly to cut these spicy chocolate sweets that include a hint of kirsch.

SWiSS basler brunsli

prep: 30 min. chill: 1 hr. bake: 12 min. per batch stand: 2 min. per batch
oven: 350°F makes: about 30 cookies

5   ounces almonds
     (about 1 cup)
¾   cup granulated sugar
¾   teaspoon ground
     cinnamon
¼   teaspoon ground
     cloves
3   ounces bittersweet
     chocolate, coarsely
     chopped
1   egg white
1   to 2 tablespoons
     kirsch
     Powdered sugar
1   recipe Powdered
     Sugar Icing

1 In a food processor combine almonds, granulated sugar, cinnamon, and cloves. Cover and process until finely ground. Add chocolate and process with several on/off pulses until finely ground. Add egg white and 1 tablespoon of the kirsch; process to form a stiff dough. If necessary, add additional kirsch, 1 teaspoon at a time, until dough holds together. Wrap dough in plastic wrap and chill about 1 hour or until easy to handle.

2 Preheat oven to 350°F. Line a cookie sheet with parchment paper or greased foil; set aside. On a surface lightly coated with powdered sugar, use a powdered sugar-coated rolling pin to roll dough until ⅜ inch thick. Using a 1½-inch star- or heart-shape cookie cutter, cut out dough. Place cutouts 1 inch apart on the prepared cookie sheet.

3 Bake 12 minutes or until edges are firm and surface is dry (center will be soft). (Do not overbake.) Let stand 2 minutes on cookie sheet. Transfer to a wire rack; cool. Decorate as desired with Powdered Sugar Icing.

powdered sugar icing: *In a bowl stir together 1½ cups powdered sugar, 1 tablespoon milk, and ¼ teaspoon vanilla. Stir in additional milk, 1 teaspoon at a time, to make an icing of drizzling or piping consistency. Decorate cookies as desired.*

To make quick work of chopping the figs and dates, use a food processor. Place 1 cup halved dates and 1 cup halved figs in the bowl. Add the 2 tablespoons granulated sugar and pulse with on/off turns until the fruit is finely chopped.

italian fruit-filled cookies

prep: 30 min. bake: 10 min. per batch oven: 375°F makes: about 40 cookies

½ cup butter, softened (no substitutes)
¼ cup granulated sugar
¼ cup packed brown sugar
¼ teaspoon baking soda
1 egg
1 teaspoon vanilla
1¾ cups all-purpose flour
2 apples, peeled and finely chopped (2½ cups)
1 cup finely chopped dried figs
1 cup finely chopped pitted dates
2 tablespoons granulated sugar
¼ teaspoon ground cinnamon
1 teaspoon finely shredded orange peel
¼ cup orange juice
½ cup finely chopped almonds
1 recipe Lemon Glaze

1 In a large mixing bowl beat butter with an electric mixer on medium to high speed for 30 seconds. Add the ¼ cup granulated sugar, the brown sugar, and baking soda. Beat until combined, scraping sides of bowl occasionally. Beat in egg and vanilla until combined. Beat in as much of the flour as you can with the mixer. Stir in any remaining flour. Divide dough in half. If necessary, cover and chill dough 30 minutes or until easy to handle.

2 Meanwhile, for filling, in a saucepan combine apples, figs, dates, the 2 tablespoons granulated sugar, the cinnamon, orange peel, and orange juice. Bring to boiling; reduce heat. Cover; simmer about 10 minutes or until apples are tender and mixture is thick. Stir in almonds. Cool to room temperature.

3 Preheat oven to 375°F. On a floured pastry cloth, roll half of dough at a time into a 10x8-inch rectangle. Cut rectangle lengthwise into two 10x4-inch strips. Spoon one-fourth of the filling (about ½ cup) lengthwise down the center of each strip. Using the cloth, lift one side of dough, then the other to cover filling and meet in the center. Pinch edges to seal. Transfer rolls to an ungreased cookie sheet.

4 Bake for 10 to 12 minutes or until light brown. While still warm, cut rolls diagonally into 1-inch slices. Transfer to a wire rack and let cool. Drizzle cooled cookies with Lemon Glaze.

lemon glaze: *In a small bowl stir together ¾ cup powdered sugar and 2 to 3 teaspoons lemon juice to make a glaze of drizzling consistency.*

note: *Store cookies as directed on page 16. Refrigerate up to 3 days. Do not freeze.*

Use a fluted pastry wheel for a ribboned edge on these chocolaty Italian cookies, named for their long, narrow shape.

mustaches

prep: 20 min. chill: 1 hr. bake: 5 min. per batch oven: 375°F makes: 60 cookies

½	cup butter, softened
¼	cup unsweetened cocoa powder
1	teaspoon baking powder
1	teaspoon ground cinnamon
	Dash ground cloves
½	cup honey
1	egg
2	cups all-purpose flour
½	cup very finely chopped almonds
½	cup very finely chopped walnuts
1	recipe Chocolate-Espresso Icing

1 In a medium mixing bowl beat butter with an electric mixer on medium to high speed for 30 seconds. Add cocoa powder, baking powder, cinnamon, and cloves. Beat until combined, scraping sides of bowl occasionally. Beat in honey and egg. Beat in as much of the flour as you can with the mixer. Stir in any remaining flour, the almonds, and walnuts. Divide dough in half. Cover and chill dough for 1 to 2 hours or until easy to handle.

2 Preheat oven to 375°F. On a lightly floured surface, roll half of the dough at a time into a 12×9-inch rectangle. Cut rectangles lengthwise into 12×3-inch strips; cut strips diagonally into 1-inch-wide strips. Place strips 1 inch apart on an ungreased cookie sheet.

3 Bake about 5 minutes or until firm. Transfer to a wire rack and let cool. Drizzle cooled cookies with Chocolate-Espresso Icing.

chocolate-espresso icing: *In a medium bowl stir together 2 tablespoons milk and 1 teaspoon instant espresso powder. Stir in 2 cups powdered sugar, 3 tablespoons softened butter, and 2 tablespoons unsweetened cocoa powder. Beat until combined. Stir in additional milk, 1 teaspoon at a time, until icing is of drizzling consistency.*

Dutch tradition calls for these cookies to be placed over a cup of hot coffee or tea to warm up their caramel filling and make it scrumptiously gooey.

stroopwafels

start to finish: 1½ hr. makes: 24 sandwich cookies

2	cups all-purpose flour
1	tablespoon baking powder
2	teaspoons ground cinnamon
3	eggs
¾	cup sugar
⅓	cup butter, melted and cooled
1½	teaspoons vanilla
1	recipe Caramel Filling

1 In a small bowl stir together flour, baking powder, and cinnamon; set aside. In a medium mixing bowl beat eggs on high speed about 4 minutes or until thick and lemon color. Gradually beat in sugar on medium speed. Beat in butter and vanilla until combined. Beat in flour mixture on low speed until combined.

2 For 3-inch-diameter cookies, heat an electric mini-pizzelle iron* according to manufacturer's directions. Place a scant tablespoon of batter in center of grid. Close lid. Bake according to manufacturer's directions. Using a spatula, transfer cookie to a paper towel; cool. Repeat with remaining batter.

3 Prepare Caramel Filling; immediately spoon 1 tablespoon onto each of half of the cookies. Top with remaining cookies.

*Look for a pizzelle iron in specialty cooking stores or in food catalogs.

caramel filling: *In a 3-quart heavy saucepan melt 1 cup butter over low heat. Add 2¼ cups packed brown sugar, one 14-ounce can sweetened condensed milk, and 1 cup light-color corn syrup; mix well. Cook and stir over medium-high heat until mixture boils. Clip a candy thermometer to the side of pan. Reduce heat to medium; continue to boil at a moderate, steady rate, stirring frequently, until thermometer registers 248°F, firm-ball stage (about 15 minutes). Adjust heat as necessary to maintain a steady boil. Remove pan from heat; remove thermometer. Stir in ½ teaspoon vanilla.*

Shortbreadlike cookies infused with the flavors of almond and lemon and topped with a shiny glaze, mantecados are popular treats in both Spain and Mexico.

mantecados

prep: 35 min. chill: 1 hr. bake: 8 min. per batch stand: 2 min. per batch
oven: 350°F makes: about 60 cookies

1 cup butter, softened
1 cup sugar
2 cups all-purpose flour
½ cup blanched almonds, very finely ground
1 tablespoon finely shredded lemon peel
1 egg, beaten
1 teaspoon water
10 ounces chocolate-flavor candy coating, melted
2 ounces vanilla-flavor candy coating, melted

1 In a large mixing bowl beat butter with an electric mixer on medium to high speed for 30 seconds. Add sugar. Beat until combined, scraping sides of bowl occasionally. Beat in flour until combined. Stir in almonds and lemon peel. Divide dough into thirds. Cover and chill dough about 1 hour or until easy to handle.

2 Preheat oven to 350°F. On a lightly floured surface, roll each portion of dough until ⅛ to ¼ inch thick. Using 2-inch desired-shape cookie cutters dipped in flour, cut out dough. Place cutouts 1 inch apart on an ungreased cookie sheet. In a small bowl stir together egg and water; brush over tops of cookies.

3 Bake for 8 to 10 minutes or until light golden. Let stand for 2 minutes on cookie sheet. Transfer to a wire rack and let cool. Dip half of each cooled cookie into melted chocolate-flavor candy coating. Drizzle vanilla-flavor candy coating onto the chocolate-dipped half of each cookie. Let stand until set.

Roll these Norwegian cookies in beaten egg, then in chopped slivered almonds to give them a delicious crunch.

serina cookies (serinakaker)

prep: 25 min. chill: 2 hr. bake: 8 min. per batch oven: 375°F
makes: 48 cookies

⅔ cup butter, softened
½ cup sugar
¼ teaspoon baking
  powder
1 egg
1 teaspoon vanilla
1½ cups all-purpose flour
1 egg, lightly beaten
1 cup coarsely chopped
  slivered almonds

1 Preheat oven to 375°F. Grease a cookie sheet; set aside. In a large mixing bowl beat butter with an electric mixer on medium to high speed for 30 seconds. Add sugar and baking powder. Beat until combined, scraping sides of bowl occasionally. Beat in 1 egg and the vanilla until combined. Beat in as much of the flour as you can with the mixer. Stir in any remaining flour. Cover and chill dough about 2 hours or until easy to handle.

2 Shape dough into ¾-inch balls. Roll each ball in beaten egg, then in almonds to coat. Place balls 2 inches apart on the prepared cookie sheet. Using a fork, flatten each ball slightly. Bake for 8 to 10 minutes or until edges are light brown. Transfer to a wire rack and let cool.

Simple as can be and truly scrumptious, these cookies are perfect for any occasion—whether it's a cozy night in or an elegant dinner party.

The dough for these cookies is baked into circles and cut into small, cookie-size wedges before cooling.

greek honey-nut wedges

prep: 30 min. bake: 15 min. stand: 10 min. oven: 350°F makes: 24 cookies

1   8-ounce package
      cream cheese,
      softened
½   cup butter, softened
2   tablespoons sugar
2   tablespoons milk
2   cups all-purpose flour
⅔   cup sugar
1½ teaspoons ground
      cinnamon
⅓   cup honey
2   tablespoons lemon
      juice
2   cups finely chopped
      walnuts
1   tablespoon sugar
⅛   teaspoon ground
      cinnamon
      Milk

1 In a large mixing bowl beat cream cheese and butter with an electric mixer on medium to high speed for 30 seconds. Beat in the 2 tablespoons sugar and 2 tablespoons milk. Beat in as much of the flour as you can with the mixer. Stir or knead in remaining flour. Divide dough into four portions. If necessary, cover and chill dough for 1 to 2 hours or until easy to handle.

2 Meanwhile, for filling, in a small bowl stir together the ⅔ cup sugar, 1½ teaspoons cinnamon, the honey, and lemon juice. Stir in walnuts; set aside. In a small bowl stir together the 1 tablespoon sugar and ⅛ teaspoon cinnamon; set aside.

3 Preheat oven to 350°F. On a lightly floured surface, roll one portion of dough into an 8-inch circle. Carefully transfer circle to an ungreased cookie sheet. Spread half of the filling to within ½ inch of edges. Roll another portion of dough into an 8-inch circle. Place over the nut-topped circle. Seal edges with a fork. Brush with milk; sprinkle with sugar-cinnamon mixture. Repeat with remaining dough and filling.

4 Bake for 15 to 20 minutes or until edges start to brown. Let stand for 10 minutes on cookie sheet. Cut each round into 12 wedges. Transfer to a wire rack and let cool.

note: *Store cookies as directed on page 16. Do not freeze.*

If you're lucky enough to live near a Dutch community, you have likely enjoyed these S-shape cookies filled with almond paste.

dutch letters (banket staven)

prep: 1½ hours chill: 40 min. bake: 25 min. oven: 375°F makes: 16 cookies

4½ cups all-purpose flour
1 teaspoon salt
1 pound butter
1 cup water
1 egg
1 8-ounce can almond paste
½ cup granulated sugar
½ cup brown sugar
2 egg whites
Milk
Granulated sugar
1 recipe Almond Glaze

1 In a large bowl stir together flour and salt. Cut butter into ½-inch slices. Stir butter into flour mixture, coating pieces to keep each piece separate. (Butter will be in large chunks.)

2 In a bowl combine the water and egg. Add egg mixture all at once to flour mixture. Mix quickly. (Flour will not be completely moistened.) Turn dough out onto a lightly floured surface; knead 10 times to form a rough-looking ball. Shape into a rectangle. (Dough will have some dry-looking areas.) Flatten slightly. On a well-floured surface, roll dough into a 15×10-inch rectangle. Fold the two short sides to meet in center, then fold dough in half crosswise to form four layers and a 7½×5-inch rectangle. Repeat the rolling and folding process one more time. Cover dough with plastic wrap; chill 20 minutes. Repeat rolling and folding two more times; chill 20 minutes more.

3 Meanwhile, in a medium bowl stir together almond paste, the ½ cup granulated sugar, the brown sugar, and egg whites; beat until smooth. Cover and chill 20 minutes.

4 Preheat oven to 375°F. Cut dough crosswise into four equal portions. (Keep unused dough chilled.) Roll one portion of dough into a 12×10-inch rectangle. Cut into four 10×3-inch strips. Spread 1 slightly rounded tablespoon of the almond mixture down center of each strip; roll up lengthwise around filling. Brush edge and ends with milk. Pinch to seal. Place rolls, seam sides down, on an ungreased baking sheet; shape each roll into an S shape. Brush with milk and sprinkle with additional granulated sugar. Bake for 25 to 30 minutes or until golden. Transfer to a wire rack; cool. Drizzle with Almond Glaze.

almond glaze: *Combine 1½ cups powdered sugar, 4 teaspoons milk, and ¼ teaspoon almond extract. Stir in additional milk, 1 teaspoon at a time, to make a glaze of desired consistency.*

These almond-studded cookie sticks get a big dose of flavor from almond extract. A drizzle of almond icing gives them a third layer of nutty flavor.

scandinavian almond bars

prep: 20 min. bake: 12 min. per batch oven: 325°F makes: 48 cookies

1¾ cups all-purpose flour
 2 teaspoons baking
     powder
 ¼ teaspoon salt
 ½ cup butter, softened
 1 cup granulated sugar
 1 egg
 ½ teaspoon almond
     extract
     Milk
 ½ cup sliced almonds,
     coarsely chopped
 1 recipe Almond Icing
     (optional)

1 Preheat oven to 325°F. In a bowl stir together flour, baking powder, and salt; set aside. In a large mixing bowl beat butter for 30 seconds. Add sugar; beat until combined, scraping sides of bowl occasionally. Beat in egg and almond extract until combined. Beat in as much of the flour mixture as you can with the mixer. Stir in any remaining flour mixture.

2 Divide dough into four equal portions. Shape each portion into a 12-inch-long log. Place two logs 4 to 5 inches apart on an ungreased cookie sheet. Flatten rolls until they are 3 inches wide. Repeat with remaining rolls on a second cookie sheet. Brush flattened rolls with milk and sprinkle with almonds. Bake, one sheet at a time, 12 to 15 minutes or until edges are light brown. While still warm on cookie sheets, slice logs diagonally into 1-inch pieces. Transfer to a wire rack and let cool. If desired, drizzle cooled cookies with Almond Icing.

almond icing: *In a small bowl stir together 1 cup powdered sugar, ¼ teaspoon almond extract, and enough milk (3 to 4 teaspoons) to make an icing of drizzling consistency.*

unbeatable ba

With flavors adapted from breads, cakes, and pies, bars offer sweet solutions to last-minute dessert dilemmas. Whether you crave multilayered bars or simple-as-can-be squares, this collection of treats is sure to please.

Dried fruit adds new flavor to traditional baklava.
Just before serving dust the bars with powdered sugar.

hazelnut **baklava** with dried fruit

prep: 50 min. **bake:** 35 min. **stand:** 20 min. **oven:** 325°F **makes:** 36 bars

2	cups hazelnuts* (filberts) and/or walnuts, toasted (see tip, page 19) and finely chopped
⅔	cup dried apples, finely chopped, and/or mixed dried fruit bits
½	cup packed brown sugar
1	teaspoon ground cinnamon
¾	cup butter, melted
12	sheets frozen phyllo dough (14×9-inch rectangles), thawed
1	cup granulated sugar
1	cup apple juice, apple cider, or water
¼	cup pure maple syrup or honey
1	2-inch piece stick cinnamon
1	tablespoon whole cloves
1	teaspoon vanilla Powdered sugar (optional)

1 Preheat oven to 325°F. For filling, in a bowl stir together nuts, dried fruit, brown sugar, and ground cinnamon. Set aside.

2 Brush the bottom of a 13×9-inch baking pan with some of the melted butter. Unfold phyllo dough. (Keep phyllo covered with plastic wrap, removing sheets only as you need them.) Layer three phyllo sheets lengthwise in the pan, generously brushing each sheet with melted butter. Sprinkle one-third (about 1 cup) of the filling on top of the phyllo layers in pan. Repeat layering of the phyllo sheets, butter, and filling two more times. Layer remaining phyllo sheets on top, brushing each sheet with butter. Drizzle remaining butter over the top. If necessary, trim ends of phyllo to fit pan. Cut through all the layers to make 36 diamonds or squares. Bake for 35 to 40 minutes or until golden. Let stand in pan on a wire rack for 20 minutes.

3 Meanwhile, for syrup, in a saucepan stir together granulated sugar, juice, maple syrup, stick cinnamon, and cloves. Bring to boiling; reduce heat. Simmer, uncovered, for 20 minutes. Strain syrup through a fine-mesh sieve into a 2-cup glass measure; discard cinnamon and cloves. (You should have about 1¼ cups.) Stir in vanilla. Pour mixture over partially cooled baklava in the pan; cool. If desired, sift powdered sugar over baklava.

✱ After toasting hazelnuts, place the warm nuts in a clean kitchen towel. Rub nuts with the towel to remove loose skins.

note: *Store bars as directed on page 16. Refrigerate up to 3 days.*

This pastry treat tastes just like apple pie. The bar shape gives it a more casual appearance.

apple pastry bars

prep: 45 min. **chill:** 4 hr. **bake:** 40 min. **oven:** 375°F **makes:** 32 bars

2½   cups all-purpose flour
1   teaspoon salt
1   cup shortening
1   egg yolk
    Milk
1   cup cornflakes
8   to 10 (about
      2½ pounds total)
      tart baking apples,
      peeled and sliced
      ¼ inch thick
      (8 cups)
½   cup granulated sugar
1   teaspoon ground
      cinnamon
1   egg white
1   tablespoon water
    Sifted powdered
      sugar (optional)
    Whipped cream
      (optional)

1 For pastry, in a large bowl stir together the flour and salt. Using a pastry blender, cut in shortening until mixture resembles coarse crumbs. Lightly beat egg yolk in a glass measuring cup. Add enough milk to egg yolk to make ⅔ cup; mix well. Stir egg yolk mixture into flour mixture; mix well. Divide dough in half. Cover and chill dough about 4 hours or until easy to handle.

2 Preheat oven to 375°F. On a lightly floured surface, roll half of the dough into an 18×12-inch rectangle. Fit dough rectangle into and up the sides of an ungreased 15×10×1-inch baking pan. Sprinkle with cornflakes; top with apples. In a small bowl stir together sugar and cinnamon; sprinkle over apples. Roll the remaining dough into a 16×12-inch rectangle; place over apples. Seal edges; cut slits in top for steam to escape. Beat egg white and the water; brush over pastry.

3 Bake for 40 to 45 minutes or until golden. Cool in pan on a wire rack. Serve warm or cool. Cut into bars. If desired, top with powdered sugar and/or whipped cream.

note: *Store as directed on page 16. Store only 2 days at room temperature.*

Compared to batch cookies, bars require only a single baking, making them perfect when time is at a premium.

Raspberry-chocolate chips enhance the delicate citrus flavor of these orange-glazed cookies.

orange and raspberry chip shortbread

prep: 25 min. bake: 25 min. stand: 30 min. oven: 325°F makes: 48 bars

1	cup butter, softened
½	cup sugar
2	teaspoons finely shredded orange peel
2¼	cups all-purpose flour
¾	cup raspberry-chocolate baking pieces
1	recipe Orange Glaze

1 Preheat oven to 325°F. In a medium mixing bowl beat butter with an electric mixer on medium to high speed for 30 seconds. Add sugar and orange peel. Beat until combined, scraping sides of bowl occasionally. Beat in flour until crumbly. Stir in the baking pieces, pressing dough together until smooth.

2 Pat dough into a 12×8-inch rectangle (about ¼ inch thick) on an ungreased cookie sheet. Bake for 25 to 30 minutes or until bottom just begins to brown and center is set. Cool on cookie sheet on a wire rack.

3 Spread Orange Glaze over cooled shortbread. Let stand about 30 minutes or until glaze is set. Cut lengthwise into three strips. Cut each strip crosswise into eight pieces, making 24 rectangles. Cut each rectangle lengthwise into two pieces.

note: *Store bars as directed on page 16. Freeze uncut and undrizzled. Thaw, drizzle, then cut before serving.*

orange glaze: *In a small bowl stir together ½ cup powdered sugar, 1 tablespoon softened butter, and 1 tablespoon orange juice. If necessary, stir in additional juice, 1 teaspoon at a time, until glaze is of desired consistency.*

*Because both the bars and the frosting contain chocolate malted
milk powder, these bars taste like a coffee-spiked chocolate malt.*

malted mocha bars

prep: 30 min. **bake:** 35 min. **oven:** 350°F **makes:** 36 bars

⅔ cup butter, softened
⅔ cup packed brown
   sugar
1¼ cups all-purpose flour
3 eggs, beaten
⅓ cup granulated sugar
2 teaspoons vanilla
1½ cups flaked coconut
¾ cup chocolate malted
   milk powder
¼ cup all-purpose flour
1½ teaspoons instant
   espresso powder
   or instant coffee
   crystals
¼ teaspoon baking
   powder
¼ teaspoon salt
1 recipe Mocha Icing

1 Preheat oven to 350°F. Lightly grease a
13×9×2-inch baking pan; set aside. For
crust, in a medium mixing bowl beat butter
and brown sugar with an electric mixer on
medium to high speed for 30 seconds. Beat
or stir in the 1¼ cups flour. If necessary, gently
knead to mix. Pat flour mixture evenly into the
bottom of the prepared pan. Bake about
15 minutes or until set.

2 Meanwhile, in a medium bowl stir together
eggs, granulated sugar, and vanilla. Stir in
coconut, malted milk powder, the ¼ cup flour,
the espresso powder, baking powder, and salt.
Carefully spread over partially baked crust.
Bake for 20 to 25 minutes more or until set.
Cool in pan on a wire rack.

3 Spread the cooled bars with Mocha Icing.
Cut into bars.

mocha icing: *In a medium bowl whisk
together 2½ cups powdered sugar, ¼ cup
malted milk powder, ½ teaspoon instant
espresso powder or instant coffee crystals,
2 teaspoons vanilla, and 4 to 5 teaspoons
boiling water. If necessary, beat in a little
additional boiling water until icing reaches
spreading consistency.*

These cakelike bars are just like brownies—only blond, hence the name. Vanilla extract and chopped nuts give them exceptional flavor.

blondies

prep: 20 min. bake: 25 min. oven: 350°F makes: 36 bars

⅔	cup butter
2	cups packed brown sugar
2	eggs
2	teaspoons vanilla
2	cups all-purpose flour
1	teaspoon baking powder
¼	teaspoon baking soda
1½	cups chopped almonds, pecans, or cashews

1 Preheat oven to 350°F. Grease a 13×9×2-inch baking pan; set aside. In a saucepan heat and stir butter and brown sugar over medium heat until smooth. Cool slightly. Stir in eggs, one at a time. Stir in vanilla. Stir in flour, baking powder, and baking soda.

2 Spread batter evenly in the prepared pan. Sprinkle with almonds. Bake for 25 to 30 minutes or until a wooden toothpick inserted in the center comes out clean. Cool slightly in pan on a wire rack. Cut into bars while warm.

Want a peanut alternative? Sprinkle these bars with chocolate pieces or additional butterscotch pieces

butterscotch bars

prep: 20 min. chill: 2 hr. makes: 48 bars

1	9-ounce package chocolate wafers
1½	cups powdered sugar
1	cup creamy peanut butter
6	tablespoons butter, melted
1	11-ounce package butterscotch-flavor pieces (2 cups)
¼	cup whipping cream
¾	cup chopped peanuts

1 Crush chocolate wafers (for a total of 2 cups); set aside. In a large bowl stir together the powdered sugar, peanut butter, and melted butter. Stir in chocolate wafer crumbs. Press mixture into the bottom of an ungreased 13×9×2-inch baking pan.

2 In a saucepan heat and stir butterscotch pieces and whipping cream over low heat until smooth. Carefully spoon and spread butterscotch mixture over crumb mixture. Sprinkle peanuts over butterscotch mixture. Cover and chill at least 2 hours. Cut into bars.

note: *Store bars as directed on page 16. Refrigerate up to 3 days.*

Remember this recipe when you have overripe bananas to use up. They are easier to mash and contribute to the sweet flavor and moistness.

banana bars
with butter-rum frosting

prep: 20 min. **bake:** 25 min. **oven:** 350°F **makes:** 48 bars

½	cup butter, softened
1⅓	cups sugar
1½	teaspoons baking powder
½	teaspoon baking soda
¼	teaspoon salt
1	egg
1	cup mashed banana (2 to 3 medium)
½	cup dairy sour cream
1	teaspoon vanilla
2	cups all-purpose flour
¾	cup toasted chopped almonds (see tip, page 19)
1	recipe Butter-Rum Frosting

1 Preheat oven to 350°F. Grease a 15×10×1-inch baking pan; set aside.

2 In a large mixing bowl beat butter with an electric mixer on medium to high speed for 30 seconds. Add sugar, baking powder, baking soda, and salt. Beat until combined, scraping sides of bowl occasionally. Beat in the egg, mashed banana, sour cream, and vanilla until combined. Beat in as much of the flour as you can with the mixer. Stir in any remaining flour and the almonds.

3 Spread batter evenly in the prepared pan. Bake about 25 minutes or until a wooden toothpick inserted in the center comes out clean. Cool in pan on a wire rack; spread with Butter-Rum Frosting. Cut into bars.

note: *Store bars as directed on page 16. Refrigerate up to 3 days.*

butter-rum frosting: *In a medium mixing bowl beat 3 tablespooons softened butter with an electric mixer on medium speed for 30 seconds. Gradually beat in 1½ cups powdered sugar. Beat in 1 tablespoon rum and 1 teaspoon vanilla. Beat in 1½ cups additional powdered sugar and enough milk to make a frosting of spreading consistency.*

This recipe packages the fruit and nut goodness of traditional fruitcake into a scrumptious bar cookie.

golden fruitcake bars

prep: 30 min. **bake:** 25 min. **stand:** 1 hr./10 min. **oven:** 350°F **makes:** 42 bars

1 cup golden raisins, coarsely chopped
1 cup dried cranberries, coarsely chopped
1 cup dried apricots, finely snipped
1 cup brandy or orange juice
1 16-ounce package pound cake mix
½ cup lightly salted, dry-roasted pistachios, chopped
1 cup powdered sugar

1 In a medium bowl stir together raisins, cranberries, apricots, and brandy. Cover and let stand for 1 hour or overnight. Drain, reserving brandy.

2 Preheat oven to 350°F. Grease a 15×10×1-inch baking pan; set aside. Mix the pound cake according to the package directions, except add one additional egg. Fold the drained fruit and the pistachios into the cake batter. Spread batter evenly in the prepared pan. (Pan will be very full.)

3 Bake for 25 to 30 minutes or until bars are golden on top and a toothpick inserted in the center comes out clean. Let stand in pan on a wire rack for 10 minutes.

4 Meanwhile, for icing, in a small bowl stir together powdered sugar and 2 tablespoons of the reserved brandy. Stir in additional brandy, 1 teaspoon at a time, to make an icing of drizzling consistency. Drizzle partially cooled bars with icing. Let cool completely. Using a serrated knife, cut into 2×1¾ inch bars.

note: *Store bars as directed on page 16. Freeze up to 1 month.*

Beloved cookie additions—pecans, coconut, caramels, and milk chocolate—pile on a buttery shortbread crust to flavor these bars.

chocolate-caramel bars

prep: 30 min. **bake:** 40 min. **stand:** 10 min. **oven:** 350°F **makes:** 48 bars

1   cup all-purpose flour
½   cup packed brown
      sugar
½   cup butter
2   cups coarsely
      chopped pecans
1   cup flaked coconut
1   14-ounce can
      sweetened
      condensed milk
      (1¼ cups)
2   teaspoons vanilla
20 vanilla caramels
2   tablespoons milk
6   ounces semisweet
      baking chocolate,
      coarsely chopped

1 Preheat oven to 350°F. For crust, in a medium bowl stir together flour and brown sugar. Cut in the butter until mixture resembles coarse crumbs. Press flour mixture into the bottom of an ungreased 13×9×2-inch baking pan. Bake 15 minutes.

2 Sprinkle pecans and coconut over partially baked crust. In a small bowl stir together sweetened condensed milk and vanilla. Pour over pecans and coconut. Bake for 25 to 30 minutes more or until set. Let stand in pan on a wire rack for 10 minutes.

3 In a small saucepan combine caramels and milk. Heat and stir over medium-low heat just until caramels melt. Drizzle caramel mixture over baked mixture. Sprinkle top with chopped chocolate. Cool completely. Cut into bars.

note: *Store bars as directed on page 16. Refrigerate up to 3 days.*

Almond toffee pieces meet bittersweet chocolate and chopped pecans for an indulgent flavor combination.

bittersweet chocolate and **toffee** triangles

prep: 25 min. **bake:** 18 min. **stand:** 1 hr. **oven:** 375°F **makes:** 48 bars

1 cup butter, softened
1 cup packed brown sugar
1 egg yolk
1 teaspoon vanilla
2 cups all-purpose flour
8 ounces bittersweet chocolate, cut up
2 tablespoons milk
¾ cup coarsely chopped pecans
¾ cup almond toffee pieces

1 Preheat oven to 375°F. Grease a 15×10×1-inch baking pan; set aside. In a large mixing bowl beat butter with an electric mixer on medium to high speed for 30 seconds. Add brown sugar. Beat until combined, scraping sides of bowl occasionally. Beat in egg yolk and vanilla until combined. Beat in as much of the flour as you can with the mixer. Stir in any remaining flour. Pat the dough evenly into the bottom of the prepared pan. Set aside.

2 In a medium saucepan heat and stir chocolate over low heat until smooth. Transfer 2 tablespoons of the melted chocolate to a small microwave-safe bowl; stir in milk and set aside. Spread the remaining melted chocolate evenly over dough in pan. Sprinkle chopped pecans and almond toffee pieces over the chocolate layer.

3 Bake about 18 minutes or until toffee pieces have melted and nuts are lightly toasted. Cool in pan on a wire rack.

4 Meanwhile, microwave the reserved chocolate mixture, uncovered, on 100 percent power (high) for 30 to 45 seconds or until smooth. Drizzle melted chocolate over bars. Let stand about 1 hour or until chocolate is set. Cut into 24 squares; cut each square in half diagonally.

Great for an adult get-together, these layered bars feature brandy-soaked fruit for their outstanding depth of flavor.

brandied cran-apricot bars

prep: 40 min. **bake:** 1 hr. **oven:** 350°F **makes:** 16 bars

⅓ cup golden raisins
⅓ cup dark raisins
⅓ cup dried cranberries
⅓ cup snipped dried
    apricots
½ cup brandy or water
1 cup all-purpose flour
⅓ cup packed brown
    sugar
½ cup butter
2 eggs
1 cup packed brown
    sugar
½ cup all-purpose flour
1 teaspoon vanilla
⅓ cup chopped pecans
    Powdered sugar

1 In a small saucepan stir together golden raisins, dark raisins, cranberries, apricots, and brandy; bring to boiling. Remove from heat. Let stand for 20 minutes; drain.

2 Preheat oven to 350°F. Grease an 8×8×2-inch baking pan; set aside. For crust, in a medium bowl stir together the 1 cup flour and the ⅓ cup brown sugar. Using a pastry blender, cut in butter until mixture resembles coarse crumbs. Press flour mixture into the bottom of the prepared pan. Bake about 20 minutes or until golden.

3 Meanwhile, in a medium mixing bowl beat eggs with an electric mixer on low speed for 4 minutes. Stir in the 1 cup brown sugar, the ½ cup flour, and the vanilla just until combined. Stir in pecans and drained fruit. Spread egg mixture evenly over baked crust.

4 Bake about 40 minutes more or until a wooden toothpick inserted in the center comes out clean, covering with foil during the last 10 minutes to prevent overbrowning. Cool in pan on a wire rack. Sift powdered sugar over cooled baked mixture. Cut into squares.

note: *Store bars as directed on page 16. Refrigerate up to 3 days.*

A brown sugar pastry crust makes these fruit-topped bars taste like a fancy French tart.

Is it a cookie or candy? Don't fret over the answer; just rest assured it's a winner.

candy bar cookie bars

prep: 35 min. bake: 10 min. oven: 375°F makes: about 117 bite-size bars

1	cup packed brown sugar
⅔	cup butter
¼	cup dark- or light-color corn syrup
¼	cup peanut butter
1	teaspoon vanilla
3½	cups quick-cooking rolled oats
1	12-ounce package semisweet chocolate pieces (2 cups)
1	cup butterscotch flavor pieces
⅔	cup peanut butter
1	cup chopped peanuts

1 Preheat oven to 375°F. In a medium saucepan heat and stir brown sugar, butter, and corn syrup over medium-low heat until smooth. Remove from the heat. Stir in the ¼ cup peanut butter and vanilla; stir until smooth.

2 For crust, place oats in a very large bowl. Pour brown sugar mixture over oats, stirring gently until combined. Press oat mixture into the bottom of an ungreased 13x9x2-inch baking pan. Bake for 10 to 12 minutes or until edges are light brown. Cool slightly in pan on a wire rack.

3 In the same saucepan heat and stir chocolate pieces and butterscotch pieces over low heat until smooth. Stir in the ⅔ cup peanut butter until smooth.

4 Sprinkle half of the peanuts over crust. Slowly pour chocolate mixture over the peanuts, spreading evenly. Sprinkle the remaining peanuts over top. Cool completely in pan on a wire rack until firm. Cut into 1-inch squares.

note: *Store bars as directed on page 16. Refrigerate up to 3 days.*

Crushed malted milk balls give these brownies an extra crunch, while toasted walnuts add a slightly chewy texture.

malt-fudge brownies

prep: 30 min. **bake:** 35 min. **oven:** 325°F **makes:** 30 bars

1½ cups all-purpose flour
⅓ cup malted milk powder
½ teaspoon salt
1 cup butter
4 ounces unsweetened chocolate, cut up
2 cups sugar
4 eggs
1 teaspoon vanilla
1 cup chopped walnuts, toasted (see tip, page 19)
2 ounces malted milk balls, crushed (about ½ cup)

1 Preheat oven to 325°F. Lightly grease a 13×9×2-inch baking pan; set aside. In a medium bowl stir together flour, malted milk powder, and salt; set aside.

2 In a medium saucepan heat and stir butter and chocolate over low heat until smooth. Remove from heat; stir in sugar. Add the eggs, one at a time, beating with a wooden spoon just until combined. Add vanilla. Stir in flour mixture, walnuts, and half of the crushed malted milk balls. Spread batter evenly in the prepared pan.

3 Bake about 35 minutes. Cool in pan on a wire rack. Cut into bars.

note: *Store bars as directed on page 16. Refrigerate up to 3 days.*

Pineapple ice cream topping and rum extract make these tropical-flavor bars taste like the favorite drink.

piña colada squares

prep: 25 min. **bake:** 30 min. **oven:** 350°F **makes:** 48 bars

2 cups all-purpose flour
2 cups quick-cooking rolled oats
1⅓ cups packed brown sugar
¼ teaspoon baking soda
1 cup butter
1 cup pineapple ice cream topping
1 teaspoon rum extract
1 cup flaked coconut Semisweet chocolate, melted

1 Preheat oven to 350°F. In a bowl combine the flour, oats, brown sugar, and baking soda. Cut in butter until mixture resembles coarse crumbs; remove 1 cup and set aside. Press remaining flour mixture into bottom of an ungreased 13×9×2-inch baking pan.

2 For filling, stir together pineapple topping and rum extract; spread evenly over crust.

3 For topping, stir coconut into the reserved flour mixture. Sprinkle over filling. Bake 30 minutes or until golden. Cool on wire rack. Cut into bars. Drizzle with melted chocolate.

note: *Store bars as directed on page 16. Refrigerate up to 3 days.*

Malt-Fudge Brownies

The rich, chocolate flavor of these cakelike brownies definitely qualifies them as a timeless classic. Another plus: They're practically foolproof. Generations of cooks have appreciated that.

buttermilk brownies

prep: 30 min. **bake:** 25 min. **oven:** 350°F **makes:** 24 brownies

2	cups all-purpose flour
2	cups granulated sugar
1	teaspoon baking soda
¼	teaspoon salt
1	cup butter
1	cup water
⅓	cup unsweetened cocoa powder
2	eggs
½	cup buttermilk
1½	teaspoons vanilla
1	recipe Chocolate-Buttermilk Frosting

1 Preheat oven to 350°F. Grease a 15×10×1-inch or a 13×9×2-inch baking pan; set aside. In a medium bowl stir together flour, sugar, baking soda, and salt; set aside.

2 In a medium saucepan combine butter, the water, and cocoa powder. Bring just to boiling, stirring constantly. Remove from heat. Add the cocoa mixture to the flour mixture. Beat with an electric mixer on medium speed until combined. Add the eggs, buttermilk, and vanilla. Beat for 1 minute (batter will be thin). Pour batter into the prepared pan.

3 Bake about 25 minutes for the 15×10×1-inch pan, 35 minutes for the 13×9×2-inch pan, or until a wooden toothpick inserted in the center comes out clean.

4 Pour warm Chocolate-Buttermilk Frosting over the warm brownies, spreading evenly. Cool in pan on a wire rack. Cut into 24 bars

note: *Store bars as directed on page 16. Refrigerate up to 3 days.*

chocolate-buttermilk frosting: *In a saucepan combine ¼ cup butter, 3 tablespoons unsweetened cocoa powder, and 3 tablespoons buttermilk. Bring mixture to boiling. Remove from heat. Add 2¼ cups powdered sugar and ½ teaspoon vanilla. Beat until smooth. If desired, stir in ¾ cup coarsely chopped pecans.*

These fudgy brownies are topped with a mound of sweet, chocolaty meringue for an out-of-this-world presentation.

top-of-the-world
brownies

prep: 20 min. **bake:** 1 hr. **stand:** 1 hr. **oven:** 350°F **makes:** 16 brownies

¾ cup butter
3 ounces unsweetened chocolate, coarsely chopped
2 cups sugar
2 teaspoons vanilla
3 eggs
1 cup all-purpose flour
3 tablespoons unsweetened cocoa powder
½ cup coarsely chopped hazelnuts (filberts) or pecans
2 egg whites

1 Preheat oven to 350°F. Line an 8×8×2-inch baking pan with heavy foil, extending the foil over the edges of the pan. Grease the foil; set aside.

2 In a medium saucepan heat and stir the butter and chocolate over low heat until smooth. Remove from heat. Using a wooden spoon, stir in 1⅓ cups of the sugar and the vanilla. Cool about 5 minutes. Add eggs, one at a time, beating just until combined after each addition. Stir in flour and 2 tablespoons of the cocoa. Spread batter evenly in the prepared pan. Sprinkle with nuts; set aside.

3 In a small mixing bowl beat egg whites with an electric mixer on medium to high speed about 1 minute or until soft peaks form (tips curl). Gradually add the remaining ⅔ cup sugar, beating on high speed just until stiff peaks form (tips stand straight) and sugar is almost dissolved. Reduce speed to low; beat in the remaining 1 tablespoon cocoa.

4 Using a tablespoon, carefully spoon the meringue in 16 even mounds on top of the brownie batter, spacing them about ½ inch apart. Or spoon meringue into a decorating bag fitted with a large star tip; pipe 16 mounds on top of brownie batter, spacing them about ½ inch apart.

5 Bake about 1 hour or until a wooden toothpick inserted in the center of the brownie portion comes out clean. Let stand in pan on a wire rack for at least 1 hour. Use the foil to lift brownies from pan. Cut brownies into 16 squares.

note: *Store bars as directed on page 16. Refrigerate up to 3 days. Do not freeze.*

Chocolate and coffee pair well, as this one-pan treat demonstrates. These brownies feature instant espresso powder, coffee liqueur, and chocolate-covered coffee beans.

triple espresso brownies

prep: 30 min. **bake:** 20 min. **oven:** 350°F **makes:** 48 brownies

¼	cup water
2	tablespoons instant espresso powder or instant coffee crystals
1	cup butter
1½	cups semisweet chocolate pieces
1½	cups granulated sugar
4	eggs, lightly beaten
1½	teaspoons vanilla
2	cups all-purpose flour
½	teaspoon salt
½	cup chopped walnuts (optional)
3	cups powdered sugar
¼	cup butter, softened
2	tablespoons boiling water
2	tablespoons coffee liqueur or 2 teaspoons instant espresso powder or instant coffee crystals
	Coarsely chopped chocolate-covered coffee beans (optional)
	Instant espresso powder (optional)

1 Preheat oven to 350°F. Grease a 15×10×1-inch baking pan; set aside. In a large saucepan combine the ¼ cup water and the 2 tablespoons instant espresso powder. Add the 1 cup butter and the chocolate pieces. Heat and stir over low heat until smooth. Remove from heat. Add sugar, eggs, and 1 teaspoon of the vanilla. Using a wooden spoon, lightly beat the mixture just until combined. Stir in flour, salt, and, if desired, the walnuts. Spread batter evenly in prepared pan.

2 Bake for 20 to 25 minutes or until a wooden toothpick inserted in the center comes out clean. Cool in pan on a wire rack.

3 Meanwhile, for the frosting, place powdered sugar in a large mixing bowl. Add the ¼ cup butter, the boiling water, coffee liqueur, and the remaining ½ teaspoon vanilla. Beat with an electric mixer on low speed until combined. Beat for 1 minute on medium speed. Spread frosting evenly over cooled brownies. If desired, sprinkle with coarsely chopped chocolate-covered coffee beans and additional espresso powder. Cut into 48 brownies.

To ensure a successful crust, be sure to use quick-cooking oats rather than regular oats in these bars.

chocolate revel bars

prep: 30 min. **bake:** 25 min. **oven:** 350°F **makes:** 60 bars

1   cup butter, softened
2   cups packed brown
     sugar
1   teaspoon baking soda
2   eggs
2   teaspoons vanilla
2½ cups all-purpose flour
3   cups quick-cooking
     rolled oats
1½ cups semisweet
     chocolate pieces
1   14-ounce can
     sweetened
     condensed milk or
     low-fat sweetened
     condensed milk
     (1¼ cups)
½   cup chopped walnuts
     or pecans
2   teaspoons vanilla

1 Preheat oven to 350°F. Set aside 2 tablespoons of the butter. In a large mixing bowl beat the remaining butter with an electric mixer on medium to high speed for 30 seconds. Add the brown sugar and baking soda. Beat until combined, scraping sides of bowl occasionally. Beat in eggs and 2 teaspoons vanilla until combined. Beat in as much of the flour as you can with the mixer. Stir in any remaining flour and the oats.

2 For filling, in a medium saucepan heat and stir the reserved 2 tablespoons butter, the chocolate pieces, and sweetened condensed milk over low heat until smooth, stirring occasionally. Remove from heat. Stir in the nuts and 2 teaspoons vanilla.

3 Press two-thirds (about 3⅓ cups) of the oats mixture into the bottom of an ungreased 15×10×1-inch baking pan. Spread filling evenly over the oats mixture. Dot remaining oats mixture over the filling.

4 Bake about 25 minutes or until top is light brown (chocolate filling will still look moist). Cool in pan on a wire rack. Cut into 60 bars.

peanut butter-chocolate revel bars: *Prepare as above, except substitute ½ cup peanut butter for the 2 tablespoons butter when making the chocolate filling and substitute unsalted peanuts for the walnuts.*

whole wheat-chocolate revel bars: *Prepare as above, except reduce the all-purpose flour to 1½ cups and add 1 cup whole wheat flour.*

If fresh cranberries are not available, look for frozen ones at your grocery. Just thaw them slightly before chopping them for the recipe.

cranberry-macadamia bars

prep: 20 min. **bake:** 10 min./30 min. **oven:** 350°F **makes:** 24 bars

1¼ cups all-purpose flour
2 cups sugar
½ cup butter
1 cup finely chopped macadamia nuts, hazelnuts (filberts), or pecans
2 eggs, beaten
2 tablespoons milk
1 teaspoon finely shredded orange peel
1 teaspoon vanilla
1 cup finely chopped cranberries
½ cup flaked coconut

1 Preheat oven to 350°F. For crust, in a medium bowl stir together flour and ¾ cup of the sugar. Using a pastry blender, cut in butter until mixture resembles coarse crumbs. Stir in ½ cup of the nuts. Press the flour mixture into the bottom of an ungreased 13×9×2-inch baking pan. Bake for 10 to 15 minutes or until light brown around edges.

2 Meanwhile, for topping, in another medium bowl combine the remaining 1¼ cups sugar, the eggs, milk, orange peel, and vanilla. Beat until combined. Pour over the hot crust. Sprinkle with the remaining ½ cup nuts, the cranberries, and coconut.

3 Bake about 30 minutes more or until golden. Cool slightly in pan on a wire rack. Cut into bars while warm. Cool completely.

note: *Store bars as directed on page 16. Refrigerate up to 3 days.*

A stellar combination of ruby red cranberries and flaked coconut tops these festive bar cookies.

For a touch of whimsy, serve these bite-size chocolate and peanut butter brownies in candy cups. If you prefer a full-size brownie, cut into 24 squares.

peanutty brownie bites

prep: 25 min. **bake:** 25 min. **oven:** 350°F **makes:** 70 bite-size brownies

1¼	cups finely crushed graham crackers (about 18 graham crackers)
1¼	cups sugar
¼	cup finely chopped dry-roasted peanuts
½	cup butter, melted
½	cup butter
2	ounces unsweetened chocolate, cut up
2	eggs
1	teaspoon vanilla
⅔	cup all-purpose flour
½	cup peanut butter-flavor pieces
1	recipe Peanut Butter Frosting
¼	cup honey-roasted peanuts or regular peanuts

1 Preheat oven to 350°F. For crust, in a medium bowl stir together crushed graham crackers, ¼ cup of the sugar, and the ¼ cup chopped peanuts. Stir in the ½ cup melted butter; press into the bottom of an ungreased 11×7×1½-inch baking pan. Bake about 5 minutes; let cool.

2 For filling, in a large saucepan heat and stir remaining ½ cup butter and the chocolate over low heat until smooth. Remove from heat. Stir in remaining 1 cup sugar, the eggs, and vanilla until combined. Stir in flour and peanut butter-flavor pieces. Spread filling over crust.

3 Bake 20 minutes more. Cool in pan on wire rack; spread with Peanut Butter Frosting. Cut into 1-inch squares. Garnish with peanuts.

note: *Store bars as directed on page 16. Refrigerate up to 3 days.*

peanut butter frosting: *In a medium mixing bowl beat ¼ cup softened butter and 2 tablespoons peanut butter with an electric mixer on low speed for 30 seconds. Gradually beat in 1 cup powdered sugar. Beat in 1 tablespoon milk and ½ teaspoon vanilla. Gradually beat in 1 cup additional powdered sugar and enough milk to make a frosting of spreading consistency.*

What a delicious way to get your family to eat their veggies!
No one will suspect the healthful ingredients these heavenly,
moist bars contain.

carrot and zucchini bars

prep: 20 min. **bake:** 25 min. **oven:** 350°F **makes:** 36 bars

1½ cups all-purpose flour
1 teaspoon baking
   powder
½ teaspoon ground
   ginger
¼ teaspoon baking soda
2 eggs, lightly beaten
1½ cups shredded carrot
   (3 medium)
1 cup shredded
   zucchini (1 medium)
¾ cup packed brown
   sugar
½ cup raisins
½ cup chopped walnuts
½ cup cooking oil
¼ cup honey
1 teaspoon vanilla
1 recipe Citrus-Cream
   Cheese Frosting

1 Preheat oven to 350°F. In a large bowl stir together flour, baking powder, ginger, and baking soda. In another large bowl stir together eggs, carrot, zucchini, brown sugar, raisins, walnuts, oil, honey, and vanilla. Add carrot mixture to flour mixture; stir just until combined. Spread batter evenly in an ungreased 13×9×2-inch baking pan.

2 Bake about 25 minutes or until a wooden toothpick inserted in the center comes out clean. Cool in pan on a wire rack. Spread cooled bars with Citrus-Cream Cheese Frosting. Cut into bars.

note: *Store bars as directed on page 16. Refrigerate up to 3 days.*

citrus-cream cheese frosting: *In a mixing bowl beat one 8-ounce package softened cream cheese and 1 cup powdered sugar with an electric mixer on medium speed until fluffy. If desired, stir in 1 teaspoon finely shredded lemon peel and/or orange peel.*

The mellow but distinctive flavor of honey comes through in these coconut and walnut bars drizzled with a sweet icing.

honey-nut bars

prep: 25 min. **bake:** 25 min. **oven:** 350°F **makes:** 24 bars

½	cup butter, softened
¼	cup shortening
1	cup honey
1	teaspoon baking powder
¼	teaspoon salt
3	eggs
1	teaspoon vanilla
1½	cups all-purpose flour
1	cup coconut
1	cup chopped walnuts
1	recipe Powdered Sugar Icing
	Chopped walnuts

1 Preheat oven to 350°F. Grease a 13×9×2-inch baking pan; set aside. In a large mixing bowl beat butter and shortening with an electric mixer on medium to high speed for 30 seconds. Add honey, baking powder, and salt. Beat until combined, scraping sides of bowl occasionally. Beat in eggs and vanilla until combined. Beat in as much of the flour as you can with the mixer. Stir in any remaining flour, the coconut, and 1 cup walnuts.

2 Spread batter in prepared pan. Bake 25 to 30 minutes or until a wooden toothpick inserted in the center comes out clean. Cool in pan on wire rack; drizzle with Powdered Sugar Icing; sprinkle with nuts. Cut into bars.

note: *Store bars as directed on page 16. Refrigerate up to 3 days. Freeze up to 1 month.*

powdered sugar icing: *In a small bowl stir together 1 cup powdered sugar, 1 tablespoon milk, and ¼ teaspoon vanilla. Stir in additional milk, 1 teaspoon at a time, until the icing is of drizzling consistency.*

Thick fudgy frosting complements the mellow chocolate flavor of these soft, cakelike brownies.

cake brownies

prep: 30 min. **bake:** 15 min. **oven:** 350°F **makes:** 48 brownies

¾ cup butter
1¼ cups sugar
½ cup unsweetened
  cocoa powder
2 eggs
1 teaspoon vanilla
1½ cups all-purpose flour
1 teaspoon baking
  powder
¼ teaspoon baking soda
1 cup milk
1 cup chopped walnuts
  or pecans
1 recipe No-Cook
  Fudge Frosting

1 Preheat oven to 350°F. Grease a 15×10×1-inch baking pan; set aside. In a large microwave-safe bowl microwave butter on 100 percent power (high) for 1½ to 2 minutes or until melted. (Or melt butter over medium heat in a medium saucepan; remove from heat.) Stir in sugar and cocoa powder until combined. Add eggs and vanilla. Using a wooden spoon, lightly beat mixture just until combined.

2 In a small bowl stir together flour, baking powder, and baking soda. Add flour mixture and milk alternately to chocolate mixture, beating after each addition. Stir in the walnuts.

3 Spread batter evenly in the prepared pan. Bake for 15 to 18 minutes or until a wooden toothpick inserted in the center comes out clean. Cool in pan on a wire rack. Spread cooled brownies with No-Cook Fudge Frosting. Cut into bars.

note: *Store bars as directed on page 16. Refrigerate up to 3 days. Do not freeze.*

no-cook fudge frosting: *In a large mixing bowl stir together 4 cups powdered sugar and ½ cup unsweetened cocoa powder. Add ½ cup softened butter, ⅓ cup boiling water, and 1 teaspoon vanilla. Beat for 1 minute with an electric mixer on medium speed. If necessary, let cool about 20 minutes or until frosting reaches spreading consistency. If frosting is too thick, beat in boiling water, 1 tablespoon at a time, until the frosting reaches a spreadable consistency.*

The spiced bars feature a luscious cream cheese frosting that makes them irresistible to any pumpkin lover.

pumpkin bars

prep: 35 min. **bake:** 25 min. **stand:** 2 hr. **oven:** 350°F **makes:** 48 bars

2 cups all-purpose flour
1½ cups sugar
2 teaspoons baking powder
2 teaspoons ground cinnamon
1 teaspoon baking soda
¼ teaspoon salt
¼ teaspoon ground cloves
4 eggs, beaten
1 15-ounce can pumpkin
1 cup cooking oil
1 recipe Cream Cheese Frosting

1 Preheat oven to 350°F. In a large bowl stir together the flour, sugar, baking powder, cinnamon, baking soda, salt, and cloves. Stir in the eggs, pumpkin, and oil until combined. Spread batter in an ungreased 15×10×1-inch baking pan.

2 Bake for 25 to 30 minutes or until a wooden toothpick inserted in the center comes out clean. Let stand in pan on a wire rack for 2 hours. Spread with Cream Cheese Frosting. Cut into bars.

note: *Store bars as directed on page 16. Refrigerate up to 3 days.*

cream cheese frosting: *In a medium mixing bowl beat half of an 8-ounce package softened cream cheese, ¼ cup softened butter, and 1 teaspoon vanilla with an electric mixer on medium speed until light and fluffy. Gradually beat in 2½ to 3 cups powdered sugar to make a frosting of spreading consistency.*

applesauce bars: *Prepare as above, except substitute one 15-ounce jar applesauce for the pumpkin.*

A coffee-with-cream layer separates two super-rich chocolate layers. For an understated yet elegant presentation, top each bar with a crunchy coffee bean.

cappuccino brownies

prep: 30 min. **bake:** 30 min. **chill:** 1 hr./30 min. **oven:** 350°F **makes:** 16 bars

½	cup butter
3	ounces unsweetened chocolate, cut up
1	cup granulated sugar
2	eggs
1	teaspoon vanilla
⅔	cup all-purpose flour
¼	teaspoon baking soda
1	teaspoon instant coffee crystals
1	tablespoon whipping cream
1	cup powdered sugar
2	tablespoons butter, softened
1	recipe Chocolate Frosting
16	whole coffee beans (optional)

1 Preheat oven to 350°F. Grease an 8×8×2-inch baking pan; set aside. In a saucepan heat and stir the ½ cup butter and unsweetened chocolate over low heat until smooth. Remove from heat; cool slightly. Stir in granulated sugar. Add eggs, one at a time, beating with a wooden spoon just until combined. Stir in vanilla.

2 In a small bowl stir together flour and baking soda. Stir flour mixture into chocolate mixture just until combined. Spread batter in the prepared pan. Bake 30 minutes.

3 Meanwhile, for topping, dissolve coffee crystals in whipping cream. In a small mixing bowl beat the powdered sugar and the 2 tablespoons butter on medium speed until combined. Beat in whipping cream mixture until creamy. If necessary, beat in additional whipping cream until topping is of spreading consistency. Spread over the warm brownies. Chill about 1 hour or until topping is set. Carefully spread Chocolate Frosting over brownies. Chill 30 minutes or until set. Cut into bars and, if desired, top each bar with 1 whole coffee bean.

note: *Store bars as directed on page 16. Refrigerate up to 3 days. Do not freeze.*

chocolate frosting: *In a small saucepan heat and stir 1 cup semisweet chocolate pieces and ⅓ cup whipping cream over low heat until smooth and mixture begins to thicken.*

Inspired by the famous shoofly pie, a Southern specialty, these bar cookies have a pastry crust and a crumbly spiced topping infused with the rich flavor of molasses.

shoofly bars

prep: 25 min. **bake:** 25 min. **oven:** 375°F **makes:** 24 bars

1¾	cups all-purpose flour
1	tablespoon granulated sugar
¼	teaspoon salt
⅓	cup shortening
4	to 5 tablespoons cold water
⅓	cup snipped dates
3	tablespoons brown sugar
⅛	teaspoon ground cinnamon
	Dash ground nutmeg
	Dash ground ginger
¼	cup butter
3	tablespoons hot water
¼	teaspoon baking soda
¼	cup molasses
1	egg, beaten

1 Preheat oven to 375°F. For crust, in a large bowl stir together 1¼ cups of the flour, the granulated sugar, and salt. Using a pastry blender cut in shortening until pieces are the size of small peas. Sprinkle 1 tablespoon cold water over part of the mixture; gently toss with a fork. Push moistened dough to side of the bowl. Repeat, using 1 tablespoon cold water at a time, until all the dough is moistened. Shape dough into a ball. On a lightly floured surface, roll dough into a 10-inch square. Carefully fit dough into an ungreased 8×8×2-inch baking pan, allowing dough to extend up the sides. Fold pastry edges over, if necessary, to make sides 1 inch high. Press pastry against sides of pan. Sprinkle dates over crust.

2 For topping, in a small bowl stir together the remaining ½ cup flour, the brown sugar, cinnamon, nutmeg, and ginger. Using a pastry blender, cut in butter until mixture resembles coarse crumbs; set aside.

3 For filling, in a small bowl stir together the hot water and baking soda. Stir in molasses and egg. Carefully pour over crust; sprinkle with crumb topping. Bake for 25 to 30 minutes or until filling is puffed and pastry is golden. Cool in pan on a wire rack. Cut into bars.

Soak the snipped dates in coffee instead of water for a pleasant bittersweet flavor in these brownies.

date-nut brownies

prep: 20 min. **bake:** 20 min. **oven:** 350°F **makes:** 16 bars

¾ cup boiling coffee or water
½ of an 8-ounce package pitted whole dates, snipped (about ¾ cup)
¾ cup all-purpose flour
¼ cup unsweetened cocoa powder
2 tablespoons granulated sugar
½ teaspoon baking powder
½ teaspoon ground cinnamon
¼ teaspoon baking soda
1 egg, beaten
2 tablespoons cooking oil
½ teaspoon vanilla
¼ cup chopped walnuts
Powdered sugar

1 In a small bowl pour boiling coffee over dates. Set mixture aside to cool. Preheat oven to 350°F. Grease an 8×8×2-inch baking pan; set aside.

2 In a medium bowl stir together flour, cocoa powder, granulated sugar, baking powder, cinnamon, and baking soda. Stir egg, oil, and vanilla into cooled date mixture. Add date mixture and walnuts to flour mixture; stir until combined.

3 Spread batter evenly in the prepared pan. Bake about 20 minutes or until edges just start to pull away from sides of pan. Cool in pan on a wire rack. Just before serving, sift powdered sugar over baked mixture. Cut into squares.

note: *Store bars as directed on page 16. Refrigerate up to 3 days.*

You can't go wrong with a bar that features America's favorite flavor—chocolate.

Choose your favorite filling for these treasured treats.
All are truly delicious.

fruit-filled oatmeal bars

prep: 20 min. **bake:** 30 min. **oven:** 350°F **makes:** 25 bars

unbeatable **bars**

1 cup all-purpose flour
1 cup quick-cooking
   rolled oats
⅔ cup packed brown
   sugar
¼ teaspoon baking soda
½ cup butter
1 recipe Mincemeat
   Filling, Raisin
   Filling, Apple-
   Cinnamon Filling,
   or Apricot-Coconut
   Filling

1 Preheat oven to 350°F. In a medium bowl stir together the flour, oats, brown sugar, and baking soda. Using a pastry blender, cut in butter until mixture resembles coarse crumbs. Reserve ½ cup of the flour mixture.

2 Press remaining flour mixture into the bottom of an ungreased 9×9×2-inch baking pan. Spread with desired filling. Sprinkle with reserved flour mixture. Bake for 30 to 35 minutes or until the top is golden. Cool in pan on a wire rack. Cut into bars.

note: *Store bars as directed on page 16. Refrigerate up to 3 days.*

mincemeat filling:*In a medium saucepan bring ¾ cup water to boiling. Add one 9-ounce package condensed mincemeat. Cover and simmer for 3 minutes, stirring often.*

raisin filling:*In a medium saucepan stir together ½ cup water, 2 tablespoons sugar, and 2 teaspoons cornstarch. Add 1 cup raisins. Cook and stir over medium heat until thickened and bubbly.*

apple-cinnamon filling:*Peel, core, and chop 2 medium apples. In a medium saucepan combine apples, 2 tablespoons water, 1 tablespoon lemon juice, ½ teaspoon ground cinnamon, and a dash ground cloves. Bring to boiling; reduce heat. Simmer, covered, for 8 to 10 minutes or until apples are tender.*

apricot-coconut filling:*In a medium saucepan combine 1 cup snipped dried apricots and ¾ cup water. Bring to boiling; reduce heat. Simmer, covered, for 5 minutes. Meanwhile, combine ¼ cup sugar and 1 tablespoon all-purpose flour. Stir into apricot mixture. Cook and stir about 1 minute more or until thick. Stir in ½ cup shredded coconut.*

When time is too short to make the almond brittle yourself, you can purchase the nut-flecked candy at most candy stores.

almond brittle brownies

prep: 30 min. **bake:** 37 min. **oven:** 350°F **makes:** 36 bars

⅓	cup slivered almonds
¼	cup sugar
1	tablespoon butter
½	cup butter, softened
½	cup sugar
1	cup all-purpose flour
¾	cup butter
4	ounces unsweetened chocolate, cut up
2	cups sugar
2	teaspoons vanilla
4	eggs
1½	cups all-purpose flour

1 Line a cookie sheet with foil. Grease foil; set aside.

2 In a heavy medium skillet combine almonds, the ¼ cup sugar, and the 1 tablespoon butter. Cook over medium heat until sugar begins to melt, shaking skillet occasionally. Do not stir. Reduce heat to low. Continue cooking until sugar is golden brown, stirring occasionally with a wooden spoon. Remove from heat. Spread almond mixture onto the prepared cookie sheet; cool completely. Place cooled almond brittle in a heavy plastic bag. Use a rolling pin to coarsely crush the almond brittle; set aside.

3 Preheat oven to 350°F. Grease and flour a 13×9×2-inch baking pan; set aside. For crust, in a medium mixing bowl beat the ½ cup butter and the ½ cup sugar with an electric mixer on medium to high speed until combined. Stir in the 1 cup flour. Press into the bottom of the prepared pan. Bake about 10 minutes or until edges are light brown.

4 Meanwhile, in a saucepan heat and stir the ¾ cup butter and the chocolate over low heat until smooth. Remove from heat. Stir in the 2 cups sugar and the vanilla. Add eggs, one at a time, beating lightly with a wooden spoon just until combined. Stir in the 1½ cups flour. Spread batter over hot crust. Bake 15 minutes. Sprinkle with crushed almond brittle; press brittle lightly into chocolate layer. Bake for 12 to 15 minutes more or until set. Cool in pan on a wire rack. Cut into diamonds.

note: *Store bars as directed on page 16. Refrigerate up to 3 days.*

Not a sherry fan? Customize these gourmet bars with kirsch, clear crème de cacao, orange liqueur, or another flavor of clear liqueur. The bars will be extra dreamy no matter which flavor you choose.

chocolate-and-sherry
cream bars

prep: 25 min. bake: 25 min. chill: 2 hr. oven: 350°F makes: 60 bars

1 cup butter
4 ounces unsweetened chocolate
4 eggs, lightly beaten
2 cups granulated sugar
1 teaspoon vanilla
1 cup all-purpose flour
4 cups powdered sugar
½ cup butter, softened
¼ cup half-and-half or light cream
¼ cup sherry
1 cup chopped walnuts
½ cup semisweet chocolate pieces
2 tablespoons butter
4 teaspoons sherry or water

1 Preheat oven to 350°F. Grease a 15×10×1-inch baking pan; set aside. For crust, in large saucepan heat and stir the 1 cup butter and unsweetened chocolate over low heat until smooth. Remove from heat. Beat in eggs, granulated sugar, and vanilla just until combined. Stir in flour. Spread mixture evenly in the prepared pan. Bake about 25 minutes. Cool in pan on wire rack. (Crust will be moist.)

2 For filling, in a large mixing bowl beat powdered sugar and the ½ cup butter with an electric mixer on low speed until combined. Gradually beat in the half-and-half and ¼ cup sherry. Stir in walnuts. Spread filling evenly over crust; chill until firm.

3 For topping, in a small saucepan heat and stir semisweet chocolate pieces and 2 tablespoons butter over low heat until smooth. Stir in the 4 teaspoons sherry. Drizzle over chilled filling. Chill slightly (until mixture is set but not firm). Using a knife, score top to outline bars. Chill about 2 hours or until firm. Cut into bars.

note: *Store bars as directed on page 16. Refrigerate up to 3 days.*

Unsweetened chocolate is the key to super-rich flavor in these spiked bars.

Minty chocolate chips make these layered bars perfect for a refreshing after-dinner treat.

chocolate mint bars

prep: 30 min. **bake:** 30 min. **oven:** 350°F **makes:** 36 bars

½   cup butter, softened
½   cup shortening
1   cup sugar
1   teaspoon baking
    powder
¼   teaspoon salt
1   egg
1   teaspoon vanilla
2¼   cups all-purpose flour
1½   cups mint-flavor
    semisweet
    chocolate pieces*
1   14-ounce can
    sweetened
    condensed milk
    (.1¼ cups)
½   cup chopped walnuts
1   teaspoon vanilla

1 Preheat oven to 350°F. In a large mixing bowl beat butter and shortening with an electric mixer on medium to high speed for 30 seconds. Add the sugar, baking powder, and salt. Beat until combined, scraping sides of bowl occasionally. Beat in egg and vanilla until combined. Beat in as much of the flour as you can with the mixer. Stir in any remaining flour. Set dough aside.

2 For filling, in a medium saucepan heat and stir chocolate pieces and condensed milk over low heat until smooth, stirring occasionally. Remove from heat. Stir in walnuts and vanilla.

3 Press two-thirds of the dough into the bottom of an ungreased 13×9×2-inch baking pan. Spread filling evenly over dough. Dot remaining dough over the filling. Bake for 30 to 35 minutes or until golden. Cool in pan on a wire rack. Cut into bars.

* If desired, substitute semisweet chocolate pieces for the mint-flavor chocolate pieces and add ¼ teaspoon mint flavoring with the vanilla.

Unsweetened chocolate makes these brownies extra fudgy.
A chocolaty cream cheese frosting adds the perfect finish.

fudgy brownies

prep: 20 min. **bake:** 30 min. **oven:** 350°F **makes:** 16 brownies

½ cup butter
3 ounces unsweetened chocolate, coarsely chopped
1 cup sugar
2 eggs
1 teaspoon vanilla
⅔ cup all-purpose flour
¼ teaspoon baking soda
½ cup chopped almonds or pecans (optional)
1 recipe Chocolate-Cream Cheese Frosting (optional)

1 Preheat oven to 350°F. In a medium saucepan heat and stir butter and chocolate over low heat until smooth. Remove from heat; let cool.

2 Meanwhile, grease an 8×8×2-inch or 9×9×2-inch baking pan; set aside. Stir sugar into cooled chocolate mixture in saucepan. Add the eggs, one at a time, beating with a wooden spoon just until mixture is combined. Stir in the vanilla.

3 In a small bowl stir together the flour and baking soda. Add flour mixture to chocolate mixture; stir just until combined. If desired, stir in nuts. Spread the batter evenly in the prepared pan.

4 Bake about 30 minutes for an 8-inch pan or 25 minutes for a 9-inch pan. Cool in pan on a wire rack. If desired, frost with Chocolate-Cream Cheese Frosting. Cut into squares.

chocolate-cream cheese frosting: *In a saucepan heat and stir 1 cup semisweet chocolate pieces over low heat until smooth. Remove from heat; let cool. In a small bowl stir together two 3-ounce packages softened cream cheese and ½ cup powdered sugar. Stir in melted chocolate until smooth.*

Be sure to cut the lavender-flecked shortbread while it is still warm or it may crumble. Look for dried lavender buds at specialty food stores.

gingery lavender shortbread

prep: 20 min. **bake:** 25 min. **stand:** 5 min. **oven:** 325°F **makes:** 32 slices

2½   cups all-purpose flour
⅓   cup sugar
2   tablespoons finely chopped crystallized ginger
1   teaspoon dried lavender buds
¼   teaspoon ground ginger
1   cup butter
    Sugar (optional)

1 Preheat oven to 325°F. Line a cookie sheet with parchment paper; set aside.

2 In a medium bowl stir together flour, ⅓ cup sugar, the crystallized ginger, lavender, and ground ginger. Using a pastry blender, cut in butter until mixture resembles fine crumbs and starts to cling. Shape mixture into a ball and knead until smooth (dough may be crumbly at first but will come together as you work it with your hands).

3 Roll or pat dough into an 11×6-inch rectangle on the prepared cookie sheet. Using a large knife, carefully cut rectangle in half lengthwise, then cut crosswise into 16 slices. Do not separate slices.

4 Bake for 25 to 30 minutes or until edges are light brown and center is set. Cut rectangle into strips again while warm. If desired, sprinkle with additional sugar. Let stand for 5 minutes on cookie sheet. Transfer to a wire rack and let cool.

Crystallized ginger and ground ginger add a pleasing bite to this buttery, rich cookie.

These chocolate-dipped, nut-sprinkled wedges will stand out on the dessert plate at a party. Don't be surprised when your friends ask for the recipe.

pistachio brownie wedges

prep: 25 min. **bake:** 25 min. **oven:** 325°F **makes:** 16 wedges

½ cup butter
3 ounces unsweetened chocolate
2 eggs
¾ cup sugar
1 teaspoon vanilla
¾ cup all-purpose flour
¾ cup coarsely chopped pecans, toasted (see tip, page 19)
1 ounce semisweet and/or bittersweet chocolate squares
1 teaspoon shortening
1 ounce white chocolate baking square (with cocoa butter)
½ cup pistachio nuts or pecans, finely chopped

1 Preheat oven to 325°F. Line the bottom of a 9×1½-inch round baking pan with waxed paper; grease waxed paper and the sides of pan. Set aside.

2 In a small saucepan heat and stir butter and unsweetened chocolate over low heat until smooth. Remove from heat; let cool.

3 In a large mixing bowl beat eggs about 1 minute or until frothy. Add sugar and vanilla; beat 2 minutes or until thickened. Beat in melted chocolate mixture. Stir in flour. Spread evenly into the prepared pan. Sprinkle with toasted pecans; press lightly into batter.

4 Bake about 25 minutes. Cool in pan on a wire rack. Remove brownie from pan. Remove waxed paper. Cut brownie into quarters; cut each quarter into 4 wedges.

5 In a small saucepan heat and stir semisweet chocolate and ½ teaspoon of the shortening until smooth. In another small saucepan heat and stir the remaining ½ teaspoon shortening and the white chocolate baking square until smooth.

6 Carefully dip outer edges of eight brownie wedges into melted semisweet chocolate mixture, then into pistachios. Dip outer edges of the remaining brownie wedges in melted white chocolate mixture, then in pistachio nuts. Place on waxed paper. Let stand until set.

note: *Store bars as directed on page 16. Refrigerate up to 3 days. Freeze up to 1 month.*

The lusciously thick filling on these all-time favorite bars gets its citrusy nuance from plenty of lemon juice and a bit of shredded lemon peel.

lemon bars

prep: 25 min. **bake:** 33 min. **oven:** 350°F **makes:** 36 bars

2 cups all-purpose flour
½ cup powdered sugar
2 tablespoons cornstarch
¼ teaspoon salt
¾ cup butter
4 eggs, lightly beaten
1½ cups granulated sugar
3 tablespoons all-purpose flour
1 teaspoon finely shredded lemon peel
¾ cup lemon juice
¼ cup half-and-half, light cream, or milk
Powdered sugar

1 Preheat oven to 350°F. Line a 13×9×2-inch baking pan with foil, extending the foil over the edges of pan. Grease foil; set aside. In a large bowl stir together the 2 cups flour, the ½ cup powdered sugar, the cornstarch, and salt. Using a pastry blender, cut in butter until mixture resembles coarse crumbs. Press mixture evenly into the bottom of the prepared pan. Bake for 10 to 20 minutes or until edges are golden.

2 Meanwhile, for filling, in a medium bowl stir together eggs, the granulated sugar, the 3 tablespoons flour, the lemon peel, lemon juice, and half-and-half. Pour filling over hot crust. Bake for 15 to 20 minutes more or until center is set. Cool completely in pan on a wire rack. Use the foil to lift baked mixture from pan. Cut into bars. Just before serving, sift powdered sugar over bars.

note: *Store bars as directed on page 16. Refrigerate up to 3 days. Do not freeze.*

These brownies, modeled after the famous Viennese apricot-chocolate sacher torte, provide a spectacular example of how celebrated desserts transform into easy bar cookies.

hazelnut sacher brownies

prep: 1 hr. chill: 20 min. bake: 32 min. oven: 350°F makes: 48 bars

½ cup butter, softened
¾ cup powdered sugar
¾ cup all-purpose flour
½ cup hazelnuts,
    toasted* and finely
    ground (see tip,
    page 19)
¾ cup apricot preserves
½ cup butter
3 ounces unsweetened
    chocolate
1 egg
1 egg yolk
1 cup granulated sugar
¼ teaspoon salt
1 teaspoon vanilla
½ cup all-purpose flour
3 ounces semisweet
    chocolate, melted
1 ounce white
    chocolate baking
    square or bar,
    melted

1 Preheat oven to 350°F. Line a 13×9×2-inch baking pan with foil, extending the foil over the edges of pan. Grease foil; set aside.

2 For the crust, in a small mixing bowl beat the ½ cup softened butter and the powdered sugar with an electric mixer on medium to high speed until combined. Beat in the ¾ cup flour and ground nuts. Pat mixture evenly into bottom of the prepared pan. Bake about 12 minutes. Cool in pan on a wire rack.

3 In a blender, cover and blend the preserves until smooth. Spread pureed preserves over the baked crust. Chill for 20 minutes.

4 Meanwhile, in a small saucepan heat and stir the ½ cup butter and the unsweetened chocolate over medium-low heat until smooth. Remove from heat; cool for 10 minutes. In a medium mixing bowl beat the egg, egg yolk, granulated sugar, and salt with an electric mixer on medium speed for 5 minutes. Beat in melted chocolate mixture and the vanilla. Stir in the ½ cup flour. Carefully spread over chilled preserves layer.

5 Bake about 20 minutes more. Cool in pan on a wire rack. Use the foil to lift brownie from pan. Carefully peel the foil from the sides of the brownie. Spread the melted semisweet chocolate over top. Let stand until set.

6 Drizzle the melted white chocolate over the semisweet chocolate layer. Let stand until set. Cut into 2×1-inch bars.

*After toasting hazelnuts, place the warm nuts in a clean kitchen towel. Rub nuts with the towel to remove loose skins.

note: *Store bars as directed on page 16. Refrigerate up to 3 days.*

No cutting required for these crisp bites. Bake the cookies in a large pan, then break them into pieces.

lemon-almond cookie brittle

prep: 20 min. **bake:** 20 min. **oven:** 350°F **makes:** 36 bars

¾ cup butter, softened
¾ cup granulated sugar
⅛ teaspoon salt
1 teaspoon vanilla
1½ cups all-purpose flour
1½ teaspoons finely shredded lemon peel
¾ cup coarsely chopped toasted sliced almonds (see tip, page 19)
Powdered sugar (optional)

1 Preheat oven to 350°F. In a large mixing bowl beat butter with an electric mixer on medium to high speed for 30 seconds. Add granulated sugar, salt, and vanilla. Beat until combined, scraping sides of bowl occasionally. Beat in as much flour as you can with the mixer. Stir in any remaining flour, the lemon peel, and half of the almonds.

2 Press dough evenly into the bottom of an ungreased 13×9×2-inch baking pan. Sprinkle remaining almonds over top; press lightly into surface.

3 Bake about 20 minutes or until top is golden. Cool in pan on a wire rack. If desired, sift powdered sugar over cooled brittle. Break into chunks.

note: *Store bars as directed on page 16. Refrigerate up to 3 days. Freeze up to 1 month.*

Lemon peel adds a refreshing burst of citrus to this almond-studded cookie brittle.

The flavors of orange and chocolate have long been a winning combination. These brownies showcase the duo and the tasty addition of toasted walnuts.

marmalade-nut brownies

prep: 20 min. **bake:** 30 min. **oven:** 350°F **makes:** 36 brownies

1½	cups sugar
1	cup butter, melted
3	eggs
½	cup orange marmalade
1	teaspoon vanilla
1	cup all-purpose flour
¾	cup unsweetened cocoa powder
1	teaspoon baking powder
¼	teaspoon salt
¼	teaspoon cayenne pepper
1	cup semisweet or milk chocolate pieces
½	cup chopped walnuts, toasted (see tip, page 19)
½	teaspoon shortening

1 Preheat oven to 350°F. Line a 13×9×2-inch baking pan with foil, extending the foil over the edges of pan. Grease foil; set aside. In a large bowl stir together sugar and melted butter. Stir in eggs, one at a time, beating well after each addition. Stir in marmalade and vanilla. Stir in flour, cocoa powder, baking powder, salt, and cayenne pepper until well combined. Stir in ½ cup of the chocolate pieces and the nuts.

2 Spread batter evenly in prepared pan. Bake about 30 minutes or until center is set. Cool in pan on a wire rack. Use the foil to lift brownie from pan. Cut brownie into 36 pieces.

3 In a small saucepan heat and stir the remaining ½ cup chocolate pieces and the shortening over low heat until smooth. Cool slightly. Drizzle chocolate mixture over brownies. Chill until chocolate is set.

*These fudgy triangles are so rich they require no frosting—
just a light dusting of powdered sugar.*

mocha-orange brownies

prep: 20 min. **bake:** 30 min. **oven:** 350°F **makes:** 24 brownies

⅔ cup butter
⅓ cup unsweetened
    cocoa powder
1 teaspoon instant
    coffee crystals
1 cup granulated sugar
2 eggs
1 teaspoon vanilla
¾ cup all-purpose flour
½ cup chopped
    semisweet
    chocolate
1 teaspoon finely
    shredded orange
    peel
   Powdered sugar
    (optional)

1 Preheat oven to 350°F. Grease an 8×8×2-inch baking pan; set aside. In a medium saucepan melt butter over medium heat. Stir in cocoa powder and coffee crystals. Remove from heat. Stir in granulated sugar. Stir in eggs, one at a time. Stir in vanilla. Beat lightly by hand just until combined. Stir in flour, the chopped chocolate, and orange peel.

2 Spread batter evenly in the prepared pan. Bake for 30 minutes. Cool in pan on a wire rack. If desired, sift powdered sugar over top of brownies. Cut into triangles or squares.

These buttery bars get their scrumptious nutty-citrus flavor from shredded orange peel and a bit of almond extract in both the dough and the icing.

orange-almond bars

prep: 30 min. **bake:** 20 min. **oven:** 325°F **makes:** about 40 bars

½ cup butter, softened
1½ cups all-purpose flour
1 cup sugar
1 egg
2 teaspoons baking powder
½ teaspoon finely shredded orange peel
½ teaspoon almond extract
⅛ teaspoon salt
Milk
½ cup sliced almonds, coarsely chopped
1 recipe Orange Icing

1 Preheat oven to 325°F. In a medium mixing bowl beat butter with an electric mixer on medium to high speed for 30 seconds. Add half of the flour, the sugar, egg, baking powder, orange peel, almond extract, and salt. Beat until combined, scraping sides of bowl occasionally. Beat in the remaining flour. Using hands, knead dough into a ball.

2 Divide dough into fourths. On a lightly floured surface, shape each portion of dough into an 8-inch-long log. Place two logs 4 to 5 inches apart on each of two ungreased cookie sheets. Flatten until logs are 2 inches wide. Brush flattened logs with milk; sprinkle with almonds.

3 Bake for 20 to 22 minutes or until bottoms are light brown. Cut warm rolls diagonally into 1-inch slices. Transfer to a wire rack and let cool. Drizzle Orange Icing over cooled bars.

orange icing: *In a small bowl stir together 1 cup powdered sugar and ¼ teaspoon almond extract. Stir in enough orange juice (3 to 4 teaspoons) to make an icing of drizzling consistency.*

The combination of chocolate-banana bars and strawberry-and-cream cheese frosting makes these brownies taste like the favorite ice cream treat.

banana split brownies

prep: 25 min. **bake:** 20 min. **oven:** 350°F **makes:** 24 bars

½ cup butter, softened
1 cup sugar
1 teaspoon baking powder
½ teaspoon baking soda
⅛ teaspoon salt
1 cup mashed banana (2 to 3 medium)
2 eggs
⅓ cup unsweetened cocoa powder
1 cup all-purpose flour
1 recipe Strawberry-and-Cream Cheese Frosting

1 Preheat oven to 350°F. Grease a 13×9×2-inch baking pan; set aside. In a large mixing bowl beat butter with an electric mixer on medium to high speed for 30 seconds. Add sugar, baking powder, baking soda, and salt. Beat until combined, scraping sides of bowl occasionally. Beat in mashed banana and eggs until combined. Beat in cocoa powder and as much of the flour as you can with mixer. Stir in any remaining flour. Spread batter evenly in the prepared pan.

2 Bake about 20 minutes or until a wooden toothpick inserted in the center comes out clean. Cool completely in pan on a wire rack; spread with Strawberry-and-Cream Cheese Frosting. Cut into bars.

note: *Store bars as directed on page 16. Refrigerate up to 3 days.*

strawberry-and-cream cheese frosting: *In a mixing bowl beat half of an 8-ounce tub cream cheese with strawberries and 1 cup powdered sugar with an electric mixer on medium speed until combined. Beat in ½ cup frozen strawberries, thawed, cut up, and well drained (about ¼ cup). Beat in 2½ to 3 cups powdered sugar to make a frosting of spreading consistency (frosting will stiffen with chilling).*

When you need something for a special occasion, try these bars that burst with citrus flavor. There's no need to toast the coconut beforehand because it toasts in the oven while the bars bake.

orange-coconut bars

prep: 20 min. **bake:** 36 min. **oven:** 350°F **makes:** 16 bars

1 cup all-purpose flour
¼ cup powdered sugar
½ cup butter
½ cup finely chopped almonds or pecans, toasted (see tip, page 19)
¾ cup packed brown sugar
2 tablespoons all-purpose flour
1 tablespoon finely shredded orange peel
¼ teaspoon baking powder
2 eggs
3 tablespoons frozen orange juice concentrate, thawed
¼ teaspoon almond extract
1 cup flaked coconut

1 Preheat oven to 350°F. For crust, in a medium bowl stir together the 1 cup flour and the powdered sugar. Using a pastry blender, cut in butter until mixture resembles coarse crumbs. Stir in almonds. Press flour mixture evenly into the bottom of an ungreased 8×8×2-inch baking pan. Bake for 18 to 20 minutes or until crust is just golden.

2 Meanwhile, for filling, in another bowl stir together brown sugar, the 2 tablespoons flour, the orange peel, and baking powder. In a small bowl combine eggs, orange juice concentrate, and almond extract. Add to brown sugar mixture. Beat with a fork for 1 minute. Stir in coconut. Spread filling over hot crust. Bake for 18 to 20 minutes more or until edges are light brown and center is set. Cool in pan on a wire rack. Cut into bars.

note: *Store bars as directed on page 16. Do not freeze.*

Coconut in three forms—milk, flakes, and frosting—puts a flavorful spin on basic white cakelike bars, while chopped dates add a bit of chewy sweetness.

coconut-date bars

prep: 30 min. bake: 30 min. oven: 350°F makes: 36 bars

2 cups all-purpose flour
1½ cups sugar
2 teaspoons baking powder
¼ teaspoon salt
1 cup butter
¾ cup canned unsweetened coconut milk
2 eggs
1 teaspoon vanilla
1 cup flaked coconut, toasted (see tip, page 19)
1 8-ounce package chopped dates (1⅓ cups)
1 recipe Coconut Frosting
½ cup flaked coconut, toasted
2 ounces white baking bar or candy coating, melted (optional)

1 Preheat oven to 350°F. Grease and flour a 15×10×1-inch baking pan; set aside. In a large mixing bowl stir together flour, sugar, baking powder, and salt; set aside.

2 In a saucepan combine butter and coconut milk. Bring just to boiling, stirring occasionally. Add butter mixture to flour mixture. Beat on medium speed until well combined. Add eggs and vanilla; beat 1 minute. Fold in the 1 cup coconut and the dates. Spread batter in the prepared pan.

3 Bake 30 minutes or until wooden toothpick inserted in the center comes out clean. Cool completely in pan on wire rack; spread with Coconut Frosting. Sprinkle with the remaining ½ cup coconut. Cut into bars.

4 If desired, place melted baking bar in a resealable plastic bag. Snip a small hole in one corner of the bag; pipe snowflake designs onto a baking sheet lined with waxed paper. Let stand until firm. Place snowflakes on bars.

note: *Store bars as directed on page 16. Refrigerate up to 3 days.*

coconut frosting: *In a medium mixing bowl beat one 3-ounce package cream cheese, softened, and 2 tablespoons softened butter with an electric mixer on medium to high speed until combined. Beat in 2 tablespoons canned unsweetened coconut milk and ½ teaspoon vanilla. Gradually beat in 4 cups powdered sugar until smooth.*

The blend of bittersweet and unsweetened chocolates gives the brownie layer an especially deep, rich taste to complement the sweet cheesecake layer.

raspberry
cheesecake brownies

prep: 25 min. **bake:** 35 min. **chill:** 6 hr. **oven:** 350°F **makes:** about 32 brownies

4	ounces bittersweet or semisweet chocolate, chopped
2	ounces unsweetened chocolate, chopped
½	cup unsalted butter
1¼	cups sugar
4	eggs
2	teaspoons vanilla
½	teaspoon salt
¾	cup all-purpose flour
1	8-ounce package cream cheese, softened
⅔	cup sugar
2	teaspoons lemon juice
2	tablespoons all-purpose flour
1½	cups fresh raspberries
1	tablespoon sugar

1 Preheat oven to 350°F. Grease and flour a 13×9×2-inch baking pan; set aside.

2 For brownie layer, in a medium saucepan heat and stir bittersweet chocolate, unsweetened chocolate, and butter over low heat until smooth. Remove from heat; let cool. Whisk in the 1¼ cups sugar and 3 of the eggs, one at a time. Whisk in 1½ teaspoons of the vanilla and the salt. Stir in the ¾ cup flour just until combined. Spread batter evenly in the bottom of the prepared pan. Set aside.

3 For cheesecake layer, in a medium mixing bowl beat cream cheese and the ⅔ cup sugar with an electric mixer on medium speed until combined. Beat in lemon juice, the remaining 1 egg, and the remaining ½ teaspoon vanilla just until combined. Beat in the 2 tablespoons flour. Spread mixture evenly over brownie layer in pan. Top with raspberries; sprinkle with the 1 tablespoon sugar.

4 Bake for 35 to 40 minutes or until top is puffed and golden and the edges start to brown. Cool in pan on a wire rack. Chill, covered, for at least 6 hours. Cut into bars. Serve cold or at room temperature.

note: *Store bars as directed on page 16. Refrigerate up to 3 days. Do not freeze.*

Who can resist a bar that stacks up so many flavors—sweet graham cracker crust; rich, chocolaty cheesecake; spicy pumpkin cheesecake; and a topping of sour cream?

pumpkin chocolate
cheesecake bars

prep: 30 min. **bake:** 55 min. **stand:** 30 min. **chill:** 4 hr. **oven:** 325°F
makes: 24 bars

2　8-ounce packages cream cheese, softened
1¾　cups sugar
3　large eggs
1　cup canned pumpkin
½　teaspoon pumpkin pie spice
½　teaspoon vanilla
¼　teaspoon salt
6　ounces semisweet chocolate, cut up
2　tablespoons butter
1　recipe Graham Cracker Crust
1¼　cups dairy sour cream
¼　cup sugar

1 Preheat oven to 325°F. For filling, in a large mixing bowl beat cream cheese and the 1¾ cups sugar with an electric mixer on medium speed until combined. Add eggs, one at a time, beating on low speed after each addition until just combined. Stir in pumpkin, pumpkin pie spice, vanilla, and salt. Transfer 1¼ cups of the filling to a medium bowl. Set both bowls aside.

2 In a small saucepan heat and stir chocolate and butter over low heat until smooth. Stir melted chocolate mixture into the 1¼ cups filling. Carefully spread the chocolate filling evenly over Graham Cracker Crust. Bake for 15 minutes. Carefully pour remaining pumpkin filling over the baked chocolate layer, spreading evenly.

3 Bake for 40 to 45 minutes more or until mixture is slightly puffed around edges and just set in center. Let stand in pan on a wire rack for 30 minutes. Meanwhile, in a small bowl stir together sour cream and the ¼ cup sugar. Cover; let stand at room temperature while cooling.

4 Gently spread the sour cream mixture over partially cooled baked mixture; cool completely. Cover and chill at least 4 hours. Cut into bars.

note: *Store bars as directed on page 16. Refrigerate up to 1 week. Do not freeze.*

graham cracker crust: *Lightly grease a 13×9×2-inch baking pan. In a large mixing bowl stir together 1¼ cups graham cracker crumbs and ¼ cup sugar. Add ⅓ cup melted butter; mix well. Press crumb mixture evenly into the bottom of the prepared pan.*

The simple dough and a drizzle of browned butter icing allow the flavor of the toasted cashews to take center stage.

browned butter and
cashew shortbread

prep: 20 min. **chill:** 1 hr. **bake:** 25 min. **oven:** 325°F **makes:** 24 bars

⅔ cup butter
½ teaspoon vanilla
1¼ cups all-purpose flour
3 tablespoons brown
   sugar
½ cup powdered sugar
2 to 3 teaspoons milk
2 tablespoons finely
   chopped toasted
   cashews (see tip,
   page 19)

1 Line an 8×8×2-inch baking pan with foil, extending the foil over the edges of pan. Set aside. In a medium saucepan heat butter over medium heat until butter turns the color of light brown sugar, stirring frequently. Remove from heat; cool slightly. Set aside 2 tablespoons of the browned butter for the icing. Stir vanilla into remaining browned butter. Chill browned butter mixture about 1 hour or until firm.

2 Preheat oven to 325°F. In a medium bowl stir together the flour and brown sugar. Using a pastry blender, cut chilled butter mixture into the flour mixture until mixture resembles fine crumbs and starts to cling. Press dough firmly into the bottom of the prepared pan.

3 Bake about 25 minutes or until firm but not brown. Immediately use the foil to lift shortbread from pan. Cut shortbread into bars. Use foil to lift and transfer bars to a wire rack; cool completely.

4 For icing, stir together reserved browned butter, the powdered sugar, and enough of the milk to make an icing of drizzling consistency. Drizzle icing over cooled shortbread. Sprinkle with cashews.

A smooth, buttery dough flecked with toffee and chocolate pieces is the perfect treat to bring to any get-together.

toffee fingers

prep: 40 min. **bake:** 20 min. **oven:** 325°F **makes:** 24 bars

1¼	cups all-purpose flour
¾	teaspoon baking powder
¼	teaspoon salt
½	cup butter, softened
¼	cup powdered sugar
2	tablespoons packed brown sugar
¾	cup toffee pieces
½	cup semisweet chocolate pieces
1	teaspoon shortening

1 Preheat oven to 325°F. Line an 8×8×2-inch baking pan with foil, extending the foil over the edges of pan; set aside.

2 In a small bowl stir together flour, baking powder, and salt; set aside. In a large mixing bowl beat butter with an electric mixer on medium to high speed for 30 seconds. Add powdered sugar and brown sugar. Beat until combined, scraping sides of bowl occasionally. Beat in flour mixture (mixture seems dry but comes together as you beat). Stir in ½ cup of the toffee pieces.

3 Press dough evenly into the bottom of the prepared pan; prick dough with fork every ½ inch. Bake about 20 minutes or until light brown. Cool slightly in pan.

4 Use the foil to lift warm bars from pan. Place bars on a cutting board and cut into eight 1-inch strips. Cut strips crosswise into three pieces, making 24 bars. Transfer bars to a wire rack placed over a sheet of waxed paper; cool completely.

5 In a small saucepan heat and stir chocolate pieces and shortening over low heat until smooth. Cool slightly. Drizzle melted chocolate over bars.* Immediately sprinkle the drizzled bars with the remaining ¼ cup toffee pieces. Let stand until set.

*To dip the cookies into chocolate instead of drizzling them, melt 1 cup chocolate pieces and 2 teaspoons shortening. Dip the ends of the cookies and allow the excess chocolate mixture to drip off. Sprinkle with toffee pieces.

unbeatable **bars**

Brazil nuts are the seeds of a giant tree that grows in South America's Amazon jungle. Look for the nuts at specialty food stores or in supermarkets around late fall.

rain forest bars

prep: 25 min. **bake:** 30 min. **stand:** 5 min. **oven:** 350°F **makes:** 40 bars

¾	cup butter, softened
1½	cup packed brown sugar
1	egg yolk
2	teaspoons vanilla
2	cups all-purpose flour
3	eggs
3	tablespoons all-purpose flour
¼	teaspoon salt
2	cups chopped Brazil nuts
1	cup flaked coconut

1 Preheat oven to 350°F. In a medium mixing bowl beat butter with an electric mixer on medium to high speed for 30 seconds. Add ½ cup of the brown sugar. Beat until combined, scraping sides of bowl occasionally. Beat in egg yolk and 1 teaspoon of the vanilla until combined. Beat in the 2 cups flour. Pat dough evenly into the bottom of an ungreased 13×9×2-inch baking pan. Bake 10 minutes. Let stand in pan on a wire rack for 5 minutes.

2 Meanwhile, in a large mixing bowl beat the remaining 1 cup brown sugar, the eggs, and the 1 teaspoon vanilla at medium speed until combined. Beat in the 3 tablespoons flour and the salt until combined. Stir in Brazil nuts and coconut. Spread nut mixture evenly over crust. Bake about 20 minutes more or until set. Cool in pan on a wire rack. Cut into bars.

note: *Store bars as directed on page 16. Refrigerate up to 3 days. Freeze up to 1 month.*

Flaked coconut and Brazil nuts make this taste-of-the-tropics cookie a great cure for the winter blues.

*Select some of your favorite
nuts or use a prepackaged mixture
for these protein-rich bars.*

mixed nut bars

prep: 25 min. **bake:** 35 min. **oven:** 350°F **makes:** 32 bars

¾	cup butter, softened
⅓	cup packed brown sugar
2	cups all-purpose flour
1⅔	cups granulated sugar
1	cup buttermilk
3	eggs
¼	cup butter, melted
1½	teaspoons vanilla
2	cups coarsely chopped mixed nuts
	Powdered sugar (optional)

1 Preheat oven to 350°F. For crust, in a medium mixing bowl beat the ¾ cup butter, the brown sugar, and 1¾ cups of the flour with an electric mixer on medium speed until well combined (mixture will be crumbly). Pat mixture onto the bottom and ½ inch up the sides of an ungreased 13x9x2-inch baking pan. Bake about 10 minutes.

2 Meanwhile, in a large mixing bowl beat granulated sugar, the remaining ¼ cup flour, the buttermilk, eggs, the ¼ cup melted butter, and the vanilla with an electric mixer on low speed until combined. Stir in nuts. Pour onto partially baked crust.

3 Bake about 25 minutes more or until golden and center is set. Cool in pan on a wire rack. If desired, sift powdered sugar over top. Cut into bars.

note: *Store bars as directed on page 16. Refrigerate up to 3 days.*

Cinnamon chips give these moist bars an intense flavor punch that is balanced by the mellow pear. If cinnamon chips are not available, white baking pieces are a delicious alternative.

pear-cinnamon
streusel squares

prep: 30 min. bake: 45 min. oven: 350°F makes: 32 bars

2 cups all-purpose flour
1¼ cups quick-cooking rolled oats
¾ cup packed brown sugar
2 teaspoons ground cinnamon
1 cup butter
2 eggs
1 cup granulated sugar
2 tablespoons all-purpose flour
¼ teaspoon baking powder
¼ teaspoon salt
2 cups chopped, peeled, and cored pears or apples
¾ cup cinnamon-flavor baking pieces
1 recipe Powdered Sugar Icing

1 Preheat oven to 350°F. Lightly grease a 13×9×2-inch baking pan; set aside. In a large mixing bowl stir together the 2 cups flour, the oats, brown sugar, and ground cinnamon. Using a pastry blender, cut in butter until mixture resembles coarse crumbs. Remove 1½ cups of the oats mixture; set aside. Press remaining oats mixture onto the bottom of the prepared baking pan. Bake for 15 minutes.

2 Meanwhile, in a medium mixing bowl beat eggs and granulated sugar with a whisk until smooth. Whisk in the 2 tablespoons flour, then the baking powder and salt. Stir in pears and cinnamon pieces. Gently spread fruit mixture over hot crust. Sprinkle with reserved oats mixture. Bake for 30 to 35 minutes more or until golden brown. Cool in pan on a wire rack. Cut into squares. Drizzle with Powdered Sugar Icing.

note: *Store bars as directed on page 16. Refrigerate up to 1 week. Do not freeze.*

powdered sugar icing: *In a small bowl stir together 1 cup powdered sugar and 1 tablespoon milk. Stir in additional milk, 1 teaspoon at a time, until icing is of drizzling consistency.*

Two favorite cookie treats—brownies and shortbread—come together for a supertasty dessert.

shortbread brownies

prep: 20 min. **bake:** 48 min. **oven:** 350°F **makes:** 24 bars

1¾	cups all-purpose flour
¼	cup packed brown sugar
½	cup butter
¾	cup miniature semisweet chocolate pieces
1⅓	cups granulated sugar
½	cup unsweetened cocoa powder
1½	teaspoons baking powder
½	teaspoon salt
3	eggs
⅓	cup butter, melted
1	tablespoon vanilla

1 Preheat oven to 350°F. Line a 9×9×2-inch baking pan with foil, extending foil over the edges of pan; set aside. In a medium bowl stir together 1 cup of the flour and the brown sugar. Using a pastry blender, cut in the ½ cup butter until mixture resembles coarse crumbs. Stir in ¼ cup of the chocolate pieces. Press flour mixture into the bottom of the prepared pan. Bake about 8 minutes.

2 Meanwhile, in a large bowl stir together granulated sugar, the remaining ¾ cup flour, the cocoa powder, baking powder, and salt. Add eggs, melted butter, and vanilla; beat by hand until smooth. Stir in the remaining ½ cup chocolate pieces; spread over crust.

3 Bake about 40 minutes more. Cool in pan on a wire rack. Use the foil to lift brownie from pan. Cut into squares.

note: *Store bars as directed on page 16. Refrigerate up to 2 days.*

This snack has the scrumptious flavor of pecan pie in the fun-to-eat shape of a bar. To easily remove bars, line the pan with foil.

pecan pie bars

prep: 25 min. **bake:** 40 min. **oven:** 350°F **makes:** 24 bars

1¼	cups all-purpose flour
½	cup powdered sugar
¼	teaspoon salt
½	cup butter
2	eggs, lightly beaten
1	cup chopped pecans
½	cup packed brown sugar
½	cup light-color corn syrup
2	tablespoons butter, melted
1	teaspoon vanilla

1 Preheat oven to 350°F. For crust, in a medium bowl stir together flour, powdered sugar, and salt. Using a pastry blender, cut in the ½ cup butter until mixture resembles coarse crumbs. Pat flour mixture into the bottom of an ungreased 11×7×1½-inch baking pan. Bake about 20 minutes or until light brown.

2 Meanwhile, for filling, in a medium bowl stir together eggs, pecans, brown sugar, corn syrup, 2 tablespoons melted butter, and the vanilla. Spread evenly over baked crust. Bake about 20 minutes more or until filling is set. Cool in pan on a wire rack. Cut into bars.

note: *Store bars as directed on page 16. Refrigerate up to 3 days. Do not freeze.*

For the ultimate treat, serve each of these gooey, pecan-filled bars with a big mound of whipped cream.

A maple syrup-flavor frosting gives these wholesome spiced bars a perfectly sweet finish.

whole wheat
gingerbread bars

prep: 20 min. **bake:** 25 min. oven: 375°F **makes:** 36 bars

½ cup shortening
1 cup all-purpose flour
½ cup whole wheat flour
½ cup mild-flavor molasses
½ cup hot water
¼ cup packed brown sugar
1 egg
¾ teaspoon baking powder
¾ teaspoon ground cinnamon
½ teaspoon ground ginger
¼ teaspoon baking soda
¼ teaspoon salt
¼ cup chopped walnuts
1 recipe Maple Frosting

1 Preheat the oven to 375°F. Grease a 13×9×2-inch baking pan; set aside. In a medium mixing bowl beat shortening on medium to high speed for 30 seconds. Add the all-purpose flour, whole wheat flour, molasses, the hot water, brown sugar, egg, baking powder, cinnamon, ginger, baking soda, and salt. Beat until combined, scraping sides of bowl occasionally. Stir in walnuts.

2 Spread batter evenly in the prepared pan. Bake about 25 minutes or until a toothpick inserted in the center comes out clean. Cool in pan on a wire rack. Spread Maple Frosting over cooled baked mixture. Cut into bars.

note: *Store bars as directed on page 16. Refrigerate up to 3 days.*

maple frosting *In a large mixing bowl beat ⅓ cup softened butter until fluffy. Slowly add 2 cups sifted powdered sugar, beating well. Beat in ¼ cup milk and ½ teaspoon maple flavoring. Gradually beat in 2½ cups additional sifted powdered sugar. Beat in a little additional milk, if needed, to make a frosting of spreading consistency.*

With walnuts, macadamia nuts, milk chocolate, and white chocolate, these bars can't help being anything but absolutely delicious.

ultimate bar cookies

prep: 20 min. bake: 30 min. oven: 350°F makes: 36 bars

2   cups all-purpose flour
1   cup packed brown
     sugar
½   cup butter, softened
1   cup coarsely chopped
     walnuts
1   3½-ounce jar
     macadamia nuts,
     coarsely chopped
     (1 cup)
1   6-ounce package
     white baking
     chocolate (with
     cocoa butter),
     coarsely chopped
     (1 cup)
1   cup milk chocolate
     pieces
¾   cup butter

1 Preheat oven to 350°F. In a medium mixing bowl beat flour, ½ cup of the brown sugar, and the ½ cup butter with an electric mixer on medium speed until fine crumbs form. Press flour mixture firmly into the bottom of an ungreased 13×9×2-inch baking pan.

2 Bake about 15 minutes or until light brown. Sprinkle walnuts and macadamia nuts, white chocolate, and milk chocolate pieces over hot crust.

3 In a small saucepan heat and stir the ¾ cup butter and remaining ½ cup brown sugar over medium heat until bubbly. Cook and stir for 1 minute more. Pour evenly over layers in baking pan. Bake about 15 minutes more or until just bubbly around edges. Cool in pan on a wire rack. Cut into bars.

note: *Store bars as directed on page 16. Refrigerate up to 2 days. Do not freeze.*

Tangy cranberries are a great match for wholesome oatmeal and sweet, creamy cheesecake in these layered bars.

oatmeal-cheesecake-
cranberry bars

prep: 20 min. **bake:** 55 min. **chill:** 3 hr. **oven:** 350°F **makes:** 36 bars

2	cups all-purpose flour
1¼	cups quick-cooking rolled oats
¾	cup packed brown sugar
1	cup butter
12	ounces cream cheese, softened
½	cup granulated sugar
2	eggs
2	teaspoons lemon juice
1	teaspoon vanilla
1	16-ounce can whole cranberry sauce
2	teaspoons cornstarch

1 Preheat the oven to 350°F. Grease a 13×9×2-inch baking pan; set aside. In a large bowl stir together flour, oats, and brown sugar. Using a pastry blender, cut in butter until mixture resembles coarse crumbs. Reserve 1½ cups of the oats mixture. Press remaining oats mixture into the bottom of the prepared pan. Bake about 15 minutes.

2 Meanwhile, in a medium mixing bowl beat cream cheese and granulated sugar with an electric mixer on medium speed until light and fluffy. Beat in eggs, lemon juice, and vanilla. Spread cream cheese mixture over baked crust.

3 In a small bowl stir together cranberry sauce and cornstarch; spoon carefully over cream cheese layer. Sprinkle with reserved crumbs. Bake about 40 minutes more or until set. Cool in pan on a wire rack. Cover and chill at least 3 hours or until firm. Cut into bars.

note: *Store bars as directed on page 16. Refrigerate up to 3 days.*

Research shows that cranberries contain a significant amount of antioxidants that may help protect against heart disease, cancer, and other diseases.

Layers of cereal, pudding, and chocolate make up these tasty, wholesome bars.

yummy no-bake bars

prep: 25 min. **chill:** 1 hr. **makes:** 64 bars

1	cup granulated sugar
1	cup light-color corn syrup
2	cups peanut butter
3	cups crisp rice cereal
3	cups cornflakes
1¼	cups butter
4	cups powdered sugar
2	4-serving-size packages vanilla instant pudding and pie filling mix
¼	cup milk
1	12-ounce package semisweet chocolate pieces (2 cups)

1 Line a 15×10×1-inch baking pan with foil; extend over the edges of pan; set aside.

2 In a large saucepan combine granulated sugar and corn syrup. Heat and stir just until mixture bubbles around edges. Heat and stir for 1 minute more. Remove from heat. Stir in peanut butter until melted. Stir in rice cereal and cornflakes until coated. Press mixture into the bottom of the prepared pan.

3 For pudding layer, in a medium saucepan melt ¾ cup of the butter. Stir in powdered sugar, dry pudding mixes, and the milk. Spread pudding mixture over cereal layer; set aside.

4 For frosting, in a small saucepan heat and stir chocolate pieces and the remaining ½ cup butter over low heat until smooth; spread over pudding layer. Cover; chill 1 hour or until set. Lift from pan and cut into bars.

note: *Store bars as directed on page 16. Refrigerate up to 3 days.*

Choose your favorite granola for this recipe; just about any kind works nicely.

apple-raisin cookie bars

prep: 20 min. bake: 30 min. oven: 350°F makes: 36 bars

4   cups granola cereal
¼   cup all-purpose flour
¼   teaspoon salt
⅓   cup butter, melted
1   cup chopped dried apple
½   cup golden raisins
1   14-ounce can sweetened condensed milk

1 Preheat oven to 350°F. Line a 13×9×2-inch baking pan with foil, extending foil over the edges of pan. Grease foil well; set aside.

2 In a food processor combine granola, flour, and salt; process just until mixture is combined. Add butter; process with several on/off turns just until mixture is combined. Press cereal mixture into the bottom of the prepared pan. Bake about 10 minutes.

3 Sprinkle dried apple and raisins over crust. Pour or spoon sweetened condensed milk evenly over top. Bake about 20 minutes more or until top is golden brown. Do not overbake. Cool in pan on a wire rack. Use the foil to lift cooled baked mixture from pan. Cut into bars.

note: *Store bars as directed on page 16. Refrigerate up to 2 days.*

These dense, superchocolaty brownies are dressed up with a sprinkling of sliced almonds.

almond-fudge brownies

prep: 15 min. bake: 20 min. oven: 350°F makes: 16 brownies

½   cup butter
2   ounces unsweetened chocolate, cut up
1   cup sugar
2   eggs
¼   teaspoon almond extract
⅔   cup all-purpose flour
2   tablespoons sliced almonds

1 Preheat oven to 350°F. Line a 9×9×2-inch baking pan with foil, extending the foil over the edges of pan. Grease foil; set aside.

2 In a medium saucepan heat and stir butter and chocolate over low heat until smooth. Remove from heat. Stir in sugar, eggs, and almond extract. Beat lightly with a wooden spoon just until combined. Stir in flour.

3 Spread batter evenly in the prepared pan. Sprinkle with almonds. Bake about 20 minutes. Cool in pan on a wire rack. Use the foil to lift brownie from pan. Cut into squares.

note: *Store bars as directed on page 16. Refrigerate up to 3 days.*

*These dark bars—
studded with chips,
chunks, and bits of
sticky goodness—offer
a wealth of flavor in their
toasty depths.*

chocolate-hazelnut
marshmallow bars

prep: 25 min. chill: 30 min. makes: 36 bars

1   10½-ounce package
     tiny marshmallows
1   cup hazelnuts
     (filberts), toasted*
     (see tip, page
     19) and coarsely
     chopped, or
     coarsely chopped
     peanuts
2½ cups semisweet
     chocolate pieces
½   cup chocolate-
     hazelnut spread
½   cup whipping cream
¼   cup butter, softened
     Powdered sugar
     (optional)

1 Line a 13×9×2-inch baking pan with
foil, extending the foil over the edges
of the pan; set aside. In a very large bowl
combine marshmallows and nuts; set aside. In
a medium saucepan heat and stir chocolate
pieces, chocolate-hazelnut spread, cream, and
butter over medium-low heat until smooth.

2 Add chocolate mixture to marshmallow
mixture; stir to coat well. Spread mixture
evenly in prepared pan, pressing down lightly.
Cover and chill for 30 minutes.

3 Use foil to lift chilled mixture from pan.
Cut into 18 bars. Cut each bar in half
diagonally. If desired, sprinkle lightly with
powdered sugar.

*After toasting hazelnuts, place the warm
nuts on a clean kitchen towel. Rub nuts with
the towel to remove loose skins.

note: *Store bars as directed on page 16.
Refrigerate up to 3 days. Keep chilled until
ready to serve.*

Flecked with pieces of semisweet chocolate, these brownies have a double dose of rich chocolate flavor.

white chocolate brownies

prep: 25 min. **bake:** 30 min. **oven:** 350°F **makes:** 20 bars

¼ cup unsalted butter
6 ounces white chocolate baking squares (with cocoa butter), coarsely chopped
2 eggs
½ cup sugar
1 cup all-purpose flour
½ teaspoon salt
½ teaspoon vanilla
1 cup semisweet chocolate pieces

1 Preheat oven to 350°F. Grease an 8×8×2-inch baking pan; set aside. In a small saucepan heat and stir butter and half of the white chocolate over low heat until smooth. Remove from heat.

2 In a medium mixing bowl beat eggs with an electric mixer on medium to high speed until foamy. Gradually add sugar; beat about 3 minutes or until thickened. Add melted white chocolate mixture, the flour, salt, and vanilla; beat just until combined. Stir in the remaining chopped white chocolate and the semisweet chocolate pieces. Spread batter evenly in the prepared pan.

3 Bake about 30 minutes or until evenly browned on top. Cool in pan on a wire rack. Cut into squares.

note: *Store bars as directed on page 16. Refrigerate up to 1 week.*

The botanical name of the chocolate tree is *Theobroma cacao,* which means "food of the gods."

The surprises—tiny marshmallows and colorful milk chocolate candies—peek out from the edges of the cereal bars.

surprise cereal bars

prep: 30 min. **stand:** 20 min. **makes:** 24 bars

1	cup sugar
1	cup light-color corn syrup
1½	cups peanut butter
6	cups crisp rice cereal
1	cup tiny marshmallows
½	cup red and green candy-coated milk chocolate pieces

1 Line a 13×9×2-inch baking pan with foil, extending the foil over the edges of pan. Butter the foil; set aside. In a large saucepan stir together sugar and corn syrup. Bring just to boiling, stirring to dissolve sugar. Remove from heat. Stir in peanut butter until melted. Stir in cereal until coated.

2 Spread about half of the mixture in the prepared pan. Sprinkle with marshmallows and candy pieces. Spoon remaining cereal mixture over top and spread to cover. Let stand 20 minutes or until firm. Cut into bars.

note: *Store bars as directed on page 16. Refrigerate up to 3 days. Do not freeze.*

apple butter bars

prep: 20 min. **bake:** 25 min. **oven:** 350°F **makes:** 36 bars

1	6-ounce package (1½ cups) mixed dried fruit bits
½	cup butter, softened
¾	cup packed brown sugar
½	teaspoon baking soda
½	teaspoon ground cinnamon
¼	teaspoon salt
2	eggs
½	cup apple butter
1½	cups all-purpose flour
	Powdered sugar

1 Preheat oven to 350°F. Grease a 13×9×2-inch baking pan; set aside. Cover dried fruit with boiling water. Drain after 5 minutes.

2 Meanwhile, in a large mixing bowl beat butter for 30 seconds. Add brown sugar, baking soda, cinnamon, and salt. Beat until combined; scrape sides of bowl. Beat in eggs and apple butter. Beat in as much of the flour as you can with the mixer. Stir in any remaining flour and the drained fruit.

3 Spread batter evenly into the prepared pan. Bake for 25 to 30 minutes or until a wooden toothpick inserted in the center comes out clean. Cool in pan on a wire rack. Sift powdered sugar over bars. Cut into bars.

note: *Store bars as directed on page 16. Refrigerate up to 3 days.*

Buttermilk adds tangy tenderness to these brownies, while chocolate and marshmallows pave a sweet path.

chunky path brownies

prep: 35 min. bake: 25 min. oven: 350°F makes: 48 brownies

2	cups all-purpose flour
2	cups sugar
1	teaspoon baking soda
¼	teaspoon salt
1	cup butter
1	cup water
⅓	cup unsweetened cocoa powder
2	eggs
½	cup buttermilk
1½	teaspoons vanilla
3	cups tiny marshmallows
1	recipe Chocolate Topper

1 Preheat oven to 350°F. Line a 15×10×1-inch baking pan with foil, extending the foil over the edges of the pan. Grease foil; set aside. In a large mixing bowl stir together flour, sugar, baking soda, and salt; set aside.

2 In a medium saucepan combine butter, the water, and cocoa powder. Bring mixture just to boiling, stirring constantly. Remove from heat. Add the chocolate mixture to the flour mixture. Beat with an electric mixer on medium speed until combined. Add eggs, buttermilk, and vanilla. Beat for 1 minute more (batter will be thin); pour into the prepared pan. Bake 25 minutes or until a toothpick inserted in the center comes out clean.

3 Sprinkle marshmallows over hot brownie. Top with Chocolate Topper. Cool in pan on a wire rack. Use the foil to lift brownie from pan. Cut into bars.

note: *Store bars as directed on page 16. Refrigerate up to 3 days. Do not freeze.*

chocolate topper: *In a medium saucepan heat and stir 2 cups semisweet chocolate pieces, ½ cup whipping cream, and ¼ cup butter over medium-low heat until smooth. Drizzle over brownies.*

unbeatable **bars**

Cocktail peanuts and caramel ice cream topping create a sweet-salty flavor combination reminiscent of peanut brittle candy.

peanut brittle bars

prep: 15 min. **bake:** 24 min. **oven:** 350°F **makes:** 36 bars

2 cups all-purpose flour
½ cup packed brown sugar
⅔ cup butter
2 cups cocktail peanuts
1 cup milk chocolate pieces
1 12.5-ounce jar caramel ice cream topping
3 tablespoons all-purpose flour

1 Preheat oven to 350°F. Line a 15×10×1-inch baking pan with foil, extending the foil over the edges of pan. Grease foil; set aside. In a medium bowl stir together the 2 cups flour and the brown sugar. Using a pastry blender, cut in butter until mixture resembles coarse crumbs. Press flour mixture into the bottom of the prepared pan. Bake about 12 minutes or until golden brown.

2 Sprinkle peanuts and chocolate pieces over hot crust. In a small bowl stir together caramel topping and the 3 tablespoons all-purpose flour. Drizzle over top. Bake for 12 to 15 minutes more or until caramel is bubbly. Cool in pan on a wire rack. Use the foil to lift baked mixture from pan. Carefully peel foil from the sides of the mixture. Cut into bars.

Inspired by the 1990s coffeehouse craze, these irresistible layered delights continue to pop up in espresso bars across the country.

toffee squares

prep: 25 min. **bake:** 33 min. **chill:** 30 min. **oven:** 350°F
makes: about 36 bars

¾ cup butter, softened
¾ cup packed brown sugar
1 egg yolk
1½ cups all-purpose flour
¼ teaspoon salt
1 14-ounce can sweetened condensed milk (1¼ cups)
2 tablespoons butter
2 teaspoons vanilla
1 12-ounce package semisweet chocolate pieces (2 cups)
1 cup almond brickle pieces or toasted chopped pecans (see tip, page 19)

1 Preheat oven to 350°F. Grease a 13×9×2-inch baking pan; set aside.

2 For crust, in a large mixing bowl beat the ¾ cup butter and the brown sugar with an electric mixer on medium speed until combined. Beat in the egg yolk. Stir in the flour and salt until well mixed. Using floured hands, press the dough into the bottom of the prepared pan. Bake about 20 minutes or until light brown. Cool in pan on a wire rack while preparing the filling.

3 For filling, in a medium saucepan heat and stir the sweetened condensed milk and the 2 tablespoons butter over medium heat until bubbly. Cook and stir for 5 minutes more. (Mixture will thicken and become smooth.) Stir in the vanilla. Spread over the crust. Bake 12 to 15 minutes more or until top is golden brown.

4 Sprinkle evenly with chocolate pieces. Bake for 1 to 2 minutes more or until chocolate pieces are shiny and melted. Remove from oven; set on a wire rack. Using a flexible spatula, immediately spread the chocolate evenly over baked layers. Sprinkle with brickle pieces. Cool completely in pan on a wire rack. Cover and chill 30 minutes or until chocolate is set. Cut into squares.

note: *Store bars as directed on page 16. Refrigerate up to 3 days.*

The delicate yet distinctive flavor of fresh bananas comes through vividly in these moist bars.

banana bars

prep: 30 min. **bake:** 25 min. **oven:** 350°F **makes:** 36 bars

½	cup butter, softened
1⅓	cups granulated sugar
1½	teaspoons baking powder
½	teaspoon baking soda
¼	teaspoon salt
1	egg
1	cup mashed banana (2 to 3 medium)
½	cup dairy sour cream
1	teaspoon vanilla
2	cups all-purpose flour
1	cup chopped pecans or walnuts, toasted (see tip, page 19)
1	recipe Powdered Sugar Icing

1 Preheat oven to 350°F. Lightly grease a 15×10×1-inch baking pan; set aside.

2 In a large mixing bowl beat butter with an electric mixer on medium to high speed for 30 seconds. Add sugar, baking powder, baking soda, and salt. Beat until combined, scraping sides of bowl occasionally. Beat in the egg, mashed banana, sour cream, and vanilla until combined. Beat or stir in the flour. Stir in pecans; spread evenly in the prepared pan.

3 Bake about 25 minutes or until a wooden toothpick inserted in the center comes out clean. Cool in pan on a wire rack. Drizzle with Powdered Sugar Icing. Cut into bars.

note: *Store bars as directed on page 16. Refrigerate up to 3 days. To freeze, wrap bars in heavy foil.*

powdered sugar icing: *In a small bowl stir together 1 cup powdered sugar, ¼ teaspoon vanilla, and 1 tablespoon milk. Stir in additional milk, 1 teaspoon at a time, to make an icing of drizzling consistency.*

This kid-pleasing treat is sure to be a hit at birthday parties.
Make it colorful by using multicolor tiny marshmallows.

chocolate peanut butter pizza

prep: 30 min. **bake:** 22 min. **oven:** 350°F **makes:** 16 wedges

½ cup butter, softened
½ cup shortening
1 cup sugar
1 teaspoon baking powder
¼ teaspoon salt
1 egg
1 teaspoon vanilla
2¼ cups all-purpose flour
2½ cups chopped miniature chocolate-covered peanut butter cups (25)
1 cup chopped peanuts
1¼ cups tiny marshmallows

1 Preheat oven to 350°F. Lightly grease a 13- to 14-inch pizza pan; set aside. In a large mixing bowl beat butter and shortening for 30 seconds. Add the sugar, baking powder, and salt. Beat until combined, scraping sides of bowl occasionally. Beat in egg and vanilla until combined. Beat in as much of the flour as you can with the mixer. Stir in any remaining flour. Pat dough into prepared pan, building up edges slightly.

2 Bake about 12 minutes. Sprinkle with chopped peanut butter cups and peanuts. Bake about 5 minutes more. Sprinkle with marshmallows. Bake about 5 minutes more or until crust is golden. Cool in pan on a wire rack. Cut pizza into wedges.

note: *Store bars as directed on page 16. Refrigerate up to 3 days.*

9

holiday favo

Cookie baking is one of the most enjoyed and anticipated traditions of the holidays. This year remember your favorites, but work in a few cookies from this collection to show your creativity.

rites

Simple triangle cutouts easily become red-nosed reindeer with the help of mini pretzels and small red candies.

reindeer cookies

prep: 40 min. bake: 8 min. per batch oven: 350°F makes: 64 cookies

½	cup butter, softened
½	cup shortening
1	cup sugar
¼	cup unsweetened cocoa powder
1	teaspoon baking powder
¼	teaspoon salt
1	egg
1	teaspoon vanilla
2¼	cups all-purpose flour
	Miniature pretzel twists
	Halved red candied cherries or red candy-coated chocolate-covered peanuts
	Miniature candy-coated milk chocolate pieces

1 In a large mixing bowl beat butter and shortening with an electric mixer on medium to high speed for 30 seconds. Add sugar, cocoa powder, baking powder, and salt. Beat until combined, scraping sides of bowl occasionally. Beat in egg and vanilla until combined. Beat in as much of the flour as you can with the mixer. Stir in any remaining flour. Divide dough in half. If necessary, cover and chill dough 1 hour or until easy to handle.

2 Preheat oven to 350°F. Shape each half of dough into an 8-inch square. Cut each square into sixteen 2-inch squares. Cut each 2-inch square in half diagonally to make 64 triangles total.

3 Place triangles 2 inches apart on an ungreased baking sheet. For each reindeer, place two pretzel twists just under the long edge of each triangle for the antlers. On the point opposite the pretzels, place a candied cherry half for the nose. Add miniature chocolate pieces for the eyes. Bake for 8 to 10 minutes or until edges are light brown. Transfer to a wire rack and let cool.

Taking the shape of a beloved Christmas symbol,
these cookies feature a popular ingredient—chocolate.

candy cane cookies

prep: 30 min. chill: 1 hr. bake: 7 min. per batch oven: 375°F
makes: about 36 cookies

⅓ cup shortening
⅓ cup butter, softened
¾ cup sugar
1 teaspoon baking powder
1 egg
2 tablespoons milk
1 teaspoon vanilla
⅓ cup unsweetened cocoa powder
1¾ cups all-purpose flour
4 ounces white baking bar
2 teaspoons shortening
½ to ⅔ cup crushed peppermint candy canes or peppermint candies

1 In a medium mixing bowl beat the ⅓ cup shortening and the butter with an electric mixer on medium to high speed for 30 seconds. Add sugar and baking powder. Beat until combined, scraping sides of bowl occasionally. Beat in egg, milk, and vanilla until combined. Beat in cocoa powder and as much flour as you can with mixer. Stir in any remaining flour. Divide dough in half. Cover and chill dough 1 hour or until easy to handle.

2 Preheat oven to 375°F. On a lightly floured surface, roll half of the dough at a time until slightly less than ¼ inch thick. Using a 4-inch candy-cane-shape cookie cutter, cut out dough. Place cutouts 1 inch apart on an ungreased cookie sheet. Bake for 7 to 9 minutes or until firm and light brown. Transfer to a wire rack and let cool.

3 In a small saucepan heat and stir white baking bar and the 2 teaspoons shortening over low heat until smooth. Drizzle a few cookies with baking bar mixture; sprinkle with crushed candy canes. Repeat with remaining cookies. Let stand until set.

Melted white chocolate serves as the glue that binds flecks of crushed candy canes to these chocolate cutouts.

To prepare the pistachios for this recipe, place 2 cups whole shelled pistachios in a food processor. Pulse several times until the nuts are finely chopped. Remove the ¾ cup to be used in the dough. Continue pulsing the remaining nuts until finely ground to use for garnish.

chocolate-pistachio trees

prep: 60 min. chill: 30 min. bake: 9 min. per batch oven: 350°F
makes: about 48 cookies

1	cup butter
⅔	cup packed brown sugar
1	teaspoon vanilla
1	egg, beaten
2¼	cups all-purpose flour
¼	cup unsweetened cocoa powder
¾	cup finely chopped pistachio nuts
¾	cup semisweet chocolate pieces
1	tablespoon shortening
½	cup ground pistachio nuts

1 In a medium saucepan combine butter and brown sugar; heat and stir over low heat until butter is melted. Remove from heat; stir in vanilla. Let butter mixture stand for 15 minutes. Stir in egg, flour, and cocoa powder until combined. Stir in the ¾ cup pistachio nuts. Divide dough in half. Cover and chill dough 30 minutes or until easy to handle.

2 Preheat oven to 350°F. On a lightly floured surface, roll half of the dough at a time until ¼ inch thick. Using a tree-shape cookie cutter, cut out dough. Place cutouts 1 inch apart on an ungreased cookie sheet. Bake about 9 minutes or until edges are firm. Transfer to a wire rack and let cool.

3 In a small saucepan heat and stir chocolate pieces and shortening over low heat until smooth. Remove from heat. Dip one-third of each cookie into chocolate mixture; roll dipped edges of cookies in ground pistachio nuts. Let stand until set.

note: *Store cookies as directed on page 16. Refrigerate for up to 3 days. Do not freeze.*

There's no better time than the holidays to indulge in these decadent chocolate goodies.

*These cozy cookies may look impressively difficult to prepare,
but making them is actually quite simple and fun.*

patchwork mittens

prep: 1 hr. chill: 1 hr. bake: 8 min. per batch oven: 375°F
makes: about 18 cookies

½   cup butter, softened
1   3-ounce package
    cream cheese,
    softened
1½ cups powdered sugar
½   teaspoon baking
    powder
¼   teaspoon salt
1   egg
½   teaspoon vanilla
2¼ cups all-purpose flour
    Paste food coloring
    (4 desired colors)
    Clear edible glitter

1 In a large mixing bowl beat butter and cream cheese with an electric mixer on medium to high speed for 30 seconds. Add powdered sugar, baking powder, and salt. Beat until combined, scraping sides of bowl occasionally. Beat in egg and vanilla until combined. Beat in as much of the flour as you can with the mixer. Stir in any remaining flour.

2 Divide dough into five portions. Place each portion into a separate bowl. Tint four of the portions different colors using paste food coloring. Knead each dough gently until it is uniformly tinted. Wrap each portion in plastic wrap or waxed paper. Chill dough about 1 hour or until easy to handle.

3 Preheat oven to 375°F. On a lightly floured surface, roll each portion of dough until ⅛ inch thick. Using a fluted pastry wheel, cut dough into 1-inch-wide strips. Cut the dough strips into squares, diamonds, and triangles. Arrange dough pieces in groups of about 10 on an ungreased cookie sheet, overlapping the edges slightly to form shapes just larger than a 3-inch mitten-shape cookie cutter. Cut out dough with mitten-shape cutter. (Reserve scraps, reroll, and cut to make multicolored marbled cutouts.)

4 Bake for 8 to 9 minutes or until edges are firm and bottoms are very light brown. Sprinkle cookies with clear edible glitter. Transfer to a wire rack and let cool.

Golden butterscotch candies create stained-glass centers in these delicate eggnog-flavored cutouts, a contemporary twist on the old-fashioned sugar cookie.

eggnog cookies

prep: 45 min. chill: 2 hr. bake: 6 min. per batch stand: 5 min. per batch
oven: 375°F makes: 24 cookies

2 cups all-purpose flour
1 cup granulated sugar
¾ teaspoon baking powder
¼ teaspoon ground nutmeg
¼ teaspoon salt
⅔ cup butter
1 egg, lightly beaten
¼ cup eggnog
½ cup finely crushed butterscotch- or rum-flavor hard candies (about twenty-five 1-inch candies)
1 recipe Eggnog Glaze Yellow colored sugar (optional)

1 In a large bowl stir together flour, granulated sugar, baking powder, nutmeg, and salt. Using a pastry blender, cut in butter until pieces are the size of small peas. Make a well in the center of flour mixture. Mix egg and eggnog together; add to well in flour mixture. Stir until moistened. Form dough into a ball. Cover and chill dough for 2 hours or until easy to handle.

2 Preheat oven to 375°F. Line a cookie sheet with foil; set aside. On a well-floured surface, roll dough until ¼ inch thick. Using 2½-inch desired-shape cookie cutters, cut out dough.* Cut smaller shapes out of larger shapes; reroll trimmings. Place cutouts 1 inch apart on the prepared cookie sheet. Fill cutout openings with crushed candies.

3 Bake for 6 to 8 minutes or until edges are firm and light brown. Let stand for 5 minutes on cookie sheet. Transfer cookies on foil to a wire rack; cool. Carefully peel cookies away from foil. Drizzle cookies with Eggnog Glaze. If desired, sprinkle with yellow sugar.

✳ Keep the dough from sticking to the cutter by dipping the edge of the cutter into flour after every few cuts.

eggnog glaze: *In a medium bowl stir together 3 cups powdered sugar, ¼ teaspoon rum extract, and enough eggnog (2 to 3 tablespoons) to make a glaze of drizzling consistency.*

*Melting colorful candies into decorative cutouts adds
a little twinkle to these buttery cookies.*

crystal-bright cookies

prep: 1¼ hr. bake: 10 min. per batch oven: 350°F
makes: about 48 cookies

18   red and green clear
      hard rectangular
      candies or 30 red
      and green fruit-
      flavor circular
      hard candies
⅔   cup butter, softened
⅔   cup shortening
½   cup granulated sugar
2   teaspoons baking
      powder
¼   teaspoon salt
2   eggs
1   teaspoon vanilla
4   cups all-purpose flour
      Powdered sugar
      (optional)

1 Preheat oven to 350°F. Line a cookie sheet with foil; set aside. Place red and green candies in separate small heavy plastic bags. Coarsely crush candies and place each color in a small container; set aside.

2 In a large mixing bowl beat butter and shortening with an electric mixer on medium to high speed for 30 seconds. Add granulated sugar, baking powder, and salt. Beat until combined, scraping sides of bowl occasionally. Beat in eggs and vanilla until combined. Beat in as much of the flour as you can with the mixer. Stir in any remaining flour. Divide dough in half.

3 On a lightly floured surface, roll half of the dough at a time until ¼ inch thick. Using 2½- to 3-inch desired-shape cookie cutters, cut out dough. Place cutouts about 1 inch apart on the prepared cookie sheet.

4 Using ½- to ¾-inch hors d'oeuvre cutters, cut out two, three, or four shapes from each larger cutout. Fill cutout openings with crushed candy. Bake about 10 minutes or until edges are light brown. Cool completely on foil. Carefully peel cookies away from foil. If desired, use a small brush to dust edges of cooled cookies with powdered sugar.

Baked treats add homespun loveliness to a Christmas tree. A set of nested scalloped cutters in several sizes is the secret to the symmetrical look. To add extra sparkle combine granulated and colored sugars to accent each layer.

double wreaths

prep: 45 min. chill: 3 hr. bake: 6 min. per batch oven: 375°F
makes: about 36 cookies

½   cup shortening
¾   cup granulated sugar
½   teaspoon baking
      powder
      Dash salt
1   egg
2   tablespoons milk
½   teaspoon vanilla
2   cups all-purpose flour
      Colored sugar and/or
         granulated sugar
      ½-inch-wide ribbon

1 Preheat oven to 375°F. In a medium mixing bowl beat shortening with an electric mixer on medium to high speed for 30 seconds. Add granulated sugar, baking powder, and salt. Beat until combined, scraping sides of bowl occasionally. Beat in egg, milk, and vanilla until combined. Beat in as much of the flour as you can with the mixer. Stir in any remaining flour. Divide dough into thirds. Cover and chill dough about 3 hours or until easy to handle.

2 On a lightly floured surface, roll one-third of the dough at a time until ¼ inch thick. Using 3¼- and 2¼-inch scalloped round cookie cutters, cut out dough making an equal number of each size. Place cutouts on an ungreased cookie sheet. Using a 1¼-inch scalloped round cutter, cut the center from each 3¼-inch cutout. Using a 1-inch scalloped round cutter, cut the center from each 2¼-inch cutout. Sprinkle cutouts with colored sugar, granulated sugar, or a combination of sugars.

3 Bake for 6 to 8 minutes or until edges are firm and bottoms are very light brown. Transfer to a wire rack and let cool.

4 To assemble, place a small wreath on top of each large wreath; tie wreaths together with ribbon. Tie ribbon, creating a loop large enough to hang cookies.

Madeleine Santas

Santa Cutouts

These tiny buttery French spongecakes effortlessly transform into jolly, big-bearded Santas. For decorating ideas, see photo, page 416.

madeleine santas

prep: 1¼ hr. bake: 10 min. per batch stand: 1 min. per batch oven: 375°F
makes: 24 cookies

2 eggs
½ teaspoon vanilla
½ teaspoon finely shredded lemon peel
1 cup powdered sugar
⅔ cup all-purpose flour
¼ teaspoon baking powder
½ cup butter, melted and cooled
1 recipe Snow Frosting (page 419)
1 recipe Powdered Sugar Icing
Assorted decorative candies
Powdered sugar
Coarse sugar

1 Preheat oven to 375°F. Grease and flour twenty-four 3-inch madeleine molds; set aside.

2 In a medium mixing bowl beat eggs, vanilla, and lemon peel with an electric mixer on high speed for 5 minutes. Gradually beat in the 1 cup powdered sugar. Beat for 5 to 7 minutes or until thick and satiny.

3 Sift together flour and baking powder. Sift one-fourth of flour mixture over egg mixture; gently stir. Stir in the remaining flour, one-fourth at a time. Stir in butter. Spoon dough into prepared molds, filling each mold three-fourths full.

4 Bake for 10 to 12 minutes or until edges are golden and tops spring back. Let stand for 1 minute in molds on a wire rack. Loosen cookies with a knife. Invert onto wire rack and let cool.

5 Decorate madeleines as desired, using Snow Frosting, Powdered Sugar Icing, decorative candies, powdered sugar, and coarse sugar. For a textured look, pipe Snow Frosting from a decorating bag fitted with a medium star tip. To add fine details, pipe Powdered Sugar Icing from a decorating bag fitted with a writing tip. Let stand until set.

powdered sugar icing: *In a medium bowl stir together 4 cups powdered sugar, 1 teaspoon vanilla, and enough milk (3 to 4 tablespoons) to make an icing of piping consistency. Tint icing as desired with paste food coloring.*

One recipe makes a variety of Santa shapes. When you use egg paint, be sure to apply it before you bake the cookies so the egg mixture fully cooks. For decorating ideas, see photo, page 417.

santa cutouts

prep: 50 min. chill: 3 hr. bake: 7 min. per batch stand: 1 min. per batch
oven: 375°F

⅓ cup butter, softened
⅓ cup shortening
¾ cup granulated sugar
1 teaspoon baking powder
   Dash salt
1 egg
1 tablespoon milk
1 teaspoon vanilla
2 cups all-purpose flour
   Egg Paint*
1 recipe Snow Frosting
1 recipe Royal Icing (page 128)
   Assorted decorative toppers and candies, such as clear and red edible glitter, plain and colored sanding sugar, miniature semisweet chocolate pieces, and candy-coated chocolate pieces

1 In a large mixing bowl beat butter and shortening for 30 seconds. Add sugar, baking powder, and salt. Beat until combined, scraping sides of bowl occasionally. Beat in egg, milk, and vanilla until combined. Beat in as much of the flour as you can with the mixer. Stir in any remaining flour. Cover and chill dough 3 hours or until easy to handle.

2 Preheat oven to 375°F. On a lightly floured surface, roll dough until ⅛ inch thick. Using desired-shape cookie cutters, cut out dough. Place cutouts 1 inch apart on an ungreased cookie sheet. Paint with egg paint.*

3 Bake for 7 to 8 minutes or until the bottoms are light brown. Let stand for 1 minute on cookie sheet. Transfer to a wire rack and let cool. Decorate with Snow Frosting, Royal Icing, and/or decorative toppers and candies as desired. Let stand until set.

*See page 25 for instructions on how to prepare and use egg paint.

snow frosting: *In a small mixing bowl beat ½ cup shortening and ½ teaspoon vanilla with an electric mixer on medium speed for 30 seconds. Gradually beat in 1⅓ cups sifted powdered sugar until smooth. Beat in 1 tablespoon milk. Gradually beat in an additional 1 cup powdered sugar and enough milk (3 to 4 teaspoons) to make a frosting of piping consistency. Tint frosting as desired with paste food coloring.*

Great for Christmas as well as Valentine's Day, these cookies get a spicy kick from black pepper and grated fresh ginger.

spicy ginger hearts

prep: 40 min. chill: 4 hr. bake: 10 min. per batch stand: 1 min. per batch
oven: 350°F makes: about 24 cookies

¾ cup butter, softened
¾ cup packed brown sugar
2 tablespoons grated fresh ginger or 2 teaspoons ground ginger
1½ teaspoons finely ground black pepper
½ teaspoon baking soda
¼ teaspoon salt
¼ teaspoon ground cinnamon
¼ teaspoon ground nutmeg
1 egg
⅓ cup molasses
2¾ cups all-purpose flour
1 recipe Royal Icing (page 128) or purchased decorator icing
Red and white nonpareils or other small red candies (optional)

1 In a large mixing bowl beat butter with an electric mixer on medium to high speed for 30 seconds. Add brown sugar, ginger, pepper, baking soda, salt, cinnamon, and nutmeg. Beat until combined, scraping sides of bowl occasionally. Beat in egg and molasses until combined. Beat in as much of the flour as you can with the mixer. Stir in any remaining flour. Divide dough in half. Cover and chill dough about 4 hours or until easy to handle.

2 Preheat oven to 350°F. Lightly grease a cookie sheet or line it with parchment paper; set aside. On a lightly floured surface, roll half of the dough at a time until ¼ inch thick. Using various-size heart-shape cookie cutters, cut out dough. Place cutouts about 1 inch apart on the prepared cookie sheet. (If you plan to hang the cookies, use a drinking straw to make holes in cutouts as needed.)

3 Bake about 10 minutes or until tops of cookies appear dry. Let stand for 1 minute on cookie sheet. Transfer to a wire rack and let cool. Decorate cooled cookies with Royal Icing and, if desired, nonpareils or other candies.

These tender cookies contain the best flavors of fruitcake in a pretty swirl.

fruitcake pinwheels

prep: 25 min. chill: 7 hr. bake: 8 min. per batch stand: 1 min. per batch oven: 350° F
makes: 92 cookies

1 cup butter, softened
½ cup granulated sugar
½ cup packed brown sugar
½ teaspoon baking powder
1 egg
1 teaspoon vanilla
2½ cups all-purpose flour
2 cups finely chopped mixed candied fruits and peels
1 cup pecans, finely chopped

1 In a large mixing bowl beat butter for 30 seconds. Add granulated sugar, brown sugar, and baking powder. Beat until combined, scraping sides of bowl occasionally. Beat in egg and vanilla until combined. Beat in as much flour as you can with the mixer. Stir in any remaining flour. Divide dough in half. Cover and chill dough for 3 hours or until it is easy to handle.

2 In a small bowl stir together candied fruits and pecans; set aside. On a lightly floured surface, roll half of the dough into a 12×8-inch rectangle. Sprinkle half of the fruit mixture over rectangle to within ½ inch of edges. Beginning with a long side, roll up dough. Pinch edges to seal. Repeat with the remaining dough and fruit mixture. Wrap rolls in plastic wrap. Chill for 4 hours or until firm.

3 Preheat oven to 350°F. Cut rolls into ¼-inch slices. Place slices 1 inch apart on an ungreased cookie sheet. Bake for 8 to 10 minutes or until edges are firm. Let stand for 1 minute on cookie sheet. Transfer to a wire rack and let cool.

Serve these minty twice-baked cookies with a mocha or rich hot chocolate.

peppermint-twist biscotti

prep: 30 min. bake: 40 min. oven: 375°F/300°F makes: about 72 cookies

⅔ cup butter, softened
1⅓ cups sugar
1 tablespoon baking powder
¼ teaspoon salt
4 eggs
½ teaspoon peppermint extract
4¼ cups all-purpose flour
1 cup coarsely chopped peppermint candy canes or peppermint candies
Red paste food coloring
1 recipe Peppermint Icing (page 423)
Chopped peppermint candy canes (optional)

1 Preheat oven to 375°F. Line a cookie sheet with foil; set aside. In a large mixing bowl beat butter with an electric mixer on medium to high speed for 30 seconds. Add sugar, baking powder, and salt. Beat until combined, scraping sides of bowl occasionally. Beat in eggs and peppermint extract until combined. Beat in as much of the flour as you can with the mixer. Stir in any remaining flour and the 1 cup chopped candy canes.

2 Divide dough in half. Tint one portion of the dough with red paste food coloring. Divide each half of dough into three portions. On a lightly floured surface, roll each portion into a 14-inch-long rope. On prepared cookie sheet, place a rope of each color side by side. Twist pairs of ropes around each other several times. Flatten twists until 2 inches wide; place about 4 inches apart on the cookie sheet.

3 Bake for 20 to 25 minutes or until light brown and tops are cracked. Cool completely on cookie sheet on a wire rack. Carefully peel foil away from twists.

4 Reduce oven temperature to 300°F. Transfer twists to a cutting board. Using a serrated knife, cut twists diagonally into ½-inch slices. Place slices, cut sides down, on an ungreased cookie sheet. Bake for 10 minutes. Turn slices over. Bake for 10 to 15 minutes more or until slices are dry. Transfer biscotti to a wire rack and let cool.

5 Drizzle cooled cookies with Peppermint Icing. If desired, sprinkle with additional chopped candy canes. Let stand until set.

peppermint icing: *In a medium bowl stir together 2 cups powdered sugar and 1 tablespoon peppermint schnapps (or use 1 tablespoon milk and ¼ teaspoon peppermint extract) until smooth. Add enough additional peppermint schnapps or milk (about 2 tablespoons) to make an icing of drizzling consistency.*

No mere nibbles, these big, beautiful cookies are substantial enough to stand in for dessert. Serve them with a light and fruity sorbet or sherbet as an elegant end to dinner.

partridge-in-a-pear-tree
cookies

prep: 45 min. chill: 2 hr. bake: 7 min. per batch oven: 350°F
makes: 16 sandwich cookies

1 cup butter, softened
2 cups powdered sugar
1 teaspoon vanilla
⅛ teaspoon salt
2 eggs
3¼ cups all-purpose flour
½ cup apricot preserves
Sifted powdered sugar
¼ cup powdered sugar
¼ to ½ teaspoon milk

1 In a large bowl beat butter for 30 seconds. Gradually beat in the 2 cups powdered sugar until combined. Beat in vanilla and salt. Add eggs, one at a time, beating after each addition. Gradually beat in as much of the flour as you can. Stir in any remaining flour. Cover dough; chill 2 hours or until easy to handle.

2 Preheat oven to 350°F. Divide dough into four portions. On a lightly floured surface, roll one portion of the dough at a time until ⅛ inch thick. Using a 4¾-inch pear-shape cookie cutter, cut out dough. Cut out a 1½-inch partridge from the center of half of the pears. Cut out one 1½-inch leaf for each cookie sandwich. Reroll dough scraps.

3 Place cutouts 1 inch apart on an ungreased cookie sheet. Bake for 7 to 8 minutes or until edges are golden. Transfer to a wire rack and let cool.

4 Spread a generous teaspoon of apricot preserves over each whole pear cookie. Sprinkle additional powdered sugar on cutout pear cookies; place on top of whole cookies.

5 In a small bowl stir together the ¼ cup powdered sugar and enough milk to make an icing of spreading consistency. Spread icing on bottoms of leaf cookies and attach them near the stems of the pear cookies.

Rolling and cutting the dough right on a cookie sheet creates the most tender trees.

lime shortbread trees

prep: 50 min. bake: 15 min. per batch stand: 10 min. per batch oven: 325°F
makes: 30 cookies

1 cup butter, softened
½ cup powdered sugar
2 teaspoons finely
   shredded lime peel
¼ teaspoon salt
2¼ cups all-purpose flour
   Green colored coarse
   sugar

1 In a large mixing bowl beat butter with an electric mixer on medium to high speed for 30 seconds. Add powdered sugar, lime peel, and salt. Beat until combined, scraping sides of bowl occasionally. Beat in flour until dough just comes together. Divide dough in half. If necessary, cover and chill dough about 30 minutes or until easy to handle.

2 Preheat oven to 325°F. On a large ungreased cookie sheet, roll half of the dough into a 13x4-inch rectangle. Score one long side at 1½-inch intervals. Starting ¾ inch from the corner of the opposite long side, score at 1½-inch intervals. With a long sharp knife, cut across the dough, connecting the scored marks and making 15 triangles (trees); do not separate trees. Remove dough scraps from edges. Sprinkle trees with green colored sugar. Shape 15 small rectangles from the dough scraps; place at bottoms of trees as trunks. Repeat with remaining dough.

3 Bake about 15 minutes or until edges just begin to brown. While cookies are still hot, recut trees with a long sharp knife. Let stand for 10 minutes on cookie sheet. Transfer cookies to a wire rack and let cool.

Impress holiday guests with these lime-scented cutouts—they'll marvel at the wonderful citrus flavor.

Each color of dough has its own special flavor—peppermint, almond, or lime—in these festive cutouts.

marbled holiday greetings

prep: 1½ hr. bake: 7 min. per batch oven: 375°F makes: 144 cookies

1 cup butter, softened
⅔ cup shortening
2 cups sugar
⅔ cup dairy sour cream
2 eggs
1 teaspoon vanilla
1½ teaspoons baking powder
½ teaspoon baking soda
⅛ teaspoon salt
5 cups all-purpose flour
Rose petal pink, violet, and leaf green paste food coloring
½ teaspoon peppermint extract
½ teaspoon almond extract
1 teaspoon finely shredded lime peel
1 recipe Decorative Icing (page 427)

1 In a large mixing bowl beat butter and shortening with an electric mixer on medium to high speed for 30 seconds. Add the sugar, sour cream, eggs, vanilla, baking powder, baking soda, and salt. Beat until combined, scraping sides of bowl occasionally. Beat in as much flour as you can with mixer. Stir in any remaining flour. Divide dough into six portions. If necessary, cover and chill dough for 30 to 60 minutes or until easy to handle.

2 Preheat oven to 375°F. Place three dough portions into separate bowls. Tint each of the three portions a different color (pink, violet, and green). Knead each dough gently until it is uniformly tinted. Leave three portions of the dough untinted. Add peppermint extract to pink dough, almond extract to violet dough, and lime peel to green dough.

3 To marble dough, break off pieces of one portion plain dough and of a colored dough. Place pieces alternately on a floured pastry cloth to form an 11x7-inch rectangle, pressing pieces together. Roll dough into a 12-inch square ¼ inch thick. Using a pastry wheel, trim edges of the marbled square; cut square into forty-eight 3x1-inch rectangles. Repeat with remaining dough portions.

4 Place rectangles 1 inch apart on an ungreased cookie sheet. Bake for 7 to 8 minutes or until edges are firm and bottoms are light brown. Transfer to a wire rack and let cool. Use Decorative Icing to pipe "Joy," "Noel," or "Peace" onto cooled cookies.

decorative icing: In a medium mixing bowl stir together 4 cups sifted powdered sugar and 3 tablespoons milk until smooth. Stir in additional milk, 1 teaspoon at a time, to make an icing of piping consistency. If desired, tint icing with paste food coloring. Pipe icing from a decorating bag fitted with a writing tip.

White chocolate gives cool, minty candy canes a warm, creamy finish. Make sure to use white chocolate that contains cocoa butter for the most tender and flavorful cookies.

white chocolate
candy cane drops

prep: 40 min. bake: 8 min. per batch oven: 375°F makes: about 50 cookies

8	ounces white chocolate baking squares (with cocoa butter)
½	cup butter, softened
1	cup sugar
1	teaspoon baking powder
½	teaspoon salt
2	eggs
1	teaspoon vanilla
2¾	cups all-purpose flour
⅔	cup finely crushed peppermint candy canes or peppermint candies

1 Preheat oven to 375°F. Line cookie sheet with parchment paper; set aside. Chop 4 ounces of the white chocolate; set aside. In a small saucepan heat and stir the remaining 4 ounces white chocolate over low heat until smooth. Set aside to let chocolate cool slightly.

2 In a large mixing bowl beat butter with an electric mixer on medium to high speed for 30 seconds. Add sugar, baking powder, and salt. Beat until combined, scraping sides of bowl occasionally. Beat in eggs and vanilla until combined. Beat in melted white chocolate. Beat in as much of the flour as you can with the mixer. Stir in any remaining flour, the chopped white chocolate, and crushed candy canes.

3 Drop dough by rounded teaspoons 2 inches apart onto the prepared cookie sheet. Bake for 8 to 10 minutes or until light brown around edges. Transfer to a wire rack and let cool.

To easily grate the large amount of ginger needed, peel and coarsely chop the root, then give it a few quick turns in the food processor.

fresh ginger cutouts

prep: 30 min. chill: 3 hr. bake: 5 min. per batch oven: 375°F
makes: 48 cookies

½ cup butter, softened
½ cup sugar
¾ teaspoon baking soda
½ teaspoon ground cinnamon
⅛ teaspoon ground cloves
1 egg
½ cup molasses
1 teaspoon vanilla
¼ cup grated fresh ginger
3 cups all-purpose flour
1 recipe Powdered Sugar Icing
    Decorative candies

1 In a large mixing bowl beat butter with an electric mixer on medium to high speed for 30 seconds. Add sugar, baking soda, cinnamon, and cloves. Beat until combined, scraping sides of bowl occasionally. Beat in egg, molasses, and vanilla until combined. Beat in grated ginger and as much of the flour as you can with the mixer. Stir in any remaining flour. Cover and chill dough about 3 hours or until easy to handle.

2 Preheat oven to 375°F. Lightly grease a cookie sheet; set aside. On a lightly floured surface, roll dough until ⅛ inch thick. Using 3-inch desired-shape cookie cutters, cut out dough. Place cutouts 1 inch apart on the prepared cookie sheet. Bake for 5 to 6 minutes or until edges are firm and bottoms are light brown. Transfer to a wire rack and let cool. Decorate cooled cookies as desired with Powdered Sugar Icing and decorative candies.

powdered sugar icing: *In a small bowl stir together 1 cup powdered sugar, ¼ teaspoon vanilla, and 1 tablespoon milk. Stir in enough additional milk (1 to 2 teaspoons) to make an icing of drizzling consistency. If desired, tint a small amount of icing with red paste food coloring.*

These baked snowflakes are crisp and fragile, so handle them gently. Be extra careful when peeling the parchment paper away from the meringues.

meringue snowflakes

prep: 30 min. stand: 1 hr. oven: 300°F makes: 10 to 12 cookies

2   egg whites
¼   teaspoon cream of
      tartar
1⅓ cups sifted powdered
      sugar
      Decorative candies,
      edible glitter,
      and/or colored
      coarse sugar

1 Preheat oven to 300°F. Line three cookie sheets with parchment paper; set aside.

2 In a medium mixing bowl beat egg whites and cream of tartar with an electric mixer on high speed until soft peaks form (tips curl). Add powdered sugar, 1 tablespoon at a time, beating well after each addition. Beat for 7 minutes on high speed. Mixture should be very thick and glossy but may not be stiff.

3 Spoon mixture into a decorating bag fitted with a medium star tip. Making lines about ¼ inch thick, pipe 4- to-5-inch snowflake shapes 2 inches apart on prepared baking sheets. Sprinkle with candies, glitter, or sugar.

4 Place the cookie sheets in the oven. Turn off oven. Leave meringues in closed oven about 1 hour or until dry and crisp but still white. Let cool on parchment paper. Carefully cut parchment paper around snowflakes. Gently peel parchment from snowflakes.

Before your eyes powdered sugar and unassuming egg whites magically transform into melt-in-your-mouth treats.

These fruit-studded cookies are reminiscent of the Italian sweet bread known as panettone, which is often enjoyed at Christmas.

panettone cookies

prep: 25 min. **bake:** 8 min. per batch **oven:** 375°F **makes:** about 48 cookies

1 cup butter-flavor or plain shortening
1 cup packed brown sugar
½ cup granulated sugar
1 teaspoon anise seeds, crushed
1 teaspoon baking soda
½ teaspoon salt
2 eggs
1 teaspoon vanilla
2½ cups all-purpose flour
½ cup golden or dark raisins
½ cup toasted pine nuts (see tip, page 19), chopped if desired
1 to 2 tablespoons finely chopped candied citron

1 Preheat oven to 375°F. In a large mixing bowl beat shortening with an electric mixer on medium to high speed for 30 seconds. Add brown sugar, granulated sugar, anise seeds, baking soda, and salt. Beat until combined, scraping sides of bowl occasionally. Beat in eggs and vanilla until combined. Beat in as much of the flour as you can with the mixer. Stir in any remaining flour, the raisins, pine nuts, and citron.

2 Drop dough by rounded teaspoons 2 inches apart onto an ungreased cookie sheet. Bake about 8 minutes or until edges are light brown. Transfer to a wire rack; cool.

Figs, citrus, and almonds, all native to Sicily, often find their way into the island's traditional Christmastime treats. Be sure to use butter, not margarine, as butter allows the dough to hold its shape better.

christmas fig cookies

prep: 45 min. chill: 3 hr. bake: 10 min. per batch oven: 375°F
makes: about 36 cookies

½ cup butter, softened
¼ cup granulated sugar
¼ cup packed brown sugar
¼ teaspoon baking soda
1 egg
1 teaspoon vanilla
1¾ cups all-purpose flour
1 recipe Fig Filling
1 recipe Lemon Glaze or powdered sugar

1 In a medium bowl beat butter for 30 seconds. Add the granulated sugar, the brown sugar, and baking soda. Beat until combined, scraping sides of bowl occasionally. Beat in egg and vanilla until combined. Beat in as much of the flour as you can. Stir in any remaining flour. Divide dough in half. Cover and chill dough about 3 hours or until easy to handle. Meanwhile, prepare Fig Filling.

2 Preheat oven to 375°F. On a floured pastry cloth, roll half of the dough at a time into a 10×8-inch rectangle. Cut rectangle into two 10×4-inch strips. Spread one-fourth of the Fig Filling lengthwise down the middle of each strip. Using the pastry cloth, lift up one long side of each dough strip and fold it over the filling. Lift up opposite side and fold to enclose filling; seal edges. Place filled strips, seam sides down, on an ungreased cookie sheet.

3 Bake for 10 to 12 minutes or until light brown. Immediately slice each strip diagonally into 1-inch pieces. Transfer to a wire rack and let cool. Drizzle cooled cookies with Lemon Glaze or sift powdered sugar over tops.

note: *Store cookies as directed on page 16. Refrigerate for up to 3 days.*

fig filling: *In a saucepan combine 1 cup dried and chopped figs, stems removed; ⅔ cup raisins, finely chopped; ½ cup orange juice; ⅓ cup diced candied fruits and peels, finely chopped; 2 tablespoons granulated sugar; 1 teaspoon finely shredded lemon peel; and ¼ teaspoon ground cinnamon. Bring just to boiling; reduce heat. Cover and simmer for 5 to 8 minutes or until fruit is soft and mixture is thick, stirring occasionally. Stir in ⅓ cup blanched almonds, finely chopped; cool.*

lemon glaze: *In a small mixing bowl stir together ¾ cup powdered sugar and enough lemon juice (2 to 3 teaspoons) to make a glaze of drizzling consistency.*

Made from hand-rolled balls of dough, these chubby snowmen look almost too cute to eat—almost.

roly-poly snowfolk

prep: 45 min. bake: 12 min. per batch stand: 2 min. per batch oven: 350°F
makes: 10 cookies

½   cup butter, softened
½   cup shortening
1   cup sugar
1   teaspoon baking powder
¼   teaspoon salt
1   egg
1   teaspoon vanilla
2¼   cups all-purpose flour
    Coarse sugar
    Miniature candy-coated milk chocolate pieces
    Miniature semisweet chocolate pieces
    Teardrop-shape sweet-sour candies
1   recipe Gumdrop Hats
    Canned vanilla frosting

1 Preheat oven to 350°F. In a large mixing bowl beat butter and shortening for 30 seconds. Add sugar, baking powder, and salt. Beat until combined; scrape sides of bowl. Beat in egg and vanilla. Beat in as much of the flour as you can. Stir in any remaining flour.

2 Shape dough into ten 1½-inch balls, ten 1-inch balls, and ten ¾-inch balls. Roll balls in coarse sugar. For each cookie, arrange a 1½-inch ball, a 1-inch ball, and a ¾-inch ball ½ inch apart on an ungreased cookie sheet. Slightly flatten the 1½-inch balls. Add candy-coated pieces for buttons, chocolate pieces for eyes, and sweet-sour candies for noses. Place snowfolk 2 inches apart on cookie sheet.

3 Bake 12 to 15 minutes or until edges are light brown. Let stand 2 minutes on cookie sheet. Carefully transfer to a wire rack and let cool. Attach Gumdrop Hats with frosting.

gumdrop hats: *Sprinkle a cutting board with granulated sugar. Place a gumdrop on the board and sprinkle with more sugar. With a rolling pin, roll gumdrop into an oval about ¼ inch thick. Curve to form a hat and press edges together to seal. If desired, bend up gumdrop edge for hat brim.*

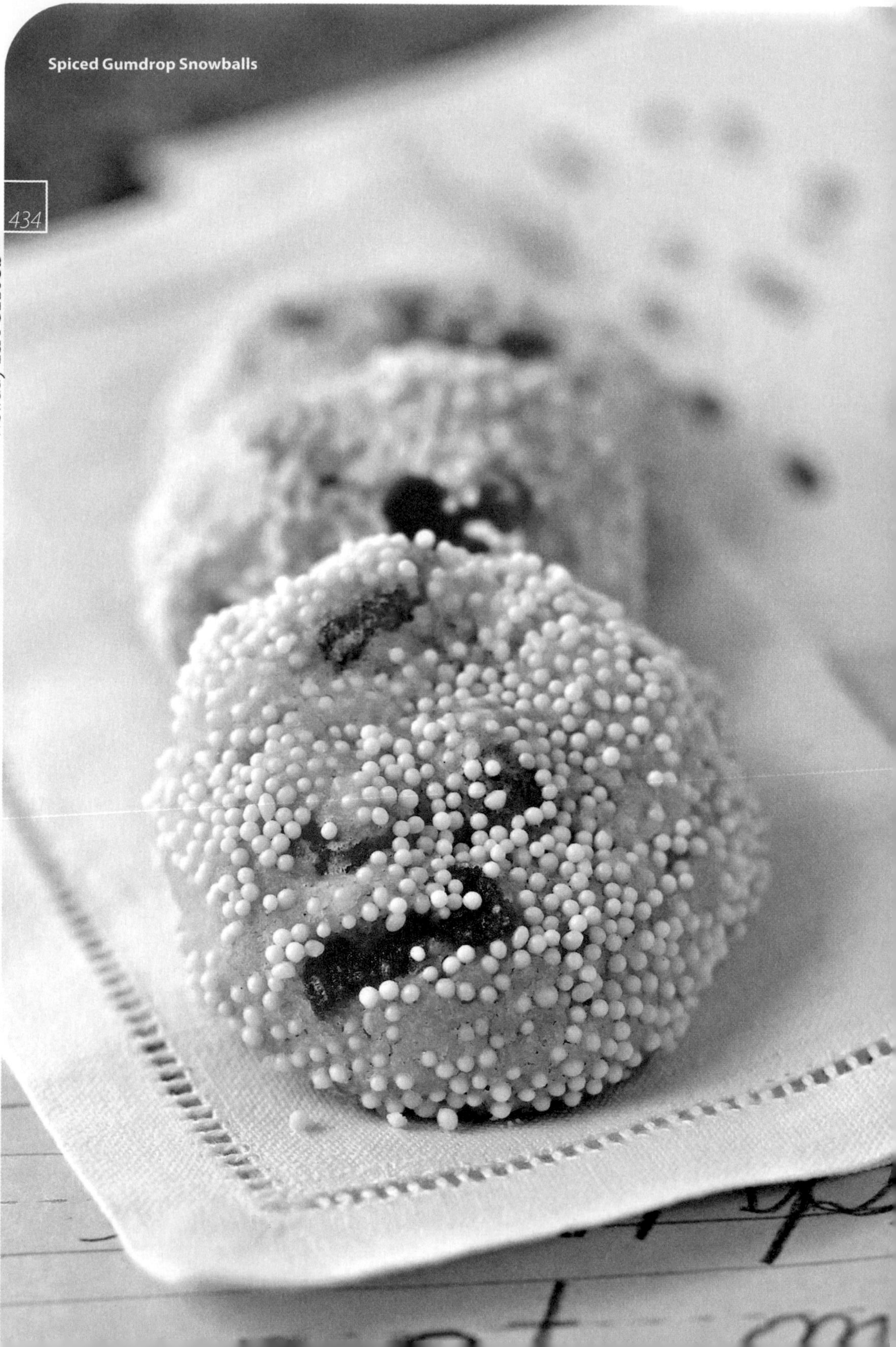

Spiced Gumdrop Snowballs

Before you quarter the gumdrops, run water over the kitchen shears to prevent them from sticking. If necessary, toss the quartered pieces with 2 to 3 teaspoons sugar to prevent them from sticking together.

spiced gumdrop snowballs

prep: 30 min. bake: 10 min. per batch oven: 375°F makes: 36 cookies

⅔ cup butter, softened
½ cup sugar
½ teaspoon ground cinnamon
2 egg yolks
1 teaspoon vanilla
1½ cups all-purpose flour
1 cup spiced red and green gumdrops, quartered
⅓ to ½ cup white nonpareils

1 Preheat oven to 375°F. Grease two large cookie sheets; set aside. In a large mixing bowl beat butter with an electric mixer on medium to high speed for 30 seconds. Add sugar and cinnamon. Beat until combined, scraping sides of bowl occasionally. Beat in egg yolks and vanilla until combined. Beat in as much of the flour as you can with the mixer. Stir in any remaining flour. Stir in gumdrops.

2 Shape dough into 1-inch balls; roll balls in nonpareils. Place balls 1 inch apart on the prepared cookie sheets. Press each ball slightly to flatten. Bake about 10 minutes or until edges are light brown. Transfer to a wire rack and let cool.

Use your favorite variety of mixed nuts in these festive drop cookies.

holiday nut drops

prep: 10 min. bake: 10 min. per batch stand: 1 min. per batch oven: 350°F makes: 24 cookies

½ cup butter, softened
¾ cup packed brown sugar
½ teaspoon baking soda
½ teaspoon salt
1 egg
1 teaspoon vanilla
1½ cups all-purpose flour
1 cup chopped unsalted mixed nuts
½ cup miniature red and green candy-coated chocolate pieces

1 Preheat oven to 350°F. Lightly grease 2 baking sheets; set aside. In a large mixing bowl beat butter with an electric mixer on medium to high speed for 30 seconds. Add brown sugar, baking soda, and salt. Beat until combined, scraping sides of bowl occasionally. Beat in egg and vanilla until combined. Beat in flour. Stir in nuts and chocolate pieces.

2 Drop dough by rounded measuring tablespoons 2 inches apart onto the prepared baking sheets. Bake for 10 to 12 minutes or until light brown at edges. Let stand for 1 minute on baking sheets. Transfer to a wire rack; cool.

Kids old enough to roll a ball of dough into a rope can help shape these sparkling canes. Color part of the dough red, if you like.

candy cane twists

prep: 30 min. **chill:** 30 min. **bake:** 8 min. per batch **oven:** 375°F
makes: 32 cookies

1 cup butter, softened
1 cup powdered sugar
1 egg
½ teaspoon vanilla
  Dash salt
2½ cups all-purpose flour
¼ cup finely crushed
    peppermint
    candy canes or
    peppermint candies
  Few drops red food
    coloring (optional)
  Granulated or colored
    sugar

1 In a large mixing bowl beat butter with an electric mixer on medium to high speed for 30 seconds. Add powdered sugar. Beat until combined, scraping sides of bowl occasionally. Beat in egg, vanilla, and salt until combined. Beat in as much of the flour as you can with the mixer. Stir in any remaining flour. Divide dough in half. Knead crushed candy canes into one half of the dough. If desired, knead red food coloring into the peppermint dough to tint slightly. Leave remaining half of dough plain. Cover and chill dough about 30 minutes or until easy to handle.

2 Preheat oven to 375°F. Work with half of each dough at a time, keeping remaining dough chilled until ready to use. For each cookie, on a lightly floured surface, shape a 1-inch ball of plain dough into a 4- or 5-inch rope. Repeat with a 1-inch ball of peppermint dough. Place ropes side by side and twist together. Pinch ends to seal. Form twisted ropes into a cane. Place canes 2 inches apart on an ungreased cookie sheet. Sprinkle with sugar. Repeat with remaining dough.

3 Bake for 8 to 10 minutes or until edges of cookies are set. Immediately transfer to a wire rack and let cool.

note: *Store cookies as directed on page 16. Freeze for up to 1 month.*

For a java-lover's gift, team these homemade coffeehouse pleasures with a bag of coffee beans and a pretty mug.

holiday biscotti

prep: 30 min. chill: 2 hr. bake: 25 min./10 min. stand: 1 hr.
oven: 350°F/325°F makes: about 48 cookies

¼ cup butter, softened
1 cup sugar
1 teaspoon baking powder
½ teaspoon baking soda
¼ teaspoon salt
4 eggs
½ teaspoon vanilla
¼ teaspoon almond extract
2¼ cups all-purpose flour
1½ teaspoons anise seeds
½ teaspoon fennel seeds
1 cup dried cranberries
¾ cup pistachios, shelled
½ cup dried apricots, snipped
1 tablespoon water

1 In a large mixing bowl beat butter with an electric mixer on medium to high speed for 30 seconds. Add sugar, baking powder, baking soda, and salt. Beat until combined, scraping sides of bowl occasionally. Beat in 3 of the eggs, the vanilla, and almond extract until combined. Beat in as much of the flour as you can with the mixer. Stir in any remaining flour and the anise and fennel seeds. Stir in the cranberries, pistachios, and apricots. Cover and chill dough 2 hours or until easy to handle.

2 Preheat oven to 350°F. Lightly grease a cookie sheet; set aside. Divide dough in half. Shape each half into a 12-inch-long log. Place logs at least 3 inches apart on the prepared cookie sheet. Flatten each log slightly until ¾ inch thick. In a small bowl whisk together the remaining egg and the water. Brush egg mixture over logs.

3 Bake for 25 to 30 minutes or until light brown. Let stand on cookie sheet about 1 hour or until completely cool.

4 When logs are cool, preheat oven to 325°F. Transfer logs to a cutting board. Cut logs diagonally into ½-inch-thick slices. Lay slices, cut sides down, on cookie sheet. Bake for 5 minutes. Turn slices over and bake about 5 minutes more or until biscotti are dry and crisp. Transfer to a wire rack and let cool.

Be sure to use paste food coloring, not liquid, to get the most intense color into the dough.

poinsettias

prep: 1 hr. bake: 12 min. per batch stand: 1 min. per batch oven: 350°F
makes: 30 cookies

½ cup butter, softened
½ cup shortening
1 cup sugar
1 teaspoon baking powder
¼ teaspoon salt
1 egg
1 teaspoon vanilla
2¼ cups all-purpose flour
½ teaspoon red paste food coloring
¼ teaspoon green paste food coloring
1 tube yellow-tinted frosting

1 In a large mixing bowl beat butter and shortening with an electric mixer on medium to high speed for 30 seconds. Add sugar, baking powder, and salt. Beat until combined, scraping sides of bowl occasionally. Beat in egg and vanilla until combined. Beat in as much of the flour as you can with the mixer. Stir in any remaining flour.

2 Divide dough into thirds. Tint two portions of the dough with red paste food coloring; tint one portion with green. If necessary, cover and chill dough for 1 to 2 hours or until easy to handle.

3 Preheat oven to 350°F. Shape red dough into thirty 1-inch balls. Shape green dough into thirty ½-inch balls. For each cookie, shape a red ball into five smaller balls. Roll each ball between palms of hands to lengthen and flatten slightly. Pinch one end, then flatten to form petals. Divide a green ball into three smaller balls and form leaves. If desired, use a toothpick to mark a leaf design in green dough. On an ungreased baking sheet, arrange five petals and three leaves to form a 3-inch poinsettia. Repeat with remaining dough, placing cookies 2 inches apart.

4 Bake about 12 minutes or until edges are firm and cookies are slightly puffed. Let stand for 1 minute on cookie sheet. Transfer to a wire rack and let cool.

5 Attach a small round tip to the frosting tube. Pipe five or six small yellow dots in the center of each cooled poinsettia.

Symbolic of a Yule log on a blazing fire, these sweet and spicy little cookies add to the warmth and fellowship of the season.

yule logs

prep: 1 hr. chill: 30 min. bake: 12 min. per batch oven: 350°F
makes: about 48 cookies

1 cup butter, softened
¾ cup granulated sugar
¼ cup packed brown sugar
½ teaspoon ground nutmeg
½ teaspoon ground ginger
1 egg
1 tablespoon dark rum
1 teaspoon vanilla
3 cups all-purpose flour
1 recipe Browned Butter Frosting
Ground nutmeg

1 In a large mixing bowl beat butter with an electric mixer on medium to high speed for 30 seconds. Add granulated sugar, brown sugar, the ½ teaspoon ground nutmeg, and the ginger. Beat until combined, scraping sides of bowl occasionally. Beat in egg, rum, and vanilla until combined. Beat in as much of the flour as you can with the mixer. Stir in any remaining flour. Divide dough into six portions. Cover and chill dough about 30 minutes or until easy to handle.

2 Preheat oven to 350°F. On a lightly floured surface, shape each portion of dough into a ½-inch-thick rope. Cut ropes into 3-inch logs. Place logs 2 inches apart on an ungreased cookie sheet. Bake 12 minutes or until light brown. Transfer cookies to a wire rack; cool.

3 Frost cooled cookies with Browned Butter Frosting. Run a fork through frosting lengthwise along log so frosting resembles bark. Sprinkle lightly with ground nutmeg. Let stand until set.

browned butter frosting: *In a small saucepan heat and stir ½ cup butter over medium-low heat until melted. Cook until butter turns golden brown. (Do not scorch.) Remove from heat. In a medium mixing bowl combine 5 cups powdered sugar, ¼ cup milk, and 2 teaspoons vanilla. Add browned butter. Beat with an electric mixer on low speed until combined. Beat on medium to high speed, adding enough milk (1 to 2 tablespoons) to make a frosting of spreading consistency.*

To create a peppermint-stick swirl of color, use red paste food coloring to tint half of the dough. Place the colored dough and plain dough side by side in the cookie press.

candy cane spritz

prep: 45 min. bake: 7 min. per batch oven: 375°F makes: about 60 cookies

¾ cup butter, softened
½ cup sugar
1 teaspoon baking powder
1 egg
½ teaspoon peppermint extract or 7 drops peppermint oil
1¾ cups all-purpose flour
6 ounces white chocolate (with cocoa butter), chopped
1 tablespoon shortening
⅓ cup finely crushed candy canes

1 Preheat oven to 375°F. In a large mixing bowl beat butter with an electric mixer on medium to high speed for 30 seconds. Add sugar and baking powder. Beat until combined, scraping sides of bowl occasionally. Beat in egg and peppermint extract until combined. Beat in as much of the flour as you can with the mixer. Stir in any remaining flour.

2 Pack unchilled dough into a cookie press fitted with a ½-inch star plate. Force dough through press to form 3½- to 4-inch-long sticks about 1 inch apart on an ungreased cookie sheet. If desired, bend ends to create candy-cane shapes.

3 Bake for 7 to 9 minutes or until edges are firm but not brown. Transfer to a wire rack and let cool.

4 In a small saucepan heat and stir white chocolate and shortening over low heat until smooth. Dip one end of each stick into melted white chocolate, letting excess drip off. Place on waxed paper. Sprinkle dipped ends with crushed candy. Let stand until set.

Candy canes originated in the seventeenth century. The first ones had different shapes than modern candy canes—they were straight, all white, and hard.

For a festive look, these giant-size drop cookies call for holiday-color candies.

mountain christmas cookies

prep: 25 min. **bake:** 8 min. per batch **stand:** 1 min. per batch **oven:** 375°F
makes: 36 cookies

½ cup butter, softened
½ cup shortening
1¼ cups packed brown
   sugar
¾ teaspoon baking soda
¼ teaspoon salt
3 eggs
2 teaspoons vanilla
3½ cups all-purpose flour
1 cup miniature red,
   green, and white
   candy-coated milk
   chocolate pieces
1 cup chopped pecans
   or walnuts

1 Preheat oven to 375°F. In a large mixing bowl beat butter and shortening with an electric mixer on medium to high speed for 30 seconds. Add brown sugar, baking soda, and salt. Beat until combined, scraping sides of bowl occasionally. Beat in eggs and vanilla until combined. Beat in as much flour as you can with the mixer. Stir in any remaining flour, the chocolate pieces, and nuts.

2 Drop dough by rounded teaspoons 2 inches apart onto an ungreased cookie sheet. Bake for 8 to 10 minutes or until golden. Let stand for 1 minute on cookie sheet. Transfer to a wire rack and let cool.

Orange peel and lemon peel give this holiday favorite a pleasing citrus flavor.

kris kringles

prep: 25 min. chill: 1 hr. bake: 20 min. per batch oven: 325°F
makes: about 26 cookies

½ cup butter, softened
¼ cup sugar
1 egg yolk
1 teaspoon finely shredded lemon peel (set aside)
1 teaspoon lemon juice
1 cup all-purpose flour
1 tablespoon finely shredded orange peel
Dash salt
1 egg white, lightly beaten
⅔ cup finely chopped walnuts
13 whole candied red or green cherries, halved

1 In a medium mixing bowl beat butter with an electric mixer on medium to high speed for 30 seconds. Add the sugar. Beat until combined, scraping sides of bowl occasionally. Beat in egg yolk and lemon juice until combined. Stir in flour, orange peel, lemon peel, and salt. Cover and chill dough about 1 hour or until easy to handle.

2 Preheat oven to 325°F. Grease a cookie sheet; set aside. Shape dough into 1-inch balls. Dip balls in egg white, then roll in chopped walnuts. Place balls 2 inches apart on the prepared cookie sheet. Press a cherry half into each ball. Bake about 20 minutes or until light brown. Transfer to a wire rack; cool.

What makes this cookie so special? It's delicious, gorgeous, and brimming with holiday flavors.

10

quick

can

Homemade candies always make delightful treats, but who has time to make them the old-fashioned way? With the help of a few convenience products and up-to-date methods, these recipes allow you to become a first-rate candy maker—no candy thermometer needed!

dy

Melt and stir. It's that easy when you use your microwave oven to make this ultrarich classic.

fabulous five-minute fudge

prep: 5 min. **chill:** 30 min. **makes:** 24 pieces

1   12-ounce package
     semisweet
     chocolate pieces
     (2 cups)
⅔   cup sweetened
     condensed milk
     (one-half of a
     14-ounce can)
1   tablespoon water
¾   cup chopped walnuts,
     toasted if desired
     (see tip, page 19)
1   teaspoon vanilla

1 Line a cookie sheet with waxed paper; set aside. In a microwave-safe bowl combine chocolate pieces, sweetened condensed milk, and the water.

2 Microwave, uncovered, on 100 percent power (high) for 1 minute; stir. Microwave about 1 minute more or until mixture is smooth, stirring every 30 seconds. Stir in nuts and vanilla. Pour onto the prepared cookie sheet and spread into a 9×6-inch rectangle. Chill about 30 minutes or until firm. Cut fudge into 1½-inch squares.

note: *Store candy as directed on page 16. Store at room temperature for up to 1 week.*

*Just four ingredients make up these melt-in-your-mouth morsels.
You don't even need to measure the marshmallows or chocolate.*

rocky road clusters

prep: 20 min. **chill:** 1 hr. **makes:** about 50 clusters

1 12-ounce package
   semisweet
   chocolate pieces
   (2 cups)
1 cup creamy peanut
   butter
1 10.5-ounce package
   tiny marshmallows
   (5½ cups)
1½ cups honey-roasted
   or dry-roasted
   peanuts

1 Line two cookie sheets with waxed paper;
set aside. In a medium saucepan combine
chocolate pieces and peanut butter. Heat
and stir over medium-low heat until smooth.
Remove from heat.

2 In a large bowl stir together marshmallows
and peanuts. Pour chocolate mixture
onto marshmallows and peanuts; stir well to
coat. Drop by heaping tablespoons onto the
prepared cookie sheets. Chill about 1 hour or
until set.

note: *Store candy as directed on page 16.
Refrigerate for up to 2 weeks.*

*For more intricate swirls, use a toothpick or a wooden
skewer instead of a spoon to marbleize the bark.*

marbled pecan bark

prep: 15 min. **chill:** 1 hr. **makes:** 1½ pounds (30 servings)

4 2-ounce squares
   vanilla-flavor candy
   coating, coarsely
   chopped
1 12-ounce package
   (2 cups) semisweet
   chocolate pieces
1½ cups toasted chopped
   pecans (see tip,
   page 19)

1 Line a cookie sheet with waxed paper; set
aside. In a saucepan heat and stir candy
coating over low heat until smooth; set aside.
In another saucepan heat and stir chocolate
pieces over low heat until smooth; stir in nuts.

2 Spread chocolate mixture thinly over
prepared baking sheet. Drizzle melted
candy coating over chocolate mixture. Using
the tip of a spoon, swirl candy coating through
chocolate mixture. Chill about 1 hour or until
firm. Break candy into pieces.

note: *Store candy as directed on page 16.
Refrigerate for up to 1 week.*

Line the baking dish with parchment paper to make it easy to remove the toffee from the dish after microwaving. Crease the paper edges along the inside edges of the dish so the liner fits nicely.

mock toffee

prep: 15 min. chill: 1 hr. makes: 12 to 16 pieces

10   graham cracker
      squares
⅓   cup chopped almonds
½   cup butter
½   cup packed brown
      sugar
⅓   cup miniature
      semisweet
      chocolate pieces

1 Line a microwave-safe 2-quart rectangular baking dish with parchment paper, extending the paper over the edges of the dish. Line bottom of the prepared dish with a single layer of graham crackers, breaking crackers as necessary to completely cover the bottom of the dish. Sprinkle almonds over crackers. Set aside.

2 In a microwave-safe 4-cup glass measure or medium glass bowl place the butter and brown sugar. Microwave on 100 percent power (high) for 3 minutes, stirring every 30 seconds. Pour over crackers and nuts in dish. (Work quickly because butter mixture separates.)

3 Place baking dish in microwave. Microwave on 100 percent power (high) for 1 minute 30 seconds. Sprinkle chocolate pieces over toffee mixture. Chill for 1 to 2 hours or until chocolate is set. Use parchment paper to lift candy from dish. Break into irregular pieces.

A graham cracker base is the secret to this candy's quick prep.

Dipped in caramel, coated with nuts, and drizzled with candy coating, these decked-out treats will be the talk of any special occasion.

triple-treat pretzel wands

prep: 30 min. **cook:** 10 min. **stand:** 1 hr. **makes:** 18 pretzels

1½	cups chopped mixed nuts
1	14-ounce package vanilla caramels (about 50), unwrapped
2	tablespoons whipping cream, half-and-half, or light cream
18	large pretzel rods
4	ounces vanilla-flavor candy coating
2	ounces chocolate-flavor candy coating
2	teaspoons shortening

1 Grease a large cookie sheet with butter; set aside. Spread nuts in an even layer on a plate; set aside.

2 In a medium saucepan heat and stir caramels and whipping cream over medium-low heat just until caramels are melted. Reduce heat to low.

3 Hold each pretzel rod by one end over the pan and spoon hot caramel mixture evenly over three-fourths of the pretzel; shake off excess. Roll coated part of pretzel in nuts, turning to coat all sides. Place pretzels on the prepared cookie sheet. Let stand about 30 minutes or until caramel is set.

4 In two small saucepans heat and stir each type of candy coating and 1 teaspoon shortening over low heat just until smooth. Drizzle some of each melted candy coating over the caramel and nuts on each pretzel. Return pretzels to baking sheet and let stand about 30 minutes or until set.

note: *Store candy as directed on page 16. Do not freeze.*

Decorated with miniature white and dark candies to resemble dominoes, these treats look just as pretty as those you find in specialty catalogs, and you can make these for a fraction of the cost.

double-dipped dominoes

prep: 20 min. **chill:** 10 min. **makes:** 24 dominoes

  6   ounces semisweet
        chocolate squares
        or pieces
  2   tablespoons
        shortening
 12   graham cracker
        squares, halved
  6   ounces white
        chocolate baking
        squares with cocoa
        butter or white
        baking pieces
        Small white candies
        Miniature semisweet
        chocolate pieces

1 Line cookie sheet with waxed paper; set aside. In a microwave-safe 2-cup glass measure place the semisweet chocolate squares and 1 tablespoon of the shortening. Microwave on 100 percent power (high) 1½ minutes or just until melted, stirring every 30 seconds.

2 Dip half of each halved cracker in the melted chocolate; place on the prepared cookie sheet. While chocolate is still soft, add white candies to resemble dots. Chill about 10 minutes or until set.

3 In another microwave-safe 2-cup glass measure place white chocolate and the remaining 1 tablespoon shortening. Microwave on 100 percent power (high) for 1½ to 2 minutes or just until melted, stirring every 30 seconds.

4 Dip the plain half of each cracker in the melted white chocolate; return to the cookie sheet. While chocolate is still soft, add miniature chocolate pieces to resemble dots. Let crackers stand until set.

note: *Store candy as directed on page 16. Freeze for up to 1 month.*

A crispy cookie crust made of graham crackers and cocoa powder pairs perfectly with a rich, minty filling.

crème de menthe cups

prep: 30 min. **chill:** 5 hr. **makes:** about 24 cups

1½ cups powdered sugar
¼ cup unsweetened
cocoa powder
2 tablespoons
whipping cream
1 teaspoon vanilla
¼ cup butter, softened
¾ cup crushed graham
crackers
1 3-ounce package
cream cheese,
softened
2 tablespoons butter,
softened
1 cup powdered sugar
1 tablespoon crème de
menthe
White chocolate,
mint chocolate, or
milk chocolate curls
(optional)

1 Line twenty-four 1¾-inch muffin cups with paper or foil liners; set aside. In a small bowl stir together the 1½ cups powdered sugar and the cocoa powder; set aside. In another small bowl stir together whipping cream and vanilla; set aside.

2 In a medium mixing bowl beat the ¼ cup butter with an electric mixer on medium to high speed for 30 seconds. Alternately beat in powdered sugar and whipping cream mixtures on low speed until combined. Beat in crushed graham crackers.

3 Shape dough into 1-inch balls; place balls in prepared muffin cups. Press dough evenly against bottom and sides of each cup. Chill for 1 hour.

4 For filling, in a medium mixing bowl beat cream cheese and the 2 tablespoons butter with an electric mixer on medium to high speed for 30 seconds. Gradually beat in the 1 cup powdered sugar and the crème de menthe. Spoon or pipe filling into chocolate cups. If desired, garnish with chocolate curls. Cover; chill for at least 4 hours before serving.

note: *Store candy in a single layer as directed on page 16. Refrigerate for up to 3 days.*

Top off these cool, minty candies
with a flourish of pretty chocolate curls.

Cherries and almonds, always a delicious pair, taste wonderful in this easy-to-make homemade fudge.

cherry-almond fudge

prep: 30 min. **chill:** 6 hr. **makes:** about 2 pounds (64 pieces)

2½   cups powdered sugar

⅔   cup milk

¼   cup butter

12   ounces white chocolate baking squares with cocoa butter, coarsely chopped

¾   cup snipped dried tart red cherries or dried cranberries

¾   cup sliced almonds, toasted (see tip, page 19)

½   teaspoon almond extract

1 Line an 8×8×2-inch baking pan with foil, extending foil over the edges of the pan. Butter the foil; set aside.

2 Butter the sides of a heavy saucepan. In the saucepan combine powdered sugar, milk, and butter. Cook and stir over medium-high heat until mixture boils and sugar dissolves. Reduce heat to medium-low. Boil gently, without stirring, for 5 minutes.

3 Reduce heat to low. Add white chocolate. Heat and stir until smooth. Remove from heat. Stir in dried fruit, almonds, and almond extract. Spread in prepared pan. Cover; chill 6 hours or until firm. Use foil to lift fudge out of pan. Cut into 1-inch squares or triangles.

note: *Store candy as directed on page 16. Refrigerate for up to 1 week.*

For a variety of finished candies, roll caramels in nonpareils, toffee, or nuts after you dip them in melted candy coating. Or let the candy coating dry and then drizzle some pieces with another color of melted candy coating.

candy-box caramels

prep: 30 min. **stand:** 1 hr. **makes:** 48 pieces

12	ounces chocolate-and/or vanilla-flavor candy coating,* coarsely chopped
1	cup toffee pieces, crushed; finely chopped pistachios; and/or nonpareils
48	short plastic or wooden skewers (optional)
1	14-ounce package vanilla caramels (about 48), unwrapped
2	ounces chocolate-and/or vanilla-flavor candy coating,* coarsely chopped (optional)

1 Line a large cookie sheet with waxed paper; set aside. In a microwave-safe 4-cup measure place the 12 ounces candy coating. Microwave on 100 percent power (high) about 3 minutes or just until melted, stirring every 30 seconds.

2 Place toffee pieces, nuts, and/or nonpareils in a shallow dish. If desired, insert a skewer into each caramel. Dip one caramel into melted candy coating; turn to coat as much of the caramel as desired, allowing excess coating to drip off. (If not using skewers, use a fork to lift caramel out of candy coating, drawing the fork across the rim of the glass measure to remove excess coating from caramel.) Place dipped caramel in toffee pieces, nuts, and/or nonpareils, turning to coat. Place coated caramel on the prepared baking sheet. Repeat with remaining caramels. Let caramels stand about 1 hour or until coating sets.

3 If desired, place 2 ounces of a contrasting color of candy coating in a microwave-safe bowl. Microwave on 100 percent power (high) about 2 minutes or just until melted, stirring every 30 seconds. Cool slightly. Transfer coating to a small heavy plastic bag. Snip a small hole in one corner of bag and drizzle additional coating over coated caramels. Let caramels stand until coating sets.

* If desired, substitute milk chocolate, dark chocolate, and/or white chocolate baking squares with cocoa butter for candy coating.

note: *Store candy as directed on page 16. Store at room temperature for up to 1 week.*

Traditional chocolate bark is dressed up with a medley of dried fruit and toasted nuts.

fruit-and-nut chocolate bark

prep: 20 min. **chill:** 1 hr. **makes:** 2¼ pounds

2 cups almonds and/or hazelnuts* (filberts), toasted (see tip, page 19) and coarsely chopped

⅔ cup golden raisins

⅔ cup snipped dried apricots

⅔ cup dried cranberries

¼ cup diced candied orange peel

12 ounces chocolate-flavor candy coating, chopped

1 7-ounce milk chocolate bar, chopped

1 Line a large cookie sheet with foil. Butter foil; set aside. In a large bowl stir together nuts, raisins, apricots, cranberries, and orange peel; reserve ¾ cup for topping. Set aside.

2 In a saucepan heat and stir candy coating and chocolate over low heat until smooth. Remove from heat. Stir into the large portion of fruit mixture; mix well. Pour onto the prepared baking sheet. Spread to about ⅜ inch thick. Sprinkle remaining fruit mixture over mixture in pan, pressing slightly. Chill candy 1 hour or until firm. Use foil to lift candy from baking sheet; carefully break candy into pieces.

*After toasting hazelnuts, place the warm nuts in a clean kitchen towel. Rub nuts with the towel to remove loose skins.

note: *Store candy as directed on page 16. Refrigerate for up to 2 weeks. Do not freeze.*

coconut-fruit truffles

start to finish: 30 min. makes: 30 truffles

½ cup flaked coconut
3 tablespoons
   powdered sugar
¾ cup chopped walnuts
8 ounces pitted dates
½ cup raisins
½ cup dried cranberries
⅓ cup flaked coconut
1 tablespoon
   unsweetened cocoa
   powder
¼ teaspoon ground
   cinnamon
¼ cup peanut butter

1 For coating, place the ½ cup coconut and the powdered sugar in a food processor. Cover and process until coconut is finely chopped. Transfer to a shallow dish; set aside.

2 For truffles, place walnuts, dates, raisins, cranberries, the ⅓ cup coconut, the cocoa powder, and cinnamon in a food processor. Cover and process until finely chopped, stopping to scrape sides of bowl as necessary. Add peanut butter. Cover and process until fruit mixture is moist enough to form a ball.

3 Using your hands, shape fruit mixture into 1-inch balls. Roll balls in coconut coating, gently patting coating onto sides of balls.

To use your microwave oven to caramelize sugar, you need a heavy-duty glass measure that can withstand high temperatures. The dish must be free from cracks and chips or it may shatter. This recipe works best in a 900- to 1,200-watt microwave oven.

mixed-nut brittle

start to finish: 15 min. makes: about ½ pound

½ cup sugar
½ cup light-color
   corn syrup
½ cup salted mixed
   nuts or peanuts
1 tablespoon butter
⅛ teaspoon vanilla
½ teaspoon baking soda

1 Grease a small cookie sheet; set aside. In a microwave-safe 4-cup glass measure stir together sugar and corn syrup. Microwave, uncovered, on 100 percent power (high) for 5 minutes, stirring twice. Stir in nuts and butter. Microwave, uncovered, on 100 percent power (high) 1 minute more or just until mixture turns golden (mixture becomes more golden when removed from the microwave). Stir in vanilla and baking soda.

2 Pour mixture onto prepared baking sheet. Use two forks to lift and pull candy into a thin sheet as it cools (to help make the brittle crisp). Cool completely. Break into pieces.

note: *Store candy as directed on page 16. Store at room temperature for up to 1 week.*

Instead of depending on a candy thermometer and long, slow simmering for its nutty flavor, this no-fuss peanut brittle relies on the timesaving technique of caramelizing the sugar.

caramelized peanut brittle

start to finish: 20 min. **makes:** 1¼ pounds (48 servings)

1 tablespoon butter
1 cup chopped peanuts
2 cups sugar

1 Line a large cookie sheet with foil. Butter foil; set aside. In a small saucepan melt the 1 tablespoon butter over low heat. Stir in chopped peanuts; keep warm over low heat.

2 Place sugar in a 12-inch heavy skillet. Heat over medium-high heat until sugar begins to melt, shaking skillet occasionally to heat sugar evenly. Reduce heat to medium-low. Cook for 12 to 15 minutes or until sugar is melted and golden, stirring only as necessary after sugar begins to melt.

3 Remove skillet from heat. Quickly stir in warm peanuts and butter. Immediately pour the mixture onto the prepared baking sheet, allowing syrup to flow and keeping nuts evenly distributed. Cool completely; break candy into pieces.

note: *Store candy as directed on page 16. Store at room temperature for up to 1 month.*

When you crave this popular treat, don't head to the candy store—you can make this peanut brittle in a flash.

So eyecatching and fast to make, this festive candy is a great treat to make when you're busy around the holidays.

peppermint bark

prep: 25 min. **chill:** 30 min. **makes:** 1¼ pounds

6 ounces chocolate-flavor candy coating, chopped

3 ounces milk chocolate bar, chopped

6 ounces vanilla-flavor candy coating, chopped

3 ounces white chocolate baking squares, chopped

¼ cup crushed peppermint candies

1 Line a large cookie sheet with foil; set aside. In a small saucepan heat and stir chocolate-flavor candy coating and milk chocolate bar over low heat until smooth. In another saucepan heat and stir vanilla-flavor candy coating and white chocolate baking squares over low heat until smooth.

2 Spread chocolate mixture over prepared baking sheet into a 10×8-inch rectangle. Pour white chocolate mixture over chocolate mixture and swirl using a thin spatula. Shake baking sheet gently for even thickness. Immediately sprinkle with crushed candies. Chill bark 30 minutes or until firm. Use foil to lift candy from baking sheet; break into pieces.

note: *Store candy as directed on page 16. Refrigerate for up to 1 week.*

Creamy **marshmallows** get a **cool finish** of **crushed candy canes** in these lollipop-shape treats.

Marshmallow Pops

Serve these minty lollipops when youngsters are around.
Kids love the fun-to-eat treats.

marshmallow pops

start to finish: 25 min. **makes:** about 36 pops

36   wooden or short
       plastic skewers
1   10-ounce package
       large marshmallows
       (about 36)
6   ounces white candy
       coating
⅓   cup crushed
       peppermint candies

1 Line a cookie sheet with waxed paper; set aside. Insert skewers into marshmallows; set aside. In a small saucepan heat and stir white candy coating over low heat until smooth. Quickly dip each marshmallow halfway into melted candy coating, allowing excess to drip off. Sprinkle with crushed peppermint candies; place on the prepared baking sheet. Let stand until set.

note: *Store candy as directed on page 16. Refrigerate up to 3 days. Do not freeze.*

easy white fudge

prep: 20 min. **chill:** 2 hr. **makes:** about 2 pounds (64 pieces)

3   cups white baking
       pieces
1   14-ounce can
       sweetened
       condensed milk
       (1¼ cups)
1   cup chopped
       almonds,
       macadamia nuts, or
       pecans
2   teaspoons finely
       shredded orange
       peel (optional)
1   teaspoon vanilla
       Coarsely chopped
       almonds,
       macadamia nuts, or
       pecans (optional)

1 Line an 8×8×2-inch or 9×9×2-inch baking pan with foil, extending the foil over the edges of the pan. Butter foil; set aside.
2 In a medium saucepan cook and stir baking pieces and sweetened condensed milk over low heat just until pieces melt and mixture is smooth. Remove saucepan from heat. Stir in the 1 cup nuts, orange peel (if desired), and vanilla. Spread fudge mixture evenly in the prepared pan. If desired, sprinkle with additional nuts; press lightly into fudge. Score into 1-inch pieces. Cover and chill about 2 hours or until firm. Use foil to lift fudge out of pan; cut into squares.

note: *Store candy as directed on page 16. Store at room temperature for up to 1 week.*
Do not freeze

note: Numbers in *italics* indicate photo pages.

index

index

metric information

The charts on this page provide a guide for converting measurements from the U.S. customary system, which is used throughout this book, to the metric system.

Product Differences

Most of the ingredients called for in the recipes in this book are available in most countries. However, some are known by different names. Here are some common American ingredients and their possible counterparts:

- All-purpose flour is enriched, bleached or unbleached white household flour. When self-rising flour is used in place of all-purpose flour in a recipe that calls for leavening, omit the leavening agent (baking soda or baking powder) and salt.
- Baking soda is bicarbonate of soda.
- Cornstarch is cornflour.
- Golden raisins are sultanas.
- Light-colored corn syrup is golden syrup.
- Powdered sugar is icing sugar.
- Sugar (white) is granulated, fine granulated, or castor sugar.
- Vanilla or vanilla extract is vanilla essence.

Volume and Weight

The United States traditionally uses cup measures for liquid and solid ingredients. The chart below shows the approximate imperial and metric equivalents. If you are accustomed to weighing solid ingredients, the following approximate equivalents will be helpful.

- 1 cup butter, castor sugar, or rice = 8 ounces = ½ pound = 250 grams
- 1 cup flour = 4 ounces = ¼ pound = 125 grams
- 1 cup icing sugar = 5 ounces = 150 grams

Canadian and U.S. volume for a cup measure is 8 fluid ounces (237 ml), but the standard metric equivalent is 250 ml.

1 British imperial cup is 10 fluid ounces.

In Australia, 1 tablespoon equals 20 ml, and there are 4 teaspoons in the Australian tablespoon.

Spoon measures are used for smaller amounts of ingredients. Although the size of the tablespoon varies slightly in different countries, for practical purposes and for recipes in this book, a straight substitution is all that's necessary. Measurements made using cups or spoons always should be level unless stated otherwise.

Common Weight Range Replacements

Imperial / U.S.	Metric
½ ounce	15 g
1 ounce	25 g or 30 g
4 ounces (¼ pound)	115 g or 125 g
8 ounces (½ pound)	225 g or 250 g
16 ounces (1 pound)	450 g or 500 g
1¼ pounds	625 g
1½ pounds	750 g
2 pounds or 2¼ pounds	1,000 g or 1 Kg

Oven Temperature Equivalents

Fahrenheit Setting	Celsius Setting*	Gas Setting
300°F	150°C	Gas Mark 2 (very low)
325°F	160°C	Gas Mark 3 (low)
350°F	180°C	Gas Mark 4 (moderate)
375°F	190°C	Gas Mark 5 (moderate)
400°F	200°C	Gas Mark 6 (hot)
425°F	220°C	Gas Mark 7 (hot)
450°F	230°C	Gas Mark 8 (very hot)
475°F	240°C	Gas Mark 9 (very hot)
500°F	260°C	Gas Mark 10 (extremely hot)
Broil	Broil	Grill

*Electric and gas ovens may be calibrated using celsius. However, for an electric oven, increase celsius setting 10 to 20 degrees when cooking above 160°C. For convection or forced air ovens (gas or electric), lower the temperature setting 25°F/10°C when cooking at all heat levels.

Baking Pan Sizes

Imperial / U.S.	Metric
9×1½-inch round cake pan	22- or 23×4-cm (1.5 L)
9×1½-inch pie plate	22- or 23×4-cm (1 L)
8×8×2-inch square cake pan	20×5-cm (2 L)
9×9×2-inch square cake pan	22- or 23×4.5-cm (2.5 L)
11×7×1½-inch baking pan	28×17×4-cm (2 L)
2-quart rectangular baking pan	30×19×4.5-cm (3 L)
13×9×2-inch baking pan	34×22×4.5-cm (3.5 L)
15×10×1-inch jelly roll pan	40×25×2-cm
9×5×3-inch loaf pan	23×13×8-cm (2 L)
2-quart casserole	2 L

U.S. / Standard Metric Equivalents

⅛ teaspoon = 0.5 ml

¼ teaspoon = 1 ml

½ teaspoon = 2 ml

1 teaspoon = 5 ml

1 tablespoon = 15 ml

2 tablespoons = 25 ml

¼ cup = 2 fluid ounces = 50 ml

⅓ cup = 3 fluid ounces = 75 ml

½ cup = 4 fluid ounces = 125 ml

⅔ cup = 5 fluid ounces = 150 ml

¾ cup = 6 fluid ounces = 175 ml

1 cup = 8 fluid ounces = 250 ml

2 cups = 1 pint = 500 ml

1 quart = 1 litre

emergency baking substitutions

Use these substitutions only in a pinch as they may affect the flavor or texture of your recipe.

If you don't have:	Substitute:
Apple pie spice, 1 teaspoon	½ teaspoon ground cinnamon plus ¼ teaspoon ground nutmeg, ⅛ teaspoon ground allspice, and dash ground cloves
Baking Powder, 1 teaspoon	½ teaspoon cream of tartar plus ¼ teaspoon baking soda
Buttermilk, 1 cup	Sour milk: 1 tablespoon lemon juice or vinegar plus enough milk to make 1 cup (let stand 5 minutes before using); or 1 cup plain yogurt
Chocolate, semisweet, 1 ounce	3 tablespoons semisweet chocolate pieces; or 1 ounce unsweetened chocolate plus 1 tablespoon sugar
Chocolate, sweet baking, 4 ounces	¼ cup unsweetened cocoa powder plus ⅓ cup sugar and 3 tablespoons shortening
Chocolate, unsweetened, 1 ounce	3 tablespoons unsweetened cocoa powder plus 1 tablespoon cooking oil or shortening
Cornstarch, 1 tablespoon (for thickening)	2 tablespoons all-purpose flour
Corn syrup, 1 cup	1 cup granulated sugar plus ¼ cup water
Egg, 1 whole large	2 egg whites; 2 egg yolks; or ¼ cup frozen egg product, thawed
Fruit liqueur, 1 tablespoon	1 tablespoon fruit juice
Ginger, grated fresh, 1 teaspoon	¼ teaspoon ground ginger
Half-and-half or light cream, 1 cup	1 tablespoon melted butter or margarine plus enough whole milk to make 1 cup
Honey, 1 cup	1¼ cup granulated sugar plus ¼ cup water
Milk, 1 cup	½ cup evaporated milk plus ½ cup water; or 1 cup water plus ⅓ cup nonfat dry milk powder
Molasses, 1 cup	1 cup honey
Pumpkin pie spice, 1 teaspoon	½ teaspoon ground cinnamon, plus ¼ teaspoon ground ginger, ¼ teaspoon ground allspice, and ⅛ teaspoon ground nutmeg
Sour cream, dairy, 1 cup	1 cup plain yogurt
Sugar, granulated, 1 cup	1 cup packed brown sugar

Weights and Measures

3 teaspoons = 1 tablespoon	1 tablespoon = ½ fluid ounce	1 teaspoon = 5 milliliters
4 tablespoons = ¼ cup	1 cup = 8 fluid ounces	1 tablespoon = 15 milliliters
5⅓ tablespoons = ⅓ cup	1 cup = ½ pint	1 cup = 240 milliliters
8 tablespoons = ½ cup	2 cups = 1 pint	1 quart = 1 liter
10⅔ tablespoons = ⅔ cup	4 cups = 1 quart	1 ounce = 28 grams
12 tablespoons = ¾ cup	2 pints = 1 quart	1 pounds = 454 grams
16 tablespoons = 1 cup	4 quarts = 1 gallon	